# Introduction to
# the SPEECHMAKING

PROCESS

Publisher and Marketing Manager: Richard Schofield

Managing Editor: Joyce Bianchini

Photo Researcher: Della Brackett

Design and Illustrations: Michelle Hipkins

Typesetter: Jacquelyn Wein

Sales Manager: Robert Rappeport

Permissions Coordinator: Suzanne Schmidt

Art Director: Esther Scannell

Soft Cover ISBN: 978-1-61882-009-9

TEXTBOOK-Plus ISBN: 978-1-61882-595-7

Loose Leaf ISBN: 978-1-61882-003-7

# BVT
PUBLISHING

**The publisher of affordable textbooks**

# Introduction to the SPEECHMAKING

PROCESS

**Fourteenth Edition**

**Raymond S. Ross**

*Wayne State University*

**Diana K. Leonard**

*The University of Arizona*

B V T
PUBLISHING

# BRIEF CONTENTS

# TABLE OF CONTENTS

# CHAPTER 3

# Audience Considerations   64

# CHAPTER 4

## Preparing and Researching the Speech                94

## CHAPTER 7
# Language Habits 194

## CHAPTER 8
## Delivering the Speech                                    228

# CHAPTER 9
## Using Visual Aids

# CHAPTER 10
## Speeches to Inform

# CHAPTER 11

## Speeches to Persuade                                      306

# CHAPTER 12

## Logical Reasoning and Argument                                                   358

# CHAPTER 13

## Unique Formats and Occasions                                                     382

# CHAPTER 14

## Speaking in Group Settings      414

# APPENDIX A

# APPENDIX B

# GLOSSARY                                                           459

# INDEX                                                             469

# PREFACE

Good communicators are almost always knowledgeable in the critical areas of the communication process, perception, language, logical thinking, and presentation. *The Speechmaking Process* addresses all of these important areas and relates them eclectically to effective and responsible public speaking.

The most important educational goals of this book are:

1.  To help students become effective critical thinkers, language users, organizers, and ethical purveyors of informative and persuasive messages.

2.  To help students learn that receivers are coactive participants in the communication process who affectively, cognitively, and/or behaviorally respond to and "co-create" messages.

3.  To help students understand that meaning is heavily dependent on one's experience and the realities their social constructions allow.

4.  To help students transfer the communication fundamentals learned from public speaking to all other forms of communication.

The more pragmatic objectives are implicit in Cicero's five essentials of public speaking:

1.  Determining exactly what one intends to say, and to whom it will be said.

2.  Arranging the materials in a proper order with good judgment.

3.  Selecting well-chosen words and carefully phrased sentences.

4.  Fixing the speech in mind (practice).

5.  Delivering it with dignity and grace.

Relevant theory and pragmatic student needs have guided the content decision for most of this book. Its basic pedagogical assumption is that students are better served by a "theory and practice" approach than by one that is all practice (or all theory, for that matter). The theory is necessary to power and steer the practice. Its obvious eclecticism is, we think, better informed than earlier editions. This edition is clearly influenced by interactionist and social construction views as well as by relevant behavioral/cognitive theories. Its rhetorical roots are also evident in its treatment of ethics, models, and practice. These generalizations from theory to practice, whether cast as rules or laws, have been simplified to facilitate understanding and application for the student. Speaking experience governed by theory, principle, and professional criticism should promote sound communication habits whatever the setting.

We are pleased that "critical thinking" scholars also identify as essential the practical skills taught in the chapters of this book: organizing, outlining, information gathering, goal setting, analysis, reasoning, and effective delivery. The theory chapters plus classroom applications are designed to lead to still richer thinking, language, and speaking skills.

The Internet continues to provide a vast and rich connection to available resources for the student and layperson. Because of its reach, and students' comfortability with its usage, we must take the time in our texts and classrooms to discuss its value and pitfalls. Hence, we have integrated discussion of the Internet in the chapter on researching and preparing the speech as well as the chapter on visual aids. We incorporated much of the previous contribution by Professors Jack Kay of Wayne State University, and Timothy Borchers of Moorhead State University as well as drawing on newer material by Cindy Elliott, MLS from The University of Arizona and Gates Matthew Stoner, MA in Communication from The University of Arizona.

# New to This Edition

1. We have moved the chapter on Language Habits to later in the book in order to allow students to focus on the pragmatics of dealing with speech apprehension, choosing topics, researching and developing outlines, before delving deeper into meanings, intentions, usage and appropriateness.

2. We decided to incorporate much of the critical thinking elements from the chapter on language into the chapter on Persuasion. We believe this will aid in conceptual continuity for the student and provide easier usage of the textbook by the instructor.

3.  The Learning Projects have proved to be useful for instructors, so we have moved them to the Online Instructor Resource Manual. This should facilitate the instructor in choosing particular chapter assignments for their students while reducing the size of the text, thus working toward maintaining a low-priced textbook.

4.  At the suggestion of review, we have made the definitions of terms easier by bolding important terms, providing the definition, and including a glossary of terms in the back of the text.

5.  On an organizational note, we have changed the headings to be more consistent throughout the text offering a stronger organizational model for students.

# Supplements for Instructors

● **Instructor's Manual**   To aid in instruction, we have provided a number of supplements that the instructor can access. The instructor is provided access to a downloadable Instructor's Manual, which is designed to assist the instructor by providing a variety of pedagogical tools. It is divided into five parts: www.bvtpublishing.com

1.  **Speech Assignments**   Although instructors should design their assignments specifically for their teaching objectives and their particular students, we provide suggestions that have been effective in similar Introductory Speech courses. Each assignment includes a pedagogical note that can help the instructor connect the assignments to the chapters and also provides examples of how other professors have approached the assignments.

2.  **Duplication/Transparency Masters**   We have created masters of some of the images found throughout the text that instructors can use to make transparencies or download to their PowerPoint slides in order to augment their lectures. We did not include lecture masters for two reasons: 1) Lectures should be dynamic and ever-changing (never stagnant). We teach our public speaking students the importance of novelty, immediacy, and currency. Likewise, as professors we need to model those same qualities. 2) Instructors are not mere conduits of information. They breathe life and interest into the content of their subjects. A good way to insure that process is by being a part of the message itself.

3.  **Evaluating and Critiquing Students**   This section is provided to assist new instructors, as well as instructors who are new to public speaking. Evaluating students' written work is a task instructors should take very seriously, but never more so than in the public presentation arena. When students stand in front of an audience, their entire self-concept is often on the line. Therefore,

we have devoted a full section to some pedagogical guidance to the instructor. We include specific grading criteria and things to consider when engaging peer or group evaluations.

**4.     Observation and Evaluation Forms**   We included a number of observation and evaluation forms that can be used "as is" or adjusted for a particular speech assignment or objective. Many of these forms have been collected from a variety of instructors and work effectively for most assignments. However, they also serve as a nice template for creating an original form that better serves the particular assignment.

**5.     Test Item File**   No college class would be complete without a few tests along the way! Hence, we have provided a comprehensive bank of 799 test items including: multiple choice, true/false, fill in the blank, and essay questions for each of the chapters in the text. We encourage instructors to create additional questions that focus on material used beyond the textbook. However, we suggest new questions follow a similar format to the ones provided for coherency and test score reliability.

● **Customize This Book**   If you have additional material you'd like to add (handouts, lecture notes, syllabus, etc.) or simply rearrange and delete content, BVT Publishing's Custom Publishing Division can help you modify this book's content to produce a book that satisfies your specific instructional needs. BVT Publishing has the only custom publishing division that puts your material exactly where you want it to go, easily and seamlessly. Please visit **www.bvtpublishing.com** or call us at **1-800-646-7782** for more information on BVT Publishing's Custom Publishing Program.

*New to this Edition!*

# BVT*Lab*

BVT*Lab* a simple, robust, online lab for college instructors and their students—provides essential teaching, assessment, and communication tools.

## Course Setup

BVT*Lab* has an easy-to-use, intuitive interface that allows instructors to quickly set up their courses and grade books, and replicate them from section to section and semester to semester. Multiple choice and true/false questions can be delivered online as practice questions, homework assignments, quizzes, and

**www.BVTLab.com**

tests—each of which draws from a separate bank of questions.

Homework, quizzes, and tests have assigned start and end times; and tests can be proctored in the computer lab or self-proctored for distance learners. Homework and quizzes offer optional hints and instructor tips. In addition, practice questions can be linked to fully worked solutions and multimedia tutorials.Instructors can preview and manually select questions assigned to students, or they can use the "quick-pick" feature in BVTLab to generate sets of questions.

## Grade Book

Using an assigned passcode, students register themselves into the grade book. All homework, quizzes, and tests are automatically graded and recorded in the grade book. In addition, instructors can manually enter or modify scores, with provisions for extra credit, attendance, and participation grades. Grade books can be replicated from section to section, semester to semester, and can be easily edited or modified if required.

## Communications Tools

Instructors can post discussion threads to a class forum and then monitor and moderate student replies. Important notifications can also be sent directly to each student via email.

# Supplements for Students

BVT*Lab* is a comprehensive online learning environment designed to help students succeed. It provides a complete online classroom, as well as the practice questions, learning aids, and communication tools that students need for success. Even if your instructor does not use the lab as a classroom, you are always welcome to take advantage of the many resources.

**Practice Questions**   Students work through hundreds of practice questions online. Questions are multiple choice or true/false and are graded instantly for immediate feedback.

**Flashcards**   **BVT***Lab* includes sets of flashcards for each chapter that reinforce the key terms and concepts from the textbook.

**Chapter Summaries**   A convenient and concise chapter summary is available as a study aid for each chapter.

**Speeches**    Mulit-media files including video, audio and text transcripts are available for over one hundred prominent speeches.

**Discussion Forum**    An online discussion forum allows students to interact with each other and the instructor to explore challenging concepts and share other resources, while providing an online community for distance learning.

**Review**    For classes taught within the lab, students can view their grades for all completed work and also review prior homework and quizzes to identify areas that require additional study.

www.BVTLab.com

## Shop Online

**1. Textbook**    For the student's convenience and pocketbook, students have the added option of purchasing this textbook at **www. bvtstudents.com**.

# Acknowledgments

We want to sincerely thank BVT Publishing for their vision in providing access to affordable textbooks for college students, who might otherwise be kept out of the high-priced textbook market. Individually, however, we must single out Robert Rappeport for his positive energy; Michelle Hipkins, Della Brackett, and Esther Scannell who tirelessly worked on many revisions; and Brae Buhnerkemper for her unparalleled endurance. As a collective, the BVT team has made working on this a text a pleasure. Dr. Laura Stafford provided extraordinary insight into what would make this 14th edition stronger, more easily used by the instructor, and more resonant with the students. She has our deep appreciation for all of her assistance.

Finally we offer our special gratitude to personal friends and loved ones.

From Ray Ross: Mark, my professor son and sometimes co-author, keeps me current, honest, and motivated. The charming Ricky, my spousal business agent and personal editor, adds to my douceur de vivre and makes the effort worthwhile.

From Diana Leonard: I offer my sincere gratitude for the opportunity to write with Ray Ross keeping this textbook in the classroom. I am eternally grateful to my former colleague, Cindy Elliott, for the guidance through the ever-changing mire of Internet sources for research purposes and for our everlasting friendship. But most importantly, I am blessed to have my friend and partner, Mary Findysz, supporting and encouraging my academic and intellectual pursuits while reminding me to laugh and play. What else should life be for?

RSR & DKL

# About the Authors

**Raymond S. Ross, Ph.D.** is Professor Emeritus, Department of Communication, Wayne State University, Detroit, MI. Born in Milwaukee, Wisconsin, Professor Ross received his Bachelor of Philosophy and Master of Arts degrees from Marquette University. He earned an interdisciplinary Ph.D. in communication and psychology from Purdue University in 1954.

Dr. Ross is best known for his several popular college textbooks: *Speech Communication,* now in its 14th edition; *Small Groups in Organizational Settings; Understanding Persuasion,* 4th ed.; *Essentials of Speech Communication,* 2nd ed.; *Communication and Interpersonal Relations;* and *Relating and Interacting: an Introduction to Interpersonal Communication.* His latest trade book, *When Your Number's Up,* 2005, is a nonfiction novel about his combat experiences in World War II. *Brother Incarnate,* a WWII novel, is now in the editing stage.

Dr. Ross is listed in American Men of Science, Directory of American Scholars, National Register of Scientific Personnel, Who's Who in the Midwest, Contemporary Authors, and Outstanding Educators of America. He is the recipient of a Distinguished Alumni Award from Marquette University and was a Distinguished Visiting Professor at Pepperdine University. He is also a member of many academic and professional organizations including the National Communication Association and the American Psychological Association.

While at Ohio State University he was appointed Mershon Professor Air Science (AFROTC). For many years Professor Ross was an educational advisor to ROTC programs and the 10th Air Force Reserve. At WSU he was a staff member of the Institute of Industrial Relations, Wayne State University/University of Michigan, where he served as director of executive development programs. He has served as a research, training and communication consultant to numerous government, military, business and industrial firms.

Dr. Ross and his wife, Ricky

Dr. Ross and his wife, Ricky, live in Traverse City, MI. They have two sons, Mark and Scott, and a golden retriever named Buddy.

**Diana Leonard**, Ph.D., is a lecturer in the Department of Communication at the University of Arizona, Tucson, Arizona. She received her Master of Arts in Communication from San Francisco State University and her Bachelor of Arts in Psychology from the University of Arizona. Dr. Leonard focused on small group communication, cultural studies, and teaching communication for her Master of Arts degree. She earned her Ph.D. in Higher Education Organization and Administration from The University of Arizona.

Currently, Dr. Leonard serves as the Director of Public Speaking at The University of Arizona, She also teaches Advanced Public Speaking and Argumentation. She has taught multiple communication courses including: Introduction to Communication; Interpersonal Communication; Communication and Human Interaction; Communication in Fiction, Film and Poetry; Communication Criticism; Communication and Instruction; as well as Introduction to Public Speaking and Small Group Communication. Prior to joining the Department of Communication at The University of Arizona, Dr. Leonard taught at various community colleges in the Bay Area, for the Department of Speech Communication at San Francisco State University, and for Northern Arizona University's Statewide Program.

Her role as faculty advisor for Communication majors at The University of Arizona inspired Dr. Leonard toward pursuing her Ph.D. in Higher Education.

Determined to understand the impact teachers have on students, she studied influences on students' decision to transfer from a two-year institution to a four-year institution. Her dissertation is titled, "Shaping Fuzzy Goals through Teacher-Student Interaction: A Detailed Look at Communication between Community College Faculty and Transfer Students."

Dr. Leonard leads communication-training seminars and also consults for private clients and organizations in decision-making processes, communication strategies, and presentation skills. In her free time, she tends to her farm animals of chickens, goats, a horse, two dogs, a cat, a tortoise, and—of course—finds time for her partner.

Diana Leonard

# Introduction to the SPEECHMAKING

# PROCESS

# PUBLIC SPEAKING
# AND COMMUNICATION

# Chapter 1

## Chapter Objectives

### The Importance of Public Speaking in Society

### The Communication Process

Meaning

Perception

Communication Models

### Speaking with Confidence

You Are Not Alone

Understanding Emotion

Controlling Speech Fright

# THE IMPORTANCE OF PUBLIC SPEAKING IN SOCIETY

Why study public speaking? A dozen or more occupations have a direct interest in public speaking. The "people professions"—law, teaching, public relations, advertising, health care, management, criminal justice, and sales—could just as well be called the "communication professions."

It has been estimated that there are over three thousand speaking platforms on any given day in Los Angeles alone, thirty thousand in Chicago, and fifty thousand in New York. These include Rotary Clubs, universities, women's groups, church groups, and conventions. In today's golden age of the lecture business, Notre Dame former football coach Lou Holtz and motivational speaker Tony Robbins command fees of $20,000 to $75,000 per appearance. Ralph Nader earns $800,000 a year speaking. Who says talk is cheap?

> Take all the speech and communication courses you can because the world turns on communication.
>
> **J. H. McConnel, CEO,**
> **Worthington Industries**

Approximately sixty thousand conventions or major meetings are held each year in hundreds of cities across America. Many of these gatherings include intelligent, entertaining, or humorous paid presentations. Add to this, unpaid speeches (for example, over three thousand program participants at the yearly National Communication Association convention), and the numbers grow quickly. Do real people ever give speeches?

A survey of the speaking habits of 478 New York adults revealed that (1) between 55 percent and 63 percent of these adults gave at least one speech in the past two years to ten or more people, with 71 percent of these speakers giving at least four speeches during that time; (2) people are more likely to give job-related speeches, and these speeches are the informative and persuasive type; and (3) people with more education and income give speeches the most frequently. Knowing this last connection, a person who wants a high-income job would be wise to get a good education and prepare to speak well. Obviously this is a skill you may need.

Still think it isn't important? In a Michigan poll, five hundred adults were asked: "What most influences your decisions about political candidates?" The respondents put party affiliation first, *speaking ability* second, appearance or good looks third, age fourth, race or ethnic background fifth, and the person's

Public Speaking is an important skill you may employ many times over the course of your life, long after your public speaking course is finished.

sex last. One would hope that honesty, issues, and intelligence might have been mentioned more often … but speaking ability is clearly critical. Although both of the above surveys have relatively small sample sizes, the point they make is strong: Public speaking is an important skill to have long after your public speaking course is finished!

Are students any good at this important oral skill? Dr. David Adamany, a university president, thinks not:

The University of Colorado faculty and students across the curriculum agree. Survey data make clear that both groups feel that students are deficient in the following:

1. Expressing ideas clearly

2. Organizing messages

3. Expressing ideas concisely

4. Using evidence

5. Using a speaking voice

6. Controlling anxiety

7. Listening effectively[1]

> It has become increasingly clear that students are significantly deficient in their ability to make oral presentations. Yet this skill has become steadily more important in a world which requires collaboration between specialists in widely varying fields and in which communications technology—by telephone, television and audiovisual tapes—implicates the ability to make effective oral presentations. Contrary to some journalistic assertions, a technological age heightens the need for human collaboration—and thus for effective oral communication—rather than diminishing it. … I ask the commission to consider how the university might improve the ability of students to make oral presentations, which is certainly one of the basic skills required of most educated persons.
>
> **David Adamany, President, Wayne State University**

There is hope that we are correcting the problem.

The national call for students to improve their critical thinking relates directly to the concepts covered in this text. "… we are teaching far more than a set of skills to use to affect others. We are also teaching structures for thinking."[2] We process information in order to "think" about it the same way we process information to share with others. When we speak to others (formally or informally) we help them understand our thinking processes by providing connections between our ideas. These "connections" depict how we reason (how we think). The interaction between how we speak and how we think is a compelling reason for learning and applying the lessons in your public speaking course.

> On higher education—"79% require speech communication in Gen Ed."
>
> **SPECTRA, April 1995**

Many researchers show that you can improve your speech skills significantly by taking a speech course. Moreover, testimonials by successful individuals have affirmed the value of speech training, and research has indicated its usefulness to you in better understanding your other university courses. The better we are at making connections, the better we are at understanding the information provided in our classes (and the better we are at showing our instructors we understand)!

Modern technology often makes speech preparation and critical thinking unusually important. In one case reported by New York state occupational education czar Willard Daggert, a speech was in IBM hard copy transcripts within 90 seconds of its completion—*and simultaneously translated into four different languages.* We'll have more to say about critical thinking in the chapters that follow.

# THE COMMUNICATION PROCESS

## Meaning

For many social theorists, communication is primarily concerned with *meaning*. Meaning for them becomes a social construction based primarily on our life experiences, our perceptions of reality, and our language habits. For *social-construction* theorists all objective reality is entirely dependent on our thinking habits and our communication abilities.[3]

This is not to say that there is not any "true" or "real" reality in the world—just that our abilities to discern it are heavily biased by our experience,

For many social theorists, communication is primarily concerned with meaning. Meaning for them becomes a social construction based primarily on our life experiences, our perceptions of reality, and our language habits.

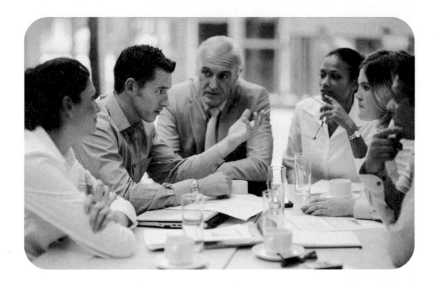

our attitudes, and our language and thinking habits. The question "What is reality?" is not a new one. In a dictionary sense the answer is, "a person, entity, or event that is actual or true," or "that which exists objectively and in fact." In philosophy, reality (realism) can mean "the doctrine that universal principles are more real than objects as sensed," or "the doctrine that the objects of perception exist independently of the perceiver."

A better question might be "Where is reality?" In the final analysis a person's individual reality, however accurate or inaccurate, is still one's individual perception of reality. The same can be said of society and its definable subgroups. One's concept and understanding of the interaction of "real" reality, individual perception of reality, and society's perception of reality can affect our ability to be objective, rational, and realistic.

Some people perceive reality better than others. They make more accurate social constructions of what they see and hear. The bias of communication professors is that these people do better because they are more knowledgeable in the critical areas of communication, perception, language, and logical thinking.

> Human action is critically dependent on the cognitive processing of information, that is, on the world as cognized rather that the world as it is.
>
> **Professor K. J. Gergen,**
> **Swarthmore College**

This book addresses all four of these areas and hopefully relates them clearly to the pragmatic dimensions of public speaking. Language and critical thinking will be covered in detail in Chapters 2 and 12.

## Perception

The perception process is really another way of looking at the communication process and how we discern or assign meanings to messages. The theory here is that we hypothesize about messages, which we then accept or reject on the basis of personal constructs based on prior learning and experience.

Have you ever been on a train that was stopped next to other trains in a railroad terminal? Have you then felt, seen, and heard all the signs indicating movement, only to find it was the other trains that were moving? Perhaps you discovered this by noticing that the other trains were gone, or by fixing your gaze on something you knew was not moving, such as the ceiling of the station, a roof support, or the ground.

The point of this is that perception is essentially two things: (1) the *sensation* caused by the stimulation of a sense organ and (2) the *interpretation* of that sensation. In our study of speech we are concerned mainly with the interpretation. As was stated earlier, it is through our knowledge and experience that we interpret or attach meaning to a symbol.

Our *mood* (or *set*), or readiness to perceive a stimulus in a certain way, affects our ability to perceive and to accept a stimulus. The consciousness defends itself by apparently refusing to accept certain messages. On the other hand, we may wish so much to hear something that, regardless of the actual message, we hear, interpret, and attach meaning to it according to what we *wish* to hear. One of the great barriers

We use both *sense* and *interpretation* to perceive the world around us; this is *perception*. We hear the noise and feel the vibration in the ground from a moving train.

to good communication is our tendency to hear what we wish to hear, see what we wish to see, and believe what we wish to believe.

A closely related perceptual and communication problem arises from our normal tendency toward **completeness**. The concept of completeness arises with our desire to fill in the missing pieces of a message or pattern to make a whole idea, picture, or message. When a communication message is only partially complete, we will fill in the unsaid part to complete the idea. If we do not have a sense of completeness about something, we often feel upset, ill at ease, confused, and unhappy about it. This tendency can be important in motivating people. Perhaps you have had a teacher who communicates just enough knowledge in a stimulating way to motivate you to do further reading and research so that you can complete or close the pattern. It is fairly easy to see Figure 1.1 as a complete triangle and by filling in the missing pieces, we can usually see a hammer and complete the question with Who's there? Problems arise, however,

Figure 1.1

KNOCK KNOCK
WH     TH     ?

when we close incomplete communication patterns in ways not intended by the speaker, or when we become frustrated by a lack of details.

Sometimes our habits and previous experiences cause us to leave things out or to not see or hear what we don't expect. Our habits and expectations contribute to what we perceive is actually there. Read the three messages in Figure 1.2 quickly. Many people see nothing unusual about these messages, even after two or three readings. The good, rapid readers seem to have the most trouble. Why should this be so? A group of second and third graders had no trouble finding the double words in each message. To a certain extent we perceive what our habits, our emotions, and our prior knowledge and experience let us perceive. A

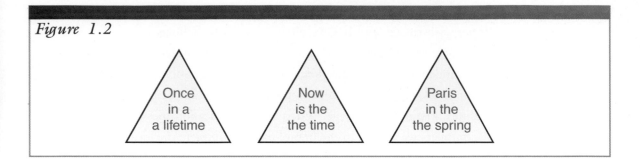

*Figure 1.2*

Once
in a
a lifetime

Now
is the
the time

Paris
in the
the spring

good reader has learned to skim and to ignore nonessential words. The beginning reader sees one word at a time.

Test your perceptual ability in Figure 1.3. Do you see anything familiar or identifiable? Do you see a message?

You should see a word in white on a partial purple field. Your experience is usually just the opposite of this pattern; here the area *between* the letters is black instead of the letters themselves. This conflict between experience and what you are actually looking at can make it difficult to hold the image for a long period

*Figure 1.3*

of time Even after you see the message it may escape you momentarily as your long-standing habits and previous patterns of experience assert themselves.

As was noted above, your *mental set*—that is, your readiness to interpret a message in a certain way—has a lot to do with what you "see." Look for a duck in Figure 1.4. You should find one quickly because a duck is what you are looking for. Keep studying the duck. You should also find another animal. This

*Figure 1.4*

might take some work. Try looking at the picture from different angles. Did you see the other animal?

A group of professional photographers found it almost impossible to "see" the photograph in Figure 1.5. What do you see?

*Figure 1.5*

Don't proceed until you see a cow looking right at you! If you haven't seen it by now, you may actually become annoyed, particularly if you've asked for help and your friends see the cow immediately. Communication is like that. We don't do our best when we begin to feel awkward, stupid, or left out.

How are you doing with LEFTY and the rabbit? Have you lost them? When experiences are new to us, we may understand or see one moment and "not see" the next.

The same person does not always perceive the same object exactly the same way every time he or she observes it. It is no wonder that other observers do not always agree on what they see.

Carl Rogers explains that every individual exists in a continually changing world of experience of which he or she is the center. This world can be referred to as the **phenomenal field** or the **experiential field**, meaning that humans exist in a sea of experiences—both conscious and unconscious. Remembering this about ourselves helps us to recognize our uniqueness. Remembering this about our audience helps us to choose the best connections to reach the uniqueness within each one of them.

## Communication Models

The word **model** generally refers to a representation of a thing or a process. We have relatively little trouble producing a model of a physical object. We can learn much about the physical behavior of trains, boats, and airplanes by building models of them. However, when we attempt to make models of more abstract things—things that are difficult to measure physically—we often oversimplify to the point of poor or dangerous representation, or we may simply be unable to agree on exactly what it is we are modeling.

The advantages of using a model are evident. The model gives you a different, closer look. It provides a frame of reference, suggests informational gaps, underlines the problem of abstraction, and expresses a problem in symbolic language when there is some advantage in using figures or symbols. Of course there are some drawbacks to using models, such as oversimplification and other dangers inherent in gross abstraction.

We may use words, numbers, symbols, and pictures to illustrate models of things, theories, or processes. In geometry, we accept the theorem that the square of the hypotenuse of a right triangle is equal to the sum of the squares of the legs. This statement is a form of **verbal model**. If we draw a picture of this theorem (Figure 1.6), we have a

*Figure 1.6*    The square of the hypotenuse of a right triangle is equal to the sum of the squares of the legs, or AKHB = ACDE + BFGC.

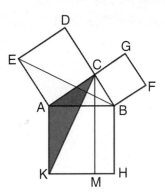

**verbal-pictorial model**. Communication experts have used mostly verbal-pictorial models in trying to give us a closer and more scientific look at the communication process.

The **transactional model** (Figure 1.7) attempts to illustrate the following definition of communication:

> A transactional process of skillfully sharing, selecting, and sorting ideas, symbols, and signs in such a way as to help listeners elicit from their own minds a meaning or construction similar to that intended by the speaker.

By **transactional** we mean that this is a socially derived process involving an unending activity that simultaneously and reciprocally affects or influences both parties. That is, we are capable of being both sender and receiver at the same time. We are, one might say, *transceivers*.[4]

The frame of the model shows the world in which this communication takes place. It suggests the importance of *situation, mood, context,* and *psychological climate*. The **situation** could range from a formal speech to a simple exchange of information. **Mood** refers to feelings of the moment. At different times your mood might be happy, angry, tense, and so on. Your mood can greatly affect what you say or hear and how you say or hear something. **Context** is the framework of other words or ideas into which yours fit. If you

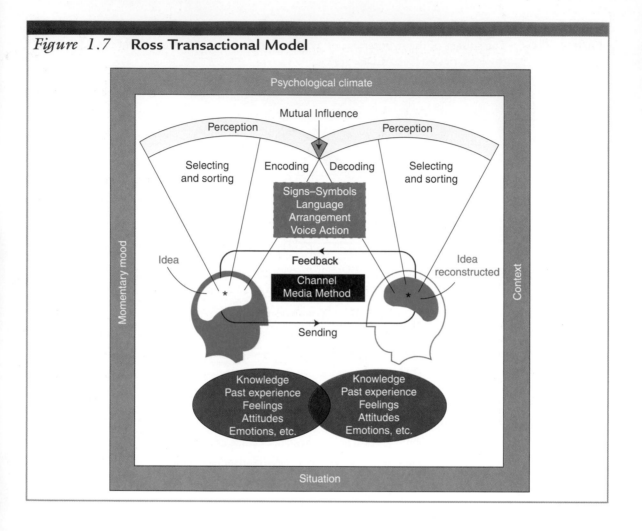

*Figure 1.7*   **Ross Transactional Model**

are talking about paper, note how the word changes in these contexts: The paper was late today (newspaper). The paper is crooked (wallpaper). It is an A paper (homework). *Psychological climate* is a lot like weather or physical climate. Just as our weather might be bitterly cold, so too might the psychological mood of a classroom or a speech occasion. A good speaker recognizes the climate of the occasion, or the mood of the audience, and adjusts for it. The speaker herself also can affect the climate negatively as well as positively. An unhappy, impersonal (cold) speaker typically hinders rather than helps communication by contributing to a negative climate. Sometimes climate is the most important part of a speaker's message.

Let's assume we have a message (which might be referred to as an *idea* or *concept* or *meaning*) that we wish to convey to another person. Our brain now sorts through our storehouse of knowledge, experience, feelings, and previous training to select and refine the precise meaning we are seeking to communicate. Before we transmit this meaning, we **encode** it; we put it into signs and symbols that we commonly think of as *language*. (Gesture, facial expression, and tone of voice may also be considered signs, symbols, or codes.)

The way in which the message is coded, the medium or channel chosen for its transmission, and the skill with which it is transmitted influence the meaning it will have for the receiver. Assuming that the medium for this illustration is simply the air between the speaker and the listener, we now have the encoded message, its transmission, and its reception by the other person. The listener then **decodes** the signal, or at least attempts to decode it. Decoding is when the listener sorts out, selects, and elicits meanings from his or her storehouse of knowledge, experience, and training until he or she constructs in his or her own mind a notion of the images and ideas contained in the mind of the sender. However, if the signal was encoded in a manner with which the listener is not familiar, such as a foreign language, the listener will not know how to decode it; and thus not much communication of any kind will take place.

Gesture, facial expressions, and tone of voice may be considered signs, symbols, or codes.

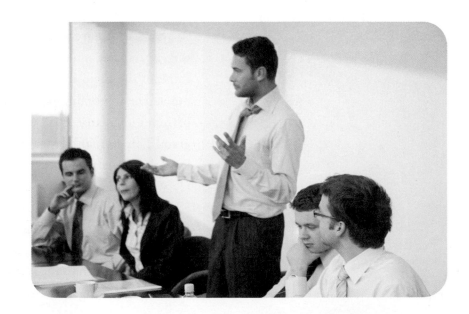

To the extent that the listener's notions or constructions are similar to the sender's images and ideas, we will usually achieve satisfactory communication. The idea, concept, or meaning in the mind of the listener is therefore very dependent upon the knowledge and experience he or she can apply to the code. The value of knowing your listeners now becomes evident. The *thoughts* you are trying to communicate and provoke are the principal energizers of the speech-making process. They are the fuel that makes a serious communication possible. However, like a car with a full gas tank, it will not go far if the sub-systems fail or if the fuel was watered down in the first place.

Let's assume that the speaker depicted in Figure 1.7 (Ross Transactional Model) is a woman who wishes to communicate a message (a thought or an idea) to an audience. The star inside her brain represents the idea.

Let's suppose the idea is an abstract one, such as *love*. Within this woman's 12 billion brain cells are stored her knowledge and past experiences, her feelings, attitudes, emotions, and many more things that make her the person she is. The brain,

The brain has a storage capacity able to accept ten new facts every second, and can hold information equivalent to 100 trillion different words.

with a storage capacity able to accept ten new facts every second, can hold information equivalent to 100 trillion different words. Our sender now sorts through and selects from this vast storehouse of knowledge and past experience, choosing items that help her define and refine what she is trying to say.

She has to have a basis upon which to perform this operation, a program if you will. We can think of the brain in some ways as a system computer. The forebrain, for example, becomes a kind of input regulator into which we feed the program. This woman's program had better include at least three questions, or she is already in trouble: (1) What do I have stored under *love?* (2) What do I know about the audience? (3) What do I have filed for this particular situation and context? You can almost visualize the program in action: assessing, accepting, rejecting, cross-referencing, and synthesizing both the information in the storehouse and in the system—in short, selecting and sorting the appropriate knowledge, past experience, and so on. In this complex process the brain actually burns electrical power. H. A. Johnson comments wryly:

*"The human brain, deep in thought, consumes about 14 watts of power. It gives some insight into world politics to consider that when three heads of state meet at the summit their combined brain power is that of a 40-watt light bulb, scarcely sufficient for reading the lines, to say nothing of reading between them."*

**Horton A. Johnson,**

**Perspectives in Biology and Medicine**

The woman must next choose her codes based on what she knows about her audience by applying a program similar to the one used in sorting ideas: (1) What do I know about my audience? (2) What codes do I have available? (3) Which codes do I believe will be most effective for this audience? She then rejects the codes she thinks might be unclear. This process is an example of encoding the message.

The woman in the model now must deliver the message. Let us assume that there is no unusual distraction or noise in the system, and that the sensory access of the audience is adequate. Assuming the audience is listening, the message is received. The auditory and other sensations experienced by the listeners are only the first part of human perception. The more critical part is the interpretation of those sensations, which is all part of the decoding process of the signs, symbols, and language of the speaker. The listeners sort through their knowledge, experiences, attitudes, and so forth and select those meanings that will allow the creation of a message concerning love. To the extent that this reconstruction or response is similar to the sender's intended message, we hopefully have meaningful communication. This reconstructed idea is largely dependent upon common knowledge, fields of experience, language, and some understanding of the communication process. This is why we say that communication is a socially constructed phenomenon

The term **feedback** in the model requires a moment of important consideration. Feedback is what the receiver provides to the speaker to let him or her know how the message is coming across to the audience and allows the speaker to make adjustments. Quizzical looks might call for clarification; nods might call for additional examples that the audience might enjoy. In engineering terms, interactional feedback also refers to some of the transmitted energy or signal being returned to the source. The automatic pilot used in airplanes is an example of self-correcting machinery that uses feedback. The general goal in both cases is to allow for small adjustments in order to correct the situation. The analogy appears to break down a bit when we consider the kind of electronic feedback all of us have observed in public-address systems or recorders, in which a reentry of some of the sound from the speaker to the microphone causes a howl or loud noise. However, even in these cases, small adjustments in the arrangement of the speakers, the volume, or where the speaker stands in relation to the microphone, can remedy the problem. Human communication is also vulnerable to disruptive feedback:, like heckling, loud argument, and fear. When this type of feedback is severe enough, a speaker may suffer encoding difficulties or even anger to the point of ending the transaction. A current example of the power of negative feedback occurred at a comedy club recently. A couple of hecklers in the balcony upset the comedian to such a degree that he lost his temper, retorted with racial epitaphs, and ended the entire show with the audience aghast. Of course, some people just don't listen well (providing poor or no feedback at all), and some speakers don't allow for feedback!

Human communication is vulnerable to disruptive feedback:, heckling, loud argument, and fear.

For most speech purposes we usually think of feedback as useful in a self-correcting sense. As our transmitted signal is "bounced off" our receivers, it feeds back information that allows us to correct and refine our signal. A curious look, a frown, a yawn, the sound of our own voice—any of these may cause us to reevaluate and recode our signals. Feedback should be considered as part of the transactional process that we should make work for us.

Obviously not every member of an audience will decode, reconstruct, and respond in the same way (Figure 1.7). This is another reminder that audience analysis is critical to message input. Recall also that the **encoder** and **decoder** can perform their functions only in terms of their own fields of experience (see the model in Figure 1.7). There must be some shared experience *common* to both in order for the communication to even begin to convey the intended message. As the receiver begins to decode a message sent to him or her, that receiver's process of encoding a response or feedback begins. The roles of encoder and decoder, speaker and audience, are interchangeable. Thus, each person in the communication process is to some extent simultaneously an encoder and decoder.

Because individuals differ, contexts differ, and speaking occasions differ, responsible speakers have an ethical obligation to match their message to these differences. A given message does not mean the same thing to all people, and perceptions and understandings vary with contexts and situations. Therefore, we have an ethical responsibility to analyze our audiences and their circumstances in order to work toward a shared interpretation and meaning of our messages. We'll talk more about analyzing our audience in Chapter 3.

According to a national survey, speech fright is the number one fear for Americans with death well down the list.

# SPEAKING WITH CONFIDENCE

## You Are Not Alone

After reading national surveys that put speech fright or what psychologists call "performance anxiety" as Americans' number one fear with death well down the list, Jerry Seinfeld cracked, "At a funeral you'd be better off in the casket than giving the eulogy."

One conclusion of all the surveys, and much of the research, is that many of you will suffer some form of speech fright of varying intensity. If it is true that misery loves company, then it will be reassuring to know that you are certainly not alone. Even professional performers report startling emotional reactions before public performances.

Beginning speech students also consider this a problem. Surveys indicate that 60 to 75 percent of a class may admit that they are bothered by "nervousness in speaking," an expectation that they have more to lose than to gain from speaking. Fourteen to 20 percent may be concerned enough to ask for help in the form of instructor conferences, specific reading assignments, or exercises that help ease speech fright. Most nervousness is typical, if not always normal. Much of it is temporary and based on expectations of anxiety in speaking situations. Most of you will find that the more formal the audience or the situation, the more speech fright there is. If you're new to speechmaking, be advised that the sooner you start facing such nervousness, the more likely you are to overcome it and subsequently do better in your remaining college courses.

> *Boy, if you tell me that four hundred people are coming in here to see me perform, I will strategically place buckets in my dressing room because my stomach cannot handle the anxiety.*
>
> **Patty Duke, actress**

Speaking or acting, like skydiving, might be an exhilarating, satisfying behavior for those who know and enjoy what they are doing, but a nightmare for the uninformed. Skills about which we have only limited knowledge frighten us and, in some instances, should. Part of speechmaking is frightening; perhaps all of it is for some speakers. It is mostly a skill, partially an art.

It helps to know that audiences do not view your fright as seriously as you do indicating that you do not appear and sound as bad as you feel. There is good evidence that audiences perceive speaker anxiety to be lower than the speakers themselves report.[5] This fact should be reassuring.

Whether or not your fear is readily apparent, the result may be the same. As in other frightening situations, you may feel dryness in the mouth, a rapid heartbeat, a sinking feeling in the stomach, difficulty with abdominal control, dysfluency, and even agitation. You may exhibit physical behaviors like trembling or reddening of the face (due to the increased heartbeat and increased adrenalin). Your voice may shake or you may find yourself speaking very rapidly (due to the lack of regular deep breathing).

Once again, evidence indicates that your classmates evaluate the physical manifestations of your feelings as modest and transitory. Hence, our fright nonverbals are not as detrimental as you think they are. Furthermore, your classmates share your same predicament. The situation is no more novel for you than it is for them, and there is no reason to feel conspicuous. Negative thoughts only increase your anxiety. If they persist to the point of panic, research confirms that the quality of your speech behavior will suffer.[6] The goal then, is to discover ways to rein in the thoughts that increase your nervousness.

> *The only difference between the pros and the novices is that the pros have trained the butterflies to fly in formation.*
>
> **Edwin Newman,**
>
> **NBC News Anchorman**

Speech courses help with this all-too-common problem of communication apprehension. Speech textbooks, course experience, and careful preparation have helped thousands of frightened students. Researchers found that after eight weeks and four speeches, observable anxiety was significantly reduced. Actual speaking experience appears to help students gain confidence. So does oral reading.[7]

For the most part, people who experience high speech anxiety do not vary from others in general intelligence, reasoning ability, or the most important aspects of personality. They may vary, however, in education, experience, linguistic ability, self-concept, and social attraction.

To a great extent, we humans are afraid of what we do not understand. Young children may be paralyzed with fear during a severe electrical storm until their mother or father explains what causes the thunder and lightning. Afterwards, the child will experience fear, but not fear of a paralyzing nature. Loud noises make all of us jump, but knowledge and understanding of what causes the loud noises make it possible for us to stop jumping between noises. Because we are dealing with the symptoms and causes of an emotional reaction, we are better able to control emotion if we know how it operates.

## Understanding Emotion

The famous philosopher and psychologist William James provides us with a relatively simple and extremely useful theory of emotion. The gist of the theory is that it is not just the *speaking* that panics us, but also our *awareness of our reactions to a frightening situation.* This awareness *is the real emotion.* James's favorite illustration of this theory was that of coming upon a bear in the woods.

*Figure 1.9*

In a nonscientific way, we might say the bear triggers the emotion of fear in us. Not so, for according to James, our body reacts almost automatically to the bear. Our natural survival devices take over to prepare us for an emergency. Our muscles tense for better agility; our heartbeat and breathing quicken to provide larger supplies of fuel; our glands secrete fluids to sharpen our senses and give us emergency energy. All of this happens in an instant. Then we become aware of these bodily reactions. We sense our heavy breathing; our muscles tense to the point of trembling; perhaps adrenalin surges into our system. It is this *awareness of our reactions* that frightens us. In other words, the awareness is the emotion. Of course, the bear still has a lot to do with our condition!

The label (fear, anxiety, and so forth) we have learned for this special awareness comes from our past experiences that fit this situation. If we observe other people acting frightened, then our own deductions are strengthened. When the cause of our emotional state is not clear, we may attribute the emotion to any available cue in the environment.

After missing a precommencement honoring ceremony because, *"I was a nervous wreck,"* and later at commencement speaking to the crowd, *"Boy am I nervous."*

**Bob Seger, musician**

It would be ridiculous to tell you that if you understand clearly all the physiological and psychological reactions described above, you have eliminated the bear. However, this knowledge and understanding will help you *control* what action you take and, thereby, improve your chance for survival. This is what we mean by emotional or speech fright control, and this is why we use the term *control* rather than *eliminate* when we speak of fear.

In the same manner that our fear of the bear is caused not by the bear itself but by our awareness of our bodily reactions to the bear, in speech fright it is our awareness of our internal and external reactions that provides us with the emotion—or at least heightens the emotion. The speech situation, though obviously less dangerous than the bear, poses a more difficult problem. Nature prepares us for *flight* or *fight*, so we either flee from the bear or attack it. When you experience anxiety in a speech situation, you are responding to a "false sense of danger." Your body doesn't realize it is a false alarm, so it is sending out messages (in the form of adrenalin) to run or fight it out. However, the speech situation rules out the use of these survival tactics. You can neither attack the audience nor run for the woods. You are stuck with a very different problem. You have to drain off some of your excess energy while holding your ground and facing a fear-provoking stimulus (the audience). In your favor, however, there are no recorded instances of an audience eating a speaker!

The point of the bear story is to help you understand the nature of emotion, for understanding and knowledge almost always promote emotional adjustment.

## Controlling Speech Fright

**OBJECTIFYING**    The principle of **objectification** is an intellectualization or pragmatic explanation of what is happening to you. Such explanations take the edge off of emotions. Imagine a great lover who, when kissing his beloved, decided to analyze exactly what he was doing. I imagine this would take a lot of the spontaneity and passion right out of that kiss!

A former student, reporting on one of his own objectification experiments, reported, "You know, Doc, it takes all the kick out of it!" By the same reasoning, detailed intellectualization of speech-fright experiences should help take some of the "kick" out of them.

Have you ever asked yourself, "Why do my arms and hands tremble? Why do I have that sinking feeling in my stomach?" The issue is not *whether* you experience these things, but rather *why?* If you do ask why and the answer is, "Because I'm scared to death," you probably only add to the emotion. This is the time to apply the principle of objectification. Remember that the emotion is largely the result of your awareness of your own bodily reactions and that an objective explanation of these reactions will take the edge off your awareness.

The sinking feeling in the stomach that we experience under stress can also be explained in great detail. When faced with a fear-provoking situation, the body calls upon its glandular secretions, notably adrenalin, for emergency energy. These secretions chemically interfere with the digestive system. This process tends to make the stomach contract and produces the sensation typically referred to as a "sinking feeling."

Analyzing these reactions should help you control fright. Emotion loses its intensity under examination and objectification. Face up to your problems and get the facts straight. *It is healthy to talk objectively about your fright.* Instructors are good listeners. Let yours help you talk out your fright. In these ways you will meet your fright on a conscious level, at which you have the most control. If your mouth feels dry, find out why. If your knees shake, find out why. If you feel faint, find out why. The *why* is usually rather mundane and unexciting, but it is extremely logical and objective.

One day on a flight from San Francisco to Tucson, I sat next to a woman who was petrified of flying. Every cell in her body was trembling. As we took off, her hands gripped the armrests leaving her knuckles albino white. When the landing gear retracted, she nearly jumped from her seat. "What's that?" she cried. It was time to start explaining how the plane works. I told her about the landing gear and the sound that would be made by the retracting flaps. I explained how a plane creates lift with the speed and design of the aircraft. When we hit a little turbulence, I told her how I loved the feeling of turbulence because I knew there was lots of atmosphere that the plane could use to stay aloft. When we landed, I explained the sounds she was going to hear and what they were in the process. We landed while talking. Her knuckles were no longer white; her body was no longer shaking. She understood how a plane worked. Your job is much simpler. Know and understand how and why your body works the way it does in order to control fright.

**ACTING "AS IF"**   Most individuals cannot experience two opposite or different types of emotional reactions at the same time. For example, at the instant when you are boiling mad, you are probably not afraid. (This is not to suggest that you should freely substitute anger for fright.) You may already have observed that when a speaker is really involved in a subject, he or she will tend to be less frightened by the platform situation. This helps explain our almost instinctive actions to ward off fright situations—why, for example, we whistle while walking through a dark alley. We are acting "as if" we are unafraid—perhaps happy, indignant, or angry. Acting "as if" has helped all of us through emotionally charged situations; it is a form of **cognitive restructuring** (which means: changing the thinking). For example, try substituting positive coping statements for negative ones: "We are all challenged by this assignment" for "I'll appear ridiculous"; "I've really prepared, and I've got something to say" for "They'll think I'm stupid"; or, if you are already into the speech, try "I'm still together—I'm getting by" for "I think I'm going to be sick." The goals of cognitive restructuring are to 1) expose errors in your thoughts (seeing how they might be just a tad bit irrational); 2) replace these irrational thoughts with rational ones (check with your instructor and others about how rational your replacement thoughts are); 3) create coping statements (like offered above); and 4) practice those coping statements so that they become second nature to you. It's a lot like the *Self-Fulfilling Prophecy*. We utilize the prophecy everyday without even thinking about it; creating experiences we think we had no control over. The Self-Fulfilling Prophecy claims that once we believe something is true or false, we act or behave accordingly. Our behavior brings about further evidence for our belief (what we believe will happen, does happen), so our belief is strengthened. To change our initial belief, we need to utilize the cognitive restructuring technique explained above.

In some cases cognitive restructuring involves a cognitive reorientation of how you view the public speaking situation. Motley and Molloy suggest that speakers who view the situation as requiring a flawless, show-biz type performance will experience more anxiety than those who concentrate primarily on sharing an important message. Indeed, they were able to achieve such an anxiety-reducing reorientation through the use of persuasive written arguments. They call this form of cognitive restructuring "Communication-Orientation Motivation."[8]

Another way of restructuring an anxious negative outlook is to visualize yourself thinking and acting in very positive and successful ways. In its simplest form, this kind of *visualization* asks you to imagine yourself making a very effective presentation. In one approach, on the day of your speech or before, start thinking positively about all aspects of the speech from the time you get up in the morning until after you've given the speech. Good evidence shows that such positive visualizations or acting "as if" reduce one's anxiety.[9] It is healthy to whistle in the dark; it is often the difference between poise and panic. Of course, actually *working* on your skills, preparation efforts, and rehearsals can also help enhance speech quality *and* your confidence level. The use of combined treatments for anxiety often works better than a single treatment.[10]

Let your emotions work for you when you can. In moments of strain, redirect your attention to other things and bring more tolerable emotions into focus. Try to become so involved in one thing that you are less aware of the other. Psychologists call this process of redirecting your attention **compensation**. It helps at the moment of truth when you must speak and also aids in visualizing during your preparation.

Your choice of a speech topic may therefore be important to you emotionally as well as rhetorically. If you are excited or can become excited about your subject, you will make theory work for you—a kind of natural and intelligent whistling in the dark. If you can find humor in your task or in your reactions to it, you may have found a very healthy distraction.

One can sometimes cognitively restructure by concentrating on the smiling and pleasant faces in the audience for moral support. Most audiences are, after all, supportive, or at worst disinterested. One professor reported that he started to overcome his speech fright when he began concentrating on the sleeping

Before your next speech, try rehearsing your presentation to enhance your speech quality and boost your confidence level.

faces. He may have been substituting anger in this instance, or he may have decided his fear was a little ridiculous if he was talking only to himself.

**CHANNELING EXCESS TENSION**    We direct our actions most usefully once we break the wall of tension with the first step. Your first problem is to release some of the extra energy that your body dutifully provides. Bodily activity will help you utilize your extra energy or tension.

In the speaking situation you need to consider how your body movements look and what the movement communicates to the audience. The strategy here is very simple. Plan and direct some of your gross bodily movement and visualize in advance—not in a stereotyped way, but nevertheless systematically, complete with options. For example, at the close of your introduction or perhaps at a transition between points, you might plan on moving a step to the side or raising a book or card for emphasis. You have the option of selecting the precise time and action, depending upon how natural it seems and how tense you are. A single cough is a natural way to expel excess energy and can provide an autonomic breathing response to get your breathing back on track. Multiple coughs will become distracting to the audience, however, so use this technique judiciously.

Another very natural kind of activity is that associated with *visual aids.* If you comment on a picture, demonstrate an object, or write on a blackboard, you have to make perfectly natural movements in the process. This is an excellent way to channel excess energy.[11]

*Pre-speech physical activity* can also help you reduce your tension and relax. One approach to dealing with speech anxiety from a physiological perspective is called **systematic desensitization**. This is a process of reducing the sensitivity one has toward certain situations. Therapists, as well as public speaking instructors, use the process of systematic desensitization to reduce apprehension. The process is simple: 1) learn relaxation techniques (e.g. deep breathing, yoga, walking, and meditation); 2) provide increased tension-provoking situations while focusing on relaxation, and finally; 3) relax on cue. Your instructor may help you learn some relaxation techniques. He or she then provides various speaking situations, often with increasing point values assigned. This reflects the systematic desensitization process. Since the goal is to relax on cue, you may take some of your learned techniques into the speaking situation.

*Figure 1.10*

If the journey from your chair to the speaker's platform is a real torture, *rehearse* this activity in an empty classroom or in measured distances at home. Keep rehearsing it until you sense monotony in the repetition. Often college debaters inadvertently repeat certain strategies and argument patterns so zealously in practice that they risk becoming stale when presenting the same ideas in debate. Football teams have had similar experiences. The point is that monotonous repetition may help drain off that keyed-up feeling.

> The only way to get over the fear of public speaking, one successful public speaker says, is "to just do it. You've got to suffer through it."
>
> **Dorothy Fuldheim, news commentator**

A moderate amount of repression of external behavior may also be in order to help you get started. By **repression** we mean a form of mental discipline in which you force yourself to get on with the business at hand. This is by no means a final adjustment because continued repression would result in extreme fatigue. However, it is neither unusual nor abnormal to use moderate repression of external behavior as a *first step* in adjusting to the speaking situation.

**HELPING YOUR MEMORY**   Beginning speakers are often frightened by just the thought of forgetting their speech. Apparently speech fright becomes a cause of forgetting, and the thought of forgetting causes or reinforces speech fright—a vicious circle.

As in redirecting attention, your topic can be important in helping your memory. The more you know about a subject and the more enthusiastic you are about it, the less likely you are to forget your material. Your attitude toward your subject, your involvement in it, and your eagerness to communicate it are all related to your ability to remember it.

In preparing your speech, the key word for memory protection is *system*. We remember better, we learn better, and we speak better if the material with which we are dealing is arranged systematically. It is easier to remember a list of twenty automobile names grouped according to some system (that is, according to manufacturer, size, horsepower, and so on) than in random order. Have you ever noticed how rapidly you can learn the names of baseball players? Obviously it is because of the system of positions they play; if you do not know the positions, you will be slower at learning the names. One of the best friends you will have when it comes to helping your memory is a well-prepared and structured outline. The outline becomes the skeleton to your speech body. Remembering that all the bones of your outline have a specific purpose and are specifically connected as you planned (the knee bone is connected to the thigh bone), makes it easy to remember what comes next. We will discuss the techniques of outlining in Chapter 6.

One of the most effective memory aids is a visual aid. If your speech uses numbers and statistics, a large poster, transparency, or PowerPoint slide with the numbers listed and identified considerably eases the pressure on your memory. Similarly, a note in your pocket containing testimony, statistics, or other details is also helpful. Just the knowledge that you have such a backup is often worth more than the material on the visual aid itself.

Research suggests that the thinking that goes into developing a visual aid will also improve the content and the delivery of your speech.[12] More on visual aids will be discussed in Chapter 9.

Despite all the protection you can give your memory, all speakers occasionally experience the frustration of "blanking out." This is often the result of **state-anxiety**, anxiety due to the particular communication circumstance, not anxiety in general, which is defined as **trait-anxiety** and refers to anxiety across many or all communication situations.[13] If you have ever watched youngsters delivering memorized poems or salutations at an elementary school convocation, you have heard them forget their lines on occasion. You have probably also noticed that they almost instinctively keep repeating the last line they *do* remember in a frantic effort to rerail their memory. This effort may help, but more often the prompter has a busy day. Word-for-word memorization is really not a very intelligent "system" because the memory cannot relate so many small, unrelated parts. However, the principle of repeating the last thing you do remember is still useful. The practical application is to review the material you have just covered.

If your memory fails toward the end of your speech, you can *summarize* the key points you have made. Practical experience indicates that such a technique does help you reawaken your memory. One student who found this suggestion useful formulated her own rule: "When in doubt, summarize."

**VISUALIZING REALISTICALLY**   We talked earlier of a professor who felt less speech fright when he discovered that most of his class was asleep. With all due respect to student audiences, an honest appraisal of them is that they are not eagerly leaning forward, straining with every muscle to record for all time the wisdom you are about to deliver. Professors know this, and so should you. Audiences may on occasion be lively, but more often than not this liveliness is due to the efforts of the speaker. Be objective about your audience. An analysis of speaker evaluations indicates that the audience sympathizes with the speaker. This means that if your audience is listening at all, it is rooting for you.

While the anxiety we experience is heavily conditioned by our individual predispositions to respond and deal with emotion, let us not forget that the specific audience we face or think we face also contributes something—such things as status inequality, dissimilarity, novel or ambiguous circumstances, or unusual formality.[14] Realistic audience appraisal at least allows us to measure and objectively analyze the beast so that we can visualize more positive situations as we prepare.

Research suggests that proper preparation, a clear understanding of your speech assignment and being adequately informed about the topic you choose, can help ameliorate anxiety.[15] Realizing that your speech will probably not be

> If you are able to talk ably on your own subject in a living room or at a dinner table, you will be safe from harm behind a lectern.
>
> **Gerald Gardner,**
> **Professional speaker**

recorded for posterity should also have a calming effect. If every speaker in a class of twenty-five gives ten speeches, any particular speech is 1 out of 250. If it is reassuring to be part of the crowd, then relax. Be realistic about your speech goals and their effect upon your audience.

Think of your speech in terms of the communication process discussed earlier, and realize the worthy purpose of speech training. Instead of worrying about the damage your ego may suffer, be afraid of not being able to *motivate* an audience to listen.

Finally, *evaluate your communication role* completely. Take heart from knowing your audience is generally sympathetic and your instructor is trained to be alert to your problems. Research in speech has given us reliable methods to help you learn: "All current practices to reduce anxiety were effective."[16] Have faith in hard-earned experience and knowledge. Have faith in the goodness of people. And have faith in yourself.

# CHAPTER REVIEW
## *Wrapping it up*

## Summary

Public speaking is a skill you will need. There are over three thousand speaking platforms on any given day in Los Angeles, thirty thousand in Chicago, and fifty thousand in New York. More education and more income predict more and more job-related speeches.

Speaking ability is more important than ever in our technological age, yet students are significantly deficient in their ability to make oral presentations. Research shows that a course in public speaking can offset this deficiency.

Communication is largely concerned with meaning. For social construction theorists, reality is dependent on our personal perceptions, our language, our thinking habits, and our communication abilities. Reality can be "real" reality, an individual perception of it, or society's perception of it. Some people are better at discerning reality than others. We can improve our social constructions of what we see and hear by being knowledgeable about the communication process, perception, language, and logical thinking.

Perception involves how we discern or assign meaning to objects and messages. The theory is that we hypothesize about messages that we then accept or reject on the basis of personal constructs we have developed through prior learning and experience.

Communication *is a transactional process of skillfully sharing, selecting, and sorting ideas, symbols, and signs in such a way as to help listeners elicit from their own minds a meaning or construction similar to that intended by the speaker.*

By *transactional* we mean that the process involves an activity that reciprocally affects or influences both parties. The word *model* refers to a representation of a thing or a process. The Ross Transactional Model (Figure 1.7) makes clear the importance of: situation, context, climate, mood, and the notion of feedback. It focuses on how ideas are processed, encoded, and delivered by a speaker and then decoded, intrapersonally reconstructed, and reacted to by receivers.

Check out our website
**www.bvtlab.com**
for flashcards, summaries, self-quizzes, and speeches.

Responsible speakers have an ethical obligation to match their message to the specific audience, context, and situation. A given message does not mean the same thing to all people, and perceptions and understandings vary with contexts and situations. We have an ethical responsibility to analyze our audiences and their circumstances.

Most beginning speech students admit that they are bothered by nervousness. Professional performers report similar feelings of tension. Significantly, though, reports indicate that you do not appear and sound as bad as you feel. Research also indicates that frightened people do not differ from the confident minority in very basic ways, such as intelligence and the important aspects of personality.

An understanding of our bodily reactions to frightening situations helps us control our emotions. Specific suggestions for controlling speech fright include: *objectification*, the intellectualization of what you are experiencing; *acting "as if"* you are not afraid, preparation in which you cognitively restructure your thought process and visualize yourself positively; *channeling excess tension,* through a process of systematic desensitization and directing your actions meaningfully; *helping your memory* through systematic topical arrangement; *visualizing realistically,* being objective about the audience and your assignment and your fears.

# Notes

1.  Sherwyn Morreale, Pamela Shockley-Zalabak, and Penny Whitney, "The Center for Excellence in Oral Communication: Integrating Communication across the Curriculum," *Communication Education,* 42, no. 1 (January 1993), 10–21.

2.  Patricia R. Palmerton, "Teaching Skills or Teaching Thinking," *Journal of Applied Communication,* 20, no. 3 (August 1992), 335–41.

3.  K. J. Gergen, "The Social Construction Movement in Modern Psychology," *American Psychologist,* 40, no. 3 (March 1985), 266–75. Also see J. Yerby, "Family Systems Theory Reconsidered: Integrating Social Construction Theory and Dialectical Process," *Communication Theory,* 5, no. 4 (November 1995), 339–65; M. D. Dixon, "Teaching Social Construction of Reality in the Basic Course" (Paper delivered at the Speech

Communication Association convention, San Antonio, Texas, 1995). For the seminal work see P. Berger and T. Luckmann, *The Social Construction of Reality* (Garden City, NY: Doubleday & Co., Inc., 1966).

4.  L. Hoffman, "Constructing Realities: An Art of Lenses," *Family Process,* 29 (1990), 1–12.

5.  C. R. Sawyer and R. P. Behnke, "Public Speaking Anxiety and the Communication of Emotion," *World Communication,* 25, no. 1 (Winter 1996), 21–30.

6.  Mike Allen and John Bourhis, "The Relationship of Communication Apprehension to Communication Behavior: A Meta-Analysis," *Communication Quarterly,* 44, no. 2 (Spring 1996), 214–26.

7.  H. M. Rose, A. S. Rancer, and K. C. Crannell, "The Impact of Basic Courses in Oral Interpretation and Public Speaking on Communication Apprehension," *Communication Reports,* 6, no. 1 (Winter 1993), 54–60.

8.  Michael T. Motley and Jennifer L. Molloy, "An Efficacy Test of a New Therapy ('Communication-Orientation Motivation') for Public Speaking Anxiety," *Journal of Applied Communication Research,* 22, no. 1 (February 1994), 48–58.

9.  Joe Ayres and Theodore S. Hopf, "The Long-Term Effect of Visualization in the Classroom: A Brief Research Report," *Communication Education,* 39, no. 1 (January 1990), 75–78; see also Melanie Booth-Butterfield and Steven Booth-Butterfield, "The Mediating Role of Cognition in the Experience of State Anxiety," *Southern Communication Journal,* 56, no. 1 (Fall 1990) 35–48.

10. Kent E. Menzel and Lori J. Carrell, "The Relationship between Preparation and Performance in Public Speaking," *Communication Education,* 43, no. 2 (January 1994), 17–26. See also R. H. Whitworth and C. Cochran, "Evaluation of Integrated Versus Unitary Treatments for Reducing Public Speaking Anxiety," *Communication Education,* 45, no. 4 (October 1996), 306–14.

11. Joe Ayres, "Using Visual Aids to Reduce Speech Anxiety," *Communication Research Reports,* 8, no. 1 (June 1991), 73–79; Joe Ayres and Tim Hopf, "Visualization: Reducing Speech Anxiety and Enhancing Performance," *Communication Reports,* 5, no. 1 (Winter 1992), 1–10.

12. Menzel and Carrell, "Relationship between Preparation," 17–26.

13. Michael J. Beatty and Matthew H. Friedland, "Public Speaking State Anxiety as a Function of Selected Situational and Predispositional Variables," *Communication Education,* 38, no. 2 (April 1990), 142–47; also see Joe Ayres, "Situational Factors and Audience Anxiety," *Communication Education,* 39, no. 4 (October 1990) 283–91.

14. J. A. Daly, A. L. Vangelisti, and D. J. Weber, "Speech Anxiety Affects How People Prepare Speeches: A Protocol Analysis of the Preparation Processes of Speakers," *Communication Monographs,* 62, no. 4 (December 1995), 383–97.

15. M. Booth-Butterfield and S. Booth-Butterfield, "The Mediating Role of Cognition," 35–48; also see Menzel and Carrell, "Relationship between Preparation," 17–26.

16. Mike Allen, "A Comparison of Self-Report, Observer, and Physiological Assessments of Public Speaking Anxiety Reduction Techniques Using Meta-Analyses," *Communication Studies,* 40, no. 2 (Summer 1989), 137–39.

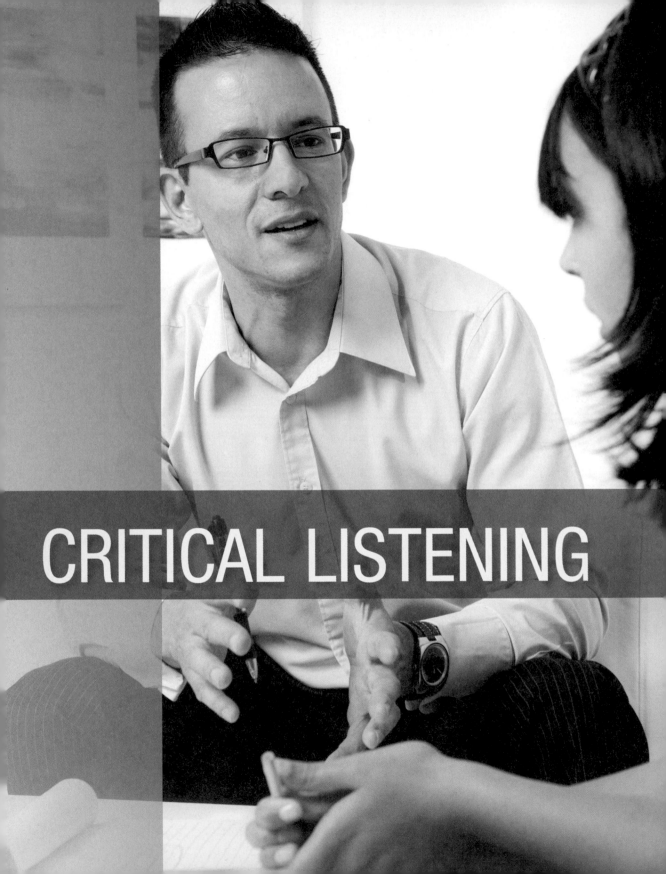

# CRITICAL LISTENING

# Chapter 2

## Chapter Objectives

# How Listening Works

Courage. There is hope! We have evidence that listening can be improved through understanding the process. Listening training improved the listening ability of elementary students. College students improved their listening comprehension through a program first designed for industry. Oral reading seems to help. There is even evidence that improving our listening skills may improve our reading skills. This bodes well for the majority of us who have poor listening habits.

> "Hearing is one of the body's five senses. But listening is an art."
>
> **Frank Tyger, author**

Good listening habits are important. Of Fortune 500 service corporations, 59 percent provide listening training to their personnel. Clearly they view listening as important.[1]

## We Assume a Style

We listen for different reasons—because we feel we have to, because we're enjoying ourselves, because we want to learn something, and because we want to argue with what is being said.

Listening experts have described types or styles of listening as active, supportive, analytic, people-centered, time-oriented, critical, appreciative, and even therapeutic.[2]

Good listening habits are important. Fifty-nine percent of the Fortune 500 service corporations provide listening training to their personnel.

Additionally, six composites of these types or styles that are often prevalent in audiences are reluctant, appreciative, empathic, comprehensive, critical, and aggressive.

**RELUCTANT**   This is the style we assume when we feel or think we had better listen, even if what is being said is distasteful. This would include classes you don't like, sermons you've heard before, and situations you would just as soon avoid but cannot.

Motivation, to say the least, is low. We must work at getting out of this style or find ways to be better listeners within the reluctant style.

*First listen, my friend, and then you may shriek and bluster."*

**Aristophanes**
**Greek playwright**

**APPRECIATIVE**    Listeners assuming the appreciative style are generally more responsive, more discerning, and more interested in the topic than reluctant types. For example, during classes that you enjoy or speeches you find stimulating, attention comes more readily because you feel that the time spent is rewarding or that the information will be of use to you. Motivation is not a problem; but you may still not be an effective listener (1) if you are so appreciative that you are not thinking objectively, (2) if it is difficult to hear the speaker, or (3) if your listening skills are poor.

**EMPATHIC**    Sometimes the situation being called for is listening in order to imagine another's experience. This can be difficult for people who want to fix things or find reason amongst emotion. Empathic listening requires that we listen as if we were in the others' shoes. A good empathic listener will refrain from listening only to the words and seek to understand the feelings of the speaker. This is supportive listening and, unlike appreciative listening, requires strong active listening skills.

Listeners assuming the appreciative style are generally more responsive, more discerning, and more interested in the topic. They choose to listen in this way because they feel that the time spent listening is rewarding, or the information useful.

**COMPREHENSIVE**    Comprehensive listening skills are what good listeners employ when trying to understand the message being delivered. When an instructor is providing novel information to the class, good listeners will be trying to understand the meaning of what is being said. This style requires suspending judgment in order to clearly understand the intent of the speaker and the depth of the material. The motivation to listen comes from the desire to understand what you previously did not.

**CRITICAL**    Critical thinking skills are fairly but firmly applied to what you are hearing whether you are pro, con, or neutral on the topic. It is a democratic but questioning, responsive mind-set. If need be, you generate your own interest and motivation to listen. When critically listening, one judges the message as being supported or not, legitimate, valid, effective, or acceptable. However, a good listener cannot critically listen if they have not comprehensively listened to the message first. If listeners have adequate access to the message, possess most of the necessary listening skills, and maintain their motivation to listen, they are on their way to becoming ideal listeners.

**AGGRESSIVE**    This is more of an opinionated, watchdog style than that used by the *critical* listener described earlier. It frequently appears when faced with high-pressure persuasion for products, political issues, or value systems. You might consider this style a "non-listening" style as it tends to prompt intrapersonal responses in the form of argument rehearsals which, if unremitting, lead to ineffective listening. One's biases intrude to the point of disruptive interpretations of what is being said.

One should strive to achieve an objective, *appreciative* style when called for; an empathic style when someone is in need or is providing a particularly emotional story; a *comprehensive* style when seeking understanding; or an even-handed, *critical* listening style when attempting to determine the validity of the message. The less rewarding *reluctant* and *aggressive* styles tend to reflect "non-listening" behaviors.

We will have more to say about critical thinking and listening shortly. First a description of the psychological mechanisms involved in the listening process.

## A Process Model

Listening is much more than paying attention and hearing. Our memory, as well as all of our senses, may be called on to "make sense" of a speaker's oral signals in a wide range of settings.[3] The verbal messages often take on quite different or sharper meaning as we observe the nonverbals that don't involve hearing—such as the eyes, gestures, body movements, and clothing. How the voice is used is also considered a nonverbal signal. As we learned in Chapter 1, "making sense" has to do with how we assign meaning, that is, how we socially construct what we think we are hearing or seeing.

Listening, like other kinds of perceptual activity, goes through a similar process: (1) sensation, (2) selection, (3) interpretation of the sensory inputs, (4) evaluation, and (5) response. The response is both internal (intrapersonal) and external (feedback). The speaker's message, as well as input from the environment (Figure 2.1), affect and in turn are affected by all steps in the process. External responses (feedback) go through a similar process as they return to the speaker.

**SENSATION**    This phase of the listening process depends heavily on hearing. However, all of our senses operate in most speaker/audience situations. Some sensory barriers are reasonably obvious. If someone is operating a jackhammer or beating a drum, you may lose the verbal signal because of sheer noise. College students frequently are given audiometric screenings (hearing tests), and some are found to have hearing losses of which they were unaware. You have learned that you hear

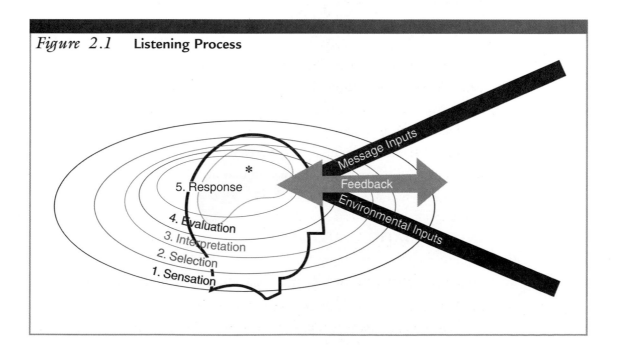

*Figure 2.1*    **Listening Process**

poorly when you are tired. *Sensory distraction* could be competing noises, other verbal messages, or distraction by the other senses. A really foul smell, temperature extremes, or an attractive face—any of these can disrupt or interrupt sensory inputs and, therefore, what we hear. Consider the first-grade teacher who has just put on the thirty-fifth pair of boots when the last child says, "These aren't my boots. They…." "Oh no, no, no," interrupts the teacher as she removes the boots counting audibly to ten. The child finishes her sentence. "…they are my sister's. I couldn't find mine this morning." The teacher is "jumping to conclusions" about what the child is saying or is trying to say. A certain amount of mindlessness may be involved at this phase. New information is not heard or truly processed. Prior experiences are stereotypically reenacted.

Think of phase one as mostly *auditory* sensation to which all other senses and distractions may contribute. Assume you have overcome the barriers and are willing to remain attentive; you are finally hearing, but may not be seriously listening. Your first sensory experience in phase one often has a lot to do with the listening style you unconsciously choose and, thereby, how you select and interpret (phases two and three that follow).

**SELECTION**   We cannot attend to all of our surroundings or else we would be so oversaturated as to not be able to distinguish one sound or idea from another. Therefore, the listening process includes *selection*. We select certain sounds over others, certain visual stimuli over others, particular ideas over others—all depending on the purpose of our listening activity and our interest. Additionally, within our focus, we tend to "listen to" the ideas with which we are familiar or can make sense out of and filter out information that is too foreign for us. Although we need the process of selection to keep us sane, it is also the first step in discounting information that may be important to our understanding the message.

**INTERPRETATION**   After adequate sensory access, and the process of selection, good message interpretation depends mostly on intrapersonal inputs. Your knowledge, past experience, beliefs, attitudes, emotional blocks, and so forth come to bear on what you've heard. Critical decoding has begun. A listener's motivations, intelligence, cognitive complexity, and attitudes will greatly affect what meaning he or she will attribute to the sensory inputs that he or she has selected.

These factors serve as additional filters that often unconsciously affect the interpretations of what we hear. Limited experiences that otherwise might help us decipher and interpret the message or non-listening skills, like prejudgments and jumping to conclusions, affect our ability to interpret the message accurately. Consider some of the following in Figure 2.2.

What does it all mean? If you understand anything the speaker is trying to say, *what* do you understand? At this point you are interpreting what you have unconsciously selected from the original message. Now you draw upon all of your inputs and your skills at managing attributions of meaning.

Listen carefully. Opportunity often speaks imprecisely.

Is the intense speaker to whom you're listening telling the truth? Is he or she perhaps under special external pressure? Is there free choice, or does the subject

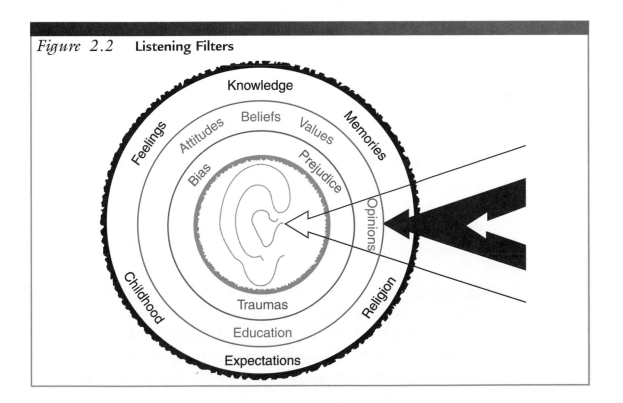

**Figure 2.2     Listening Filters**

or the speaker's role dictate all or part of the behavior? Does the hostage speak true treason, or is there a gun at his family's head?

**Attribution theory** deals with how and what we infer about the behaviors, attitudes, and intentions we observe or know, or think we know, in others and in ourselves. The **discounting effect** is an important part of attribution theory. The discounting effect suggests a given cause should be discounted if other plausible causes are also present. For instance, if a speaker is speaking quietly and is difficult to hear, we might attribute this behavior to speech anxiety. However, if we know that this student has been ill, we might discount the anxiety explanation since her illness is another plausible cause. Before inferring meaning, one should consider how these behaviors relate or **covary** (change together in a predictive manner over time).

The **covariation principle** suggests that we often misattribute meanings and causes because we tend to work backward from behavior to inferences about causes and often overlook the other critical influences that covary. Therefore, we need to choose the appropriate listening style to accommodate our tendency toward misattribution. If we are listening in an aggressive style and the situation calls for an appreciative style, we are apt to take things more literally than we should. The appropriate style or mind-set would allow us to discount some of what we heard and stay true to the intended message.

**EVALUATION**   Once the sensory stimuli have been selected and narrowed down to something manageable for the listener, and then interpreted for meaning (based on the knowledge, belief, attitude, and experience), the process moves to evaluation. We begin to decipher whether or not the message is accurate, truthful, helpful, justified, etc. We evaluate to accept or reject the message. One suggestion is to withhold evaluation until we have heard the person out. Once we have evaluated the message, we respond.

**RESPONSE**   *Internal* responses deal with the final results of your perceptual and attributional efforts during the interpretation and evaluation phases. This is an ongoing process. One does not have to be at the end of the to respond. These internal responses may signal understanding or confusion, approval or disapproval, and so on. It is the start of vigilant critical thinking that leads to external response.

> *... helping a student unlock his or her thoughts for others, the communication teacher also unlocks a potentially demanding citizen, a citizen with the mental agility to listen between others' lines when they speak and to remember her or his own bottom line when responding to them.*[4]
>
> **Roderick P. Hart**

*External* responses are the overt manifestation of those internal signals—**feedback**. They can be both verbal and nonverbal. Nonverbal feedback may consist of nods, indicating the listener is still listening and is encouraging the speaker to continue. Quizzical facial expressions may indicate the need for further clarification. Leaning forward often indicates interest. Nonverbal vocal expressions can be in the form of **back channeling** (uh-huh, hmmm, and other sounds that encourage the speaker to continue). *Verbal feedback can be in the form of direct questions or encouragements to continue ("Please continue." "Excuse me I am not sure I understand.").* Verbal and nonverbal responses can help an alert speaker adjust his or her message. Unfortunately, they can also confuse and occasionally unnerve a speaker. A blank stare might indicate to the speaker that the listener is not interested when, in fact, the listener is mesmerized by the novel information being provided. The job of the listener in creating the message is just as important as it is for the speaker. It begins with presence to sensory stimuli, is followed by the unconscious selection of what will be attended to and proceeds to interpreting what has been selected, evaluates the message for acceptance or rejection based on the interpretation, and finally ends with a response. Good listening habits include providing fair, but also forthright feedback. The job of listening is hard work!

Feedback can be both verbal and nonverbal. Verbal feedback can sometimes be in the form of direct questions or encouragements to continue.

## LISTENING IMPROVEMENT AREAS

Three specific areas where we can pragmatically improve our listening behavior are *motivation, access,* and *skills.* These take place in a sea of knowledge and beliefs that affect our thinking habits and might, therefore, seriously affect our listening behavior. First, consider the specific areas.

Consider three students all clearly confused after a lecture on primitive art.

---

*Figure 2.3*    **Listening Improvement Areas**

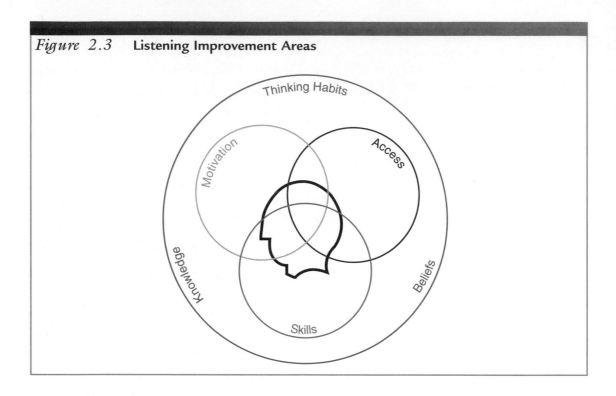

John: "I really don't dig this stuff, bore—ing!"

Hamza: "Good, but I no understand too much."

Ruth: "Okay, I guess, but my notes are meaningless."

John's listening barrier is a lack of *motivation.* Assuming Hamza has interest and motivation, his problem is *access:* specifically, a language barrier. Ruth has primarily a *skill* problem. She has interest and access, but her ability to organize what she's heard (note-taking) is poor.

## Improving Motivation to Listen

Rudolph, a theater major and a reluctant listener, falls asleep in his chemistry class. His interest is zero. Why is he taking chemistry? He is taking chemistry because it meets the science requirement and is the only class that fits his play rehearsal schedule. Not much motivation here—perhaps Rudy is a lost cause. But wait—concentrate on what motivation there is. Rudy needs to meet a science requirement. This

Three specific areas where we can pragmatically improve our listening behavior are *motivation*, *access*, and *skills*.

class allows him his first love, namely, acting; and if he fails the course, he could lose it all. In short, he has sought motivation in a larger system of interest.

Although it is unlikely that Rudy will ever develop a consuming interest in chemistry, perhaps he can somehow relate the class to his theater interests. "Maybe I'll play a mad chemist in a Broadway play." "I'll have a better feel for *Arsenic and Old Lace.*" "Perhaps I can *act* like a chemistry major for one term." On the other hand, perhaps discretion is the better part of valor, and Rudy will quietly withdraw and take a different course at another time.

In review, to improve motivation to listen, (1) look for motivation (positive or negative) in a larger area of interests; (2) relate the topic at hand to your own selfish interests; and (3) translate the problem to an intellectual challenge: "I'll figure out this turkey subject!"

Rudy should also carefully read the material on improving listening skills, which follows shortly.

## Improving Listening Access

If the listening channel is blocked by physical noise, fatigue, or even a hearing deficiency, there are some obvious ways to improve things. Eliminate or move away from the noise, get some rest, move closer to the speaker, and/or see a hearing specialist. In short, clear the channel of pragmatic problems.

The following are some clues indicating when hearing loss diminishes access:

1.    Voices sound muffled.

2.    Male voices seem clearer than female voices.

3.    People assert that you're not listening.

4.    You frequently ask people to repeat themselves.

When the problem is language, as in our foreign student Hamza's case, the answer is not as easy. Assuming Hamza's reading of English is not equally deficient, he can start there. He should also seek out those campus support groups that work to improve language proficiency. The language block is not restricted to foreign students. Chemistry has a language and a vocabulary of its own—as Rudy discovered. To clear the channel of such barriers one must work on the jargon and vocabulary to gain access to what's being said. Reading is thought to be related to **auding**, or good listening, probably because it adds to our vocabulary, thereby giving us more meaningful access[5]. Finally, when the terminology of the speaker is unfamiliar and he or she has failed to provide explanations or definitions, good listening requires that we ask for clarification. Asking questions is part of the listening process as well as the learning process.

In review, we can improve our *access* to listening by doing the following: (1) managing or eliminating noise, (2) avoiding fatigue, (3) accommodating our hearing deficiencies, (4) learning relevant language and vocabulary especially through reading, and (5) asking for clarification.

## Improving Listening Skills

The skills area overlaps the areas of motivation and access. The following material should also help your efforts in those areas.

**NOTE-TAKING**   Recall that Ruth was confused after the lecture on primitive art. She was *motivated* to listen, and she had reasonable *access;* but her note-taking skills not only failed in function but also actually contributed to the cause of the confusion. Skillful note taking helps one concentrate on what's important as well as serves as an intelligent, brief record of what you've heard.

Ruth's first mistake was trying to take down too much material (trying to listen for every word). That effort lasted about one minute, and she was hopelessly behind. In her panic she switched styles and went to a partial sentence, abbreviated word style. When that failed, her notes became almost gibberish and her listening efficiency dropped to a frustrating zero. The following are Ruth's notes on the lecture:

In general primitive art is about the graphic and plastic arts of prehistoric cultures; the term is loosely applied to the art of tribal cultures, of untrained artists in our own culture, as well as of trained artists cultivating a self-consciously primitive style; these last are more properly termed primitivistic.

Paleolithic or Quaternary art dates back to about 30,000 B.C. The hunting peoples of Ice Age Europe made paintings of their game animals, including many now extinct. This initial chapter of human art was concentrated in Western Europe, although manifestations have appeared in Central Europe, which remained free of ice during the Quaternary Era, and in Russia and Siberia. Women's and children's handprints next to the drawings indicate this early rupestrian, or cave, art may have been art for decorative purposes, rather than based on magic as originally assumed.

The Magdalenian period, during which the peak of this art was reached, was followed by the Mesolithic period between 8,000 and 4,000 B.C., when another cycle of particularly beautiful art was created in the mountains of the Spanish Levant. Its development resembles a last echo of the great art of the Paleolithic. It appears to have been the work of hunting people who even at that late date lived a life similar to that of the Paleolithic age, despite development of agriculture and herding in the fertile valleys and the coastal slopes of the Levant. These Levant artists were the first to make use of composition. Although simple, their works are full of movement: they had already begun to realize the problems of perspective. Moreover, the principal subject of their art was the people themselves rather than the animals they hunted. Thus in the rock shelters of the Spanish Levant we see paintings of people hunting, fighting, preparing weapons, dancing, and gathering fruit.

Ruth's note-taking would have been far less frustrating and her listening much improved if she had listened for ideas and facts, that is, main points and supporting data. Her notes would make more sense for review if sub-points were indented in a consistent manner. System is the secret. Be consistent in form, note key words—not everything you hear—and identify supporting evidence.

> "I find it especially difficult to converse with philosophers. They're so busy trying to cut you up that they often don't take the time to listen."
>
> **Thomas S. Kuhn**
>
> **Philosopher of Science**

Here are the notes of a more skillful notetaker and better listener.

Of course, not all speakers are well organized, and nothing is more frustrating than trying to organize the unorganizable. It is sometimes advisable to first attempt to figure out what scheme a speaker is using and then adjust your note-taking accordingly. An important skill of a good listener is the ability to decipher the speaker's organization or figure the organization that the speaker is attempting.

**MANAGING DISTRACTIONS**  Distractions range from the physical that deny us listening access (noise, smell, vocabulary, etc.) to the intrapersonal that distorts our ability to listen objectively. Some intrapersonal distractions may be (1) a speaker whose personality, appearance, or manner upsets you enough to disrupt good listening; (2) language that you consider substandard, inappropriate, or obscene; (3) topical opposition that reaches a disruptive emotional level; (4) misinformation and erroneous beliefs.[6]

Training advice is hard to come by; even the listening experts resort to rules and admonishments in these matters. The assumption is that many people will manage distractions better if their bad habits are simply called to their attention. Are you guilty of any of these?

Skillful note taking helps
you concentrate on what's
important and provides a
brief record of what
you've heard.

1.    *Overly criticizing the speaker:*    Try to disregard a person's appearance or speech mannerisms when they offer you an excuse for not listening.

2.    *Avoiding new and challenging topics:*    Some topics are difficult and complex, and insisting that they are too complicated is a way of avoiding them.

3.    *Calling the topic stupid or uninteresting:*    This is a great way to duck listening. Work hard at relating the topic to something you do like or do find interesting.

4.    *Prejudging:*    Jumping to the conclusion that you understand the speaker's meaning before it is fully expressed can cause misunderstanding. Worse yet, it often means preparing and rehearsing answers to questions or points before fully understanding them.

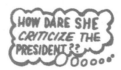

5.    *Reacting emotionally:*    If you hear something that challenges your most deeply rooted prejudices, you become overstimulated. You mentally plan a rebuttal to what you hear, or you develop questions designed to embarrass the speaker. Emotionally loaded words distract you.

6.    *Seeking distraction:*    You look out the window for something, anything, that might be more interesting. You concentrate on

another person who excites you, or you daydream or actually cause distraction.

7.    *Faking attention:*    You only pretend to listen, and your act gets pretty good. You smile, nod, blink, and so forth; you may even fool the speaker. That is why this bad habit is so cruel. You may be fooling (and cheating) both yourself and the speaker.

The Sperry Corporation program is concerned mainly with improving listening skills. The company and its listening consultant, Dr. Lyman Steil, have developed ten keys or rules to effective listening shown in Table 2.1.

All speakers are entitled to *some* listening effort and rule concordance by their audience. In the case of a required course that is notoriously dull and taught by an even duller teacher, you may dramatically discover your own listening responsibilities when you fail the midsemester examination!

# CRITICAL THINKING AND LISTENING

A 1982 poll of high school students revealed that more than 25 percent actually believed that the moon landing never occurred and was a matter of propaganda, fake photography, or CIA conspiracy. In 1993 David Koresh and the Branch Davidian cult believed that he was the Lamb mentioned in the Book of Revelations and that he could bring about the end of the world.

According to the late Carl Sagan, 1994 surveys indicate that 25 to 50 percent of adult United States citizens didn't know the Earth goes around the Sun once a year. This lack of knowledge or lack of attention to our world continues today. According to Dr. Jon D. Miller, Director of the Center

> *One of the best ways to persuade others is with your ears—by listening to them.*
>
> **Dean Rusk,**
>
> **former U.S. Secretary of State**

of Biomedical Communications at Northwestern, one adult American in five thinks the Sun revolves around the Earth! Are we just not listening or just not thinking?

*Table 2.1*    **10 Keys to Effective Listening**

| KEYS TO EFFECTIVE LISTENING | THE BAD LISTENER | THE GOOD LISTENER |
|---|---|---|
| 1. Find areas of interest | Tunes out dry subjects | Opportunizes—asks What's in it for me?" |
| 2. Judge content, not delivery | Tunes out if delivery is poor | Judges content; skips over delivery errors |
| 3. Hold your fire | Tends to enter into argument | Doesn't judge until comprehension is complete |
| 4. Listen for ideas | Listens for facts | Listens for central themes |
| 5. Be flexible | Takes intensive notes using only one system | Takes fewer notes; uses 4–5 different systems, depending on speaker |
| 6. Work at listening | Shows no energy output: fakes attention | Works hard, exhibits active body state |
| 7. Resist distractions | Is easily distracted | Fights or avoids distractions, tolerates bad habits, knows how to concentrate |
| 8. Exercise your mind | Resists difficult expository material; seeks light, recreational material | Uses heavier material as exercise for the mind |
| 9. Keep your mind open | Reacts to emotional words | Interprets color words; does not get hung up on them |
| 10. Capitalize on fact that thought is faster than speech | Tends to daydream with slow speakers | Challenges, anticipates, mentally summarizes, weighs the evidence, listens between the lines to tone of voice |

Source: "Your Personal Listening Profile," p.9. © Sperry Corporation

> Mountains of evidence—both in the form of statistical studies and personal testimonies—establish that the American people are suffering from a new and perhaps unprecedented form of mental incapacitation for which I have coined the word *dumbth*.
>
> **Steve Allen,**
> **Comedian and *Tonight Show* founder**

The state of California has had it with "*dumbth*" and has instituted a *critical thinking* requirement in its schools. The executive order reads as follows:

Instruction in critical thinking is designed to achieve an understanding of the relationship of language to logic, which would lead to the ability to analyze, criticize, and advocate ideas, to reason inductively and deductively, and to reach factual or judgmental conclusions based on sound inferences drawn from unambiguous statements of knowledge or belief. The minimal competence to be expected at the successful conclusion of instruction in critical thinking should be the ability to distinguish fact from judgment, belief from knowledge, and skills in elementary inductive and deductive processes, including an understanding of the formal and informal fallacies of language and thought.

In many ways the most difficult audience a speaker can engage is not a *dumbth* one or even a hostile one but rather one that holds uninformed, erroneous beliefs, has little mind for facts, and prefers not to even think about reassessing them. "Don't confuse me with the facts; I'm happy with what I think." It's a laid-back refusal to engage in any serious thinking or listening effort.

What can we as *listeners* do to avoid these problems? Obviously we should strive to be better informed. We should also review how we know what we know or think we know. We should learn to suspend our laid-back demeanor long enough to hear what the "word spinners" are saying. We are frequently wrong. Aristotle thought that male babies were conceived in a strong north wind!

Critical thinking should be defined as exercising intelligent, objective, cautious judgment and evaluation. Although in some contexts "critical" means harsh, caustic, and unfavorable evaluation and may be successful in some influence situations, its habitual, unconstrained use often leads to a proneness to seek out irrelevant issues and to raise objections based on narrow prejudices. However, as long as we apply the positive, more scientific meaning of critical to our thinking and strive to give events and ideas meaning through fair hearing and logical analysis, we're off to a good start.

Assuming we are not suffering complete "dumbth," what can we do to improve the critical evaluations of messages we attend to? All of the chapters offer

> *...perhaps we are the only existing species capable of sustained logical thought, such thought does not come easy to us. Very few of us ever get very good at it—to most it remains difficult and even alien.*
>
> **Leon Festinger,**
>
> **Social psychologist**

partial answers to that question, but here are some general areas for improving your thinking and listening habits.

## Interpretations of Chance Events

We hear satanic messages in garbled music. We make bets on the chanciest of data. We find acceptable prediction in astrology. Consider that 58 percent of college students agree that astrological predictions are valid.

A predisposition exists in all of us to seek order and meaning in even the most random of data. That is not all bad. It may lead to the solving of a crime or the discovery of a new star. However, to see order in chance events when there is none becomes a real thinking trap. See if the events or data are indeed representative or ordered in some way. Even the basketball fans "hot-hand" theory is invalid and has been proven so statistically.[7] Watch for invalid predictions or arguments based on chance events or random data. Poor thinking is often the result of our normal tendency to seek order in all things. We sometimes mistakenly find that order because we have not taken a really critical look at the data.

## Secondhand Information

"A reporter told me, based on reputable sources . . ." We're really talking third-hand here. The further away we get from direct experience, the shakier the facts become. This is an ever-present problem since most of the messages we receive are indeed based on secondhand information. We must, for example, rely on Professors Gilovich, Bartlett, Allport, and Postman[8] for what we are relaying to you regarding the following concepts of **sharpening** and **leveling**. What the relayer has been found to do was (1) *sharpen* or emphasize the gist of the message, and (2) *level* or de-emphasize less essential details. As we choose to discuss different topics with you throughout the text, we sharpen areas that we believe get at the heart of a theoretical concept and level those extraneous details we feel might be confusing. Hence, the message is necessarily changed from its original form. To complicate matters even more, the actor in all of us often leads to story enhancement, which may further distort the original message. If you have ever played, telephone, the game of passing along a message orally to see how much distortion takes place by the time it reaches the last person at your party, you have a good idea of what this critical thinking suggestion is all about. First-hand information, "out of the horse's mouth" will be the most accurate.

## Wishful Thinking

While listening to the campaign manager touting your favorite political candidate, you may overvalue the argument and overestimate your candidate's chance of winning. Most post-debate (Dole–Clinton) evaluations revealed that supporters all thought *their* candidate won the debate.

There is nothing wrong with being an optimist or even engaging a considered bias as long as you can be objective. It's also healthy to be skeptical but not close-minded.

If an assembly of like-minded people wants desperately to have their wishes fulfilled, an emergent group mentality may completely destroy critical thinking. Why else did 912 cult members commit mass suicide at Jonestown in 1978?

When our pre-existing beliefs are extremely strong, we may blindly accept new information and direction if it is consistent with those beliefs. New information that contradicts those beliefs is ignored or flatly rejected. The tendency to see and hear what we may desperately want to see and hear is a major threat to critical thinking and listening.

Over a century ago in George Eliot's book *Felix Holt,* the Reverend Rufus Lyon counseled the hot-tempered hero as follows: "Therefore I pray for a listening spirit, which is a great mark of grace…. The scornful nostril and the high head gather not the odors that lie on the track of truth."

Ask yourself:

1.   How biased or impartial am I on this topic?

2.   Are the sources cited credible to detractors?

3.   Are the arguments exaggerated?

4.   Is the evidence relevant and adequate?

5.    Are emotion and desire overwhelming my critical thinking?

The topics of support, reasoning, and argument will be discussed in detail in subsequent chapters.

# "Conventional Wisdom" and "Wise Sayings"

Some people still agree with Sir Francis Bacon that warts can be cured by rubbing them with bacon. Most architects still avoid numbering the thirteenth floor because many people believe it's bad luck to be housed there.

Conventional wisdom is not always helpful and is frequently fraught with unwarranted assumptions. Critical thinkers need to know also that logical, scientific thinking may start with first premises or assumptions that are false and go unchallenged. It is, therefore, possible to be logical and yet dead wrong. Critical thinking involves examining first our major premises and challenging them when necessary.

A group of British engineers concluded that coupling a diesel engine with a locomotive was scientifically impossible. After observing a test model in operation in Detroit, they shook their heads and said, "How could we have been so wrong?" Boss Kettering, the president of General Motors Corporation, replied astutely, "You weren't wrong. You just didn't start out right."

"Wise" sayings or proverbs are also part of some unwise actions. Critical thinkers usually have the good sense to apply them either humorously or after the fact—that is, to support actions or decisions already taken. L. J. Peter of "Peter Principle" fame demonstrates the contradictions in this kind of conventional wisdom:

"Wise" sayings or proverbs are also part of some unwise actions. Critical thinkers usually have the good sense to apply them either humorously or after the fact.

1.    Look before you leap.

He who hesitates is lost.

2.    You can't teach an old dog new tricks.

It's never too late to learn.

3.    Where there's a will, there's a way.

Time and tide wait for no man.

4.    Out of sight, out of mind.

Absence makes the heart grow fonder.

5.    Two heads are better than one.

If you want something done right, do it yourself.

6.    Never look a gift horse in the mouth.

All that glitters is not gold.

7.    You can't tell a book by its cover.

Clothes make the man.

8.    Many hands make light work.

Too many cooks spoil the broth.

9.    Better safe than sorry.

Nothing ventured, nothing gained.

> "Language will have maximum usefulness when it properly corresponds to what it is supposed to represent."
>
> **Irving J. Lee, Professor of Semantics,**
> **Northwestern University**

Steve Allen points out that some old sayings are really dangerous: " 'All's fair in love and war.' Really? No civilized society has ever thought so, even though unspeakable atrocities and savagery are all too characteristic of the behavior of humans engaged in war. As for love, there is no moral code in the world that sanctions the commission of any act—rape, adultery, incest, kidnapping, child abandonment, and so forth—simply because the committer is, or perceives himself to be, seized by the emotion of passionate love."[8]

## Language Confusion

During the World War II "Blitz" in Great Britain, people wounded during the bombing were rushed to the nearest aid station where they were given first echelon treatment and then relayed to field hospitals. The War Department called these stations "evacuation hospitals." Harsh criticism of these temporary treatment stations followed because of their "unhospital-like" treatment of patients. When the name was changed to "evacuation posts," the criticism stopped.

> *Language is a wonderful thing. It can be used to express thoughts, to conceal thoughts, but more often, to replace thinking.*
>
> **Kelly Fordyce**

Our perceptions of and our thinking about events and things are in large part at the mercy of our language. It becomes very clear that critical thinking suffers if we are not extremely careful about how we **decode** (make sense out of) (and **encode**) (imbue meaning into) our language. How one manages language is a large part of speaking, listening, and critical thinking. That is why an entire chapter is devoted to "Language Habits" (Chapter 7).

## SPEAKER RESPONSIBILITIES

Listening is a difficult process even under the most favorable conditions. One reason for this is that *we think much faster than we talk. This is referred to as* **thought speed**.[10] The average rate of speech for most Americans is about 120 to 180 words per minute. However, we can listen to and process between 400 and 800 words per minute without a significant loss in comprehension. This is not to say that speakers should sound like a machine gun, but too slow a rate does give listeners more free time to distract themselves.

As speakers, we are also responsible to a large extent for both attentive hearing and objective listening. An audience that is inattentive and half-asleep may not be *hearing* very efficiently because our voice or delivery pattern is dull and monotonous, or because our topic is poorly organized, poorly explained, or both. The audience may not be *listening* for the same reasons. In trying to promote critical listening, the speaker has an ethical responsibility to avoid language confusion, reckless overgeneralizations ("They're all yuppies," "fascists," "commies," and so forth), irrelevant arguments and unrepresentative evidence, and to avoid attacking personalities.

A capable speaker needs to consider the total communication process (Figure 1.7) in trying to elicit good listening habits. Remind yourself that communication is a coactive, two-way process. Watch closely for feedback signs. Listeners usually let you know, one way or another, if you are not being understood or have been tuned out.

# CHAPTER REVIEW
## *Wrapping it up*

## Summary

*Good* listening does not guarantee success, but *poor* listening will stand in the way of its attainment. We listen for different reasons and assume different styles of listening: reluctant, appreciative, empathic, comprehensive, critical, and aggressive.

Listening is a five-phase process: (1) sensation, (2) selection, (3) interpretation, (4) evaluation, and (5) response. Responses can be (a) internal or intrapersonal, or (b) external or feedback. The process is affected by environmental inputs as well as the speaker's message and also produces feedback. Interpretation is improved by better understanding perception and attribution theory.

Basic areas for listening improvement are motivation, access, and skills. These three are interactional and interdependent. To improve motivation one can (1) look for *motivation* in a larger area of interests, (2) relate the topic at hand to one's own selfish interests, and (3) translate the problem to an intellectual challenge.

Improving listening *access* can be accomplished by managing or eliminating noise; avoiding fatigue; accommodating our hearing deficiencies; learning relevant language and vocabulary, especially through reading; and asking for clarification.

We can improve our listening skills by learning the skills of key word note taking and of managing distractions. Note taking should concentrate on ideas, main points, subpoints, facts, and evidence. Notes should be recorded in a consistent, systematic, brief manner and form.

Major listener distractions range from the physical (for example, noise) to the intrapersonal. They include the speaker's appearance or manner, the speaker's language, topical opposition to the point of emotional disruption, and misinformation and erroneous beliefs.

Bad habits that distract us from efficient listening include overly criticizing the speaker, avoiding new and challenging topics, calling the topic stupid or uninteresting, prejudging, reacting emotionally, seeking distractions, and faking attention.

The Sperry Corporation listening program offers the following ten "Keys" or rules for good listeners: (1) find areas of interest, (2) judge content not delivery, (3) hold your fire, (4) listen for

Check out our website
**www.bvtlab.com**
for flashcards, summaries, self-quizzes, and speeches.

ideas, (5) be flexible, (6) work at listening, (7) resist distractions, (8) exercise your mind, (9) keep an open mind, and (10) utilize the difference between thought and speech speed.

Critical thinking is exercising intelligent, objective, cautious judgment and evaluation. Areas of influence that need to be recognized in order to improve critical thinking and listening are the following: how we interpret chance events, how we use secondhand information, the impact of wishful thinking, our reliance on conventional wisdom and wise sayings, and language confusion.

Responsible speakers promote objective listening by avoiding language confusion, overgeneralization, irrelevant arguments, and personality attacks. Good speakers are alert to feedback and help audiences listen by adapting their speech material, mood, and mode of delivery to the total speechmaking situation in which they find themselves.

## Notes

1. Andrew D. Wolvin and Carolyn Gwynn Coakley, "A Survey of the Status of Listening Training in Some Fortune 500 Corporations," *Communication Education,* 40, no. 2 (April 1991), 152–64.

2. Andrew Wolvin and Carolyn Gwynn Coakley, *Listening,* 5th ed. (Dubuque, Iowa: Brown & Benchmark Publishers, 1996), pp. 151–54. Also see J. B. Weaver and M. D. Kirtley, "Listening Styles and Empathy," *Southern Communication Journal,* 60, no. 2 (Winter 1995), 131–40.

3. For more on memory and verbal recall, see L. T. Thornos and T. R. Levine, "Disentangling Listening and Verbal Recall: Related by Separate Constructs," *Human Communication Research,* 21, no. 1 (September 1994), 103–27.

4. Roderick P. Hart, "Why Communication? Why Education? Toward a Politics of Teaching," *Communication Education,* 42, no. 2 (April 1993), 103.

5. Theodore Mueller, "Auding Tests," The Modern Language Journal, 43, no. 4 (April 1959), 185.

6. For more on these matters see Thomas Gilovich, *How We Know What Isn't So* (New York: The Free Press, 1991).

7. Ibid., pp. 11–12.

8. Ibid., p. 91.

9. Steve Allen, *Dumbth* (Buffalo, New York: Prometheus Books, 1991), p. 156.

10. Florence I. Wolff, Nadine C. Marsnik, William S. Tacey, and Ralph G. Nichols, *Perceptive Listening* (New York: CBS College Publishing, 1983), p. 154.

# AUDIENCE CONSIDERATIONS

# Chapter 3

## Chapter Objectives

### Considering the Setting

The Occasion

Physical Arrangements

Ritual and Protocol Orientation

### Demographics

Ethnic-Cultural Identity

Religion

Group Membership

Gender

### Audience Behavior

Stimulation Effects

Patterns of Audience Interaction

Types of Audiences

Age

Sexual Orientation

Education

### Value Orientation

Ultimate Values

Everyday Values

### Topic Orientation

(Phone rings) "Hello. Joe Dakota here."

"Joe, this is your old coach, Vince Gipper, from Bay View High School."

"Hi Coach. What can I do for you?"

"Joe, Bay View is having a convocation on teamwork. As our only all-state alumnus and now a university student, we'd like you to say a few words. It's next Monday."

"Sounds interesting Coach. What time?"

"Seven thirty. Will you do it?"

"Sure, sounds like fun. See you Monday."

Joe is already in big trouble! He knows nothing about the total setting: the program, his role in it, the physical arrangements, and nothing about the audience. On Monday Joe arrives promptly at 7:30 in the Bay View gym, of course. Another mistake because the program is in the auditorium and is ready to start. Joe left no time to accommodate last minute program changes or problems.

Joe guessed wrong about almost everything. It wasn't in the gym. It wasn't high school students. "Who are these people? What is Professor Brainy doing here? Why didn't Coach tell me what I was getting into?!"

It turns out that Coach Gipper was calling as a member of the local Chamber of Commerce, who were using the high school auditorium for their program on "Teamwork in the Workplace." Coach was also at fault, of course, but Joe should have asked for more details and considered the setting and the people in the audience. It was a long, awkward evening for Joe Dakota.

Unlike Joe, we most often know the general type of audience we will meet (for example, business people, teachers, hospital volunteers). In your classroom speeches you will get to know the specific audience. The speeches of self-introduction give you a marvelous opportunity to gain insights into your specific audience, which can make a real difference. Suppose in planning your "Role of a Manager" speech you discovered that your audience was composed of management majors instead of freshmen liberal arts students. You might want to revise your purpose and your speech as follows: "To review the five managerial functions of planning, organizing, controlling, coordinating, and communicating to an audience of management majors," or perhaps concentrate on just one function. Unless you felt very well informed or had unusual credibility, you might even choose to change topics.

What follow are insights and suggestions on how to better understand the setting and how to describe an audience demographically and psychologically. The advice extends beyond the classroom since you will be giving speeches and reports in other classes and programs and beyond.

# CONSIDERING THE SETTING

## The Occasion

Joe Dakota forgot to ask about the *program* and its *purpose*. With only very general answers to these questions, he could have pursued more specific questions. "Why have I been chosen to speak?" Is he a second or a third choice? Is he being paid? Is this a special meeting called for the specific purpose of hearing him? Did the audience pay for this experience? Were they forced to come? Is this one of a series of programs? Is he the headline attraction, or are there other events or speakers on the program? If there are other speakers, when, in what order, and for how long will each person speak? How large is the audience? Will there be an open forum?

The time at which the speech is scheduled is often a critical factor. Occasionally, A.M. and P.M. have been incorrectly assumed. The concept of "company time" versus "our time" often applies; hence speakers might need to regulate not only the content but also the length of their speech accordingly. It has been observed that industrial and business audiences often are more generous when they are listening on company time. Remember to arrive early (even for a classroom speech) or you may wind up like Joe Dakota.

Assuming you understand the time, place, and speech length, you are ready to ask about the physical setting and arrangements.

## Physical Arrangements

*Physical arrangements* include seating configuration, type of room, lighting, sound system, and so forth and are an important part of adapting to the setting. The pulpit in a church adds something to the minister's message. In like manner, the raised dais in the House of Representatives imparts extra authority to the Speaker's words. What we do with lighting, music, and pomp is also part of the physical setting and ritual. The same message uttered in a church, a restaurant, and a fraternity house might be sacrilege in the first, rudeness in the second, and understatement in the third. People have different expectations in different settings as well as in different situations.

The proximity of the speaker to the audience is also thought to be important. If you are on an elevated platform far removed from the first row of the audience, your style of delivery should be different from the style you would use if you were close to the group.

> It is not enough to know what to say—
> one must also know how to say it.
>
> **Aristotle**

The *seating arrangement* of the audience also affects how listeners react to persuasion and influence. Logical, factual persuasion is probably more effective when listeners are separated, and emotional appeals are probably more successful when listeners are close together.

The noise level of the room is often a problem, as are the lighting and ventilation. Many of these circumstances can be controlled, or at least improved, if you consider them early enough.

If you'll be using a PA system, it may have an important effect on the way you use your visual aids. Most microphones fade if you move more than two feet away from them. It's a good idea to check such things *before* you speak.

The effectiveness of visual aids is closely related to environmental factors. The size of the visual aid should be appropriate to the size of the room and the size of the audience. A chart big enough for a group of twenty-five may be hopelessly small for a group of several hundred. A series of slides may be useless if the room will not darken, and a tape recording may not be heard in a room filled with echoes.

Seating arrangement, closeness, and the like are clearly an important aspect of the setting. Advance information on the physical setup can save you a lot of surprises. Consider some of the configurations in Figure 3.1; their

*Figure 3.1*

*(continued)*

*Figure 3.1* **(continued)**

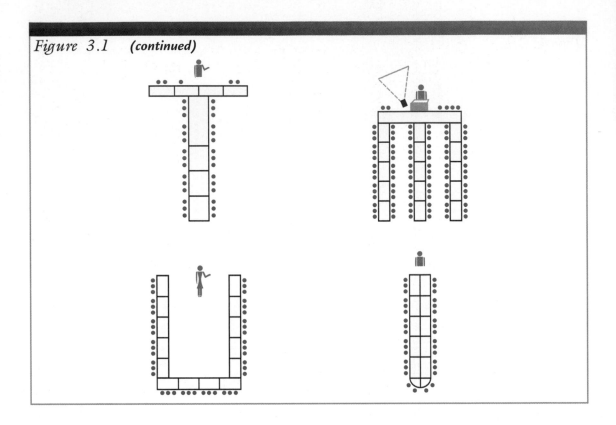

identifying names are usually derived from their appearance: herringbone, T, U, and so forth. Look at the different seating arrangements. Can you figure out which seating arrangement goes with each of the following names: Boardroom, Theater, Classroom, T, Perpendicular, Lecture Hall, U, Cluster, Modified classroom, Herringbone (also known as "Chevron")? Which seating arrangement would be most conducive for training, a sales pitch, an office meeting, or an award ceremony?

## Ritual and Protocol Orientation

In somewhat polarized or formal audiences, the *ritual* and associated *protocol* may become a critical part of your audience consideration.

We take the rituals of our social clubs, veterans' organizations, temples, and churches in stride. However, speakers should be cautious and pragmatic about the rituals of their audiences. The old public-speaking adage against using foul language is a useful one, especially when ritual is part of the occasion.

If possible, you should know the special rules, habits, rituals, and practices you are likely to encounter. For example, organizations such as the Kiwanis, Rotary, Lions, Eagles, and Elks clubs have relatively standard meeting formats. Many of these same organizations have certain "fun" rituals, which, although great sport if you are warned in advance, can be a nightmare if you are unaware. A speaker was once fined a dollar before saying his first word because he was wearing a red necktie! Dress codes are often part of the protocol. See that you are not under- or overdressed. Know your audience so well that you can take language, ritual, and protocol into account in your preparation. If you are the youngest person in the room, don't dwell on it.

Often part of the ritual and protocol is the inevitable *speech of introduction.* (If you are the introducer, read Chapter 13 now.) A bad speech of introduction can make life very difficult for the speaker. Seldom do introducers mean any harm. Quite the contrary! If they give a lengthy speech, it is meant to be complimentary. They may even be so enthusiastic about your subject that they give part of your speech for you.

The chairperson or introducer almost always asks the speaker for help with the introduction, and the novice or incautious speaker almost always answers with a blush and says, "Oh, it doesn't really matter." It *does* matter, however; so *do* give them help. They will appreciate it, and you will reduce your risks at the same time. On one occasion a speaker was asked to give a ten-minute critique of a championship debate. The university's public relations department had sent a standard release to the person chairing the debate; this consisted of about four pages of biographical material, including a listing of every award the speaker had received and every publication with which he had been associated. You can guess what happened. The well-intentioned chairman read every word, and took ten embarrassing minutes to do it, before introducing the speaker.

# DEMOGRAPHICS

The average American is a 32.7-year-old married white woman living in a mortgaged suburban three-bedroom home heated by natural gas. She's also a myth. The family has been dramatically redefined by delayed marriage, deferred childbirth, and divorce. More than 50 percent of American children will live in a single-parent household at some point in their childhood; more than one-third are born to an unmarried parent, and one in four children are living with a single parent at any one time.[1] Six in ten mothers with four children are in the labor force; three in a hundred households conform to the family made up of a working husband, his wife, and their two children.

If you're planning a speech for the public school students of New York City, consider that nearly 15 percent of them are not proficient in English and speak a different native language—including ninety thousand who speak primarily Spanish, thirteen thousand who speak Chinese, seven thousand who speak Haitian Creole, five thousand who speak Russian, and five hundred who speak Farsi.[2] Clearly this is a demographic (or census analysis) to be wrestled with, helpful but not controlling since each school and each class may vary considerably. If you are campaigning for mayor or school superintendent, these demographics take on a different significance.

*Demography* refers to the study of groups in terms of their common vital statistics. Demographic classroom audience description is typically a statistical averaging of your classmates' ages (e.g., eighteen to twenty-two), their education (e.g., twelfth grade), their politics (e.g., 70 percent Republican), and more or less common characteristics. Not all elements will be relevant to your particular speech, of course, but others obviously will be. One needs to determine to which characteristics one must attend and which do not need to be considered. For example, you might want to adjust your speech promoting abortion quite carefully if you knew that your audience was 90 percent Catholic. Yet, if your topic were on the necessity of regular automotive maintenance, the religious demographics of your audience would be of little or no concern.

Furthermore, most demographics are conditioned by other demographics. The education of a group often alters the inferences we might make from their age or gender. The point being that one should look at relevant demographics in concert and as interacting descriptive measures.

In psychological studies of social relationships, it was found that we assess people first in terms of *cultural* information, second in terms of *sociological* information (social groups, roles, and so forth), and third in terms of *psychological* information. The latter is the most personal and most specific. Your audience demographic analysis might profit from similar ordering of assessments. The following are some demographics or general descriptive measures you might consider follow.

# Ethnic-Cultural Identity

Almost all audiences in America are becoming more diverse and are proud of it. There are many different racial, ethnic, and cultural groups, each with very special customs, attitudes, language, and behavior patterns. In addition to the larger African-American and Hispanic American groups, you will meet classmates of other cultural identities including Asian, Arab, Native American, European, and African. Latest estimates by the U.S. Census Bureau indicate that by the year 2050, Blacks, Latinos, and Asians may constitute a majority of the U.S. population. Some groups view gender quite differently; crime and punishment standards vary since they often reflect quite different political philosophies. Hence, it is important to consider your language choices very carefully. Ross Perot lost ground in the 1992 presidential election when he used the words "you people" with an African-American audience. Do your homework on this measure, and be prepared to be wrong.

Almost all audiences in America are becoming more diverse. If you glance around during your next class, you will most likely notice at least some variety of races, ethnic, and cultural groups, each with particular attitudes, language, and behavior patterns.

## Religion

Five Pentecostal students walked out of a class when the speaker used "d…" and "h…" in his speech. One mostly Catholic class tuned out a pro-choice speaker. In one case a Jew and an Arab student shouted at each other until the professor told them they needed a good Christian attitude. Class dismissed! Find out if your audience is fundamentalist Christian, Orthodox Jew, Muslim, and so forth or some combination. One's religion does not, of course, predict one's attitude or behavior on each and every social issue, but speakers are well advised to carefully consider religious orientations when they are central and closely related to their topic.

## Group Memberships

If the Alpha Kappas or the Delta Sigma Rhos dominate your class, find out about them. The same is true of other groups that offer insights into attitudes you may encounter—Young Republicans, Young Democrats, the debate team, varsity basketball players, National Rifle Association, Vietnam veterans, National Organization for Women, Hillel Foundation, ROTC, Arab-American club, and many others. Even more "average" audiences are often highly polarized if they all have some special interest in common. A small community with a winning high school basketball team may unceremoniously ignore a guest speaker who is unaware of this special interest. Sometimes these interests are temporary, but a speaker will do well to seek out and become familiar with any special interests about which the audience expects him or her to know something.

## Gender

An audience of twenty men may, on a given subject, differ considerably in outlook from an audience of twenty women. Likewise, an audience of ten men and ten women may be different from either of the previous homogeneous audiences. An audience of nineteen men and one woman may cause a male speaker to alter many of his remarks and examples, not necessarily because of the one woman, but because of the expectations of the nineteen men that the speaker will be conscious of the one woman. Language is a special case. Many modern

The gender composition of your audience is important to consider when choosing your language. The presence and ratio of either gender can significantly change the way your presentation is received.

men are unintentionally sexist in their use of pronouns, and some women's groups are unforgiving. See Chapter 2, "Language Habits."

## Age

It is obvious that an audience of ten-year-olds will call for considerably different preparation by the speaker than will a group of forty-year-olds, even if the subject is Little League baseball. Even a few children in an otherwise all-adult audience sometimes present a problem. Although you may choose (or are advised) to ignore them, you can assume that the audience will not; rather, they will establish norms of appropriateness and understanding based on the presence of the youngsters. Some language is less well received when even a single child is present. In one study young people experienced greater pressure to comply with the persuasion of seventy-year-old speakers and they expected more direct, forceful language from them.[3] However, then, all seventy-year-olds, like all twenty-year-olds, are not alike!

## Sexual Orientation

Like religion and group membership, yet unlike gender and age, the speaker cannot ascertain the sexual orientation of his or her audience members unless the speaking situation indicates sexual orientation. Asked to speak at an event sponsored by GLAD (Gay and Lesbian Advocates and Defenders), one would be cognizant enough to use the term "partner" instead of "husband" or "wife." However, not also employing the term "partner" in a heterogeneous audience, may discount a portion of the audience, reducing audience connection to you as the speaker and, thereby, reducing the impact of your message.

## Education

A person's education is the sum of that person's learning. Do not confuse schooling with education, for schooling is no guarantee of an education. There are many uneducated college graduates. Nevertheless, formal schooling is, in many cases, a faster and more systematic way of acquiring knowledge than are the other ways. Your language and vocabulary should be adapted to your audience's educational level and previous schooling. Moreover, an audience with a highly technical education will require a different approach than will one with a religious or a liberal arts background. Better-educated people usually know more about current events and have a wider range of interests. Hopefully, they are more tolerant of change and differences of opinion. Don't count on it, however. Much depends on the issues and their values orientation.

# VALUE ORIENTATION

*Values* are powerful life-guides of right and wrong, good and evil. They are related to some of the demographics discussed earlier. Values are systems or frameworks that hold our various beliefs and attitudes together. The more you know about these central audience orientations, the easier and better your message adaptation should be. This knowledge can help you choose appropriate illustrations, arguments, and forms of support. Considering a given audience's special values orientation allows you to anticipate controversies and sensitivities. A "Nationalizing the Coal Industry" speech given to an audience fiercely holding a "free-enterprise" value orientation would take some special adaptation. Not to know that your audience had such a prominent value orientation could make for a difficult experience. Try an audience that heavily values "Right-to-Life," and your speech on planning parenthood may need some special adaptation.

Many sociologists, psychologists, and communicologists have suggested some benchmark value orientations. One way of applying values analyses is to think of these benchmark as lenses through which you will analyze your audience. The widest-angle lens will capture the large value systems within which our beliefs and attitudes emerge. These can be referred to as **ultimate values**. A normal lens will capture more specific value systems in which we will find our **everyday values**, attitudes and beliefs. If you add a telephoto lens we can focus on the finer details of everyday values we might need to consider in creating our speech. See Figures 3.2, 3.3, and 3.4.

## Ultimate Values

Understanding your audience and the values that orient them toward their world-view can help you in choosing how to construct your speech. The **ultimate values** are the large value systems that hold our various beliefs and attitudes together. For example, equality is an ultimate value that holds equal opportunity and civil liberties dear. Valuing orderliness may instill an attitude of predictability and a belief in law and civic control. Freedom as an ultimate value may house the belief in self-determination and a negative attitude toward coercion or constraint

*Figure 3.2:* **Ultimate Values**

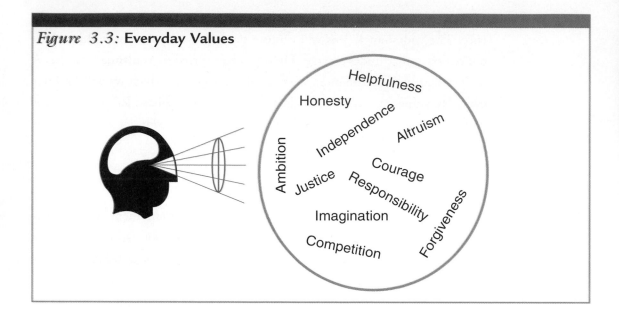

*Figure 3.3:* **Everyday Values**

- *Equality*    Belief in equal opportunity for all, civil liberties, legal rights, responsible citizenship

- *Orderliness*    Law, control, and predictability; rational, pragmatic behaviors

- *Freedom*    Desire for an absence of necessity, coercion, or constraint—often a desire for moral self-determination

## Everyday Values

Your normal lens might pick up more specific value systems, what have been called **everyday values**. See Figure 3.3. These terms capture slightly more specific value systems and suggest still more attitudes and beliefs. For example:

- *Ambition*    Willingness to compete, a desire to achieve occupational success and personal achievement

- *Independence*    A strong belief in individualism, dignity, and integrity; a resistance to strong authority, which is often construed as exploitation

- *Altruism*    Unselfish regard for or devotion to the welfare of others; charitableness and generosity

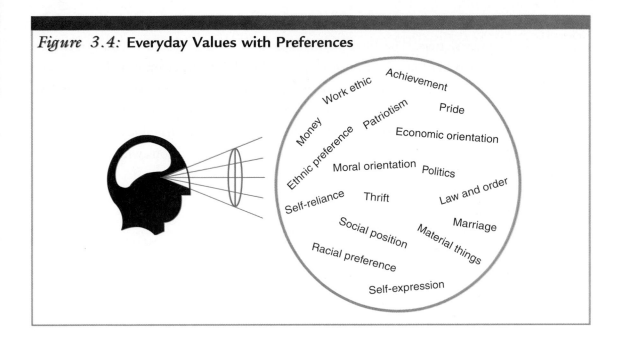

*Figure 3.4:* **Everyday Values with Preferences**

A close-up, or telephoto lens should help describe even more of these everyday value systems and reveal preferences as well as attitudes. These everyday values and preferences might relate more closely to the specific purpose of your speech. See Figure 3.4.

The following three everyday values might lead to these kinds of inferential analyses:

- *Work ethic*   Belief that one should earn one's own way; hard work is the only way to achieve anything, laziness is evil

- *Patriotism*   Two types: (A) "Semper Fidelis," those always faithful to the American way; (B) those loyal to our national institutions so long as they don't contradict the larger values (see Figure 3.2)

- *Moral orientation*   Can be a strong belief in an organized religion; a strong, law like notion of ethics and human behavior; honesty

These lenses can be of real assistance in your audience analysis, but they only help classify or categorize the information you find, and they are only as good as your information. Don't overlook the obvious sources of such information. *Ask* about the group; check its literature, from bylaws to newsletters. The library, Chamber of Commerce, and friendly members are other sources of information. A helpful chairperson can also assist you in getting a handle on the group's prominent values. Keep your analysis fresh even as you speak. Audiences don't change their basic value systems frivolously, but they do make different interpretations where related attitudes and beliefs are concerned. A 1976 survey suggested that Americans most valued security and self-fulfillment. By 1990 they were more concerned with a sense of accomplishment and warm relationships with others, and then in a 2006 PEW Research report, most Americans reflected a desire to find common ground across political and ideological spectrums. People change!

> *The only man who behaves sensibly is my tailor; he takes my measure anew each time he sees me, whilst all the rest go on with their old measurements and expect them to fit me.*
>
> **George Bernard Shaw,**
> **Irish playwright**

One final warning: We are assuming a certain amount of audience homogeneity in this discussion, which is obviously not the case with all audiences. It is a good idea to take a second look.

Be realistic in your analysis as you plan your speech message. You can't win 'em all! Current events change things ... happy or sad moods can't always be anticipated ... some attitudes under some circumstances become almost totally inflexible.

# TOPIC ORIENTATION

Your speech topic should be chosen with your own interests in mind, but you should also be considering audience interests at the same time. To adapt your topic successfully to your audience, getting answers to the following questions would be very helpful:

1.    How important is the subject to the audience?

> Very important
>
> Casual interest
>
> Not very important

2.     What does the audience know about the subject?

>      A great deal

>      They've heard of it …

>      Very little

3.     How do they know what they know?

>      Available facts

>      Opinions and sentiments

>      Biased sources

4.     What is the audience attitude toward the subject?

>      Positive

>      Neutral

>      Negative

>      Mixed

>      Polarized (positive and negative)

>      What percentage of the above?

5.     How do they assess my topical credibility?

Answers to these questions are not always easy to find. In your classroom speeches you can often sound out a few students or refer back to your notes on the speeches of introduction. In the real world, such as Joe Dakota faced, Coach Gipper might have been able to answer most of these questions. Joe could have also asked other members of the local Chamber of Commerce. Look also for newsletters, annual reports, and other documents that a specific group might have generated.

You may be asked to do a brief, formal audience survey for one of your classroom speeches. The first four questions in the box above can easily be converted to an oral or written survey. For example, suppose you were considering a topic supporting "Human Organ Donating."

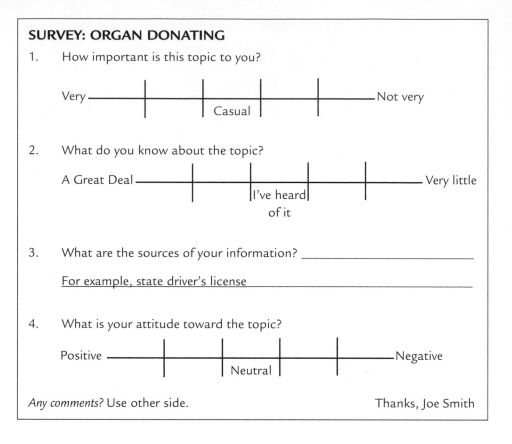

**SURVEY: ORGAN DONATING**

1.    How important is this topic to you?

Very ———————————————————— Not very
                        Casual

2.    What do you know about the topic?

A Great Deal ———————————————— Very little
                  I've heard
                    of it

3.    What are the sources of your information? _____

For example, state driver's license _____

4.    What is your attitude toward the topic?

Positive ———————————————————— Negative
                  Neutral

*Any comments?* Use other side.                              Thanks, Joe Smith

Keep your survey simple and brief or it may be ignored. Allow for some open-ended comments (as shown). One comment offered on a survey similar to this one was, "I wouldn't be in class today without a donor transplant." The speaker made good use of this information by pursuing an interview that provided vital testimony and a great attention step.

# AUDIENCE BEHAVIOR

## Stimulation Effects

In speech-communication training the emphasis is generally on passive audiences. However, the modern speaker also meets active, expressive, even aggressive collections of people. In recent times we have seen demonstrations, panics, riots, and other types of collective behavior that challenge long-standing rhetorical advice. If *crowd* is the most general term for a collection of people, then *mob* better describes these aggressive groups, leaving the word *audience* for the more restrained and often prearranged groups.

Another way of visualizing these different types of crowds is to supply an arbitrary universe—say, fifty persons—and targets of behavior (Figure 3.5). The bull's eye in each target represents the most *focused* behavior.

Most research and theorizing assume relatively passive audiences. We can understand standard audiences by looking at what happens in more stimulated groups. Some thirty years ago, on December 3, 1979, eleven young Cincinnatians were stampeded to death in tragic mob insanity while waiting for The Who rock concert. Some of the following randomly collected comments by psychologists try to explain:

A blurring suggestibility occurs.

The sense of self is lost.

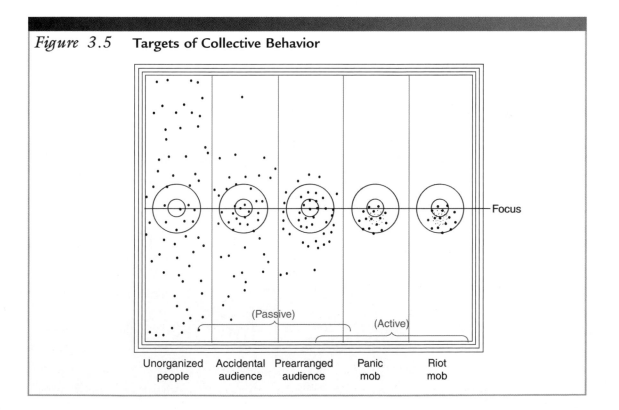

*Figure 3.5*    **Targets of Collective Behavior**

The mob becomes your identity.

Regressive, irresponsible behavior results.

Peer pressure is contagious.

A loss of restraint occurs.

Guilt is lost in anonymity.

More recently, in November 2008, a Walmart employee was trampled to death on Black Friday, the day after Thanksgiving when the crowd of shoppers decided it was time to open the doors. When a crowd becomes a mob, as in a panic, we see people at their worst. Early social psychologists Gustave Le Bon and E. D. Martin suggest that when a crowd is focused into a mob, a *psychological law of mental unity* comes into play. The participants become a sort of *collective mind* or crowd mentality, and conscious personality is lost. Each person thinks and behaves quite differently from the way he or she would if acting alone. It is as if our animal nature, or id, were unleashed, and we indulge ourselves in a kind of temporary insanity by all going crazy together. For Le Bon and Martin, the mob lurks under the skin of us all. In this view, mobs may be weapons of revenge.

> A riot at bottom is the language of the unheard.
>
> **Martin Luther King, Jr.**

When a crowd becomes a mob, as in a panic, we see people at their worst. A marching crowd protesting the war has a very different attitude and strength than a protesting, politically enraged mob.

They are always uncompromising in their demands, and in no way do they respect individual dignity. Even their achievements are less a testament to their leadership than a consequence of their unbridled fury.

For Le Bon, Martin, and others, the mob is a group in which people's normal reactions become secondary to unconscious desires and motivations. The major mechanisms leading to a state of collective mind or mob mentality appear to be **anonymity, contagion**, and **suggestibility**. One who is lost in the press of the mob loses much of his or her sense of responsibility. This anonymity produces an inflated feeling of power. It is a kind of high-speed, infectious and contagious mayhem.[4] A heightened state of suggestibility leads to hasty, thoughtless, and rash action. We get swept up by the moment. Many of our restraining emotions are lost. Fear is often gone in battle; pity retreats in a riot or a lynching.

A complete concept of collective mind includes, of course, the ethical and legal issues of sanity and guilt or innocence. We can argue that stupidity, suggestibility, and irrationality exist in individuals as much as in mobs, and that individuals vary in their degree of participation in mob action. We can also argue that mobs simply supply a form of **social facilitation,** whereby an individual desires are stimulated merely by the sight and sound of others making similar movements.

## Patterns of Audience Interaction

In a typical audience there is far less emotionality and irrationality than in a mob; the "group mind" is nowhere near as evident. Mobs may regress to adolescence or violence—audiences, rarely. Nevertheless, similar motivational forces are present even in very casually organized audiences. More formal audiences—such as classes of students, church groups, and lecture gatherings, which are intentionally and purposefully organized—are motivated by more readily identifiable forces.

Audiences, like mobs, can vary considerably in size. The small group is special enough to be considered separately in Chapter 14; here we are concerned with relatively formal, intentional audiences of roughly twenty or more persons. We are concerned mainly with audiences that are present physically. When you are dealing with vast, unseen audiences, as in the mass media, you are for the most part beyond interpersonal influence and must utilize a more sociological and political analysis. Nevertheless, much of what follows will also apply to the mass media audience.

When you are dealing with audiences in the mass media, such as on the *Today* talk show, you are, for the most part, beyond interpersonal influence and must utilize a more sociological and political analysis.

Most of what was said in Chapter 1 applies here. An audience model obviously has a larger potential for collective stimulation and its consequences, and the problems of physical setting and feedback are more important. The analysis of audiences by types becomes an averaging process, and we must realize that such generalizing inevitably fits some members of the audience poorly and others perhaps not at all. Accordingly, the model in Figure 3.6 places some of the members outside of the general audience concept.

The audience has frequently been considered as a statistical concept—a means of assembling a large amount of information about individuals into manageable form (average age, income, nationality, education, and so forth). Audiences have also been classified into many general types, such as organized-unorganized, unified-heterogeneous, apathetic-hostile, polarized-bipolar. More will be said about types of audiences shortly.

In general, the audience we are talking about is a fairly formal collection of individuals who assemble for a specific purpose. Patterns of interaction are reasonably predictable in such groups, if one is given enough information. Three of these patterns are polarization, interstimulation, and feedback-response.

**Polarization** describes unusually homogeneous audience attitudes, polarized around a particular belief or attitude. When two relatively homogeneous but opposing factions are present in an audience, the audience is referred to as

*Figure 3.6:* **Audience Interaction Model**

bipolar *(exhibiting two polar opposite attitudes, beliefs or behaviors).* Debates often attract bipolar audiences. Heterogeneous audiences differ from bipolar audiences in that they are made up of a wide variety of attitudes, beliefs, and demographics and not polarized. The pattern of **interstimulation** is often present in polarized audiences and refers to some of the volatile behavior characteristic of mobs and more specifically to the concept of social facilitation. Members of an audience motivate each other using ritual, suggestions, and the reinforcement from similar behavior occurring at the same time. When all of those around us are angry, we are apt to be angry; when all are happy, we are apt to be happy. During social facilitation and interstimulation, individual reasoning decreases and suggestibility increases. **Feedback-response** is a *positive* response to the efforts of the speaker; a *negative* response is quite another matter. If the speaker is strongly reinforced by positive feedback, he or she may become closely identified with some ideal. With strong interstimulation, this identification may lead to exceptional, if only temporary, polarization among the speaker's listeners—an enviable situation as long as the persuader can control it and live with the results over a period of time. An aroused audience, we remember, is only a few steps removed from a mob.

## Types of Audiences

H. L. Hollingworth made the categorization of five classic types of audiences: pedestrian, discussion-passive, selected, concerted, and organized audiences. Hollingworth's categories make sense not only for dyadic and small-group situations but also for more formal settings. Hollingworth used the term *orientation,* by which he meant "the establishment of a pattern of attention, when the group is considered, or a set and direction of interest, when we consider the individuals comprising the group."[5] See Figure 3.7.

The **pedestrian audience** is a temporary audience, such as a group of pedestrians on a busy street corner. No common ties or lines of communication bind the members of the audience to the speaker. The first step, *catching attention,* is crucial. How far the process goes beyond that varies with the purpose of the speaker.

The **discussion group** or **passive audience** is one whose attention is already secured or guaranteed by rules of order. The persuader's initial problem is more likely to be the second step, that of holding attention or interest. Again, how long the persuader can do so depends upon the occasion or the success of the persuader.

The **selected audience** is one whose members are assembled for some common purpose, but not all are sympathetic to one another or to the speaker's point of view. Impression, persuasion, and direction characterize the speaker's undertaking here.

The **concerted audience** is one whose members assemble with a common, active purpose in mind,

Young street buskers entertain passers by with music. Their audience is considered a temporary audience, or a *pedestrian audience.*

*Figure 3.7* **Hollingsworth's Categories of Audiences and Tasks**

| Pedestrian audience | Discussion and passive audience | Selected audience | Concerted audience | Organized audience |
|---|---|---|---|---|
| | | . . . . | . . . . | . . . . |
| Attention | | . . . . | . . . . | . . . . |
| Interest | Interest | . . . . | . . . . | . . . . |
| Impression | Impression | Impression | . . . . | . . . . |
| Conviction | Conviction | Conviction | Conviction | . . . . |
| Direction | Direction | Direction | Direction | Direction |

From H. L. Hollingworth, *The Psychology of the Audience* (New York: American Book Co., 1935, 1977), p. 21.

with sympathetic interest in a mutual enterprise, but with no clear division of labor or rigid organization of authority. A sense of conviction and delegation of authority are the speaker's chief responsibilities.

The **organized audience** is a group with a rigid division of labor and authority supported by specific common purposes and interests. The tasks of members are well learned, having already been assigned by the leader. The persuader only issues instructions, because the audience is already persuaded.

Before appearing in front of the audience, Hollingworth suggests the speaker ought to secure as full knowledge as possible of the mode and degree of the audience's orientation. The speaker must be prepared to shift tactics if first reactions show that the initial judgment was wrong.

Hollingworth's five fundamental tasks of a persuader are attention, interest, impression, conviction, and direction. From these we can gain a better picture of what distinctions he saw among the five types of audiences. In Figure 3.7 we have listed these five tasks under the types of audiences to which they are most relevant. For instance, the principal tasks of a person speaking before a concerted audience are to instill conviction and to delegate authority.

According to Hollingworth, the craving for an audience is one of humanity's fundamental needs. The type of audience that most readily motivates their thought and conduct indicates one of the most significant characteristics of individuals. There is often a striking conflict between our craving for an audience and our fear of it. We probably seek a certain amount of confrontation and at the same time resist it.

# CHAPTER REVIEW
## Wrapping it up

## Summary

Check out our website
**www.bvtlab.com**
for flashcards,
summaries,self-quizzes,
and speeches.

Considering the setting includes learning about the occasion, the purpose and specifics of the program, the physical arrangements, and the rituals and protocols. Audience analysis should include seating arrangements. These configurations have names derived from their appearance: herringbone, T, U, etc.

Demography refers to the study of groups in terms of their common vital statistics. General audience demographics discussed include age, gender, group memberships, ethnic-cultural identity, sexual orientation, religion, and education.

Values are benchmark life-guides that hold our various beliefs and attitudes together. These benchmarks serve as lenses through which one can analyze audiences. The most global values are called *ultimate;* more specific values are called *everyday.*

The following are useful questions for topical orientation: (1) How important is the subject to them? (2) What do they know about it? (3) How do they know? (4) What is their attitude toward it? (5) How do they assess my topical credibility?

*Crowd* is the most general term for a collection of people; *mob* describes aggressive groups; *audience* describes more restrained groups. The major mechanisms leading to mob mentality are anonymity, contagion, and suggestibility.

When an audience is hyperinterstimulated, normal reactions become secondary to unconscious or repressed desires or motivations. To cope with this problem, carefully consider your audience, your topic, and your language.

An audience may be considered as a statistical concept: average age, income, nationality, education, etc. Three patterns of audience interaction are *polarization, interstimulation,* and *feedback-response.* Hollingworth described five types of audiences: (1) pedestrian, (2) discussion/passive, (3) selected, (4) concerted, and (5) organized. The five fundamental tasks of a persuader are attention, interest, impression, conviction, and direction.

# Notes

1. Perri J. Bomar, *Promoting Health in Families: Applying Family Research and Theory to Nursing Practice*, 3rd edition (Philadelphia, PA: Saunders, 2004), p. 486.

2. Sam Roberts, *Who We Are* (New York: Times Books/Random House, 1994).

3. James Price Dillard, Karen Henwood, Howard Giles, Nikolas Coupland, and Justine Coupland, "Compliance Gaining Young and Old: Beliefs about Influence in Different Age Groups," *Communication Reports,* 3, no. 2 (Summer 1990), 84–91.

4. For more on these matters, see Jaap vanGinneken, *Crowds, Psychology and Politics 1871–1899* (Cambridge, England: Cambridge University Press, 1992).

5. H. L. Hollingworth, *The Psychology of the Audience* (New York: American Book Co., 1935, 1977), p. 21.

# PREPARING AND RESEARCHING THE SPEECH

# Chapter 4

## Chapter Objectives

**Selecting a Topic**

**Stating Your Purpose and Central Idea**

General Purpose
Specific Purpose
Central Idea

**Gathering Materials**

Conversation and Interview

**Forms of Support**

Illustration or Example
Analogy or Comparison
Statistics
Testimony
Restatement

The Library
The Internet
Note-Taking

The cornerstones of speech preparation are the speaker's goal or *specific purpose* followed closely by the *central idea*—the major thought upon which the speech evolves. The speaker obviously has a lot to do with these matters, but so does thinking critically about the larger world that may pertain to and constrain the topic. Consider a defense lawyer whose goal in the legal system is clear: defend the client. However, even the rule-bound legal system offers choices: plead innocent, plead guilty, or plea-bargain—whatever best defends the client. To make these choices and prepare and plan the defense, our lawyer considers the audience, which, in this case, is the jury, the media, and the public at large. Most of us are stuck with the audiences we get. Lawyers can sometimes alter their audience by dismissing a juror or requesting a change of venue and literally moving the trial environment. The point of this illustration is that a speaker's purpose, however charged, convinced, or predisposed, must also consider the audience simultaneously — a kind of synchronic thinking and preparation.

Practicing the speech preparation suggestions that follow will make you feel more confident, speak more fluently, and generally improve the content and quality of what you say.[1]

## SELECTING A TOPIC

The lawyer in the earlier illustration has no trouble finding a speech topic; neither does Department of the Treasury, Timothy Geithner or Dr. Mehmet Oz, author of the *YOU* health books and regular guest on Oprah. Your job, expertise, current interests, timely events, and the occasion—all will help dictate what your speech topic will be, its length, and so on.

In some ways speech class is more difficult simply because you have so much topic freedom. At one university almost all of the students had either full-time or part-time jobs usually related to their major course interest. Topics were abundant: "Marketing at Krogers," "What a Law Clerk Does," "A PR Internship at GM," "My Quality Circle at Ford," "House Husbandry," "Buying a Used Car," "Psychology at McDonald's," "Soul Food," "How Films Are Made," "Auto Body Repairs," "The Peace Corps."

Don't forget your school major or main academic interests. Your school catalog and its course descriptions offer hundreds of topics where you may already have information and interest.

In some ways speech class is more difficult simply because you have so much topic freedom. To narrow things down, consider your own personal interests and hobbies as fertile sources of speech topics.

Your personal interests and hobbies are other fertile sources of speech topics: "Running," "Yoga," "Umpiring Little League," "Scuba Diving," "Sailboarding," "Ballooning," "Kite Fighting," "Archery," "Birding," "Falconry," "Dog Training," "Photography," "Web Page Design," "Pop Culture."

People who interest you make good topics—an unusual family member, a celebrity you've met, or a person you admire: "Mahatma Gandhi," "Martin Luther King, Jr.," "F.D.R.," "John F. Kennedy," "David Letterman," "Oprah Winfrey," "Dr. Phil," "The Red-Hot Chili Peppers," "Hillary Rodham Clinton," "President Barack Obama," "Eleanor Roosevelt," "Michael Jordan."

Consider processes and events that interest you, the how-to speeches from "Ski Racing" to "Home Cooking," the "I was there" from "South Africa" to "The World Series."

Problems that are in the news or your environment are worth informing people about in more detail. If you have opinions on these matters, you may have found topics for your persuasive speech: "Acid Rain," "Blockbusting," "Peace," "Child Abuse," "Hand Guns," "Meth," "Drunk Drivers," "Teen Violence," "Grade Changes," "Potholes," "Parking," "Teenage Pregnancy," "Political Advertising," "Terrorism."

> Nothing is said that has not been said before.
>
> **Terence, 150 B.C.,**
> **Roman comic poet**

Start a speech topic list. Collect interesting information from magazines, newspapers, your other classes, radio, and television. No topic is too simple, too tired, or too old if you make it interesting and tell it well. "The Topic Locator" in the Appendix has an array of ideas if you find yourself stumped.

Topics and titles might be worded identically. If your topic is "Prehistoric People," your title could be the same or it could be "Cave People," "Whence

Human," "Early Ancestors," and so on. It is typically inserted at the top of the outline proper.

**Topic:**      Prehistoric People

**General Purpose:**      _____

**Specific Purpose:**      _____

**Central Idea:**      _____

CAVE PEOPLE

 The title of your speech is important for several reasons. First, it forces you to consolidate your thoughts and progress toward a speech purpose. A clever title helps promote interest. "Reach out and touch someone" is more provocative than "Use the phone." Titles should also fit the audience and occasion as well as your central idea. "Objective Exams?" might fit your classmates but sound boring to other groups. Keep titles brief. Long titles turn off many audiences and upset program planners who have to list them in publicity and use them in introductions.

# STATING YOUR PURPOSE AND CENTRAL IDEA

## General Purpose

The insurance agent who comes to your door with policy in hand is interested mainly in selling you a policy. Even though he or she may present an armload of objective and practical *information* that explains the risks of not having insurance and that describes how the policy works, the general purpose is to *persuade*. A speech billed as an "Informative Talk on the Arts" may turn out to be a highly belittling piece of persuasion on abstract painting, even if most of the material is informative and perhaps very entertaining. These examples illustrate the difficulty of intelligently dividing the purposes of speaking into even the apparent ones of *informing, persuading,* and *entertaining*.

 There is probably no such thing as a purely informative, purely persuasive, or even purely entertaining speech. Even the most over-generalized, flowery oratory probably presents at least a bit of information. Entertainment ranging from court jesters to comedy players has for ages been the means of subtle and effective persuasion. Some very effective persuasive speeches have sounded like informative talks; some, in fact, have been composed almost wholly of information.

By itself the sheer number of informative, entertaining, or persuasive elements in a speech does not determine the kind of speech or the speaker's purpose. The arrangement of the material, the knowledge possessed by the audience, the speaker's style and voice, the length of the speech, and many more factors also must be considered.

If your instructor asks you to prepare an informative speech for the next class, and you state your purpose as being "to inform the class why it should join the Republican Party," you had better be prepared for criticism. The instructor will probably suggest that you save the subject for the persuasive speech assignment and that you then state your purpose more accurately as being "to *persuade* the class to join the Republican Party." You might use as your purpose "to inform the class about the history of the Republican Party." The speech then becomes either informative or persuasive, depending upon the treatment and emphasis you use.

Your real purpose can be determined by the primary reaction you want from your audience. Rhetoricians have described these as enlightening understanding, influencing the will, moving the passions, and pleasing the imagination.[2] These fit the general purposes that follow:

| PURPOSE | GOALS |
| --- | --- |
| To inform | Clarity |
| | Interest |
| | Understanding |
| To persuade | Belief |
| | Action |
| | Stimulation (Inspiration) |
| To entertain | Interest |
| | Enjoyment |
| | Humor |

**TO INFORM**   One of the most frequent purposes of speaking is to inform people of something about which you either have more knowledge or know in a different or more specific way. This is the purpose of the typing teacher who is showing students how to use the keyboard. The instructor lectures primarily to inform. The speaker who would inform has the obligation of making the information or instruction clear and interesting as well as easy for the audience to learn, remember, and apply. To achieve these goals, a speaker should know something of how humans learn.

Briefly, we learn through our previous knowledge and experience; and we do so more easily when the material is arranged in some logical sequence. We remember better because of reinforcement (strengthening the message through repetition), verbal emphasis, organization, effective use of voice, and other techniques. (More on learning in Chapter 10.)

The goals in informative speaking are *clarity, interest,* and *understanding.* One key means to these goals is appropriate *organization of material.*

**TO PERSUADE**   The general goals of a persuasive speech are to convince people to *believe* something, convince them to *do* something, and *stimulate* them to a higher level of enthusiasm and devotion.

These divisions (belief, action, and stimulation), like the general purposes of speaking, often overlap and are not easily recognized at first. When no immediate action is warranted, the speaker may be attempting to convince or to induce *belief.* This purpose might be illustrated by persuasive speech topics such as "Foreign Policy," "The Threat of Terrorism," or "Upholding the United Nations." No specific and immediate action or performance is asked of the audience. Rather, the listeners are asked to agree with the speaker and to believe and be convinced. This assumes that the audience does not have the power to act except in some distantly related way. If the audience were the United States Congress, these belief purposes could become action purposes.

When the audience is asked to do something specific immediately following the speech, the purpose is *action.* A speech asking for donations to the Red Cross that ends with the passing of a container for contributions from the audience is an obvious example. Election speeches asking people to vote or to sign petitions are further examples. Most sales talks are action speeches—even though the TV announcer does not really expect you to run out and buy a Ford

Persuasive speeches, such as those one hears during an election year, are meant to incite people into action by voting.

at 11:30 p.m. The desired action is typically specific and typically available in the very near future.

When a speaker is seeking a higher degree of audience involvement, enthusiasm, or devotion on issues and beliefs that the audience already holds, the purpose is one of *inspiration* or *stimulation*. Examples might be a speech for party unity at a political convention after the nominee has been selected or a football coach at the half—"win this one for the Gipper." In short, the purpose of stimulation is found in those situations in which the speaker is (1) not trying to change any basic attitudes but rather to strengthen them, (2) not trying to prove anything but rather to remind the listeners, or (3) not calling for any unusual action but rather to inspire the listeners to a more enthusiastic fulfillment of the actions to which they are already committed.

**TO ENTERTAIN**   When your purpose in speaking is to help people escape from reality, and when you sincerely want them to enjoy themselves, your general purpose is to *entertain*. The "fun," after-dinner, or radio-television speeches are the most typical examples. These speeches contain jokes, stories, and a variety of humor, all of which depend upon the experience, skill, and personality of both the speaker and the audience. In a speech designed solely to entertain, the audience should understand that purpose and be encouraged to relax and enjoy themselves.

Fun, humorous radio-television presentations are the most typical examples of speeches that are meant to entertain, such as Brian Regan's stand-up comedy acts.

Sometimes people like to hear witty rather than profound speakers. Most of us can learn to be more humorous but some seem blessed. Adlai Stevenson was one of the blessed. "I saw a woman there (Democratic convention) who was eight months pregnant and carrying a sign that said…(pause), 'Stevenson's the man.'"

A word of warning is in order for both beginning and experienced speakers. Other things being equal, the speech to entertain is the most difficult kind of speech to give. Probably, and perhaps fortunately, this is the least likely speech you will be asked to present. Even when you try to be entertaining or humorous within more conventional speeches, consider your audience carefully and practice, practice, practice. There is little doubt when a funny story or joke does not succeed. The effect of such failure on the speaker is often demoralizing, and the presentation of the rest of the speech may suffer. Helpful suggestions will be detailed in Chapter 13.

## Specific Purpose

After you have decided or been assigned your general purpose and chosen a topic, you are ready to limit your purpose to one specific aspect of the topic. The *specific purpose* attempts to describe precisely what it is that you want your audience to understand, to believe, to feel, or to do. Said another way, the specific purpose is the *outcome, objective,* or *response* that your speech is supposed to achieve. A teacher, for example, prepares lesson plans; the specific purpose is called a learning outcome (a desired objective or response). A geometry teacher has the general purpose of informing (about geometry); the specific purpose or learning outcome for a given class might be to inform the class about the applications of geometry to map and chart reading.

If you are interested in flying, you might start preparing your speech with the general idea (purpose) of informing the class about flying. Obviously, the general subject of flying is far too big a subject for a short speech. You'll want to *restrict* your subject to what you can reasonably cover in the time available. Deciding what to leave out is often the most difficult decision you'll have to make. In many respects a short speech is more difficult to prepare than a long one. President Woodrow Wilson discerned, "If you want me to talk for ten minutes, I'll come next week. If you want me to talk for an hour, I'll come tonight." Here's how one student restricted the "Flying" topic.

| | |
|---|---|
| **Topic:** | Flying |
| **General Purpose:** | To inform |
| **Specific Purpose:** | To inform the audience about the principle of aerodynamics that allows a wing to "lift" |

Perhaps you feel that your particular audience would find aerodynamics too abstract. A more concrete and interesting choice might be as follows:

| | |
|---|---|
| **Topic:** | Jennies |
| **General Purpose:** | To inform |
| **Specific Purpose:** | To inform the audience how weapons were propeller-synchronized in World War I Jenny airplanes |

Because one must always consider the audience, you will probably want to check to see if you have a class comprised of AFROTC students who may already be informed on such topics.

The more exactly you can state what you are trying to say or do, the more systematic and intelligent your preparation and communication will be. In some speeches to persuade, you may not wish to state your purpose to the audience; however, when preparing and outlining your speech, you should always start with a precise statement of your specific purpose. This will help you to create a tightly organized speech that has focus and clarity.

Do not confuse speech topics—"Flying," "Jennies," "Propeller and Weapon Synchronization," "How to Shoot Through a Propeller,"—with a statement of specific purpose. Specific purposes should be full infinitive statements—clearly defined, concrete, and limited.

A speech entitled "To persuade that rock music is far out" fails (as a statement of specific purpose) on almost all counts. It is unclear, incomplete, and figurative ("far out") instead of concrete. This student wanted to say that rock music has significant social impact. He was trying to persuade the class that rock music brings social problems to light and seriously affects individual and group social behavior. He might better have done the following:

| | |
|---|---|
| **Topic:** | Rock Music |
| **General Purpose:** | To persuade |
| **Specific Purpose:** | To persuade this audience that rock music has significant social impact |

# Central Idea

A *central idea* is the core of what you are going to say. It is an expansion of your specific purpose. In the case of an informative speech, it summarizes the information or main thoughts you are trying to communicate. In a persuasive speech it states the claim you are making and suggests the action or belief you wish the audience to adopt. In both cases, the central idea is worded in a *complete sentence*. This complete sentence is referred to as the thesis. In the rock music example it might look like this:

> *Don't undertake to tell your audience everything it ever wanted to know about your subject but were afraid to ask.*
>
> **Gerald Gardner,**
>
> **Professional speaker**

| | |
|---|---|
| **Topic:** | Rock Music |
| **General Purpose:** | To persuade |
| **Specific Purpose:** | To persuade the audience that rock music has significant social impact |
| **Central Idea:** (thesis statement) | Rock music illuminates and reflects societal problems; therefore, its individual and group impact should be viewed objectively. |

Suppose you're a management major and choose the topic "Managing Effectively" or "Role of a Manager." What you're really intending to talk about are basic management functions. Your central idea:

**Topic:** The Role of a Manager

**General Purpose:** To inform

**Specific Purpose:** To inform my audience of five basic management functions

**Central Idea:** Five basic management functions are planning, organizing, directing,

**(thesis statement)** coordinating, and controlling.

In this case you have a mini-outline. The five functions become the five major points or body of the speech. A clearly stated central idea, or thesis statement, is important to speech preparation because it helps you organize your ideas, arrange and outline your speech, and direct your research of relevant speech materials. As previously mentioned, the central idea should be stated as a full sentence. It should not be constructed as an infinitive phrase, like your specific purpose statement. Use concrete terms and be specific.

> The best way to be boring is to leave nothing out.
>
> **Francois Voltaire,**
> **French writer and philosopher**

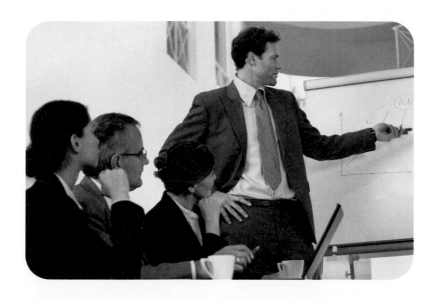

Perhaps you're a management major and choose the topic "Managing Effectively" or "Role of a Manager." What you're really intending to talk about are basic management functions.

The language and the wording of specific purposes and of central ideas are worth some extra effort because these help you clarify where your speech is going. For example, an informative speech on sailboats might be developed in several ways:

**Topic:**          Sailboats

**General Purpose:**     To inform

**Specific Purpose:**    (different emphases)

1. To explain how wind powers a sailboat
2. To explain the various classes of sailboats
3. To describe the Coast Guard sailing regulations
4. To inform the class about sailboat racing
5. To offer advice on buying a sailboat
6. To describe a harrowing sailing experience
7. To sell your Lightning sailboat (General purpose changes to persuade.)

**Central Idea:**    **thesis statement** (varies with specific purpose)

1. Sail power is based on angle to the wind and sail position-close haul, reach, downwind.
2. Sailboat designs are carefully controlled by class to assure fairness in competition-size, weight, sail area, crew, and so forth.
3. Coast Guard regulations for sailboats include safety, right-of-way, signal recognition, and sailor qualification.
4., 5., 6., 7., etc.

When your purpose is clearly to *persuade,* the language of your central idea (thesis statement or claim) helps direct your audience (and yourself) to the reasons why you are arguing as you are. To say "The proposed bypass around Petosky, Michigan, should be condemned" makes your *purpose* clear but not your *central* reasons *why.* The reasons could be ecological (it destroys wetlands); practical (it won't handle enough traffic); economic (it's too expensive); or political (the mayor owns the land).

# GATHERING MATERIALS

Once you have thoroughly considered your topic, specific purpose, and central idea and related them to your audience and the occasion, you are ready to start collecting the materials that will make up the speech. The question now is, "Where do I find these materials?"

## Conversation and Interview

An obvious way to gather materials is to talk with people about your topic, to "try it out" on somebody. If you discover someone with firsthand or secondhand experience with your topic, you may be in luck. If there are known experts on your topic who are available for consultation on your campus or in your community, you may be able to set up a formal interview. Before you interview someone, always do some preliminary research: inventory your own knowledge, observe or poll your friends, and create a list of brief and clear questions you would like to ask of your subject. Make sure your questions are open-ended and that you explain early in the conversation why you want this person's opinion or information. Avoid loaded or biased questions (even though you may have a bias) and try to be objective. Note any

An obvious way to gather materials is to talk with people about your topic, to "try it out" on somebody. If you are fortunate, you may find someone with experience with your topic. Create a list of brief and clear questions you would like to ask of your subject.

sources your interviewee mentions. The goal is to listen carefully, letting the other person do most of the talking.

Conversations with knowledgeable people can be very valuable. However, any serious interviewing or corresponding should usually follow some reading and observing. The purpose of starting your research early is to help you understand what the important questions are. If, for example, you were going to interview a professor of electrical engineering on the subject of information theory, you would be well advised to browse through one or two of the classic books or articles in the field to obtain maximum value from the interview. The same would be true if you were going to interview a speech professor on such subjects as semantics, psycholinguistics, or debate.

Once you are ready for your interview appointment, be sure you have the right place, day, and time. Briefly review your purpose and listen to the informant. He or she should do most of the talking. Don't argue, and do respect your informant's time. Be on time and stop on time. Say thanks, and find a quiet place to review and rewrite your notes while you can still remember what you heard.

## The Library

The largest source of speech materials is your library catalogue, and most universities and colleges have their catalogues online. You can search by author, subject, title, as well as by specific word-search. The library website is a vast treasure house of information, so take advantage of it. Most sites are user-friendly. Help screens and instructions are provided; and if you still find yourself in a fix, you can always contact the librarian by email, by phone, and yes, even in person!

Almost every library has the *Reader's Guide to Periodical Literature*. This source lists magazine articles by author, title, and subject. It is online in volumes by year or is found bound in the reference section of the library. You can use it much as you would the computer catalogue. You might also look through *Books in Print,* the *Cumulative Book Index* and its predecessor, *The United States Catalog;* these sources do for books what the *Reader's Guide* does for magazines. The *Book Index* is arranged according to author, title, and subject. *The New York Times Index* is online and can be a real timesaver. There is also an *Index to the Times of London.*

A good selection of general encyclopedias (such as *Britannica, Americana, New International, World Book)* and special ones (such as the *International Encyclopedia of Communication, International Encyclopedia of the Social Sciences, New Catholic Encyclopedia,* the *Jewish Encyclopedia,* and the *Encyclopedia of Religion and Ethics)* are found in many libraries and are now available online as well. Very often, these sources present the best short statement on a given subject to be found anywhere. Printed encyclopedias are usually kept current by annual supplements called yearbooks. The online versions are more easily updated. Encyclopedias, however, should not be the sole source of your information.

Do not overlook your dictionary. Good ones carry much more than a good vocabulary. Again, you can find dictionaries online, and they might be a little less dated than the one on your desk. The following are some quality dictionaries:

- *American Heritage College Dictionary*

- *The American Heritage Dictionary of the English Language, 4th ed.*

- *Random House College Dictionary*

- *Webster's New Collegiate Dictionary*

- *Webster's Third New International Dictionary*

Many of the above-mentioned reference books and dictionaries, as well as the following sources, are provided online and can be accessed for a fee. Your college library will probably have paid subscriptions to the sources allowing you free access with your student identification. For descriptions of cultural and political events, see *The Official Associated Press Almanac or Facts on File;* for geographical topics, see *The Information Please Almanac. The Reader's Digest Almanac* offers facts and household hints and advice. When you need statistics and short statements of factual data, see *The Statesman's Yearbook, The World Almanac and Book of Facts,* and the

*Statistical Abstract of the United States* from the U.S. Bureau of the Census. This last source covers social, political, and economic facts of a wide range. Smaller general encyclopedias, such as *Columbia* or *Everyman's,* also contain compact statements and facts. Finally, an atlas can provide political facts as well as detailed maps. Try *The Hammond Citation World Atlas,* the *National Geographic Atlas of the World* or the *Rand-McNally Commercial Atlas and Marketing Guide.* Whether you use an online version or a desk copy, make sure to check the date of publication or revision on all of these sources; the world has changed dramatically in the last few years.

To learn more about famous individuals, you can consult some of the better-known directories and biographical dictionaries, such as *Current Biography, Who's Who in America, Who's Who in American Education, Who's Who in Engineering, American Men of Science,* and the *Directory of American Scholars.* For information on prominent Americans of the past, see *Who Was Who in America, Dictionary of American Biography, Lippincott's Biographical Dictionary,* and *The National Cyclopedia of American Biography.*

Most professional or trade associations publish journals of their own. Some of these organizations are the American Bar Association, the American Bankers' Association, the American Medical Association, the National Communication Association, the American Psychological Association, and the AFL-CIO. Many of the articles in the journals published by these organizations are indexed and often available online: *Biological and Agricultural Index,* the *Art Index,* the *Index to Legal Periodicals, Index Medicus, Psychological Abstracts, Psychology Books, Encyclopedia of Associations,* and many more.

In addition to the *Statistical Abstract of the United States,* mentioned earlier, other government publications can be excellent sources of speech materials. The *Commerce Yearbook,* the *U.S. Government Manual,* and the *Monthly Labor Review* provide much valuable information. The *Congressional Record* is an especially fruitful source for speech students. It includes a daily report of the House and Senate debates—indexed according to subject, name of bill, and representative or senator—and it has an appendix that lists related articles and speeches from outside of Congress.

Other sources of speech materials are the thousands of organizations that issue pamphlets and reports, often at no cost. You can write directly to these organizations for information; in some cases (for example, Planned

Parenthood League, the World Peace Foundation, the American Institute of Banking, and the AFL-CIO), you may receive a speech outline or manuscript in return. If you would like to know the addresses of these or other organizations, refer to *The World Almanac* under the heading, "Associations and Societies in the United States." You can also search for any of the organizations online to learn more about them and to obtain contact information.

If you cannot find enough information in these sources, or if you would like to start out with a printed bibliography on your subject, some libraries provide an index of bibliographies called the *Bibliographic Index.* Online databases such as *ERIC, Academic Search Premier, Lexis-Nexis,* and *PsycInfo* are also available. Most college and community libraries have access to these online search services. This usually means that the fee is paid for by the college and not by the individual student! Information searches that would have taken eight hours just a few years ago can now be done in seconds. The subjects one can search for cover the entire range of human thought from law and medicine to philosophy and current events.

Indexes list both materials available on the Internet and those found in traditional books and periodicals. A number of these indexes are available in online databases: newspaper indexes, *Social Science Index, Humanities Index,* and the *Reader's Guide to Periodical Literature.* Find out which indexes are available at your library. Your library may have the index you seek but not own copies of all of the materials you want.

## The Internet

Many of the resources you once would find in the brick and mortar library, you can now find online. As mentioned above, most libraries have created online catalogues and currently subscribe to online reference materials including encyclopedias, dictionaries, and indexes. However, the Internet provides additional resources beyond the individual college or university library. The Internet is a vast collection of thousands of smaller networks used by people all over the world.[3] In 1995, it was estimated that forty million people were connected to the Internet worldwide. As of December 30, 2006, the *Internet World Stats* homepage (http://www.internetworldstats.com/stats.htm) reported that there were 1,091,730,861 Internet users worldwide. And as of March 31, 2011 they reported 2,095,006,005 Internet users. That is two billion, ninety-five million, six

The Internet contains vast resources of information. Many libraries have online catalogues and subscribe to various online reference materials that may be helpful in your research.

thousand, and five users worldwide—a full 30 percent of the world population!

**AVAILABLE INFORMATION**   The practical benefits of using the Internet are potentially limitless. Internet research can save you time in gathering speech materials. Government, commercial organizations and institutions, scholars and individuals provide unlimited information to the Internet. Vast amounts of materials are available. Information is available on everything from earthquakes and NASA to gardening and dog training. You can communicate with others who share your interests, or you can search libraries all over the world. All it takes is a computer, a modem, a server, and an Internet connection. As a student you may be able to connect to your school's computer from home and connect to the Internet that way. If you do not have a computer of your own, school libraries and public libraries are now equipped with multiple computer stations that can access the Internet.

The federal government has made available a great deal of information. Information about virtually every matter before Congress and the White House is available online. Congress has set up an extensive Internet location that describes bills it is considering and provides background on the proposed legislation. Full text of the *Congressional Record* is also available, and it is searchable by keyword. You can follow your president and your legislators through their personal websites. The judicial branch has court opinions and case histories available as well. Finally, many state and local governments have documents of local interest online. For persuasive speeches, the government information available online is a virtual gold mine. The following two locations are good places to start your government research: http://thomas.loc.gov/ and http://www.whitehouse.gov

Commercial news organizations have full texts of their publications online. These sources have search features that allow the user to access articles in current and previous publications. Many of these sources do charge a fee for access, particularly for archived materials. Some of the most popular sources include *The New York Times, The Wall Street Journal, Time* magazine, the Associated Press, Reuters, CNN, National Public Radio, the Voice of America, *Sports Illustrated,* and *People.*

In addition to news information, diverse information about many subjects exists as well. Between commercial organizations, university researchers, and private individuals, there exist many articles, publications, and technical documents. In addition, many think-tank groups or other special interest organizations have posted information. Information comes not only from sources in the United States but also from most countries throughout the world. You will find information about virtually any topic on the Internet, and from many different political, social, and cultural viewpoints!

**USING THE INTERNET**    One of the problems of using the Internet is that much of the information is often poorly organized and difficult to find. The Internet can be thought of as a big library with no single card catalog or index. Each organization that has a site on the web uses its own indexing system. The key, then, is mastering the art of navigating the Internet. Just as the best way of learning to use a library requires you to visit the building, you will find that accessing the Internet and exploring what is there is the best way to become an effective researcher.

Another key to being able to research using the Internet is to be able to use various "search engines." One of the most popular search engines is Google (http://www.google.com). In fact, the word "google" is now being used as a verb, "If you don't know where to look, 'google' it." There are plenty of other search engines besides Google (Yahoo!, AltaVista, AOL—just to name a few), with new ones appearing quite frequently. Most search engines function in two ways. First, they work as a "search" tool. You simply type in the word or words that you are looking for and the site lists on your computer screen links to sites that may or may not be related to your search. Try to be as specific as possible when entering key words. For example, instead of typing "President," type "President Barack Obama." You then scroll through the links the search engine provides in order to find specific information. A search using "President Barack Obama" would return thousands of links. Some addresses (or Internet links, also known as URLs) would refer to news articles about the president, some to web sites devoted to Obama, and some to official government locations. Using key words would make the search more precise. For example, type "Obama Stimulus Package" to obtain those sites only about President Obama and the different stimulus packages.

Second, the search tools function as an index, or a directory. You would follow the menus to find information. For example, you could follow the "Government" listing on the page to find the site for the White House. From there, you could follow links relating to Obama and public statements he has made. In other words, the search engines function as a phone book with a long list of categories, subcategories, etc.

The various search tools of the Internet can help you narrow your topic and locate specific and useful information. For example, you may wish to do a speech on "racism." There are many different aspects of racism so you would be wise to focus the topic. You could turn to one of the Internet's search engines and enter the term "racism." You could then sift through the numerous files that would be returned about racism until a more specific aspect of racism catches your attention. For example, you could find information about discrimination in housing and use that as the more focused topic of your speech. Then, you could return to the search engine and type "housing discrimination" and find a great deal of information about discrimination in housing that could be used as support material for your speech. Thus, the Internet can help you narrow a speech topic.

**QUALITY OF INTERNET RESEARCH**   Because the Internet is so vast and so accessible, anyone can create a site and post material that may or may not be reliable. Supporting material you rely on for your speech needs to be tested and reviewed by qualified individuals. Sources such as published books, journals and newspapers such as *The New York Times, Wall Street Journal,* and the *Washington Post* can generally be counted on as accurate. However, information posted by many individuals is posted without review and, oftentimes, without expertise. Hence, you should take extra precautions before using unverifiable sources. The rule of thumb would be to look for corroborating evidence from other non-biased sources to strengthen the source's credibility. If you cannot find corroborating sources and you cannot determine the qualification of your source, simply do not use it! Continue your research elsewhere.

Another thing to consider when relying on the Internet is that it does not house all the books, journal articles, and references that your library does. Many older volumes and editions have not been uploaded to the Internet yet. Make sure to include your library in your search for information.

## Note-Taking

While you are reading and absorbing all the materials discovered through the sources discussed above, you must consider how to select, sort, evaluate, and finally record the material. You will find that you need an efficient system of taking notes in order not to be overwhelmed by the sheer amount of information available to you. Not remembering exactly what you read or where you read it is frustrating, and if this failure of memory results in a return trip to the library or the Internet, you have lost preparation time as well.

A very general "yes-no" selection of your potential major sources is usually possible after rapid browsing. After this preliminary sorting, you are ready to record the details that are most likely to support your specific purpose and audience analysis. One more suggestion, though, before you begin writing things down. You may wish to revise or add to your specific purpose as a result of your browsing, which may turn up important guidelines for choosing the materials you will use in your speech, selecting the issues you will discuss, or establishing the order in which you will present your topics. In other words, set up *temporary categories* of speech materials, issues to be discussed, and so forth. You can add, omit, or subdivide later as your search becomes more specific. This categorizing will also give you a head start on the organizing and outlining of the speech itself.

Now you are ready to start taking systematic notes. The emphasis is on the word *system*. As long as you have done the rough sorting suggested above and are taking notes with a purpose, you may

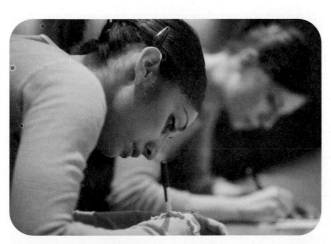

An efficient note taking system is essential in order to not be overwhelmed by the sheer amount of information you discover during the research process.

use any system that works for you. The most common system in library searches is the use of three-by-five or four-by-six file cards. You should write only one subject, source, classification, and note on each card. The big advantage of file cards

*Figure 4.1*

```
(Subject) Creativity                    (Classification) Mental
                                                         functions

1. Absorptive - the ability to observe, and to apply attention
2. Retentive - the ability to memorize and to recall
3. Reasoning - the ability to analyze and to judge
4. Creativity - the ability to visualize, to foresee, and to
                generate ideas.

SOURCE: Alex F. Osborn, Applied Imagination
        (New York: Scribner's, 1973), p. 1.
```

over a notebook is that you can rearrange the file cards and thus reclassify or subclassify your material very easily. This shuffling of cards becomes very useful when you organize and outline your speech.

*Figure 4.2*

```
(Subject) Prehistoric man               (Classification)
                                                Dinosaurs

". . . you will often see cartoons showing cave men being
chased by dinosaurs. But this could never have happened.
The physical anthropologists tell us which bones are the
bones of the prehistoric men who lived in caves. The paleon-
tologists tell us which bones are the bones of giant reptiles.
The geologists tell us that the human bones come from layers
of earth that are 50,000 years old, and the dinosaur bones
come from the rocks 150,000,000 years old.

SOURCE: Donald Barr, Primitive Man (New York: Wonder Books,
1987), p. 10.
```

The next problem is what to write on the card. If you have found a general source that you may or may not wish to use later, a short summary in your own words would be in order. You will then be better able to decide at a later time whether you wish to reread the source. If you find a statement by an authority that you wish to use, record it *word for word and put quotation marks around it.* Be sure to record the name and qualifications of the authority in both situations. Fully referencing your source on your note card (including the page numbers and all URL data from an Internet source) will allow you to return to the source easily and will also make creating your reference list much easier. In taking down testimony or statistics, make sure you record the date; people change their minds, and so may your sources. If you insert explanations or interpretations of your own, put brackets around these words so that later on you will not confuse your words with those of your sources.

*Figure 4.3*

```
(Subject) Problem-Solving                    (Classification)
          Systems                                   General
                                                  Background

Chapter 2 (Reasoning) of this book covers four special read-
ings, including some special problems. Included are the follow-
ing: 1. Reasoning in Humans; 2. An Exper. Sty. of P. S.; 3. The
Sol. of Prac. Probs.; 4. Prob. Sol. Proc. of Col. students.
(Looks impressive)

SOURCE: T. L. Harris and W. E. Schwahn, The Learning Process
        (New York: Oxford University Press, 1991), pp. 29–79.
```

In your English class you may have been taught a certain system of taking notes for a term paper. Whatever the system, it should be useful here. Whether you use classifications at the top of the card or footnotes at the bottom will depend in part upon your training and preference, as well as upon your specific purpose and subject. Some sample note-taking systems are illustrated in Figures 4.1 through 4.4.

Although the note-taking process we have described relies on hard-copy notes, some software programs also offer note-taking abilities. If you are comfortable moving files around on your computer desktop, you might investigate the latest iterations of note-taking and research software. Our personal biases lean toward the hard copy, hands-on approach. Like shuffling a deck of cards, you can place them in categories and then easily shift between the categories as you accumulate unexpected areas of interest. Nonetheless, whatever system or process you choose is not important—only that you choose one and stick to it.

*Figure 4.4*

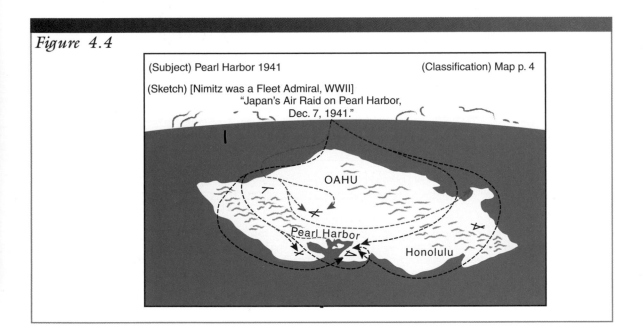

## FORMS OF SUPPORT

### Illustration or Example

An education major, who was a student teacher, had as her specific purpose "to inform the class of the basic principles of overcoming discipline problems in the fourth grade." She could have proceeded to discuss "projections of insecurity and overt cognitive intellectualization assistance from an interacting teacher." The class was fortunate because she elected instead to *draw specific examples* from her own experience to illustrate and clarify the complex problems of discipline, and this approach was much more interesting. She opened her speech by describing her experience with George and his habit of putting gum in little girls' hair. She followed this with the story of Richard, who, though a gifted child, took special delight in swearing. Next she explained the psychological reasons for such behavior, the things a teacher should not do, and the proper principles of discipline to apply. In a sense the whole speech was an extended example, and it helped make her point clear. The more detailed and the more vivid the incident, the more interesting it usually is. Very often pictures or actual objects (perhaps a recording of Richard's language) can aid verbal illustration considerably.

If your subject is one with which you have had no firsthand experience, you can often draw your examples from people who do have such experience. A student who had never been in an airplane used examples and pictures from the experiences of three veteran stunt pilots and delivered an excellent speech on aerial acrobatics.

Clarify a point with your own experiences and add personal interest at the same time. One student who had recently survived a DC-b plane crash opened his speech on "Unsafe Air" with a detailed description of what happened and how he felt.

An illustration or example may also be a *hypothetical* story (a made-up story that is reasonable and fair to the facts). Such an example usually starts: "Suppose you were …" or, "Put yourself in this predicament." The hypothetical example does not carry the weight of a real or factual illustration; but it does have the advantage of adaptability to the point being made, since you may tell the story as you please. The major problem is an ethical one. Make sure the hypothetical example is never taken for a factual one, and make sure it is consistent with known facts.

Illustration or example is a powerful, efficient way of clarifying and supporting a point. In choosing your illustrations, make sure that they are truly related to the point being made and that they represent the general rule. An example out of context or an example that is an exception to the general rule only confuses the audience and the message in the long run. In addition to being reasonable and fair, your illustrations and examples should contain enough details and excitement to add to the interest of the subject.

# Analogy or Comparison

We all spend money on everyday things like postage stamps and cups of coffee. We usually buy them without thinking much about what they cost or about the value we get for the price.

But if you take the 0.42 for a postage stamp and the $1.50 cents for a cup of coffee and apply it to electricity, you will discover some surprising values.

For example, for the price of the stamp you put on a letter, you can run your home stereo system for four hours per day for six days.

> For the price of a $1.50 cup of coffee, you can wash six loads in your dishwasher or watch your color television for more than three and a half hours each night for a week. What you pay for a gallon of milk—about three dollars—can take you even further electrically. Three dollars worth of electricity can dry about ten loads of clothes in your electric dryer, operate your electric range for about two weeks, or run your refrigerator for five days.

So next time you mail a letter, think of the value electricity gives you for the price of your stamp.

Analogy is often the most useful device a teacher or speaker can use in making a point vivid and clear. The nature of an analogy is to *point out similarities* between something already known or understood and something not known (in other words, going from the known to the unknown). If you were trying to explain the microscopic size of a molecule or the gigantic size of our galaxy, the analogies in Figures 4.5 and 4.6 would be both vivid and useful.

*Figure 4.5*

If molecules of water were poured into a drinking glass at the rate of one per second, it would take 100,000,000 years to fill it.

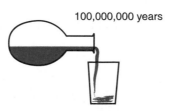

100,000,000 years

## Figure 4.6

There is so much empty space inside an atom that if the atom could be magnified to a diameter of 100 yards, the nucleus would appear to be only the size of a billiard ball.

At 186,000 miles per second light travels six trillion miles a year, a distance equal to 240 million trips around the earth. At this rate we could reach the sun in eight and a half minutes, the next nearest star in four and a half years. If we started at age twenty and moved at the speed of light, we would be eighty before we reached the star Aldebaran. The really distant stars in our galaxy would take us thousands of years to reach!

Abraham Lincoln made good use of analogy and comparison not only for clarification but also for persuasion. During the Civil War there were those who loudly criticized his method of conducting the war. At that time, a tightrope walker named Blondin was famous for walking and for riding a two-wheel bicycle on a rope strung across Niagara Falls. In explaining the dangerous position of the nation, Lincoln directed the following analogy at his critics:

> Gentlemen, I want you to suppose a case for a moment. Suppose that all the property
> you were worth was in gold, and you had put it in the hands of Blondin, the famous
> ropewalker, to carry across the Niagara Falls on a tightrope. Would you shake the rope

while he was passing over it or keep shouting to him, "Blondin, stoop a little more! Go a little faster!" No, I am sure you would not. You would hold your breath as well as your tongue, and keep your hands off until he was safely over. Now the government is in the same situation. It is carrying an immense weight across a stormy ocean. Untold treasures are in its hands. It is doing the best it can. Don't badger it! Just keep still, and it will get you safely over.

# Statistics

The use of numbers to help make a point clearer or more specific is not as simple as it may seem. Statistics are frequently used to support a point in a persuasive speech, but they are powerful evidence only if they are (1) *meaningful* to the audience and (2) *related* to the point under consideration. However, when statistics are overly precise and complicated, they may cloud rather than clarify an issue. Have you ever been given directions like these? "You go down Norfolk Street exactly 3.2 miles, turn left on Baker Street and go 2.4 miles to a Y intersection, turn right about 120 degrees onto Charlie Street and go 0.3 miles, then turn right and go 150 yards and you're there." Some details are most helpful, but not these! Even if you were able to keep them straight, you would probably cause an accident by watching your odometer instead of the road. Of course, the other extreme ("You go up Norfolk quite a little piece and then a couple of miles or so on Baker to a kind of wide-angle left turn and then…") isn't any better. A "little" piece and a "fur" piece can vary by a good many miles.

**MAKE STATISTICS CONCRETE AND INTERESTING**    By themselves, statistics are abstract; make them concrete by relating them to known things. To say that Latin America has serious economic problems because the average family income is $650 per year is reasonably clear; to compare this figure with the $39,308 annual family income of the United States, or to show that $650 comes to only $1.78 a day, is clearer.

Some students were shocked when an economics major explained that the state budget of $9 billion would buy 3,495 bottles of Stroh's beer for every resident of the state of Michigan—not including the deposit!

Wall Street's Black Monday, October 19, 1987, became more meaningful with the use of these statistics:

The Dow Jones Industrial Average fell 508 pts., or 22.6 percent (In 1929 it fell only 12.8 percent.)

By 10:30 a.m. the number of shares traded was equal to the number traded on a normal day, 140 million.

The total number of shares traded was 604 million.

The value of stocks plunged $500 billion. (Equal to the Gross National Product of France)

A community library used statistics effectively in seeking (and getting) a tax increase.

---

**BALDWIN PUBLIC LIBRARY IS A GREAT INVESTMENT!**
**UNLIMITED OPTIONS: SECURE DIVIDENDS**

We are in the business of serving people. Our responsibility is to gather books and nonprint materials and make them available to you. If Baldwin's borrowers had purchased individually the books and services they received during the last fiscal year, they would have spent over $4,000,000.00!

For instance:

You borrowed 382,122 books and other items. Buying them at our average price, you would have spent . . . . . . . . . . . . . . . . . . . . . . . . . . . . $3,630,169.00

Newspapers were read on at least 4,680 occasions saving you . . . . . . . 936.00

We secured 21,317 for you from our closed stacks. You could have paid one dollar each for them . . . . . . . . . . . . . . . . . . . . . . . . . . . . . . . . . . . . 21,317.00

You viewed 10,534 reels of microfilm and saved . . . . . . . . . . . . . . 126,408.00

You hung 2,054 art prints in your home or office. You could have spent more than . . . . . . . . . . . . . . . . . . . . . . . . . . . . . . . . . . . . . . . . . . . . 262,912.00

We secured 1,056 interlibrary loans; some of these books were not available for purchase at any price . . . . . . . . . . . . . . . . . . . . . . . . . . . . . . . . . 10,032.00

We answered 65,423 reference and research questions. Saving you . 65,423.00

Twenty-one film programs were presented to about 850 people at the Library. They could have paid more than this at a theater . . . . . . . . . . . . . . . . 850.00

At least 3,000 children attended Story Hours . . . . . . . . . . . . . . . . . . 3,000.00

FOR A TOTAL OF . . . . . . . . . . . . . . . . . . . . . . . . . . . . . . . . . $4,121,037.00

All of these services cost the citizens of Birmingham . . . . . . . . . . $362,558.00

**USE STATISTICS CORRECTLY**    We live by statistics. We accept data on births, deaths, and accidents as facts. However, using statistics as a method bewilders many people. You do not have to be a statistician to realize that the *mean* (an average) is not always the most representative measure. To illustrate, let's consider eleven hypothetical educators and their yearly incomes in Table 4.1.

The mean income of these eleven educators is $38,136. The problem is obvious: Two educators (the administrators) make the figure unrepresentative, particularly if you are more concerned with teachers than with administrators. Counting halfway down the list of salaries, we find $34,000. This is the *me-*

*Table 4.1:* **Hypothetical Annual Incomes**

| EDUCATOR | SALARY |
| --- | --- |
| Educator A (Administrator) | $60,000 |
| Educator B (Administrator) | 55,000 |
| Educator C | 45,000 |
| Educator D | 40,500 |
| Educator E | 35,500 |
| Educator F | 34,000 |
| Educator G | 33,000 |
| Educator H | 32,000 |
| Educator I | 29,500 |
| Educator J | 28,000 |
| Educator K | 27,000 |

*dian*— in this case a much more meaningful and representative figure. If we do not include the two administrators, the average income of the teachers is $33,833, and the median is $33,000. You could then figure the amount by which each income differs from the average; the average of these differences is the *average deviation.* If you were to translate these deviations from the average onto a so-called normal distribution, you could then determine the *standard deviation* (also known as *sigma).* Figure 4.7 depicts some of the confusion many students experience when dealing with statistical measurements. We will leave further explanation of this to your statistics instructor!

**COMBINE STATISTICS WITH OTHER FORMS OF SUPPORT**    More and more we live by statistics that predict things. From Unisys's vote predictions to insurance rates, from the number of cancer-causing things in a carton of cigarettes to the average number of cavities in a given group of children, we are in an age of specific, predictive statistics. We have learned to combine statistics with analogies or comparisons to make sense of the astronomical numbers of outer space. We express speed as Mach 1, 2, or 3 instead of miles per hour, and speak of distance in terms of light years.

Statistics can give a speech a sense of precision if you remember to relate the statistics to known things and to make them meaningful and dramatic to the audience. It also helps to round your numbers and to use visual aids.

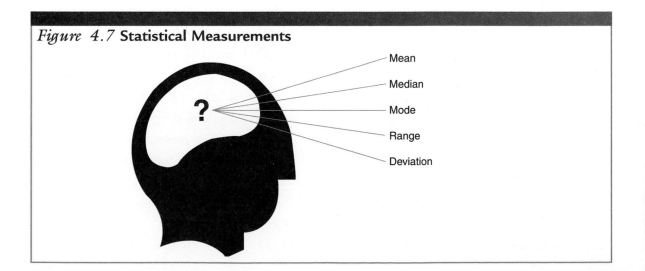

*Figure 4.7* **Statistical Measurements**

— Mean
— Median
— Mode
— Range
— Deviation

**IDENTIFY YOUR SOURCES**   To hear that at one time 72 percent of the students who entered high school in Detroit did not graduate is a startling statement, but easy to dismiss unless you know that the statistic came from the Detroit superintendent of schools. The statistics on teacher incomes might vary considerably if they were drawn from metropolitan Los Angeles or some impoverished, remote area of the country.

Some excellent sources of statistics in general are: the *Statistical Abstract of the United States* from the U.S. Bureau of the Census, *The Statesman's Yearbook, Statistical Reference Index, The World Almanac and Book of Facts,* the *Statistical Yearbook* published by the United Nations, and even the *Guinness Book of World Records.*

## Testimony

Like statistics, *testimony* has great use in speeches to persuade but is also valuable for its ability to clarify. In a speech to inform, it may add considerable interest to what might otherwise be straight explanation.

**EXPERT AND NONEXPERT TESTIMONY**   The idea or statement being supported determines in part who the experts are. If you are trying to prove that the person who crashed into your car ran a red light, the one who knows and can testify is the lone person who was standing on the corner and saw the whole thing. With this kind of nonprofessional (or nonexpert) testimony, you often need more than one witness. If you are trying to prove that you have observed a bird that is considered extinct, such as the passenger pigeon, you will need the testimony of a qualified ornithologist. This expert will insist on first-hand observation of the bird in this exceptional case.

Authorities are qualified to give expert testimony by their closeness to a first-hand observation and by their training in observing the phenomenon in question. The authority should be an expert *on the topic under discussion.* All experts are not equal in all things. You would not ask an aeronautical engineer to testify about heart transplants; you might be equally off target if you asked a gynecologist. And you certainly would not ask a maestro to diagnose a problem in an airplane engine!

In most cases you will be using *expert* testimony from people who are recognized authorities or experts in their fields. Their testimony adds interest and credibility to your own thoughts and indicates that you are not alone in your opinions.

One student speaking on "choosing a medical internist" suggested using both kinds of testimony. First, ask friends who have been patients of internists for recommendations; second, ask another physician or medical professional that you respect and who has made referrals in the past. Of course, a physician who is right for one person may not be right for another. The more your friends' general preferences match your own, the more likely you are to like the physician.

In choosing testimony—expert or ordinary citizen—make sure that it fits or relates to the speechmaking system in which you find yourself. Some "fits" are quite subtle. All Bible testimony is not equal. Some groups put quite different values on it depending whether it is from the Old or the New Testament, and some groups would not value testimony from either.

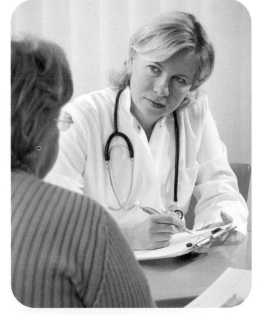

A physician who is right for one person may not be right for another. The more your friends' general preferences match your own, the more likely you are to like the physician.

Obviously your expert should be qualified, but in a specific way. Audiences are suspicious of expert testimony when self-interest is obvious. A qualified nuclear physicist who is a member of the Joint Chiefs of Staff may be right in supporting limited nuclear armaments, but his self-interest diminishes his testimony. Furthermore, once an individual becomes an expert in a particular field, he or she actually has more of a bias toward their expertise. Our best-qualified sources come from reluctant testimony—testimony from experts that goes against what they would normally expect or lean towards.

## QUOTE ACCURATELY AND IN CONTEXT

The shortening or paraphrasing of testimony can be troublesome. One IRS speaker stated, "However undemocratic the new tax law appears to be, we will never achieve true democracy until we embrace and enforce it." The material was paraphrased, as "The new tax law appears to be undemocratic." In this case the inaccuracy was deliberate and therefore unethical.

Identify your authorities unless they are fully accepted by all. You may have an excellent quote from John Doe regarding your position on the federal deficit; but if the audience never heard of him, you must explain why his testimony is expert. For example, "John Doe is professor of economics at the University of Michigan and a member of the U.S. Tax Commission." This contextualizes his knowledge and credibility as an expert on your topic.

# Restatement

*Restatement* is more than simple repetition. It is saying the same thing in a different and reinforcing way, usually at a later point in the message. This is particularly useful if the material is complex or the vocabulary specialized. For example, restatement provides a better and more dramatic explanation of how many people go through the giant Macy's department store in a single day: "Everyday more people crowd into Macy's New York department store than live in Des Moines, Grand Rapids, or Salt Lake City."

> You can observe a lot just by watching.
>
> **Yogi Berra**

If you reread Chapters 1 through 3 of this book, you will find restatements of the definitions of speech communication; all trying to say the same thing. One definition is a model, another consists of a short paragraph, and yet another may reduce the definition to encoding and decoding. This is an example of restatement for clarification. If the meaning is not clear in one place because of sentence structure or vocabulary or in another because of context, you are given still more choices. If you understood all the definitions at first glance, fine. Assuming that it was not too extended, this repetition should have reinforced the learning.

To restate the value of restatement: It is more than simple repetition. It is saying the same thing in different ways to reinforce learning, and it is particularly useful if the subject is complex or if the vocabulary is specialized or strange to the audience.

# CHAPTER REVIEW
## *Wrapping it up*

## Summary

The cornerstones of speech preparation are the speaker's goals or *specific purpose* followed closely by the *central idea* or major thought on which the speech evolves. When selecting speech topics, consider your job, expertise, interests, hobbies, people, experiences, and problems in the news. A good title helps you consolidate your thoughts and your purpose. General purposes for speaking are to inform, to persuade, and to entertain. The specific purpose attempts to describe precisely what it is that you want your audience to understand, believe, feel, or do, and it is typically worded in a full infinitive statement. Your central idea is an expansion of your specific purpose. It is worded as a full sentence, also called the thesis statement, which encompasses the core of your speech and can sometimes encompass the preview as a mini-outline of what you are going to say. When your purpose is clearly to persuade, your central idea (thesis or claim) helps direct you and explain to your audience why you are arguing as you are.

Major ways and aspects of gathering speech materials are: conversation and interview, using the library, and exploring the Internet. The Internet is a vast forum for information but must be navigated with judicious creativity. Much of what is found on the Internet is questionable or just plain false. Therefore, it is imperative to check the qualifications of your sources. Just like non-Internet sources, look for expertise, biases, and corroboration from other sources. Creating a systematic note-taking procedure will help you accurately refer to and relocate sources. Make sure to record bibliographic references while you do your research to make creating your reference list much easier.

Forms of support include (1) illustration or example, (2) analogy or comparison, (3) statistics, (4) testimony, and (5) restatement. In using the forms of support, especially testimony and statistics: make these concrete and interesting, use them correctly, combine them with other forms of support, and identify your sources. Restatement is more than repetition. It is saying the same thing in different ways to reinforce learning.

## *Notes*

1.  Kent E. Menzel and Lori J. Carrell, "The Relationship between Preparation and Performance in Public Speaking," *Communication Education,* 43, no. 1 (January 1994), 17–26.
2.  William L. Benoit, "Campbell's *The Philosophy of Rhetoric* and the Advancement of Rhetorical Theory: The Integration of Philosophical Antecedents," *Communication Studies,* 41, no. 1 (Spring 1990), 89–100.
3.  Allen C. Benson, *The Complete Internet Companion for Librarians* (New York: Neal-Schuman Publishers, 1995). Also see Richard J. Smith and Mark Gibbs, *Navigating the Internet* (Indianapolis: Sams Publishing, 1994); *Communication Education,* 43, no. 2 (April 1994).

# ORGANIZING
# THE SPEECH

# Chapter 5

## Chapter Objectives

### Organizing the Body of the Speech

Main Points

Ordering Main Points

Cohesion: Connecting Ideas

### Planning the Introduction

Functions

Model Introductions

### Planning the Conclusion

Functions

The *introduction, body* and *conclusion* are the basic parts of a speech. Aristotle points to the importance of organization and structure in fulfilling *logos,* one of his three proofs of an argument (more will be said on this in the chapter on persuasion). Almost all of the serious message organizing goes on in the body. Because the body is the longest and most important part, it is the logical place to begin your critical thinking and planning. Introductions and conclusions are easier to prepare after you have a clear understanding of your message and how you intend to develop it.

| Introduction | Body | Conclusion |
|:---:|:---:|:---:|
| I | II | III |

# ORGANIZING THE BODY OF THE SPEECH

## Main Points

**LOCATING MAIN POINTS**   If you've carefully worded your specific purpose and your central idea or thesis, you have already seen some main points emerge. Chapter 4 discussed Aristotle's first canon, *invention,* which involves preparing and researching the speech. Aristotle's second canon, *disposition,* is the focus of this chapter: how to organize the speech. A well-thought-out central idea often becomes a mini-outline for the body of a speech. Recall the student speech on management functions in Chapter 4.

| | |
|---:|:---|
| **Topic:** | The Role of a Manager |
| **General Purpose:** | To inform |
| **Specific Purpose:** | To inform my audience of five basic management functions |
| **Central Idea (Thesis):** | Five basic management functions are planning, organizing, directing, coordinating, and controlling. |

### *Body*

**Main Points:**

I.  The planning function serves as the foundation for your management decisions.

    **A.**

    **B.**

II.  The organizing function provides the step-by-step process that needs to be followed.

    **A.**

    **B.**

    **C.**

III.  The directing function guides the employees through the organized process of the plan.

    **A.**

    **B.**

IV.  The coordinating function sees that different aspects of a plan are being handled without overlapping.

    **A.**

    **B.**

V.  The controlling function of a manager suggests that the decision is ultimately yours.

    **A.**

    **B.**

        **1.**

        **2.**

Some main points follow a logical, 1–2–3 order and become evident in your early preparation as well as your central idea.

**Topic:**    Finding a Job

**General Purpose:**    To inform

**Specific Purpose:**    To explain to the class the proper way to find and apply for a job

**Central Idea (Thesis):**    Getting a job involves: listing employers, data preparation, letters, interview preparation, and, finally, personal appearance.

### Body

**Main Ideas:**

I.    Prepare a complete list of prospective employers.

II.    Prepare data for an employment application.

III.    Prepare three-part letters.

IV.    Prepare what you will say in an interview.

V.    Plan your dress and grooming.

Speeches to persuade are often more difficult to outline because influence is involved, evidence must be found, and reasons for your viewpoint explained. Look at basic reasons or arguments for your main points. One student sorted out a great many facts and opinions on a controversial topic and settled on two reasons, which then became the two main points.

**Topic:**    Promiscuity

**General Purpose:**    To persuade

**Specific Purpose:**    To persuade the audience that promiscuity has too high a price

**Central Idea (Thesis):**    (thesis or claim) Promiscuous persons face new and unusual risks from herpes and AIDS.

**Main Points:**

I.    Promiscuity has become a major transmitter of genital herpes.

II.    Promiscuity has become a major transmitter of AIDS.

## RHETORICAL ADVICE

*Number of Points*    Classroom speeches are typically short and limited to one central idea. Three to four main points are usually all that can be covered. Should you need more than four or five main points, it will be necessary to cover each one more superficially; as a result, clarity may suffer. Try eliminating some of them on a rank-order of interest or importance. Try combining points that may overlap. Eliminating and/or combining, which is the hardest part of speech preparation, is very important because it also directs future research of your topic.

***Unity with Central Idea***    This advice, based on a long-standing rhetorical principle, refers to how well your speech organization hangs together and promotes an undivided total effect. As we learned in Chapter 4, we should be able to capture much of the speech in the title, the specific purpose, and the statement of central idea. If you are simply tacking interesting main points to your outline with no clear notion of how or whether they fit the total effect you are hoping to achieve, they should probably be cut. Your speech outline is like the plot of a play. If it gets too tricky, complicated, or strays too far from the point, the audience gives up.

***Relatively Equal Merit***    A district attorney arguing a murder case has three main points:

   **I.**    Means

  **II.**    Opportunity

 **III.**    Motive

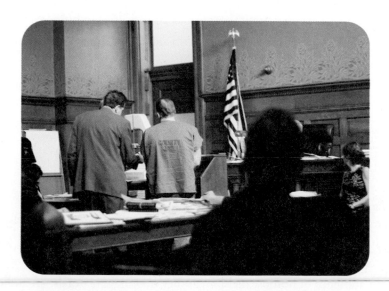

A district attorney arguing a murder case has three main points: means, opportunity, and motive.

These points have equal merit relative to her purpose. She must prove all three. However, if the defense concedes *means* and part of *opportunity,* the D.A. will spend more time on *motive.* Equal merit does not necessarily mean equal time or equal emphasis.

If our D.A. adds a fourth point concerning the fact that the accused is an expert marksman, she has then injured her speech organization. "Expert marksman," while important, is not of equal merit with the others. It should be a subpoint under "Means."

Your main points should also be judged on equal merit relative to your purpose. Although you will need to spend a reasonable amount of time on each main point (like the D.A.), it is not necessary to allot equal time and emphasis to each point. A careful assessment of your audience often helps decide time, space, or emphasis.

Suppose your purpose is "To inform the audience about listening." The three points you chose as having equal merit are:

I.    Sensory access

II.   Motivation

III.  Skills

Suppose the audience is composed of healthy, motivated seminarians. Because most of your time and effort will be spent on "Skills," perhaps these three points are not of equal merit. Because merit is relative to purpose, you may need a different purpose to accommodate this audience and this rhetorical advice: "To inform the audience about the skills used by effective listeners."

Wrestling with the question of equal merit not only helps you coordinate your main points but also gives you a good check on your specific purpose and your audience adaptation.

## Ordering Main Points

Ordering your main points depends heavily upon the audience and the setting, as well as your purpose. A speech on the U.S. economy depends on the economic sophistication of the audience as well as the latest news from Wall Street. A speech on AIDS might be ordered quite differently for an audience of drug abusers, an audience of homosexuals, an audience of heterosexuals, an audience of physicians, and so on. Nevertheless, several inherently sensible, useful, almost generic methods exist and are used by successful speakers.

**CHRONOLOGICAL ORDER**   Materials are arranged according to the order in which events took place. In speaking on "Life on Earth," we would probably discuss the following geologic periods chronologically:

| | |
|---|---|
| **Topic:** | Life on Earth |
| **General Purpose:** | To inform |
| **Specific Purpose:** | To inform the audience about the geologic periods of the planet Earth |
| **Central Idea (Thesis):** | Life on earth developed through six geologic periods, from the Archeozoic to the present. |
| **Main Points:** | (chronologically) |

      I.    The Archeozoic period

     II.    The Proterozoic period

   III.    The Paleozoic period

   IV.    The Mesozoic period

    V.    The Cenozoic period

   VI.    The Present period

This large topic would have to be severely limited to some specific aspect that cuts across all of the periods, such as changes in life forms. Creating full sentences in your outlining helps you see the development of your central idea and how well you have supported your main points. This, then, assists you in editing your ideas to fit the parameters of the assignment. Perhaps the first four main points discussed above could be covered superficially with the emphasis on the Cenozoic period when the mastodons, mammoths, and saber-toothed tigers first appeared. Historical subjects lend themselves readily to this method; so do processes of a sequential (1–2–3) order, such as film developing. Remember, however, that these subjects can be handled in other ways. History is often more interesting and meaningful if discussed topically.

**DIFFICULTY ORDER**   For some subjects, particularly technical ones, it may help to organize your materials according to order of difficulty, proceeding from the easiest aspect to the most difficult one. In discussing general principles of electricity, you might arrange a series of ideas as shown below.

|  |  |
|---|---|
| **Topic:** | Electricity and Magnetism |
| **General Purpose:** | To inform. |
| **Specific Purpose:** | To inform the audience about the effects of electromagnetic phenomena |
| **Central Idea (Thesis):** | Electricity and magnetism are companion physical forces that are responsible for most modern technology. |
| **Main Points:** | (in order of difficulty) |

    I.   Electrostatic force occurs between stationary charges.

    II.   Magnetic force occurs between charges in uniform motion.

    III.   Electromagnetic induction and varying current are companion forces.

    IV.   Electromagnetic radiation and accelerating charges create current and electrons.

One electrical engineering student, sensing that her classmates might find all of her main points most difficult, focused them differently to better fit her audience and scaled them down as in Figure 5.1. She still developed her points from easiest to more difficult.

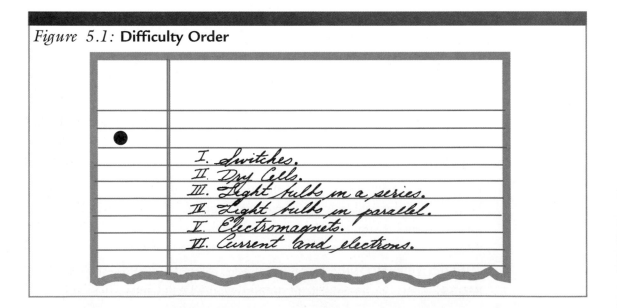

*Figure  5.1:* **Difficulty Order**

    I. Switches.
    II. Dry Cells.
    III. Light bulbs in a series.
    IV. Light bulbs in parallel.
    I. Electromagnets.
    II. Current and electrons.

**SPATIAL ORDER**   This method is particularly useful for certain types of geographic or physical-order subjects. In a speech about the United Nations headquarters in New York, you might first describe each building and then discuss the offices in each building one floor at a time; the ideas are thereby organized spatially. This discussion could also be organized topically if the audience was familiar with the general political structure of the United Nations. In discussing "Nationalism in Africa," you might organize according to geographic location and simply divide the ideas from north to south and east to west. Chronological history might also be a useful method of organizing this speech. A speech on the various peoples of Africa and where they are or are not found could also be ordered and discussed geographically.

| | |
|---|---|
| **Topic:** | Different Africans |
| **General Purpose:** | To inform |
| **Specific Purpose:** | To inform the class about four regions of differing African peoples |
| **Central Idea (Thesis):** | Differing African peoples are found across four distinctly different African regions. |
| **Main Points:** | (arranged spatially) |

    I.    The Sahara

    II.   The Nile Valley

    III.  The Great Rift Valley

    IV.  The Kalahari Desert

**LOGICAL ORDER**   This causal-order method uses generally accepted or obvious cause-and-effect relationships, whether we are talking about the fall of the Japanese empire or the building of a house or a boat. When the order is naturally present in the subject or when the association of ideas is evident, it may be convenient to organize your speech materials accordingly. This method differs from the topical method in that the subpoints almost always illustrate or explain to what they are subordinate, unless the audience (for example, experienced boat builders) already knows the logical relationship. If you were talking to boat builders about excessive hull vibration, you might deal first with effects and work back to causes. You must study your audience very thoroughly before using this method. Persuasive speeches often employ the logical method.

| **Topic:** | Crack |
|---|---|
| **General Purpose:** | To persuade |
| **Specific Purpose:** | To persuade my audience that cocaine is a returning threat to society |
| **Central Idea (Thesis):** | Cocaine is being widely used and is a threat to public health. |
| **Main Points:** | (causal order) |

    **I.**   Cocaine or crack use is accelerating alarmingly.

        **A.** Statistics on use

        **B.** Statistics on reduced cost

    **II.**  Cocaine use is destroying public health.

        **A.** Loss of sensory impressions

        **B.** Recent evidence that its use leads to stroke

**NEED-PLAN ORDER** Materials are organized according to problems *(needs)* and solutions *(plans)*. The speaker first presents the need or the problem that currently exists and then supplies a plan or solution to the problem. The first goal is to get agreement on the existence of the problem. Sometimes this takes more development than others. If the problem was increased tuition, most of the classroom audience should be aware already. Therefore, showing the existence of the problem might need no more than a precursory introduction and a focus on the harmful effects. The second goal is to provide the audience with the plan or the solution. In this case, perhaps the plan would be to suggest alternate resources. The speaker needs to fully develop the plan and, most importantly, show how the plan actually will solve the problem.

If the cocaine speech illustrated under the *logical* (cause-effect) method were expanded to the problem of drug use generally, a *need-plan* or problem-solution order might be a better organizational option.

| **Topic:** | "H", Crack, Smack, and "Mary Jane" (also the speech title) |
|---|---|
| **General Purpose:** | To persuade |
| **Specific Purpose:** | To persuade the audience that a national policy is necessary to control widespread drug use |
| **Central Idea (Thesis):** | The federal government needs a radical new mandatory educational program to stop the flow and use of drugs. |

**Main Points:**    (Need-plan order)

> Need
>
> **I.**    The deleterious effects of drug use are out of control.
>
> **A.**
> **B.** } Evidence and argument
> **C.**
>
> **II.**    The uninhibited trafficking in illegal drugs is leading to horren-
> dous crime statistics.
>
> **A.** } Evidence and argument
> **B.**
>
> Plan
>
> **III.**    A federal program of mandatory drug education is necessary.
>
> **A.**
> **B.** } Details of plan (and how it will solve the problem)
> **C.**

An organizational tool often used for problem-solution or persuasive speeches is Monroe's Motivated Sequence. A full description of this organizational format will be presented in Chapter 11—Speeches to Persuade.

**TOPICAL ORDER**  In the topical method, materials are often ordered according to general topics or classifications of knowledge. For example, a history professor might concentrate on the history of religion, war, government, education, or science. The importance of the topic may or may not be such that the presentation of the topic violates historical time. Some topics are better designed to be broken down into parts, or subtopics. These subtopics become your main points. Although the topical method is a useful way to start breaking down very broad topics, you should first assess the other, more specific ordering systems before deciding upon this more general ordering system. A broad topic like integration of the races can be looked at in several topical ways—educationally, socially, militarily, economically, and so forth. A city may be described topically in terms of its industry, employment opportunities, recreational facilities, schools, and climate.

| | |
|---|---|
| **Topic:** | Faltering Integration |
| **General Purpose:** | To persuade |
| **Specific Purpose:** | To persuade the audience that racial integration needs to be pursued more aggressively |
| **Central Idea (Thesis):** | Racial integration is uneven across standard societal measures. |
| **Main Points:** | (topics) |

    I.    Educational integration is not working.

    II.    Economic integration is weak at higher income levels.

    III.    Housing integration is mostly unsuccessful.

    IV.    Social integration is improving.

    V.    Military integration is the most apparent.

In the above example, a need-plan organization might also be used if you have a plan or a chronological order can be used to show the improvement or the lack of it over time.

An audience can be easily confused with the topical method if you mix your main points in terms of function. For example:

| | |
|---|---|
| **Topic:** | The Real Zodiac |
| **General Purpose:** | To inform |
| **Specific Purpose:** | To inform the audience about the latest news on solar system components |
| **Central Idea (Thesis):** | The solar system is composed of nine planets plus moons, planetoids, comets, meteors, and particles that reflect zodiacal light. |
| **Main Points:** | (topical) |

    I.    Nine planets and thirty-three moons

    II.    One thousand six-hundred planetoids or asteroids

    III.    Comets and meteors

    IV.    Reflectors of zodiacal light

    *V.    Space travel

Note that the first four main points are logically consistent, each serving the same function of describing *parts* or components of the solar system. The fifth point, "Space travel," deals not with constituent parts but with another topic (or dimension) completely. This is not to say that a brief anecdote or startling illustration about space travel wouldn't make a good attention-getting *introduction* for such a speech. I suppose one could also organize this speech spatially.

In general, main points should be (1) related in function, (2) unitary (one idea per point), (3) consistent in wording, (4) roughly equal in speech time needed, and (5) ordered to achieve appropriate emphasis.

# Cohesion: Connecting Ideas

This includes all efforts at showing that your ideas *cohere;* that is, they relate, connect, or hang together in some meaningful way. The principle means are *previews* and *reviews* of main ideas and effective *transitions* between them.

**PREVIEWS**   Your announcing, in advance, how your main points are connected may make them clearer.

"Today I will explain three reasons why we should support Senator Foghorn."

1. First she has a clear record of accomplishments

2. She is a woman of deep and sustained character

3. And lastly, she doesn't mind getting her hands dirty

The preview of your speech is found as the last point in your introduction. Some speech instructors might separate the preview out of the introduction to stand alone between your introduction and the body of your speech.

**REVIEWS**   Make your main points more cohesive—and better understood by your audience—by *reviewing* or *summarizing* your points. In Chapter 4, we talked about the importance of restatement for audience comprehension. However, you can be creative by avoiding direct repetition. Restate the ideas in your summary, not each word directly.

1. What is clear about Senator Foghorn is that her record of accomplishments is unparalleled.

2. Her character is unquestioned by all who know and have worked with her.

3. When it comes to work, Senator Foghorn gets involved

**TRANSITIONS**   These specific language segments connect one idea to another. They can be short and direct indicating a move to the next point, or they can be elaborate internal previews and internal reviews that help the audience hold the points together. Whichever the case, they are the bridges of words and phrases indicating that you have finished one thought and are moving on to another.

In the case of speeches that follow a fairly clear chronological order, you may need little by way of transitional statement.

"To continue…"

"Step two in this process…"

"On the third day…"

"To sum up…"

These are just simple *signs* that hopefully will replace the excess verbalizations often used by inexperienced speakers—"Let's see," "ah," "um," "okay," "so…"

You can also use connecting phrases as *signposts* designed to emphasize or indicate a shift in focus.

"More important than my previous points…"

"My next argument is crucial…"

"Now hear this…"

"Most of all…"

"In this case…"

For lack of a simple connecting word or phrase, these additional situations sometimes provide awkward moments for speakers. The following are some suggestions:

1. *Comparing:* from another point of view, in like manner, in contrast with this

2. *Citing:* by way of illustration, a case in point is, under this head

3. *Judging:* this being true, such being the case, under these circumstances

4. *Excepting:* with this exception, waiving this question, excluding this point

5. *Opposing:* were this not so, on the contrary, in spite of this

6. *Conceding:* to be sure, it must be granted, admitting the force of

7. *Making reference:* in point of, with respect to, as related to

As mentioned earlier, you can also employ internal previews and internal reviews between your points as transitions.

**INTERNAL PREVIEWS**    You can preview each main idea as you come to it in a more developed transition. Previewing a main point within the body of the speech is referred to as an internal preview. Think of them as elaborate transitions. Here is an example of how an internal preview is used as a transition within the body of a speech.

> "My second important reason to support Senator Foghorn has to do with her strength
> of character, including her willingness to stand by what she says"

We would expect that the following point would cover examples of character and explain what is meant by "stand by what she says."

**INTERNAL REVIEWS**    Sometimes a complicated point needs a summary before moving forward, and might be necessary to show the logic of the point as it relates to what is coming. This transition style is referred to as an internal review. Although the speech on Senator Foghorn contains points that are hardly complicated, we will stay with that example here.

> "Now that I've established that Senator Foghorn is a woman of character by following
> through with her promises, standing by what she says, and dependably responding to
> her constituents, let's move to work ethic."

There are also times that internal previews and internal reviews can be combined. This can be particularly helpful with complicated points. However, it can also be cumbersome. Speakers use these transitions judiciously.

# PLANNING THE INTRODUCTION

## Functions

*Securing attention* is the first requirement of an introduction, and is one of great importance. An uninterested audience means your message will not get across. Your introduction should also attempt to establish or strengthen *goodwill* among you, the group you represent, and the audience. In those rare cases in which goodwill is scarce (when you're facing a hostile audience), you need to establish an atmosphere for a *fair hearing,* meaning that you create enough credibility and trustworthiness that the audience is willing to hear you out. For example, statesman Adlai Stevenson used humor to establish rapport with a tough Labor Day audience. "When I was a boy, I never had much sympathy for a holiday speaker. He was just a kind of interruption between hot dogs, a fly in the lemonade."

Another function of the introduction is *orientation.* The speaker must orient the audience by supplying certain background explanations or definitions to help the audience understand the main body of the speech. Certain terms may be unfamiliar, and *not* to define them is to confuse the audience (for example, cybernetics, carcinoma, ROM/RAM, method acting, and organon). Not all definitions need to occur in the introduction; however, if a term or concept is central to your speech, it should be addressed at this point.

Finally, unless some special strategy of persuasion is involved, the introduction seeks to make your *central idea* and *purpose* clear: What is the main thrust of your topic and what are you seeking from your audience? Almost always it offers a *preview* of what will follow in the main body.

In sum, the general functions of an introduction are as follows:

1.    Secure *attention*

2.    Establish goodwill and credibility

3.    Assure a fair hearing

4.    Orient your audience to the subject

5.    Make your *central idea* and *purpose* clear

6.    Offer a preview

**SECURE ATTENTION**    One student with a persuasive speech on chest X-rays secured attention with the following *startling statement*:

There is a subtle killer loose in the room. It killed forty thousand people last year. It likes young people—no one is immune to tuberculosis.

It was topic relevant (X-rays reveal TB), it was audience relevant (young people are most susceptible), and it was startling. How much better than:

A yearly chest X-ray is the best way to avoid TB.

Audiences usually respond to the unique, the strange, and the bizarre. One student speaking against terms that stereotype people aroused attention and curiosity with the following *rhetorical questions*:

1.    What if this week Dr. Ross asked us to define who we are, or what our roles are? In doing so I wonder how many of us would use such terms as "man," "woman," "male," "husband," "wife," "mother," "father," "masculine," "feminine"? And if so, I wonder how many of us would be stereotyping ourselves?

The following elements of her introduction to secure attention highlight the use of *reference to subject*:

2.    For far too long clichés—such as: "Little boys are made of snakes and snails and puppy dog's tails; and little girls are made of sugar and spice and everything nice"—have represented the image of the male and female in society. Traditionally, males have been depicted as heroic, active, and aggressive, while females pale in the shadow of masculinity.

The title of the student's speech was "A War on Words," which was an attention-getting device in itself when announced by the student chairperson.

Another student speaking on the social impact of rock music used *audio equipment* and opened with music examples—plenty of attention here.

Statistics make great attention-getters, particularly if not commonly known. They are sometimes very poignant when put in question form to a relevant audience. Here are some examples:

Do you know that 72 percent of the freshmen in the Detroit public high schools don't graduate?

Eighty percent of the books written are read by 10 percent of the people.

Fewer than one out of five books published covers expenses.

*Quotations* are often good openers and attention-getters. Here are some that students have used:

A speech on the future:

> *I am not afraid of tomorrow for I have seen yesterday, and I love today.*
> **William Allen White (journalist)**

A speech on publishing difficulties:

> *A person who publishes a book willfully appears before the populace with his pants down.*
> **Edna St. Vincent Millay**

A speech on human insensitivity:

> *The young man who has not wept is a savage, and the old man who will not laugh is a fool.*
> **George Santayana**

A speech on critical thinking:

> *I am not afraid of tomorrow for I have seen yesterday, and I love today.*
> **William Allen White (journalist)**

A speech on inexperienced deer hunters:

> *A little learning is a dangerous thing; Drink deep, or taste not the Pierian spring; There shallow draughts intoxicate the brain, And drinking largely sobers us again.*
>
> **Alexander Pope**

This student not only moved on to a discussion of inadequate training in gun handling but also, through a play on words, to the problems of drinking and hunting. We'll have more to say about attention and interest factors in Chapter 10, "Speeches to Inform."

**ESTABLISH GOODWILL AND CREDIBILITY**    Goodwill and credibility are especially important with a controversial subject and a hostile audience. As we shall learn in more detail in Chapter 11, "Speeches to Persuade," some concession to the opposition helps establish goodwill and indicates that you know something about the other side of the argument. So does humor. When Jimmy Carter was campaigning for the presidency, he became used to difficult audiences. Upon finally being greeted by a quieter, more contemplative group, he commented, "It certainly is nice to have people waving at me with all five fingers." Establishing goodwill is another way of connecting to the audience. A speaker wants the audience to trust him or her and minimizing differences is a good start.

In a student speech *against* the repeal of Michigan's container (bottles and cans) law, the speaker opened as follows:

I know that soft drinks cost a dollar a case more in Michigan due to extra handling and storage. I also know that some glassmaking jobs are lost and that some energy is lost because of extra transportation. However, let me tell you about litter reduction and the costs saved there …

Credibility can be established by revealing your experience, training, or any other reason why you are qualified to speak on your chosen topic. Trying to do that without sounding boastful can be a problem.

A speech on scuba diving was opened with a display of equipment and the following words:

I've only been diving for two years and my deepest dive was only 80 feet to the wreck of the schooner Kukla. I'd like to review some basics …

It was clear to all of us (even the divers) that this speaker had credibility and that he wasn't trying to inflate his qualifications.

Other ways to establish credibility include stating some startling statistic or referring to a source that is an expert on your topic. This shows the audience that you have faithfully been doing your homework for the speech and have come to the presentation prepared.

**ASSURE A FAIR HEARING**    This function is much like securing good-will and perceptions of credibility and is not necessary in speeches where the audience is not hostile. The container-law speech was a good example of an appeal for a fair hearing because the audience had concern about increased costs on their beverages. Hostile audiences are the main problem particularly if they keep rehearsing arguments to what they *think* you're going to say. The concession suggestion is also a good one here, but sometimes a direct appeal is appropriate.

I know that most of you are opposed to the by-pass road proposal. I have heard your arguments—it's only American fair play that you hear the other side. I promise to be as objective as I can.

Other methods of securing fair hearing include *appreciation:* ("I understand and appreciate your concern—and most of all your willingness to hear both sides"), *personal reference:* ("I've lived all of my life in this community and I want only the best for its citizens.…") and *humor* ("Your spokesperson just paid me a compliment—I think. He said, 'It must be difficult for you to soar among eagles when you work with turkeys [the road commission].' ")

**ORIENT YOUR AUDIENCE TO YOUR SUBJECT**    As in establishing goodwill by connecting to the audience; the audience also needs you to connect them to your topic. It may be important to you, but why is it important or interesting to them? Sometimes an audience also needs to become better acquainted with technical aspects, definitions, diagrams, or terms that you will use in the body of your speech. Review these in the introduction; a visual aid helps too. A speech on the history of firearms made more sense to the audience after the speaker first oriented audience members to the basic nomenclature (names of the parts) of a rifle. He did this by using an enlarged diagram, thus giving the audience a vocabulary and a sense of function that greatly assisted understanding. Had his speech been on the firearms themselves, and not the history, naming the parts of a rifle might have worked better as a first point. The point of orientation is to give the audience the information they need to better follow the rest of the speech and to see how it relates to them.

Other ways to orient your audience to the topic may include a brief historical sketch, an extended example or short narrative, or a hypothetical story.

**CLARIFY YOUR CENTRAL IDEA AND PURPOSE**    If, after a rousing speech introduction, your audience says, "Okay, but what are we talking about?" or "Whadhesay?" we might have a problem of clarity in the purpose, the central idea, and/or poor orientation. Unless strategy is involved, the introduction should clarify what you are going to discuss (the central idea), why your audience should listen (orientation), and what you expect from them (purpose).

The central idea is clarified with a thesis statement that captures and summarizes your speech in a full, declarative sentence. As a complete sentence, the thesis will help focus the speaker in creating the main points and help focus the audience on what to expect. A student speaking on music theory started his introduction with a violin demonstration (attention) and for his central idea provided the following thesis statement:

> There are three elements shared by all instruments that need to be understood in order to play any of them

He then revealed the purpose of the speech by making it clear to the audience that there was simplicity to the instruments:

> Although you, yourself might not play an instrument, knowing what they all have in common can better help you to appreciate the necessary knowledge all musicians share.

**PREVIEW THE BODY OF YOUR SPEECH**   The old rule of "Tell 'em what you're going to tell 'em, tell 'em, tell 'em what you've told 'em" makes some sense. The preview is "what you're going to tell 'em." The preview is the last element of a good introduction and lets your audience know precisely what you are going to cover in the body of your speech. It can serve as a transition to the body, but more often is followed by a transition to the first main point.

The above student, giving his speech on music theory, ended his introduction with a forthright preview of what was to follow.

> I have three points to make that I will relate to playing an instrument: the kinds of notes, the musical staff, and methods of counting the notes.

You need not always be as specific as the example above. Look at the following direct preview and its more creative counterpart:

> Today, I am going to speak about how to reduce, reuse, and recycle.

> Instead;

> Reducing what we consume, reusing what we purchase, and recycling what we no longer want are ways we can contribute to a greener environment.

**PITFALLS TO AVOID IN INTRODUCTION**   The following examples illustrate problems that speakers often find in working their introductions. False starts, unnecessary apologies, and overstatements are three general pitfalls you will want to avoid. All three result in a reduction of your credibility.

### *False Starts*

> "Before I begin …"

> "Well, I guess it's time to start …"

> "Is it all right if I sit down?"

> "Before saying anything important …"

> Statements such as these generally irritate audiences and label you as ineffective.

### Unnecessary Apologies

"I'm not very good at this ..."

"I hope you'll pay attention ..."

"I didn't have much time to prepare ..."

"I never had a speech course ..."

"I'm sorry if this sounds complicated ..."

If any of these apologetic statements are true, the audience will find out soon enough. Don't destroy your credibility before you even get started.

On the other hand, if you are late for the speech, lost your visual aids, or caused the schedule to be rearranged, a brief explanation, if not an apology, is in order.

"I'm late because my ROTC instructor held the class overtime."

"My luggage along with my slides was stolen."

"I apologize to the other speakers and appreciate their accommodating my travel problems."

***Overstatement***   This pitfall includes distortion, imprudence, misrepresentation, and over exaggeration to get attention. Don't promise more than you can deliver.

A social science teacher opened a lecture on nuclear power by asking each student to cut off a lock of hair and deposit it in a metal container. The teacher then burned the hair, which gave off a nauseating stench. This, he explained, was what human flesh smelled like when exposed to nuclear radiation. Next he showed a two-minute film clip of the most grisly pictures of hideously burned people after the atomic bomb raid on Hiroshima. Finally, he snuffed out an ant farm in a fraction of a second by burning up the oxygen with hot magnesium, much, he explained, as people are destroyed in a nuclear explosion.

Attention here all right! But will it help introduce the body of the speech? Not if it is so overpowering that it destroys future concentration or so emotional that it actually turns people off to the point of rejection of the speaker and the speaker's message. Will it assure a fair hearing? Is it a fair hearing? Is it a fair orientation to the subject? Does it confuse the purpose? Is it a case of overkill and misplaced emphasis?

Attention at any price is a mistake. Attention-getting strategies should be relevant to both the topic and the audience, no matter whether it's a joke, a story, an example, or a demonstration. However, some topic-relevant devices are not always audience relevant. One student speaker opened a speech on presidential politics with a joke about one of the more profligate candidates. The story had two four-letter words in it. Half of the audience were members of the Pentecostal Church; more than half of the audience walked out before he got to the message.

Do not be afraid to startle or titillate an audience especially with an important but dull topic, but look for the boomerangs.

Certainly, gaining the listeners' *attention* is an important requirement of the beginning of a speech, but one can overdo as well as underdo attention-gaining devices. The number of attention devices to be used also depends on what attention level the audience has already achieved. In other words, if the listeners are on the edge of their seats and ready to hear what you have to say, a lengthy introduction designed to arouse their attention will be unnecessary.

## Model Introductions

The inaugural address of John F. Kennedy, which follows, illustrates most of the functions and requirements of a good introduction. Note that they both lack a preview of main points to follow.

*Attention*     My fellow citizens:

We observe today not a victory of party but a celebration of freedom—symbolizing an end as well as a beginning—signifying renewal as well as change. For I have sworn before you and Almighty God the same solemn oath our forebears prescribed nearly a century and three-quarters ago.

*Orientation*     The world is very different now. For man holds in his mortal hands the power and Goodwill to abolish all forms of human poverty and to abolish all forms of human life. And, yet, the same revolutionary beliefs for which our forebears fought are still at issue around the globe—the belief that the rights of man come not from the generosity of the state but from the hand of God.

*Fair Hearing*    We dare not forget today that we are the heirs of that first revolution. Let the word go forth from this time and place, to friend and foe alike, that the torch has been passed to a new generation of Americans-born in this century, tempered by war, disciplined by a cold and bitter peace, proud of our ancient heritage—and unwilling to witness or permit the slow undoing of those human rights to which this nation has always been committed, and to which we are committed today.

*Central Idea* And *Purpose*    Let every nation know, whether it wish us well or ill, that we shall pay any price, bear any burden, meet any hardship, support any friend, or oppose any foe in order to assure the survival and success of liberty. This much we pledge—and more.

In still more specific terms, an introduction may utilize appreciation, personal reference, quotations, humor, and related stories or experiences. When the purpose of the speech is relatively obvious and the speaker and subject are well known, a related story, incident, or narrative with built-in attention often reinforces the purpose and gives the audience a fresh orientation. Booker T. Washington's introduction to his classic address at the Atlanta Exposition is a case in point.

*Attention*    Mr. President and Gentlemen of the Board of Directors and Citizens: One-third of the population of the South is of the Negro race. No enterprise seeking the material, civil, or moral welfare of this section can disregard this element of our population and reach the highest success.

*Goodwill*    I but convey to you, Mr. President and Directors, the sentiment of the masses of my race when I say that in no way have the value of manhood of the American Negro been more fittingly and generously recognized than by the managers of this magnificent Exposition at every stage of its progress. It is a recognition that will do more to cement the friendship of the two races than any occurrence since the dawn of our freedom.

*Fair Hearing*    Not only this, but the opportunity here afforded will awaken among us a new era of industrial progress. Ignorant and inexperienced, it is not strange that in the first years of our new life we began at the top instead of at the bottom; that a seat in Congress or the state legislature was more sought than real estate or industrial skill;

that the political convention or stump speaking had more attractions than starting a dairy farm or truck garden.

*Orientation*    A ship lost at sea for many days suddenly sighted a friendly vessel. From the mast of the unfortunate vessel was seen a signal, "Water, water; we die of thirst!" The answer from the friendly vessel at once came back, "Cast down your bucket where you are." And a third and fourth signal for water was answered, "Cast down your bucket where you are." The captain of the distressed vessel, at last heeding the injunction, cast down his bucket, and it came up full of fresh, sparkling water from the mouth of the Amazon River.

*Central Idea* and *Purpose*    To those of my race who depend on bettering their condition in a foreign land or who underestimate the importance of cultivating friendly relations with the Southern white man, who is their next door neighbor, I would say: "Cast down your bucket where you are—cast it down in making friends in every manly way of the people of all races by whom we are surrounded."

President Franklin D. Roosevelt also used a story in an introduction to one of the many appeals he made for the purchase of war bonds.

Once upon a time, a few years ago, there was a city in our Middle West, which was threatened by a destructive flood in a great river. The water had risen to the top of the banks. Every man, woman, and child in that city was called upon to fill sandbags in order to defend their homes against the rising waters. For many days and nights destruction and death stared them in the face. As a result of the grim, determined community effort, that city still stands. Those people kept the levees above the peak of the flood. All of them joined together in the desperate job that had to be done—businessmen, workers, farmers, and doctors, and preachers—people of all races.

To me that town is a living symbol of what community cooperation can accomplish.

# PLANNING THE CONCLUSION

## Functions

A good conclusion offers *review, reinforcement, and a call to action.* To these we sometimes add *visualization, restatement,* and *impression.* All of these devices intend to rekindle attention and to assist the memory. Aristotle suggested that the major purpose of the conclusion is to help the memory. An attention-getter used here is a good idea just as it was in the introduction.

The conclusion is generally shorter than the introduction. It may, and generally should, include a short summary that reinforces the central idea, thus making it easier to understand. It may provide clearly stated directions if certain actions are part of the speaker's purpose. When your purpose has been inspiration, you may need a more impressive conclusion. Some of the devices suggested in the discussion on introductions (an impressive quotation, incident, or experience) apply here. The three major functions of a good conclusion are as follows:

1. Review the central idea.

2. Reinforce belief or action desired.

3. End with impact and impress when appropriate.

**REVIEW THE CENTRAL IDEA**    "Tell 'em what you told 'em." Sometimes the speaker summarizes the central idea in his review. Other times, the speaker reviews each main point covered in the speech. A detailed speech about the dietary laws of the Jewish people, including the biblical and pragmatic reasons behind them, concluded as follows:

CONCLUSION

I. In review, an observing Jew may not:
   A. Consume meat that comes from animals that do not possess cloven hoofs and that do not chew their cud.
   B. Consume fish that do not have both scales and fins.
   C. Consume or cook meat and dairy foods together.
   D. Eat any part of a living animal.
   E. Consume blood (hence, koshering).
   F. Consume meat from an animal that has not been ritually slaughtered.

In a speech about the future six wonders of the world, where the central idea was to show their useful purposes compared to the ancient seven wonders, this student offered an interesting and detailed review:

CONCLUSION

I.   These new six wonders have useful purposes.

   A. Snowy Mountains Scheme makes Australia's desert lands places of lush vegetation.

   B. Chesapeake Bay Bridge Tunnel enables people to travel more easily from Norfolk to the Delmarva Peninsula.

   C. The Netherlands' Delta Plan secures the land from the damaging storms of the sea.

   D. The New York Narrows Bridge allows traffic to cross the entrance of New York Harbor.

   E. The Mont Blanc Tunnel allows year-round travel through the Alps.

   F. The English Channel Tunnel connects Britain and France by rail transporting passengers and their cars.

II.   These constructions are more wondrous than the ancient ones.

   A. Ancient wonders were noted primarily for art, size, and beauty.

   B. The modern wonders each have all of these plus unchallenged utility.

**REINFORCE BELIEF OR ACTION**   A speaker can, of course, reinforce by simply reviewing as shown in the illustrations above. However, in persuasive speeches one may also wish to be a little more explicit or manifest. In a speech where the central idea was that nonsmokers have rights and should speak up for them, after a review of actions to be taken, the student uses reinforcement to emphasize the belief and action she is requesting. Her concluding statement is a direct **call to action**, giving the audience specific actions they can adopt immediately:

CONCLUSION

I.   In summary, smokers infringe on the health and well-being of nonsmokers with the secondhand smoke of their burning cigarettes.

   A. Secondhand smoke can cause lung cancer in adults who do not smoke.

   B. Exposure to secondhand smoke also increases the risk of heart disease in the nonsmoker.

C. In children, exposure to secondhand smoke can cause asthma, increase the risk of SIDS, and increase the risk of lower respiratory track and middle ear infections.

D. The United States Environmental Protection Agency has created the smoke-free home and car program.

E. We should follow the EPA program guidelines and secure smoke-free environments for nonsmokers and children.

II. There is no reason there can't be places for smoking as well as places not to smoke.

A. I don't think anyone has ever really died of a "nicotine fit" from not smoking for an hour or two during a class period.

B. You really should stand up for your rights and support movements to designate places to smoke and places not to smoke.

C. So, the next time you're in a car or other enclosed place and someone asks you, "Do you mind if I smoke?" be sure to reply, "Yes, I mind!"

In a speech where the central idea was that latchkey children can survive very nicely if parents will practice specific rules, a student reviewed and reinforced the actions as follows:

CONCLUSION

I. In review, these are actions to take if you have a child who will have to stay alone.

A. Teach children to use the phone and lock the doors.

B. Don't let the child display a key in public.

C. Instruct children to tell callers that the parent is busy and unable to come to the phone.

D. Structure activities for the child.

E. Arrange for the child to spend some afternoons with friends.

F. Get a pet.

G. Teach children that independence and resourcefulness are virtues but don't overload the circuits.

II. Latchkey children can lead normal lives without fear, drugs, or crime.

A. The proof is standing here in front of you;

B. I was a latchkey child.

In the above example, the student is covertly asking for the audience to re-consider their beliefs. Although he provides actions a parent can take, he is not requesting the audience to any particular action or overt change. In fact, depending on how he organized the speech, his review could signal it was either an informative or persuasive speech. His reinforcement leads us to believe it was designed as a persuasive speech.

**END WITH IMPACT AND IMPRESS WHEN APPROPRIATE**    All speeches should end with a strong final statement that leaves the audience with something to consider or resonates with the audience long after the speech is over. This is referred to as **ending with impact**. Most classroom speeches other than *special-occasion* assignments don't call for superdramatic, elevated conclusions, but a dramatic or pointed, relevant quotation like those shown in the discussion of introductions usually works well in all speeches. A very touching speech by a handicapped student on the "Promise of Tomorrow" was concluded using the same quotation with which she had opened her speech.

Other choices to end a speech can include restating a startling fact given earlier in the speech, providing a rhetorical or hypothetical question, offering a thought-provoking comment that invites the audience to further consideration, or requesting or calling the audience to action in a persuasive speech.

Special-occasion speeches typically do call for a more elevated style of language and a more impressive presentation at their conclusion. Martin Luther King, Jr. provided a classic inspirational conclusion in his famous speech in support of civil rights legislation before an estimated two hundred thousand people. Note that his review is much more than a mere repetition of his main points, and that his purpose is made abundantly clear.

So let freedom ring—from the prodigious hilltops of New Hampshire, let freedom ring; from the mighty mountains of New York, let freedom ring—from the heightening Alleghenies of Pennsylvania!

Let freedom ring from the snowcapped Rockies of Colorado!

Let freedom ring from the curvaceous slopes of California!

But not only that; let freedom ring from Stone Mountain of Georgia!

Let freedom ring from Lookout Mountain of Tennessee!

Let freedom ring from every hill and mole hill of Mississippi.

From every mountainside, let freedom ring,…

When we allow freedom to ring, when we let it ring from every village and every hamlet, from every state and every city, we will be able to speed up that day when all of God's children, black men and white men, Jews and Gentiles, Protestants and Catholics, will be able to join hands and sing in the words of the old Negro spiritual, "Free at last! Free at last! Thank God almighty, we are free at last!"

A presidential inauguration is a very special occasion and the "Ask Not" speech of John Fitzgerald Kennedy made an impression that will be long remembered. The conclusion deserves a piece of marble.

And so, my fellow Americans, ask not what your country can do for you: Ask what you can do for your country.

My fellow citizens of the world: Ask not what America will do for you, but what together we can do for the freedom of man.

Finally, whether you are citizens of America or citizens of the world, ask of us here the same high standards of strength and sacrifice which we ask of you. With a good conscience our only sure reward, with history the final judge of our deeds, let us go forth to lead the land we love, asking His blessings and His help, but knowing that here on earth God's work must truly be our own.

## PITFALLS TO AVOID IN CONCLUSIONS

As in introductions, there are pitfalls that speakers want to be sure to avoid in their conclusions. Three typical pitfalls include deprecation of a speaker's own effort in creating and presenting his/her speech, overamplification by restating points with too much emphasis or even worse, adding new material, and prolonging the close.

### Deprecation of Effort

"I should have had more time to prepare."

"I'm sorry I couldn't say it better."

"I guess there are more important points as well."

"I'm not an orator, but I hope you got something out of this."

These kinds of apologies are almost always superfluous and damaging to your credibility. Apologies and qualifiers germane to other issues may sometimes pertain, but should probably have been stated earlier.

***Overamplification*** Overamplification refers to a disproportionate expansion of the points already covered in the body of the speech. A speaker can creatively restate, but should not elaborate on points already covered in the speech. In its worst example of overamplification, new material is introduced. New material should never appear in the conclusion. Main points with their support belong in the body of the speech, not in the conclusion.

> I am not afraid of tomorrow for I have seen yesterday, and I love today.
>
> **William Allen White**

***Prolonged Close*** Most important, make it clear when you are finished; consider your exit lines carefully. Speakers who do not know when to finish appear awkward and frustrate the audience. Furthermore, an awkward conclusion reduces the credibility he may have gained throughout the speech. The never-ending conclusion leaves you with so many things to tie together that you cannot conclude your speech in any unified manner. The lesson is obvious; prepare your conclusion as carefully as the rest of your speech. Doing so serves as a good check on organic unity. Quit while you're ahead. Don't let an audience hypnotize you so much that you ruin a good speech by an overly long or overly dramatic conclusion.

# CHAPTER REVIEW
## *Wrapping it up*

## Summary

The introduction, body, and conclusion are the basic parts of a speech. Main points emerge from your central idea and early preparation. In persuasive speeches, look at your basic reasons or arguments for the main points. Rhetorical advice regarding main points includes: limit them to three or four, keep them unified with your central idea, and give each relatively equal merit.

Methods of ordering main points include: chronological, difficulty, spatial, logical, need-plan, which includes considering Monroe's Motivated Sequence, and topical. The principal ways of connecting main ideas include: a preview in the introduction, a review in the summary, and transitions between main points (which include internal previews and internal reviews or summaries as well as brief statements and signposts).

Six functions of the introduction part of a speech include: securing attention, connecting to the audience by establishing goodwill and credibility, assuring a fair hearing when the audience is opposed or hostile to your topic, orienting the audience to the subject of your speech, clarifying your central idea and purpose, and offering a preview of your main points. Pitfalls to avoid include: false starts, unnecessary apologies, and overstatement.

Three functions of the conclusion include: reviewing the central idea, reinforcing the belief or action desired, and ending with impact while impressing when appropriate. Pitfalls to avoid include: deprecation of effort, overamplification, and a prolonged close.

Check out our website
**www.bvtlab.com**
for flashcards, summaries, self-quizzes, and speeches.

# OUTLINING
# THE SPEECH

# Chapter 6

## Chapter Objectives

### Where to Start

**Purpose and Central Idea**

**Rough Draft**

### Outlining Principles

**Symbolization**

**Subordination**

**Simplicity**

**Discreteness**

**Coordination**

**Progression**

### The Complete Outline

**General Rules**

**Model Complete Outline**

### The Speaking Outline

**General Rules**

**Model Speaking Outline**

### Exemplar: Outline Development

The outline is to a speech what a blueprint is to a house. A good, clear outline can help you discover mistakes, weaknesses, and unnecessary information *before* you speak, just as the builder or architect can often save costly mistakes by taking a hard look at the plans before starting to build the house.

This chapter begins with practical suggestions for a rough draft outline, then describes basic principles of outlining, and closes with explanations of how to prepare, really, two outlines. The first is a complete sentence outline, the one many instructors ask you to turn in for a grade; the second is your speaking outline, a shorter version of the first.

# WHERE TO START

## Purpose and Central Idea

Review the assignment. Has your general purpose shifted from *inform* to *persuade* when to *inform* was the charge? Then review your *specific* purpose and central idea. If your central idea is clearly stated, it may be a mini-outline. Recall the central idea for the "Role of the Manager" speech in Chapter 4. "Five management functions are planning, organizing, directing, coordinating, and controlling." These five functions can be viewed as the five main points of the speech. As we said in Chapter 5, start with the main points in the body of the speech, make a note of any ideas for the introduction or conclusion, and hold them for the time being. You'll want to review your research notes and ideas to see if they suggest still more main points or perhaps a way to rewrite or combine them.

The examples that follow are informative speeches. Strategic outlining suggestions for the persuasive speech are found in Chapter 11, "Speeches to Persuade." If you are still searching for a subject, see the "Speech Topic Locator" in the Appendix.

## Rough Draft

Mark Scott loved his anthropology course and decided to look for his informative speech topic in that general area. The study of human beings was, of course, too broad a topic for a four- to five-minute speech so he thought of two areas of that broad topic that interested him: "The Races of Man" and "The Beginnings of

Mankind." Preliminary research in these areas indicated that anthropologists have divided the world's population into three, general racial types—Caucasoid, Mongoloid, and Negroid. Mark also found that *Homo sapiens* (human beings) first appeared in the Pleistocene epoch of the Cenozoic era. The Cenozoic era began about 70 million years ago and humans had mastodons, mammoths, and saber-toothed tigers with which to contend. Mark was fascinated by stories of "Peking man," the oldest discovery. This person may have lived 6 million years ago. Other prehistoric people varied somewhat and were discovered near Neanderthal, Germany, and Les Eyzies, France. The latter were called Cro-Magnon, which is the French word for "great hole" or "cave" in which they were found.

That provided great materials for a speech, perhaps two or three, but what an overload of confused information! Mark started by listing the more important and interesting points and ideas.

| | |
|---|---|
| Races of man | Pleistocene epoch |
| Beginnings of man | Cenozoic era |
| Anthropology | Peking man |
| Caucasoid | Java man |
| Mongoloid | Neanderthal man |
| Negroid | Cro-Magnon man |
| Homo sapiens | |

Now it was time to combine, subordinate, discard, and generally reduce the list. *Anthropology* covered everything—discard. *Homo sapiens* and human being mean the same thing—discard *Homo sapiens*. *Caucasoid, Mongoloid,* and *Negroid* are all the races of humans-subordinate them.

I.  Races of man
  A. Caucasoid
  B. Mongoloid
  C. Negroid

The *Pleistocene* epoch is part of the *Cenozoic* era …? *Peking, Java, Neanderthal,* and *Cro-Magnon* are all early, archaeological discoveries that describe the *beginnings of man.* They can be subordinated.

I.  Beginnings of man
    **A.** Neanderthal man
    **B.** Cro-Magnon man
    **C.** Peking man
    **D.** Java man

Mark wisely decided that he had enough ideas here for two speeches. He selected "Beginnings of Man" because he found it more interesting, and he thought the word "Negroid" might offend some of his classmates. Oh yes, he also had more research material on prehistoric humans.

Because all of this information referred to prehistoric times, Mark decided that "Prehistoric People" might be a better topic title than "Beginnings of Man." It also occurred to him that the constant use of the word "man" might offend his female classmates. Note also that there is a natural, chronological order to archaeological findings. An outline began to emerge.

## PREHISTORIC PEOPLE

INTRODUCTION

BODY

I.  Peking man (6,000,000 to 125,000 years BC)

II.  Java man (6,000,000 to 125,000 years BC)

III.  Neanderthal man (125,000 to 25,000 years BC)

IV.  Cro-Magnon man (25,000 to 8,000 years BC)

CONCLUSION

Mark's revised specific purpose and central idea now focused his research on the archaeological findings related to these three periods of early humans and to their inferred characteristics and behavior. His rough outline follows.

## ROUGH OUTLINE

**Topic:** Prehistoric People

**General Purpose:** To inform

**Specific Purpose:** To inform the audience about the characteristics of early humans

**Central Idea:** There are three main periods of early humans based on archaeological finds.

WHENCE HUMAN

INTRODUCTION

BODY

      I.    "Peking man" (6,000,000 to 125,000 years BC; also Java "Man" and other finds of this period)

      II.   Neanderthal people (125,000 years to 25,000 years BC; also other finds of this period)

      III.  Cro-Magnon people (25,000 to 8,000 BC; also other finds of this period)

CONCLUSION

    A review of characteristics and behaviors

Mark is now ready to develop his complete, finished outline. However, first let's review the classic principles of outlining in general.

# OUTLINING PRINCIPLES

The **complete-sentence outline** is the most detailed and specific of all the forms. For speech class purposes all main- and first-level subpoints are complete sentences, and second- and third-level subpoints may be explicit phrases or sometimes simply words. Check with your instructor on this matter. The use of complete sentences helps clarify the relationship between main points and their major subdivisions. Your rough draft is called a **topical outline**, one in which phrases or groups of words carry the essential meanings intended. Its disadvantage as a final working outline is that ideas may be difficult for you to visualize as complete thoughts; hence it is far more difficult to develop and support these phrases or partial ideas.

A **key-word outline** is an abbreviated topical outline and is usually created out of the complete-sentence outline to be used as a *speaking outline*. In terms of indentation and symbols it looks the same as the complete-sentence outline. The key-word outline is usually easier to remember, and it makes the extemporaneous reordering of ideas much easier when the situation calls for such adaptation.

Combinations of these forms are often advisable when you are speaking on a subject with which you are thoroughly familiar. The main points might be complete sentences, the subpoints phrases, and the subsubpoints key words. We'll describe the *speaking outline* in more detail at the end of this chapter.

# Symbolization

**Symbolization** means that similar symbols (I, A, 1, a, and so on) should represent items of equal importance. The symbol and its indentation should indicate the relative importance of the item that follows. Roman numerals represent the top level of importance in an outline. Sometimes these will be indicators of the introduction, body, and conclusion. Often however, the introduction, body, and conclusion are just titled and the main points are symbolized with the Roman numerals. Beginning in this fashion, major subpoints then capital letters, minor subpoints are Arabic numerals, further examples and elaborations are symbolized by lowercase letters, and so on.

Logical outlining includes (1) divisions of ideas and (2) headings that make these divisions clear. If a topic is divided, there should be two or more parts. In other words, if you're going to have a *1,* you should also have a *2;* if you're going to have an *A,* you should also have a *B.* If your *2* or *B* is not important to your speech, the first point should be incorporated into its superior heading. For example:

A.        Wagon trains

1.          Role in development of West

                becomes

A.        Wagon trains factored in development of West

The numbers and letters used as labels must be consistent. Let your symbols show clearly that the main ideas are relatively equal in importance and that the subpoints are secondary to the main points, and relatively equal to each other

The standard system of symbols and indentations is shown in Figure 6.1.

In order to be true main points and not subdivisions, your main points should be of approximately equal importance. Each main point should be worded carefully and completely and should contribute to the central idea of the speech. The order in which you present your main points should aid in the logical development of your speech and strengthen audience motivation, remembering, and understanding.

# Subordination

*Subordination* means that related lesser points supporting a general category or statement should be grouped separately from the category, usually by means of indentation. Items of equal importance should be given equal billing.

**Figure 6.1     Standard System of Subordination**

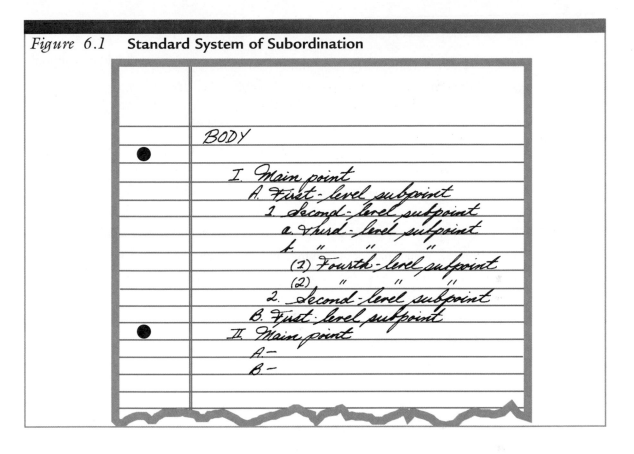

BODY

I. Main point
   A. First-level subpoint
      1. Second-level subpoint
         a. Third-level subpoint
         b.  "      "      "
            (1) Fourth-level subpoint
            (2)   "      "      "
      2. Second-level subpoint
   B. First-level subpoint
II. Main point
   A. —
   B. —

WRONG ⊗

**A.** Learning to type

   1. Preliminary preparation

   2. Addressing the keyboard

   3. Practice exercises

   4. First-level maintenance

      a. Unsticking the strikers

      b. Cleaning the keys

      c. Replacing the ribbon

   5. Selecting a typewriter

      a. Mechanical machines

      b. Electric machines.

      c. Kinds of type

RIGHT ✓

**A.** Learning to type

   1. Preliminary preparation

   2. Addressing the keyboard

   3. Practice exercises

**B.** First-level maintenance

   1. Unsticking the strikers

   2. Cleaning the keys.

   3. Replacing the ribbon

**C.** Selecting a typewriter

   1. Mechanical machines

   2. Electric machines

   3. Kinds of type

# Simplicity

*Simplicity* means that each numbered or lettered statement should contain only one idea.

WRONG ⊗

**I.** I wish to cover the following major steps in music theory:

    A. The kinds of notes and the musical staff

    B. Methods of counting and the relation of these to an instrument

RIGHT ✓

**I.** I wish to cover the following steps in music theory:

    A. The kinds of notes

    B. The musical staff

    C. Methods of counting the notes

    D. The relation of these methods to an instrument

# Discreteness

*Discreteness* means that each item in an outline should be a distinct point and not overlap other items.

WRONG ⊗

    **A.** Tennis strokes

    1. The serve

    2. The forehand

    3. The backhand

    4. Various shots

RIGHT ✓

    **A.** Tennis strokes

    1. The serve

    2. The forehand

    3. The backhand

    4. The volley

    5. The approach shot

    6. The overhead

# Coordination

**Coordination** means that a subordinate list of topics must have a common relationship.

WRONG ⊗

**A.** Manufacturing companies in Detroit

    1. General Motors Corporation

    2. Ford Motor Company

    3. Chrysler Corporation

    4. American Motors Corporation

    5. Campbell Ewald Advertising Company

    6. American Automobile Association

    7. Benedict and Moore Insurance

RIGHT ✓

**A.** Manufacturing companies in Detroit

    1. General Motors Corporation

    2. Ford Motor Company

    3. Chrysler Corporation

    4. American Motors Corporation

**B.** Service companies in Detroit

    1. Campbell Ewald Advertising Company

    2. American Automobile Association

    3. Benedict and Moore Insurance

## Progression

*Progression* refers to the arrangement of related items in some sort of natural sequence, such as chronology, time, genre, or space. Keep the items in sequence and don't switch patterns. The following example is based on difficulty and natural sequence.

WRONG ⊗

**A.** Courses in mathematics

    1. Algebra

    2. Arithmetic

    3. Calculus

    4. Solid Geometry

    5. Trigonometry

    6. Plane Geometry

RIGHT ✓

**B.** Courses in mathematics

    1. Arithmetic

    2. Algebra

    3. Plane Geometry

    4. Solid Geometry

    5. Trigonometry

    6. Calculus

## THE COMPLETE OUTLINE

Your rough outline should eventually become a *complete* or *complete-sentence outline* (one in which all main- and first-level subpoints are written out as complete sentences). This form will force you to think your way through the material and help you avoid embarrassing moments on the platform. The complete-sentence outline will also make it easier for your instructor to evaluate and help you with your speech planning. It is the outline that may be graded by your instructor.

If you intend to use the speech again or if others may have to speak from it, a complete-sentence outline becomes valuable. After this kind of thorough outlining, it is easier to redo the outline in a topical or key word form for use on the speaking platform.

# General Rules

State your topic.

State your general purpose.

State your specific purpose.

State your central idea.

Label the introduction, body, and conclusion.

Label and state, in complete sentences, the various elements of the introduction and conclusion.

State main points in complete sentences.

State major subpoints in complete sentences.

In addition to these standard rules, your instructor may ask you to insert transition (connecting) language between main points or between introduction and the body and conclusion. Label these transitions. If you are using some special arrangement system (for example, Monroe's Motivated Sequence of attention, need, satisfaction, visualization, and action), use those labels to the left of the standard three divisions. This will help you to stay true to your organizational plan.

INTRODUCTION

(Attention)  **I.**    _____

**II.**   _____

      **III.** _____

      **IV.** _____

Transition to Body:

          BODY

(Need)   **I.** _____

(Satisfaction)   **II.** _____

(Visualization)   **III.** _____

Transition to Conclusion

      CONCLUSION

      **I.** _____

(Action)   **II.** _____

Because your *complete* outline reflects your research, attach a bibliography of your major sources of information: books, articles, conversations, interviews, and so forth. Your instructor will tell you which referencing format is required for your complete-sentence outline. Make sure to follow the format consistently. Some instructors will want you to place in a reference list only the sources you reference in your speech, not all the sources that have contributed to your knowledge. Other instructors will want a bibliography of all the sources from your research that contributed to your knowledge on the topic. Usually, all instructors will want you to show references in your outline where you intend to cite them.

## Model Complete Outline

We return to Mark Scott and his interest in prehistoric humans. After more research and thinking, he decided on the title (or topic) "Cave People." He's been more precise in his statement of specific purpose, and the central idea is more detailed but still quite limited. Compare what follows to his rough draft earlier in this chapter. Note the kind of natural extension and development of those earlier thoughts.

MODEL COMPLETE OUTLINE

**Topic:**  Prehistoric People

**General Purpose:**  To inform

**Specific Purpose:**  To inform the class about changing human characteristics over the last 6 million years

**Central Idea:**  There are three distinct periods of prehistoric human development based on archaeological discoveries.

CAVE PEOPLE

INTRODUCTION

(Attention)  **I.**  You will often see cartoons showing cave people being chased by dinosaurs. This is impossible!

(Orientation)  **A.** Human bones are from earth 50,000 years old,

**B.** Dinosaur bones, however, are from rocks 15 million years old (show cartoons of Alley Oop and the Flintstones).

(Credibility)  **II.**  According to Professor of Anthropology, Dr. Moss, we can surmise the changing human characteristics over the last 6 million years by looking at the distinct periods of prehistoric humans.

(Central Idea/Thesis) **III.**  There are three distinct periods of prehistoric human development based on archaeological discoveries.

(Preview)  **IV.**  I would like to describe briefly the three main periods of prehistoric humankind and explain how they looked and behaved, namely: Peking person, Neanderthal person, and Cro-Magnon person.

Transition:  First, we need to talk about the Peking Period.

BODY

**I.** Peking People lived 6 million to 125,000 years BC

**A.** There have been three major archaeological discoveries of the Peking period.

1. The Peking discovery
2. The Java discovery
3. The South Africa discovery

(Cite source)     **B.** According to Timothy Sevrin, in his book *Vanishing Primitive Man*, Peking period people had particularly different characteristics and behavior than people of later periods. (Show encyclopedia map and magazine pictures.)

(Visual Aid)     1. They had ape-like ridged fore heads and receding chins.

2. They had 3/4 of modern human's brain capacity.

3. They made fire and primitive weapons from deer antlers.

(Chronological Organizational Method)

Transition:     The next prehistoric period is called the Neanderthal period.

**II.** Neanderthal People lived 125,000 to 25,000 years BC

(Cite source)     **A.** According to Dr. E. Cullota, in her 1991 *Science* article entitled, "Pulling Neanderthals Back into Our Family Tree," four major archaeological discoveries reveal the Neanderthal period.

1. Neanderthal, Germany, was the site of the first discovery.

2. The Rhodesia discovery

3. The Gibraltar discovery

4. The Monte Cicero, Italy, discovery

(Visual Aid)     **B.** The characteristics and behavior of the Neanderthal people were much different from those of the Peking period (pictures).

1. They were 5 feet tall with heavy, thick necks.

2. They had low foreheads, but no ridges.

3. They buried their dead.

4. Scraping tools were found, but no needles or awls were used.

Transition:     The final prehistoric period is known as the Cro-Magnon period.

(Cite Source)     **III.** Leaky and Lewin, in their 1992 book titled, *Origins Reconsidered*, determined Cro-Magnon people lived 25,000 to 8,000 years BC

**A.** Three major archaeological discoveries of the Cro-Magnon period occurred in France, Czechoslovakia, and New Mexico.

1. The Dordogne, France, discovery

2. The Moravia, Czechoslovakia, discovery

3. The Folsom, New Mexico, discovery

(Visual Aid)     **B.** The characteristics and behavior of the Cro-Magnon people differed sharply from both the Peking and Neanderthal people (pictures).

1. They were nearly 6 feet tall.

2. High forehead, wide cheekbones, big nose and chin were common.

3. Needles and awls were used.

4. They liked ornaments (carved bone, etc.).

5. They did wall cave paintings of animals.

Transition:     Six million years is a long time that has allowed slow, but distinct, changes in human characteristics.

CONCLUSION

(Review)     **I.**     Three distinctly different cave people walked the earth between 6 million and 8,000 years BC.

A. The Peking people

B. The Neanderthal people

C. The Cro-Magnon people

(Reinforcement)     **II.**     Twentieth-century humankind appears to have changed, greatly from our prehistoric ancestors but there is much we don't know. Old discoveries are being challenged and refined; new discoveries are still being made.

(Impact)     **III.**     Which cave people do you think are YOUR ancestors?

## BIBLIOGRAPHY (SOURCES)

Culotta, E. (April 19, 1991). "Pulling Neanderthals Back into Our Family Tree," *Science*.

Leaky, R. E. and Lewin, R. (1992). *Origins Reconsidered: In Search of What Makes Us Human* New York: Doubleday.

Moss, Leonard. (Lecture: Changing Human Characteristics Over the Ages")

Severin T. (1990). *Vanishing Primitive Man.* New York: McGraw-Hill.

Trinkaus, E. (1994). *The Neanderthals and the Slanidar Neanderthals* New York: Alfred A. Knopf.

Note: your instructor may request a particular citation style for your references. MLA or APA style references are often required.

> **Author's Comment**
>
> Before you speak, check the latest news! As Mark Scott was rehearsing his speech, the news carried a new "find" by anthropologist Susan Antone suggesting that all three cave people may have lived at the same time. More research and rewrite may be in order.

# THE SPEAKING OUTLINE

The speaking outline is an abridged version of your complete-sentence outline and functions to help you remember your message and smooth out your delivery. It represents your notes to yourself on how to proceed. It allows for extemporaneous delivery; that is, the ideas flow smoothly, but you still have freedom to adapt your language as you speak. Some speakers put their outline on index cards.

## General Rules

*Keep it brief.* The idea is to keep you from being too dependent on your notes.

*Double- or triple-space your entries.* This allows you to follow your notes more easily and avoid losing your place. It also allows you room for last-minute additions and notes to yourself (but don't clutter it).

*Use phrases and key words* unless you have a complex, critical idea that must be stated precisely. In that case write it out as a complete sentence.

*Write out complex statistics or long quotations.* Either put them on index cards or frame them as cards in your speaker's outline.

*Use personal cues for memory joggers and for visual aids.* Use a different color type or ink for these.

## Model Speaking Outline

Typically a speaking outline should be contained on one side of one page. It avoids full sentences, except for quotes and occasional transitions. Some students prefer to use note cards. They, too, should be written on only one side to avoid the distraction of flipping cards and, should be limited in number (usually designated by your instructor, but one card per main point, plus an intro and a conclusion card is a good rule of thumb to follow). Here is Mark Scott's speaking outline based on his complete outline. Note how it uses the same symbolization and subordination as he used in his complete outline. Outlining your note cards or speaking outlines helps you to stay organized during your speech.

MODEL SPEAKING OUTLINE: CAVE PEOPLE

INTRODUCTION

    **I.**    Attention: Humans, Dinosaurs, Alley-Oop, the Flintstones, BC

(Impossible!)

    **II.**

Credibility: Professor Moss

    **III.**    Thesis: Three distinct periods

    **IV.**    Preview: Peking, Neanderthal, Cro-Magnon

Transition:    First, Peking period

BODY

    **I.**    Peking "Man" (6 million–125,000 BC)
    **A.** Archaeological discoveries
    **B.** Appearance and behaviors

Transition:          Next, Neanderthal period

**II.**    Neanderthal people (125,00–25,000 BC)

**A.** Archaeological discoveries

**B.** Appearance and behaviors

*use vu-graph, slide #3*

Transition:          Final Period: Cro-Magnon

**III.**    Cro-Magnon people (25,00–8,000 BC)

**A.** Archaeological discoveries

**B.** Appearance and behaviors

*use vu-graph slide #4*

Transition to Conclusion:    Six million years a long time; distinct changes

CONCLUSION

**I.**    In review, three prehistoric periods include: Peking, Neanderthal, and Cro-Magnon reveal an ever changing human kind.

*use vu-graph slide #5*

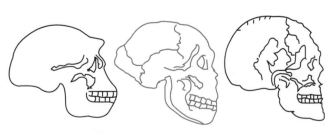

Peking          Neanderthal          Cro-Magnon

    **II.**    This is not the final proof of evolution, but clearly twentieth-century humankind is different and has changed.

   **III.**    Which cave people are YOUR ancestors?

# EXEMPLAR: OUTLINE DEVELOPMENT

All classroom speeches aren't as academic as Mark Scott's "Cave People" speech on prehistoric humans. Robert, a student at Wayne State University, gave a perfectly delightful speech on the problems and theories associated with being left-handed. It was entertaining as well as informative. Here is how the outlines developed.

ROUGH OUTLINE

|  |  |
|---:|:---|
| **Topic:** | Left-handedness |
| **General Purpose:** | To inform |
| **Specific Purpose:** | To inform the class about handedness theories and problems |
| **Central Idea:** | Lefties have problems, but society is trying to help. |

INTRODUCTION

Humor

Central Idea

Credibility

Preview

BODY

    **I.**    Theories of why

   **II.**    Advantages/disadvantages

  **III.**    How many?

  **IV.**    Who are they?

   **V.**    Help for lefties

CONCLUSION

Things are improving.

Humor

After research into some famous left-handers and theories of cerebral dominance, Robert decided to concentrate on problems and what's being done about them. Interviews at a sporting goods store and at the music department were most helpful. He decided that two of his main points could be combined (who and why), one should be divided (advantages/disadvantages), and that the order should be changed from *topical* to more of a *difficulty* order. He sharpened the purpose and central idea and came up with a great title.

Oprah Winfrey, talk show host and "left-hander of the year". Left-handed people are normal with special problems that society is helping to solve.

### COMPLETE OUTLINE

| | |
|---|---|
| **Topic:** | Left-handedness, "The Left Wing" |
| **General Purpose:** | To inform |
| **Specific Purpose:** | To inform the audience about handedness: problems, solutions, and theories |
| **Central Idea:** | Left-handed people are normal with special problems that society is helping to solve. |

### THE LEFT WING

**INTRODUCTION**

I. Left-handed luminaries include:
   A. Oprah Winfrey, left-hander of the year
   B. Bill Clinton, top left-hander in politics

Attention
   C. Alan Thicke, top left-handed male entertainer
   D. Phil Collins, tops in the music category
   E. Even Michelangelo and Leonardo da Vinci

    **II.** Are you one of those people who have been described as temperamental, unstable, unintelligent, pugnacious, or, in a word, left-handed? Like me!

(Central idea/Thesis)  **III.** Left-handed people are normal with special problems that society is helping to solve.

    **IV.** Even if you're not a lefty, you should know some facts about this sometimes-persecuted group.

Preview
    **A.** Their number and famous left-handed people

    **B.** Their advantages and

    **C.** Their disadvantages

    **D.** Assistance given to lefties

    **E.** Theories as to why they are left-handed

Transition
    One of the first things people often ask is, "who are the southpaws?"

BODY

(Main Point)   **I.** There are many southpaws, and many are famous.

(Visual Aid)     **A.** Statistics reveal a substantial number of lefties. (Show slide with statistics.)

      **1.** One-quarter of North Americans are originally left-handed.

      **2.** Schools report an 8 percent increase in left-handed students.

(Visual Aid)     **B.** As mentioned in the introduction, some lefties are famous people. (Show second slide.)

      **1.** Present-day lefties

      **2.** Historic lefties

  **II.** Unbeknownst to many non-lefties, there are advantages of being left-handed.

(Visual Aid)     **A.** Mirror-writing is easy. (Show example)

    **B.** Sports, in most cases, benefit the lefty.

      **1.** Since there are fewer lefties than non-lefties, their style is more unusual and therefore can surprise non-lefties.

    **2.** According to John Walsh in a 2007 article entitled, "The Advantage of Batting Left-handed," in *The Hardball Times*, "Major-league left-handed batters, on average, hit better than their right-handed counterparts."

**III.** However, there are also disadvantages of being left-handed.

    **A.** Eating can be embarrassing.

(Visual Aid)     **B.** Musical instruments are mostly right-handed.

    **C.** Knitting is difficult.

    **D.** Office machines are programmed for righties.

**IV.** Help for left-handers is on the way.

    **A.** The Association for the Protection of Rights of Left-Handers (APRLH) provides fun and support to lefties.

        **1.** Oaths for fun and fellowship

        **2.** Meetings for some serious issues

        **3.** The *Lefthander Magazine*

    **B.** Manufactured goods for lefties are a reality.

(Visual Aid)         **1.** You can purchase golf clubs designed for the lefty.

        **2.** According to Harold Arnaldi, Director of Wayne State University School of Music, there are some musical instruments that accommodate the lefty.

        **3.** Some tools are also now designed for lefties.

**V.** Theories concerning southpaws are inconclusive.

    **A.** One theory is that of Cerebral Dominance

        **1.** Most left-brained dominant people are right-handed.

        **2.** This theory suggests that left-handedness may be caused by dominance in the right brain.

    **B.** A second theory relies on Heredity

        **1.** This theory suggests that it was passed from your parents or ancestors through genes.

        **2.** It is also suggested that it might be determined in the womb when the mother passes along high levels of testosterone.

**C.** A third theory suggests that people can learn to use their left hand when there has been some injury.

Transition to Conclusion:    As stated earlier, these theories are inconclusive, but there is much we do know about left-handed people

CONCLUSION

(Review)    **I.**    If you are left-handed, be comforted in that:

    **A.** Though your numbers are small, you are not alone or inferior.

    **B.** Your disadvantages are being reduced and, in fact, you have some clear advantages.

    **C.** Society is trying to help by recognizing that some things simply work better for lefties when designed for left-handed usage.

    **D.** The theories make you more interesting, even though they don't really tell the whole story.

(Reinforcement)    **II.**    For the "righties" you now know what it is like for a lefty to live in a right-handed world.

(Impact)    **III.**    Let's all keep a "right" attitude about the left wing.

BIBLIOGRAPHY (SOURCES)

*Lefthander Magazine* (December 1987). The Association for the Protection of Rights of Left-Handers (APRLH).

Walsh, J. "The Advantage of Batting Left-handed." *The Hardball Times*, November 15, 2007. Retrieved from www.hardballtimes.com

Interview, Acme Campus Sporting Goods.

Interview, Harold Arnoldi, Director, Wayne State University School of Music.

*Note:* your instructor may request a particular citation style for your references. MLA and APA style references are often required.

MODEL SPEAKING OUTLINE: THE LEFTWING

INTRODUCTION

     **I.**   Luminaries include Oprah Winfrey, President Clinton, Alan Thicke, Phil Collins, Michelangelo, and Leonardo da Vinci.

     **II.**   Are you called temperamental, unstable, pugnacious? You must be lefthanded like me!

     **III.**   Left-handed people are normal with special problems that society is helping to solve.

     **IV.**   Preview main points: pointsstatistics, advantages, disadvantages, society acceptance and accommodation, theories.

BODY

(Visual Aid)   **I.**   Statistics on southpaws

(Visual Aid)       (Also list some famous lefties.)

     **II.**   Advantages

(Visual Aid)   **A.** Mirror-writing *(Demonstrate) Bring a mirror!*

     **B.** Sports

     **III.**   Disadvantages

     **A.** Eating *(Demonstrate)*

(Visual Aid)   **B.** Music

     **C.** Knitting

     **D.** Office machines

     **IV.**   Help is on the way.

     **A.** APRLH

(Visual Aid)   **B.** Manufactured goods *(Show a left-handed golf club.)*

     **C.** *Lefthander Magazine* awards

     **V.**   Theories

     **A.** Cerebral dominance

     **B.** Heredity

     **C.** Learned

CONCLUSION

| | | |
|---|---|---|
| (Review) | **I.** | Many lefties, advantages, disadvantages, social acceptance and accommodation, and theories that try to explain. |
| (Reinforcement) | **II.** | "Righties" now know what it is like for a lefty to live in a right-handed world. |
| (Impact) | **III.** | We all should now have a right attitude about the left wing. |

Robert could also have used the six numbered cards he had prepared. The visual aids served as his memory jogger for the statistics on lefties, the list of famous left-handed people, and the details of the cerebral dominance theory. The cards are shown on the following pages.

---

| INTROD. | THE LEFT WING | 1 |

I Winfrey, Clinton, Thicke, Collins, Michelangelo

II ARE YOU — tempermental, unstable, etc. like me?

III Preview
    More famous Lefties & Statistics
    advantages / disadvantages
    Society
    Conflicting theories

---

| BODY | | 2 |

I. Famous Lefties & Statistics USE VISUAL AID (STATS)

II. Advantages
    sports — 1st base, pitch, etc

    Mirror writing Demonstrate

    (Bring a mirror)

---

| | | 3 |

III Disadvantages

    Eating (demonstrate)

    Music      role-play?

    Knitting

    Office machinery

_Transition Help on the way_    | 4 |

IV Social Awareness

    Assoc. to protect Left-handers

    New products

        – golf clubs (show one)

        – fish reels

        – instruments

    Left-handers awards

---

V. _Theories are inconclusive_    | 5 |

    A. Cerebral dominance

        USE VISUAL AID (BRAIN)

    B. Heredity

    C. Learning

( what I think – if time permits )

---

| CONCLUSION |    | 6 |

Review – Lefties abound (restate stat)

    Advantages might assist your sports aspirations

    Disadvantages could be cause of embarrassment

    or extra work

    Society is becoming aware

    Theories are still inconclusive but possibly case

Reinforcement – you now know what it's like

Impact – Let's all keep a right attitude about the left wing.

# CHAPTER REVIEW
## *Wrapping it up*

## *Summary*

An outline is to a speech what a blueprint is to a house. Start with the main points in the body of the speech, review your research, and refine your most important ideas or points. Prepare a rough draft of your specific purpose, central idea, and main points. This becomes your brief topical outline. A complete outline and a speaking outline will follow.

Basic outlining principles include symbolization, subordination, simplicity, discreteness, coordination, and progression.

All major- and first-level subpoints are written out as complete sentences in the complete outline. This is the outline that many instructors will grade Your instructor will usually ask for a bibliography or a reference list to be attached at the end this outline.

The speaking outline is an abridged version of your complete outline. It represents your notes to yourself on how to proceed and allows for extemporaneous delivery. Some speakers put their speaker's outlines on index cards. Use phrases and key words; keep it brief, but write out quotes and statistics. Use personal cues for audio and visual aids and to jog your memory. Use the model outlines in the chapter as guides for your own outline.

Check out our website
**www.bvtlab.com**
for flashcards,
summaries, self-quizzes
and speeches.

# LANGUAGE HABITS

# Chapter 7

## Chapter Objectives

# THE IMPORTANCE OF LANGUAGE

The greater the size of one's vocabulary, the easier it is to communicate and to be understood. The more words from which we have to choose, the greater the likelihood that we will choose the correct word for the idea we are trying to impart. Words are somehow learned and used with reasonable facility, but not always.[1] Sometimes words can be strung together awkwardly. Consider these church bulletins.

1.   The ladies of the church have cast off clothing of every kind, and they may be seen in the church basement on Friday.

2.   Thursday at 5:00 P.M. there will be a meeting of the Little Mothers Club. All wishing to become little mothers please see the minister in his study.

3.   At the evening service tonight, the sermon topic will be "What Is Hell?" Come early and listen to our choir practice.

4.   Wednesday the Ladies Liturgy Society will meet. Mrs. Jones will sing, "Put Me in My Little Bed," accompanied by the pastor.

The situation worsens when we learn, thanks to computers, that the five hundred most commonly used English words show more than fourteen thousand recorded dictionary uses. Robert Pula, former Director of the Institute for General Semantics, suggests three main sources of these "same term" differences:

- *lexical*—"same" term, different definition, e.g., fast (abstain), fast (stuck), fast (morally loose), fast (quick), etc.

- *contextual*—"same" term, different situation: Even if we know "all" of the accepted uses and definitions of a term, we still need sensitivity to context to determine which use is intended by a speaker or writer.

- *neurological*—"same" term, different brain—even if a speaker and listener agree on the particular use of a term in a given context, idiosyncratic structural and experiential differences of each brain (nervous-system-as-a-whole) will generate to varying degrees, different semantic reactions.[2]

Clearly, vocabulary alone is often a sensitive matter and is capable of altering or even short-circuiting meaning. To compound the problem many words *sound* exactly the same but have startlingly different meanings. One student speaker was shocked that some listeners decoded his description of erratic personalities as erotic personalities. In addition, how do "Fat Chance" and "Slim Chance" come to mean the same thing?

The language problem is often worse for the speaker than the writer because the listener has more **concomitant signals** to deal with than the reader. Concomitant signals are the nonverbals that accompany and operate at the same time as the words. Your *voice,* for example, is a wonderfully sensitive instrument with a powerful influence upon the meaning the listener attaches both to your words and to you, the speaker. The appearance of the speaker—dress, movements, facial expressions, and gestures and other signals that affect how language is decoded.

> It is not enough to know what to say—one must also know how to say it.
>
> **Aristotle**

Another less obvious point to be made is that these codes and signals affect one another. Sometimes they work together and strengthen the meaning intended by the speaker. We call this **congruence**. When things go together as we expect them to, they are congruent. At other times, however, they conflict with one another and distort the intended meaning to the point where the listener is confused, suspicious, or frustrated. This is referred to as **incongruence**. Consider the sloppy student presenting a speech on the value of personal neatness, or the professor with a frozen grin discussing the possibility of a student's failing the course. We often act in a way contrary to what we really intend. The cause may be tension, emotional involvement, or poor language and thinking habits. The audience notices the contradiction (or incongruence) between the words being stated and the accompanying behaviors. In fact, we notice behaviors or words that are *incongruent*, more than we notice when they are *congruent*.

*Where* you are from or are currently living often affects your language; "L. A. speak" is for real. Generic names are out, it seems; it's Kleenex, Nike, and Ray-Bans. "Valley Talk" is, of course, "totally awesome." In the South, it is "y'all;" and in universities today you'll hear "peace-out." Generic names are out, it seems; it's Kleenex rather than tissue, Nikes rather than tennis shoes, and Ray-Bans rather than sunglasses.

There are also simple slips of the tongue called *bloopers* or *Spoonerisms* (named after Professor Spooner) from which recovery is sometimes impossible. Try the emcee that blooped, "We now have Dr. Christian Barnard who will talk about his now famous rear transplant—I mean rare transplant." Or the sports announcer who was laughed out of the booth after stating, "Toronto hockey fans will be glad to learn that their goalie made his first *girl* ever in the last ten seconds of play" (that's *goal,* not *girl).* ).

Language as a system is *holistic,* that is, the whole of it is greater than the sum of its parts. Perhaps that explains how Yasin, a student from Kuwait with a good sense of communication but weak, barely adequate English, was able to give a well-received speech on his reaction to American women. However, another foreign student with somewhat better English skills failed miserably. If language is so poor or so inappropriate that it makes simple decoding impossible, then, of course, the entire system goes down.

This is good reason to not only use our language in the best and most appropriate way possible but also to take every opportunity to improve our language ability. Perhaps this helps explain why some communications fail with one group and work with another. Your code was proper for one set of receivers but perhaps incomprehensible for the rest.

# LANGUAGE AND CRITICAL THINKING

Our understandings and perceptions of the world are thought to be inextricably tied to language, particularly its grammar. In other words, language is said to create reality by affecting the ways in which we conceptualize our world. Language does not merely describe our world. If this long-standing *Whorf-Sapir hypothesis* is true, then our very thinking is largely governed by this powerful language system.[3]

Critical thinking involves exercising intelligent, objective, cautious judgment and evaluation of the language we use and receive and decode from others. More will be said about logical thinking and formal argument in Chapter 12. In this chapter, however, we can come to understand the power of language

> .... If we lacked the ability to use language we would not be able to even think in any meaningful sense.
>
> **John Chaffe,**
>
> **Author of Thinking Critically**

and how it can serve or hinder our message depending on how we use it.

# Meaning and Abstraction

The heart of the difficulty with language is the confusion of the word with the thing for which it stands. The thing itself is called the **referent**. The further we are from this thing—the referent—the more problems of meaning arise. **Concrete** language is language that is closest to the referent and **abstract** language is language furthest from the referent. If we use the word *dog* while pointing to a Golden Retriever, we are indeed close to a *concrete* referent and the **denotation**, or literal meaning, is quite clear. If we are talking about someone who is *dog-tired,* or perhaps a *"dirty dog",* we are seeking a more distant and *abstract* referent and are infusing it with an emotional element. This added meaning usage is called **connotation**. Therefore, denotation is the literal meaning or the dictionary definition of a word and connotation is the feelings or emotional responses tied to the word. As we move from a concrete physical object to an abstraction, the connotation increases.

So how does all of this work in terms of creating messages or meaning? When we receive a symbol or sign (like the word, chair), it travels to our thought or reference center. We then consult our storehouse of experience to find our own representation of the thing or *referent* to which the symbol refers. Line A in Figure 7.1 indicates what a person ideally perceives as a *correct symbol,* in this case the word *chair.* Line B represents the cognitive selecting and sorting of knowledge and experience that ideally represents an *adequate referent.* The broken line C indicates that the *word* chair and a *real* chair are not the same, making very clear the crucial point that the symbol and its referent are not *directly* related. The *word is not the thing!* You cannot *sit* on the word *chair!*

Clear communication calls for a referent, a reference, and a symbol. This concept leads us to the subject of misuse of abstractions. **Abstracting** is a process of thinking in which we selectively leave out details about concrete or real things. We have learned previously that perception has at least two elements: (1) sensation and (2) interpretation of this sensation. Interpretation is controlled by our individual knowledge, experience, and emotional set. For this

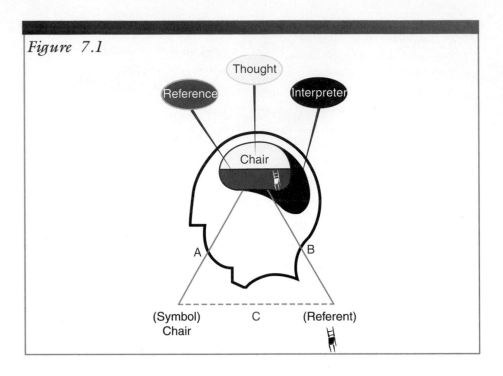

Figure 7.1

reason, as well as because of the limitations of our language system, all language contains an element of abstraction.

In abstracting, we go beyond the specific fact or thing that is usually observable or demonstrable. For example, if one were giving a speech on "flying machines," one could be talking about balloons, gliders, blimps, helicopters, and airplanes. A speech on "airplanes" would be more specific (or less abstract). "Fighter aircraft" narrows the topic even more. "World War I Jenny" is quite specific. Think of abstracting as a stepladder with the most specific item on the first rung and the most general on the third or fourth (Figure 7.2). As we move from lower- to higher-order abstractions, we tend to consider fewer and fewer details of the specific, original object.

Another way of looking at abstraction is to consider firsthand observations as facts, but as facts that may never be described completely. If we move away from firsthand descriptions, we will be in a different order of abstraction—**inference**. An inference is drawing a conclusion based on possibilities *beyond* what is observed. If an ambulance is in your driveway when you return home, you may conclude, "One of my family has been seriously hurt." This is an inference.

*Figure 7.2*   **Abstraction Stepladder**

You must go into the house to see if it is valid. Upon entering your house, you may find a close friend telling your healthy family about his new business venture of converting station wagons into ambulances. When we are in the realm of inference, then, we are dealing with *probability* rather than with *certainty.*

## Classifying Concepts and Things

The five hundred most commonly used English words have more than fourteen thousand dictionary definitions. The problem is that there are an infinite number of things and concepts, each worthy of its own label. In short, if we did not use a limited number of words to represent an infinite number of things, we could hardly reason or communicate at all.

For example, if each *individual* chair in the world had its own label, we would have

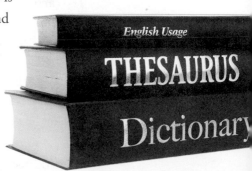

to have dictionaries of chairs. Even with the general classifying word *chair,* we have developed a large vocabulary of chair words-for example, Windsor, Hitchcock, stuffed, swivel, rocking (Figure 7.3). Despite our useful and necessary dictionaries, no word has real meaning except in the particular **context** in which it is used. The meaning of a word is never quite the same from one

*Figure 7.3*

occasion to another, although the variation in meaning may not always be great. Word meanings change when we take words for granted and think of them as *actual* things rather than as what they really are—*representations* of things. A good speaker must always ask, "What does *this* word mean to this audience in *this* situation, in *this* context, as used by *this* speaker at this time?" (see Figure 7.4)

The propositional nature of language can be a word problem in some language systems. Even absurd statements can be grammatically correct. Try these:

Red is Green

Tony: "What color is the sky?"

Cleo: "Blue."

Tony: "Wrong!"

*Figure 7.4*

Because of the propositional nature of language, we may become too literal and too rigid in our evaluation of words. These characteristics often lead to poor thinking and misunderstanding.

When we arrange words into the context of a sentence—that is, when we create **syntax**—we are really fitting generalizations together. The meaning of an English sentence is determined not by its words alone, but by the whole arrangement and sequence of the words. In one sense, the communication pattern of a sentence is the systematic exclusion of meanings the listener might attach which are *not* intended by the speaker. In short, the sentence may define meanings *not* intended.

A distortion of this process has been called "**doublespeak**", often used to soften bad news, shift blame, or, if completely unethical, to cover up the truth. Firing of workers has been referred to as: "consolidating operations," "derecruitment," "rationalizing marketing efforts," even "career change opportunities." All so-called doublespeak is not unethical. Some is really a more tactful way of explaining harsh realities. Tact versus forthrightness can make for difficult language choices for ethical speakers.

The particular character you give your language usage is important to your messages. The most characteristic language pattern of schizophrenics is an apparent confusion between words and things. Because objective abstraction is difficult for schizophrenics, they tend to be extremely one-sided and opinionated. The sobering thought in discussing abnormal language habits is that we all exhibit these habits to some degree. It behooves us to be aware of our language patterns lest we, too, represent a one-value world of words without referents.

Almost any speech course, whatever its context, puts a high premium on language habits. The instructor will criticize you diligently, knowing that proper language habits will make it easier for you to adjust to the linguistic demands of life in college and after.

# MEANING MANAGEMENT

## Specificity and Accuracy in Language

Were Confucius alive today, he might well be pained by our fascination with slang and jargon. He once said, "The first step in finding out the truth is to call things by their right names." **Jargon**, is specialized language, accepted and used in a specific context or industry. However, using jargon can confuse or even stop communication. Try this gem from the Department of Housing and Urban Development:

> *Any simple-minded person can come up with an obvious idea in a simple, straightforward way; only a true scholar can come up with an obvious idea in a complex, incomprehensible way.*
>
> **Ronald F. Reid, Rhetorician**

Action-oriented orchestration of innovative inputs, generated by escalation of meaningful indigenous decision-making dialogue, focusing on multi-linked problem-complexes, can maximize the vital thrust toward a non-alienated and viable urban infrastructure.

Confusion about what language means is often very frustrating. Note the speech given at a freshmen orientation session:

At this university, education for the undergraduate has as purposes the fostering of the intellectual and personal growth of the individual student. The student, ultimately responsible for his or her own development in both of these areas, must be an active participant in framing his or her own education. A central aspect of this development is the relationship of the student with professors and fellow students and with the material they approach together. Structures, rules, and regulations of the university should facilitate these relationships and should provide the student with the maximum opportunity to formulate and achieve his or her educational objectives.

"KISS," said one student (keep it simple, stupid) and translated as follows:

THE TRANSLATION:

> There are no course distribution requirements. If you make mistakes in choosing courses, you have only yourself to blame. Ask the advice of your professors and peers if you would like help in choosing your courses.

Consider that Lincoln's Gettysburg address contained only 272 words and that 196 of them were of one syllable. There are only 297 words in the Ten Commandments and 300 in the entire Declaration of Independence—a good lesson for long-winded speakers.

The confusion isn't always caused by windy jargon. Sometimes our desire to be specific is not always conditioned by critical thinking and careful preparation. Here are the exact words of a witness in an arbitration case. See if you can figure them out.

> Now, there is two obligations on them here in the plan, and I think one is more controlling over the other, and that is to do what they said they were going to do, and if they can't do what they said they were going to do in the manner in which they said they were going to do it, I don't feel that they are relieved from the obligation of doing what they said they were going to do, even if it had to be done in a manner other than what they said they were going to do, in as much as doing what they said they were going to do is consistent with their obligation under the agreement to do what they said they were going to do, and anything else would be inconsistent.

Aristotle, in his treatise on rhetoric, had this to say about the use of language: "… language that does not convey a clear meaning fails to perform the very function of language."[4] Accurate word choice is a must for speakers to be effective. A debater of religion who really does not know the difference between atheism and agnosticism is apt to raise confusion to a still higher level. Atheism denies the existence of God. Agnostics merely claim not to know if God exists, a critical difference if critical thinking is to occur. To use either term incorrectly changes the meaning of the message and negatively affects the debate.

In his treatise on Rhetoric, Aristotle stressed that accurate word choice is a must for speakers to be effective.

Naming things or people can make a difference. Remember "Who is on first!"? Try this one:

There were four people named Everybody, Somebody, Anybody, and Nobody. There was an important job to be done, and Everybody was sure that Somebody would do it. Anybody could have done it, but Nobody did it.

Somebody got angry with that, because it was Everybody's job. Everybody thought Anybody could do it, but Nobody realized that Everybody wouldn't do it. It ended up that Everybody blamed Somebody when Nobody did what Anybody could have.

Sometimes language inaccuracy seems deliberate. Why else would the military refer to a bullet hole as a "ballistically induced aperture in the subcutaneous environment" or a parachute as an "aerodynamic personnel decelerator"?

Perhaps there are some times when **obfuscation** (to make obscure or unclear; to confuse) is justified. Imagine being asked by your best friend how you like her new "funk" jacket for which she just spent $250.00. You might think, "Funk? That looks more like Junk," but it would be unwise to be quite that direct. Instead, you might choose to *obfuscate* your response: "I think it is interesting how styles change to incorporate new materials in new ways."

> *Some people have a way with words.*
> *Some no have way.*
>
> **Steve Martin**

## Principles and Rules

**OVERGENERALIZATION AND OVERSTATEMENT**   One of the most widespread "thinking" faults of student speakers is **overgeneralization**. Overgeneralization (or false generalization) is stating a conclusion based on too little evidence. This is the problem of selectively leaving out details and concluding after only a superficial examination that a thing is true beyond any shadow of a doubt. For example, if upon driving into Detroit for the first time you (1) witnessed a serious accident, (2) observed a truck exceeding the speed limit, and (3) had your fender dented at a busy intersection, you might be tempted to draw some strong conclusions and speak in strong language about Detroit drivers. However, you would have to examine comparative safety records, driver education programs, and driver insurance rates before participating in any intelligent discussion about Detroit drivers. Even then, you might want to hedge your generalizations by noting that Detroit has more cars per person than any other city in the world.

The irony of overgeneralization is that it is usually not intended. It seems so obvious that all Detroit drivers are crazy! All male politicians are sexist! All whites are racist! All Democrats feel one way and all Republicans feel another! However, that is not the case. All Democrats are *not* alike, *nor* are all Republicans alike. We should think in terms of Democrat 1, Democrat 2, Democrat 3, and so on. This is called **indexing** and is used to disaggregate a group into individual members. It is a safeguard against taking stereotypes seriously and failing to appreciate individual differences. Even entire states differ from one another. Fifty-five miles per hour may mean sixty-two in Illinois, but when you cross into Wisconsin on Highway 41, you are greeted by the sign in Figure 7.5.

*Figure 7.5*

With the **either/or response** type of overgeneralization, one's language habits conceal differences of degree. Either/or responses don't offer possibilities outside of the two or three provided, nor do they recognize individual differences. The absolute ruler and the demagogue use this device regularly. All of us in moments of frustration or desperation seem to revert to "They're all no good," "You're either for me or against me," or "You'll never understand." When we routinely use words such as *all, nobody, everybody* and *never,* we are guilty of a **false-to-fact** use of language, statements that cannot be supported

*Figure 7.6*

by the facts. The speaker guilty of these exaggerations runs risks of creating resentment, particularly among sophisticated audiences.

An extremely irritating form of the either/or response is what we might call *arrogant dismissal.* "That's ridiculous!" "Out of the question!" "Nonsense!" The responder clearly indicates that the discussion is over; the speaker and the topic are dismissed as stupid. Individuals who consistently engage in this kind of behavior are considered by some psychologists to have serious adjustment problems. Simplistic language, such as that above, usually reflects simplistic thinking or a high degree of emotional involvement.

The communication problems of generalization are complicated, frustrating, and often dangerous. Once you understand this clearly, you have already solved much of the practical problem; for it is when you are *aware* of abstracting and generalizing that you begin to restrain your own overstatement and reckless generalization. A practical way of using this awareness is to **qualify** your statements with great care. Qualifying a statement is adding a comment to indicate what you are saying may not be true in all

> *He can compress the most words into the smallest ideas of any man I ever met.*
>
> **Abraham Lincoln**

situations. The danger in using too many qualifiers is that the message can become vague and weak. Although ethical speakers want to employ qualifiers to avoid overstatement, they run the risk of appearing as if they have dodged their obligations and responsibilities.

## Helpful Rules

1.  *The index rule* reminds us to beware of stereotypes and other forms of overgeneralization. We should think in terms of actually indexing or cataloguing Christian 1 (Catholic), Christian 2 (Lutheran), Christian 3 (Methodist), Christian 4 (Baptist), and so on. Then there are liberal and conservative indexes to be considered as well, some within the previous index. The index rule is a warning against taking stereotypes seriously and failing to appreciate individual differences.

2.  *The "is" problem* is related to the principle of nonidentity. The map is not the territory as anyone who has ever been misled by an old map can readily tell you. The injunction to "call a spade a spade" is profoundly misleading because it implies that we call it a spade because that's what it is. Language and thought are not identical. Words are not the things signified (the *referents*). Dictionaries give only the meanings that people have given to words.

3.  *The et cetera rule* is related to the principle of "nonallness." In a sense, this rule also refers to the awareness of abstracting—an awareness that we are leaving something out. One cannot say everything on a given

matter; there is always more to be said. Thus the good speaker leaves listeners with the impression that he or she has not attempted to say the last word on a subject.

4.    *Dating your language* Often the specific date of an event significantly affects the meaning a listener will attach to it. "At last the Japanese people have taken the actions that will restore their rightful dignity." Certainly, we would attach different meanings to this hypothetical statement by the Emperor of Japan according to whether it was uttered on

January 7, 1925 (no special significance)

December 7, 1941 (Pearl Harbor)

September 2, 1945 (surrender of Japan)

*July 1, 1968 (return of Okinawa)

January 1, 2009 (?)

A favorite exam question of one psychology professor was, "What are Thorndike's laws of learning?" This question is challenging because Thorndike changed his mind about some of his laws of learning and made this clear in his most recent writings. The student who had read only his early writings would inevitably give the wrong answer.

5.    *Discerning presymbolic language* It should be evident by this time that it is impossible for a person to "say exactly what one means." Much of our language behavior is **presymbolic**—that is, it may function even without recognizable speech, or perhaps with symbols approaching an **idiom**. An idiom is an accepted expression, shared by a culture or group of people, with a meaning different from the literal. A grunt from my office partner at 8:00 A.M. means, "Good morning, it's good to see you." When you pass a friend on the street and she says, "Hi," how does this really differ from "How are you?" Does "Nice day" mean just that and no more?

When language is used in a presymbolic sense, we have to look beyond the words to obtain the real meaning intended. In our efforts to become alert, critical listeners, we must take care not to become so literal that we mistake tact and social grace for foolishness, hypocrisy, or stupidity. Much of what we refer to as "small talk" is in part presymbolic language. In order to become an objective and honest sender or receiver, we must strive to distinguish presymbolic from symbolic language.

# COLORFUL LANGUAGE

## Vividness

When speech is vivid, it provides a colorful, vibrant image for the mind to grasp. Consider this passage from Ecclesiastes:

> I returned and saw under the sun, that the race is not to the swift, nor the battle to the strong, neither yet bread to the wise, nor yet riches to men of understanding, nor yet favor to men of skill; but time and chance happeneth to them all. (9:11)

Now consider George Orwell's less colorful, more pedantic translation of the passage from Ecclesiastes found in his essay "Politics and the English Language."

> Objective consideration of contemporary phenomena compels the conclusion that success or failure in competitive activities exhibits no tendency to be commensurate with innate capacity, but that a considerable element of the unpredictable must invariably be taken into account.

**Imagery** is a form of vividness that employs figures of speech to produce mental pictures in the mind's eye of the listener.

Mental pictures, images, or word pictures are typically accessed through sensory recollections. One can almost *hear* (auditory) "a voice that would fracture glass," or *see* (visual) "a flash of blinding insight," or *feel* (tactual, touch) "the cold, north wind icing its

> Words strain, crack, and sometime break under the burden.
>
> **T. S. Eliot**

way through the pines," or *smell* (olfactory) "the foul, whiskey-soaked breath of the bully." You probably wouldn't sell much *sushi* if you described it as "cold, caked, sour rice soaked in vinegary liquid covered with raw dead fish." For some it may not be much better as "rice dressed with vinegar, shaped into small cakes, and topped with garnishes of raw fish" (*taste,* gustatory). "The queasy, faintish, life-weary feelings of a young soldier too long on the battlefield" stimulates *internal feelings* (organic). "The fatigue ridden, paralytic numbness of legs on a march too far..." produces a mental picture of *muscle strain* (kinesthetic).

The French have a way with imagery when they are upset. Here is French writer Jean Cau describing the EuroDisney theme park near Paris:

> It is a horror made of cardboard, plastic, and appalling colors, a construction of hardened chewing gum and idiotic folklore taken straight out of comic books written for obese Americans.

On a higher note, consider the beautiful close of General Douglas MacArthur's speech after accepting an award for service to the nation:

> ... the soldier, above all other people, prays for peace, for he must suffer and bear the deepest wounds and scars of war. But always in our ears ring the ominous words of Plato, that wisest of all philosophers, "Only the dead have seen the end of war."

> The shadows are lengthening for me. The twilight is here. My days of old have vanished tone and tint; they have gone glimmering through the dreams of things that were. Their memory is one of wondrous beauty, watered by tears, and coaxed and caressed by the smiles of yesterday.

> I listen vainly, but with thirsty ear, for the witching melody of faint bugles blowing reveille, of far drums beating the long roll. In my dreams I hear again the crash of guns, the rattle of musketry, the strange, mournful mutter of the battlefield.

But in the evening of my memory, always I come back to West Point. Always there echoes and re-echoes Duty-Honor-Country.[5]

One of the most vivid and moving speeches of our time was delivered to some two hundred thousand people from the steps of the Lincoln Memorial in Washington, D.C., on August 28, 1963, by Martin Luther King, Jr. Consider these selected paragraphs from the speech, "I Have a Dream."[6]

I have a dream that one day this nation will rise up and live out the true meaning of its creed, "We hold these truths to be self-evident, that all men are created equal."

I have a dream that one day every valley shall be exalted, every hill and mountain shall be made low, the rough places will be made plane and the crooked places will be made straight, and the glory of the Lord shall be revealed, and all flesh shall see it together.

So let freedom ring from the prodigious hilltops of New Hampshire. Let freedom ring from the mighty mountains of New York. Let freedom ring from the heightening Alleghenies of Pennsylvania!

Let freedom ring from the snowcapped Rockies of Colorado! Let freedom ring from the curvaceous slopes of California!

But not only that. Let freedom ring from Stone Mountain of Georgia!

Let freedom ring from Lookout Mountain of Tennessee!

Let freedom ring from every hill and molehill of Mississippi. From every mountainside, let freedom ring.

And when this happens, when we allow freedom to ring—when we let it ring from every village and every hamlet, from every state and every city—we will be able to speed up that day when all of God's children, black men and white men, Jews and Gentiles, Protestants and Catholics, will be able to join hands and sing in the words of the old Negro spiritual, "Free at last! Free at last! Thank God almighty, we are free at last!"

# Figures of Speech

That crook is drowning in money.

**Figures of speech** are expressions used outside their literal meanings. These are statements that can add vividness, spunk, and delight to your message but, they can create confusion if used in excess. Twenty-five major types have been identified. Some examples follow:

•   **Metaphor:** an implied comparison that transports the listener from the thing itself to a sensory image or experience.

"Fiery temper, thirsty sword"

"She's a pussycat."

•   **Metonymy:** substituting the name of an item associated with a larger concept for the idea.

"Sword" for war

"Brass" for military officers

•   **Synecdoche:** the use of a part for the whole or the whole for a part or parts.

"All hands on deck."

"She wears a jewelry store."

- **Hyperbole:** an exaggeration.

  "His arms dangled a mile out of his coat sleeves!"

- **Prosopopoeia:** having the dead speak.

  "If Washington were here, he would say…."

- **Paradox:** a seemingly self-contradictory, ironic, or absurd statement.

  "We'll teach these natives democracy even if we have to shoot every last one of them."

- **Catachresis:** somewhat abusive phraseology, involving the use of an incompatible word.

  "He threatened me a good turn."

  "I am not guilty of such virtues."

- **Euphemism:** a mild, inoffensive substitute for a "bad" or negatively connoted word.

  "Grandpa passed away."

  "Pleasingly plump"

- **Onomatopoeia:** words that imitate the sounds to which they refer.

  "Buzz," "snarl," "tintinnabulation"

- **Oxymoron:** use of incongruous or contradicting details.

  "Cruel kindness"

  "Make haste slowly."

- **Alliteration:** the use of words beginning with the same letter.

  "Over stock and stone"

  "Through thick and thin"

- **Simile:** a comparison of things, similar to a metaphor, made with "like" or "as."

"The present administration is bobbing around like a cork in a stormy sea."

There is clearly more to language than denotative meaning. When arranged with elegance and style, words can connote strength, grace, and all manner of meanings beyond the dictionary. Vivid messages are also more persuasive than those presented in a less colorful manner.

# APPROPRIATENESS

## "Politically Correct" Language

"Shooting from the lip" has killed or injured the careers of many public figures. Insensitivity goes beyond language, of course, but some word and language choices are really self-destructive.

### Marge Schott

Cincinnati Reds' owner suspended from baseball for making racial slurs against African Americans, Jews, and Asians.

### Ross Perot

While running for president, unknowingly offended an African-American audience by repeatedly referring to them as "You people."

### Edward Derwinski

Veterans Affairs Secretary who referred to illegal Hispanic immigrants as "wetbacks."

### Evan Mecham

This Arizona governor, who was impeached, defended use of the derogatory word "pickaninny" in a textbook, said Japanese "got round eyes" when talking about golfing, and told Jews they live in a "great Christian nation" where "Jesus Christ is the lord of the land."

In Dangerous English, a guidebook written for foreign visitors to the United States, Elizabeth Claire defines her topic as "… words that may be embarrassing for the speaker to say, or cause the listener to feel insulted, to become angry, or to judge the speaker in a negative way."[7] She cautions foreign visitors that "some words for racial or national groups are so dangerous they have caused violence and even murder." Sad perhaps, but true—there are words speakers should probably never use, foreign or domestic.

**ETHNIC/RACIAL NAMING**    "What do I call you?" Mark asked his new friend, Mr. Chippewa. "Chip," replied Mr. Chippewa. "No," said Mark. "I mean, do you prefer *Indian* or *Native American?*" "I can live with either, but the younger folk prefer *Native American.*" Good advice for speakers. Go with the preferred or stick with "Chip."

*Meeting News* had one of their consultants talk to a variety of people from varied backgrounds to see what kind of naming was most appropriate. She found the following:[8]

> **Native American:**  Native American is more widely accepted than Indian.
>
> **Hispanic:**  Responses varied. Many people in Texas were comfortable with Mexican American while others felt Hispanic was the only correct term. On the West Coast, Latino is common. The vote from the experts: If in doubt, ask. If you can't ask, use Hispanic.
>
> **African American:** There appeared to be great confusion among professionals whether to use Black or African American. An administrator with Project Family in Little Rock, Ark., visited Africa and prefers African American. She likes the connection and heritage the term represents. Yet, many who prefer the term Black resent African American.
>
> **Asian American:**  Asian American is usually appropriate. However, in order to recognize individuals from Guam or other Pacific Islands, many use the term Asian-Pacific Islander. The term Oriental is still used, but it is becoming less acceptable. Too many different ethnic backgrounds fall under its umbrella.

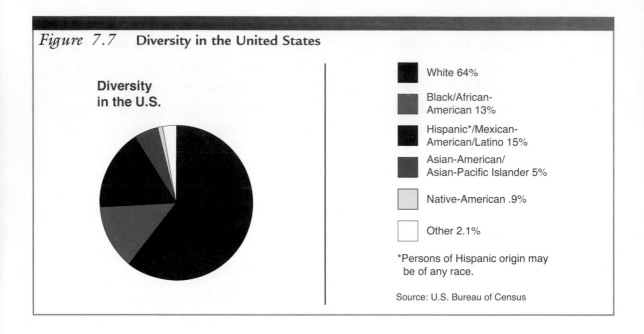

*Figure 7.7*    **Diversity in the United States**

**Diversity in the U.S.**

White 64%

Black/African-American 13%

Hispanic*/Mexican-American/Latino 15%

Asian-American/Asian-Pacific Islander 5%

Native-American .9%

Other 2.1%

*Persons of Hispanic origin may be of any race.

Source: U.S. Bureau of Census

Knowing what is offensive is not always an easy matter. Cultures are changing rapidly and their linguistic preferences are sometimes in flux. If you're going to ask someone about these preferences, ask, "What is your heritage?" not "What do I call you?"

Overlapping all previous categories of appropriate language is the question of gender-specific or sexist language.

## Sexist Language

In 1990 the Sacramento, California city officials considered the term "manhole" too sexist for utility holes in their streets and adopted the term "maintenance hole" to replace "manhole" on official maps and documents.

Gender research proceeds at a near explosive rate—some contradictory, some not. Social roles, especially female, are changing rapidly and with these changes come changes in social orientations and the communication patterns they govern. Sex roles and gender are not the same notion. Some females are quite masculine; some males are quite feminine. Some people combine the roles and are described as androgynous.[9]

In 1990 the Sacramento, California city officials considered the term "manhole" too sexist for utility holes in their streets and adopted the term "maintenance hole" to replace "manhole" on official maps and documents.

In the area of sexist language, both research and experience have provided stable data, suggestions, and important rules. Speakers should be aware of the following:[10]

**GENDERED PRONOUNS**    Modern audiences are very much aware of the *"he," "she," "he/she," "she/he"* problem and expect speakers to know when they may or may not use gender-specific pronouns. For the moment, a Catholic priest may be referred to as "him" but not so for a minister who may be a woman. Gender-specific activities may be referred to in masculine terms. So far, football is male; basketball is not. Mother is female, father is male; however,

> *Does HuMan become Huperson? What about the SON in person? What this country needs is a good 5-cent neuter pronoun …*
>
> **Columnist Matt Roush**

much of what was once gender specific is no longer so. When in doubt, *speak in the plural.* "They" can refer to males or females; "their" or "theirs" to the possessive form "his" or "her" (or "hers"); "them" to the objective form "him" and "her." Perhaps, one day, grammarians will provide us with a generic personal pronoun, but until they do speakers must beware of the masculine pronouns.[11]

**GENDER INFLECTIONS**　We speak here of the changes in form that words undergo, not of voice. "Fireman" is an inappropriate gendered inflection unless one is talking about a specific male person. Even here, one is better advised to use "firefighter" and avoid all risks. It's also easier for a speaker to say, "Attention firefighters" than "Attention firemen and firewomen." How about "Fellow fire-fighters?" "Fellow" is pretty much a neutral noun, but don't count on it.

Other gendered nouns that speakers may trip on abound—"mailman, "po-liceman," "chairman." Try "mail carrier," "police officer," "chairperson," or "chair". "Person" can also desex many of these male-gendered occupational designations.

**SEXIST ANECDOTES**　These are explanations, illustrations, jokes, and "humorous" comments that foster stereotypes or social roles based on gender. This kind of inappropriate discrimination is mostly directed against women. However, this type of inappropriateness can be directed at any group.

A Secretary of Agriculture was forced to resign when, in a "joke," he said blacks, whom he called "colored," wanted three things. In obscene, derogatory terms, he described alleged preferences for dress, sex, and bathroom habits.

A celebrity lost her job promoting Florida oranges when in an effort to defeat a gay rights ordinance in Miami she said that letting children be exposed to ho-mosexuals was close to feeding them garbage.

One professional comedian with a large collection of Polish, "women" and gay jokes decided to im-prove his image by changing all his ethnic, sexist, and gay designations to Ecuadorians. The insulted groups figured it out, and he's been banned in Ecuador.

It is decidely safer to use the word "police officer", as opposed to "policeman". Apply the same tactic to other words, such as "firefighter" instead of "fireman".

# Verbal Obscenity

This is also part of the modern scene. Words can hurt us. Shockingly obscene words have a way of affecting the rationality of both those who use them and those to whom they are addressed.

The riots at the 1968 Democratic National Convention in Chicago entailed much obscenity and counter-obscenity. John Bowers and Donovan Ochs maintain that, "the tactic that probably prompted the 'police riot,' the violent suppression witnessed by millions on television, was the use of obscenity."[12]

The ancient rhetoricians stated without qualification that profanity should be rejected as a legitimate rhetorical strategy. J. Dan Rothwell, however, suggests the following:

> Despite centuries of negative criticism, verbal obscenity has become a more frequent rhetorical device. It is successful in creating attention, in discrediting an enemy, in provoking violence, in fostering identification, and in providing catharsis. Its effects are governed by a variety of circumstances that need to be understood more fully. It has precipitated a police riot, brutal beatings, and even death. Hoping it will go away will not make it so.[13]

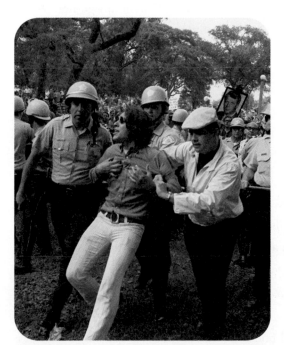

Words are powerful and can incite reaction like the riots at the 1968 Democratic National Convention in Chicago.

Vulgar words and phrases are unfortunately being used more frequently. The younger generation seems to have fewer hang-ups with such terms than do older folk. As with any other words, whatever power they have is lost if a person uses them all of the time on any topic. Our mass media still forbids many of them and they are almost always bad news for public speakers.

Research also indicates some shifting of beliefs regarding appropriate language for males and females. However, this same research did find that speakers using obscene phrases were rated lower in "socio-intellectual status" and "aesthetic quality."

Modern research also tells us that using profanity generally has a detrimental effect on the credibility of the speaker. Suitable language is a necessary part of human social behavior. Some people are seriously offended on a religious basis, others on a social basis.

## Language Overstatement

An antiunion student speaker opened one of his speeches with the words: "Unions are ruining this country. I am going to prove to you that these Bolsheviks are entirely corrupt and more dangerous than terrorists." This language was enough for his opponents to throw up an emotional communication barrier; and, as a result, he was not very persuasive. The most interesting part of this story is that the pro management listeners were most critical of the speech. Even when a sophisticated audience agrees with your point of view, it can be offended by extreme overstatement and overgeneralization, for these are indications of immaturity or emotional insecurity.

When strong attitudes intrude, strong, intense language and word choice often follow. "Guardians of the peace" is a much more positive, less intense description of the police force than "brass-hatted pigs." Language does not stand-alone. The audience and the situation should help decide the potency of your language. If you're not potent enough, you may lose audience interest. If you're too potent you may lose them altogether. When strong "…ist" words intrude in your communication ("sexist," "racist," "elitist," etc.), such charges not only precipitate conflict, but also make it difficult to find resolution. In plain English, you may get more than you bargained for!

A highly polarized audience (in your favor) may welcome intense language of even bizarre proportions, but beware of such behavior should you try the same language on a more neutral or sophisticated audience. To add to your problems, language that is appropriate one day may be a disaster the next. Some topics, audiences, or speakers seem to be more language tolerant, yet ignorance is seldom excused and insensitive language is mostly perceived as bias. A long look at the total situation and audience you're facing can save you much chagrin and embarrassment later on.

## Ode to Sensitivity

Knowing what is appropriate and politically correct in every speaking situation is often a frustrating, but an absolutely necessary effort if we are to be effective and sensitive speakers.[14]

Using politically correct language does not mean that we must abandon our beliefs or positions on socially sensitive subjects. It is fair to use appropriate naming when the discussion or speech concerns *gays* in the military, radical feminism, inner city African Americans, Native-American casinos, and so on.

The meaning of any speech is also in the mind of the listener—it is an *interactive* process. You must choose your language so it helps your listeners sort and select from their word representations something approximating your purpose. Is there room for humor regarding political correctness?

Considerable controversy exists in these matters, and even the academic debates have become polarized and extreme in their arguments.[15]

That speakers may sometimes feel threatened by unreasonable demands for political correctness is a serious matter. Columnist Charles Osgood addresses this problem in a lighter and less threatening way.

**An Ode to Being Sensitive**

Today folks are so sensitive about what's said or sung that one must always watch one's step, and also watch one's tongue. One's career can be ruined and one's life completely wrecked, if one says something that is not politically correct.

Beware of anything that smacks of sexism or racism, of lookism or ageism, of timeism or placeism. There are so many isms it will drive you up the wall, and it's terribly important that you recognize them all.

To say that someone "failed" is much too negative, you see.

What you want to say is that they have "achieved deficiency."

If you're opposed to "otherness," that's called "assimilationism." If you question Mr. Darwin, they'll accuse you of "creationism." There's heightism and fatism, and good old isolationism. Don't complain or you are guilty of "anti-ismizationism."

Nobody is disabled, "handi-capable's" what's said, and you're "terminally inconvenienced" now instead of simply dead. To say that someone "failed" is much too negative, you see. What you want to say is that they have "achieved deficiency."

You do not want to be "centrist" either anthropo or eu. So never say you want to see the "Middle Eastern" bureau. For by now you should have noticed at the very, very least that's considered eurocentric now. There is no "middle east."

You are not supposed to ever give anyone a "test." A "needs assessment" is the term that's now considered best. If you're drunk, you are "sobriety deprived" we can report, and "vertically challenged" if you're too tall or too short.

The active voice is much preferred by Messrs. Strunk and White, but the PC crowd is not so sure politically that's right... To say how you see something is nowhere near as keen as saying what the subject of discussion is now "seen as."

By whom, in this construction, you do not have to say, so sometimes you can get completely off the hook that way. A fact which in too many ways exploiters have exploited, so both the active and the passive voice should be avoided.

Which doesn't leave you room for saying what you want to say, but the way things are, most likely you are better off that way. If all this seems quite strange to you, it's just as I have feared, and you better get that handbook by Chris Cerf and Henry Beard.[17]

*Reprinted by permission: Tribune Media Services*

# CHAPTER REVIEW
## *Wrapping it up*

## Summary

The greater the size of ones vocabulary, the easier is to communicate effectively. The five hundred most commonly used words have more than fourteen thousand uses. These same-term differences may be described as lexical, contextual, and neurological. A listener has more concomitant signals to deal with than a reader. Voice, for example, has a powerful influence upon meaning. A speaker's appearance and gestures are other concomitant signals that affect the listeners.

Language as a system is holistic—the whole of it is greater than the sum of its parts. Language that is appropriate one day may be a disaster the next. Our understandings and perceptions of the world are thought to be inextricably tied to language and particularly to its grammar. If this long-standing *Whorf-Sapir Hypothesis* is true, then critical thinking is governed by this powerful language system.

Denotation refers to literal meaning; connotation refers to added, more abstract meaning. Meaning has three elements: a person having thoughts, a symbol (or sign), and a referent.

A word is a kind of symbol. A word is a generally accepted representation of a thing. There are obviously more things and concepts in the world than there are words, so a word may be thought of as a representation or generalization with a meaning in accordance with its context. A speaker should ask, "What does *this* word mean to *this* audience in *this* situation, in *this* context, as used by *this* speaker at *this* time?" A good sentence systematically excludes meanings the listener might attach that are not intended by the speaker—in short, it qualifies by defining meanings *not* intended. A perversion of this process has been called "doublespeak."

The propositional nature of language can be a problem in some language systems. If we become too literal and rigid, logic and language habits may be impaired and misunderstanding may result.

Specificity and accuracy in language behooves us to eliminate as much jargon as possible, to date events, and to make accurate word choices.

Check out our website
**www.bvtlab.com**
for flashcards,
summaries, self-quizzes,
and speches.

Helpful rules include indexing, "is," "et cetera," dating your language, and discerning presymbolic language. Colorful language includes vividness and imagery. Vividness suggests that there is more to language than denotative meaning. When arranged with elegance and style, words can connote strength, grace, and all manner of meanings not in the dictionary. Imagery refers to vivid figures of speech that produce mental pictures in the mind's eye of listeners. Figures of speech include metaphor, hyperbole, euphemism, simile, and others.

Language does not stand-alone. The audience should help decide the specificity and intensity of your language. Insensitive language is mostly perceived as bias. "Shooting from the lip" has injured the careers of many public figures.

Language that is not "politically correct" has been described as *dangerous English*…words that may be embarrassing for the speaker to say, or cause the listener to be insulted, to become angry, or to judge the speaker in a negative way.

Ethnic/racial naming advice includes: Use the currently preferred designations (e.g., African American, Hispanic, Asian American) and make sure that naming is relevant and necessary.

Research and experience in the area of sexist language provide important rules for speakers. These rules include the use of gendered nouns and pronouns, gender inflections, and sexist anecdotes.

Shockingly obscene words have a way of affecting rationality of both those who use them and those to whom they are addressed. Profanity, generally, has a detrimental effect on the credibility of the speaker.

Knowing what is appropriate and politically correct in every speaking situation is often a frustrating, but absolutely necessary effort if you are to be an effective and sensitive speaker.

Critical thinking involves exercising intelligent, objective, cautious judgment and evaluation of the language we use and the language we receive and decode from others. One of the most widespread thinking faults is overstatement and overgeneralization.

Language habits reflect your personality. Seriously maladjusted individuals can often be identified by their language habits.

That speakers may sometimes feel threatened by unreasonable demands for political correctness is a serious matter. See "Ode" within this chapter.

# *Notes*

1. Paula J. Schwanenflugel, ed., *The Psychology of Word Meanings* (Hillsdale, NJ: Erlbaum, 1991).

2. Robert P. Pula, "A General Semantics Glossary (Part VI)," ETC., 50, no. 4 (Winter 1993–94), 493.

3. B. L. Whorf, *Language, Thought and Reality* (New York: John Wiley & Sons, 1957). See also John A. Lucy, *Grammatical Categories and Cognition: A Case Study of the Linguistic Relativity Hypothesis* (Cambridge, England: Cambridge University Press, 1992); Janet Yerby, "Family Systems Theory Reconsidered: Integrating Social Construction Theory and Dialectical Process," *Communication Theory,* 5, no. 4 (November 1995), 339–65.

4. Lane Cooper [translator], The Rhetoric of Aristotle, (Englewood Cliffs, N.J.: Prentice-Hall, 1932), p. 185.

5. Douglas MacArthur, "Duty, Honor, Country," speech delivered at West Point Military Academy, May 12, 1962.

6. Martin Luther King, Jr., "I Have a Dream," speech delivered in Washington, D.C., August 28, 1963.

7. Elizabeth Claire, *Dangerous English* (Dundee, IL: Delta Systems Co., Inc., 1990), p. 1.

8. *Meeting News,* March, 1993, p. 23.

9. For a broader discussion of gender and communication, see: J. C. Pearson, L. H. Turner, W. Todd-Mancillas, *Gender and Communication* (Dubuque, Iowa: W. C. Brown, 1991); also H. Giles and R. L. Street, "Communication Characteristics and Behavior," in M. L. Knapp and G. R. Miller, eds. *Handbook of interpersonal Communication* (Beverly Hills, Calif.: Sage), 1985; also see B. Bate, *Communication and the Sexes* (New York: Harper & Row, 1988); for a radical feminist view, see Cheris Krarrarae and Paula A. Treichler, *A Feminist Dictionary* (London, England: Pandora Press, 1985).

10. For more on gender issues in the classroom, see *Communication Education,* 40, no. 1 (January 1991).

11. For a radical feminist view see Julia Penelope, *Speaking Freely: Unlearning the Lies of the Fathers' Tongues* (New York: Pergamon Press, 1990).

12. John Bowers and Donovan Ochs, The Rhetoric of Agitation and Control (Reading, Mass.: Addison-Wesley, 1971, 1991), p. 70.

13. Dan Rothwell, "Verbal Obscenity: Time for Second Thoughts," *Western Speech,* 35, no. 4 (1971), 242.

14. See Michael Burgoon and William Baily, "PC at Last! PC at Last! Thank God Almighty, We Are PC at Last," *Journal of Communication,* 42, no. 2 (Spring 1992), 95-104; also see Barbara J. O'Keefe, "Sense and Sensitivity," *Journal of Communication,* 42, no. 2 (Spring 1992), 123–30.

15. Richard Bello, "A Burkeian Analysis of the 'Political Correctness' Confrontation in Higher Education," *The Southern Communication Journal,* 61, no. 3 (Spring 1996), 243–52.

16. Charles Osgood, "An Ode to Being Sensitive." Reprinted by permission: Tribune Media Services. Also see Henry Beard and Christopher Cerf, *The Official Politically Correct Dictionary and Handbook* (New York: Random House, 1992, 1993.)

# DELIVERING THE SPEECH

# Chapter 8

## Chapter Objectives

**Effective Delivery**

**Types of Delivery**

Reading from a Manuscript
Memorization
Impromptu Delivery
Extemporaneous Delivery

**The Nature of Nonverbals**

Nonverbals Always

**Communication (Kinesics)**

Unconscious Nonverbal
  Communication
Types of Body Action
Standards of Good Body Action

**Voice and Articulation (Paralanguage)**

Voice and Personality
Variable Characteristics of Voice

Communicate Something
Nonverbals Are Bound to the
Situation
Nonverbals Are Believed
Nonverbals Are Seldom Isolated
Nonverbals Affect Our
  Relationships

**Body Action**

Articulation Control
Pronunciation

**Related Nonverbal Behaviors**

Object Language (Clothes and
  Things)
Space and Distance (Proxemics)
Time (Chronemics)

# EFFECTIVE DELIVERY

Your first objective is not to be dull! When told that Calvin Coolidge, the dullest speaker on record, had died, satirical author Dorothy Parker responded, "How could they tell?" In this chapter we are interested in(1) the *types* or *ways* of effectively delivering a speech and (2) the nonverbal signals, especially bodily action and voice, that accompany your message.

> The art of delivery has to do with the voice: with the right management of it to express each several emotion—as when to use a loud voice, when a soft, and when the intermediate; with the mode of using pitch—high, low, and intermediate; and with the rhythms to be used in each particular case. These are, in fact, the three things that receive attention: volume, modulation of pitch, and rhythm.
>
> **Aristotle**

When combined with the verbal message, nonverbal signals are quite effective in conveying ideas, particularly emotional concepts such as love and hate. People display quite different nonverbal responses to various emotional situations. Research suggests that some people are more sensitive than others to nonverbal signals and also that young people are less sensitive to nonverbal signals than are older people. No wonder that in some speeches our voices and our actions speak so loudly that our words are often unheard or are not very persuasive.

Speakers should bear in mind that our nonverbal behavior may be unintentionally contrary to our verbal message. We express attitudes through body action, voice and articulation patterns, the objects we wear or own, our use of time and space, as well as our language and verbal messages.[1] There is even good evidence that people rely primarily on nonverbal cues to judge truthfulness.[2] Hence, when the verbal message and the nonverbal message don't coincide, we are more apt to believe what we understand the nonverbal message to be rather than the verbal one.

The *context* and *situation* can radically change the meaning of our nonverbals. One student arrived in class wearing a trenchcoat over a leotard. Lots of nonverbals here, none appropriate for speechmaking, one might presume; however, she was giving a demonstration speech on aerobics (and a good one), and her leotard took on a whole different meaning and was suddenly appropriate.

Many characteristics are associated with effective delivery and some are associated with ineffective, even annoying, delivery. Some of the more relevant, positive characteristics include:

1.   A well-paced, moving delivery

2.   An alertness of body and mind that indicates enthusiasm

3.   Controlled, yet flexible, body activity that reinforces meaning

4.   Some direct eye contact that indicates a sense of communication

5.   A clear, pleasant, conversational voice and articulation

Various speech studies undertaken to determine what specific aspects of delivery are unpleasant, ineffective, or annoying to audiences help us recognize effective delivery. The following are those aspects considered annoying:

1.   Stiff body action

2.   Refusal to look at the audience

3.   Excessive nervousness or fidgeting

4.   Monotonous, stiff reading or delivery from a manuscript

5.   Weak, or overly loud, unclear, or monotonous voice

6.   Mumbling of words

7.   Too many mispronunciations and grammatical mistakes

Gerald Ford was not a gifted speaker but better than "Silent Cal." (President Calvin Coolidge, "Silent Cal," was known for not talking and getting more sleep than any other president in the White House!) Gerald Ford worked to be a better speaker by writing cues in the margin of his notes: "Smile," "Pause," "Move." Perennial presidential candidate Pat Paulsen mused, "Whenever I heard Gerald Ford speak on TV, I thought I had lost the color on my set."

It has been observed that Bill Clinton's nonverbals helped him make "contact" with his audiences and that Senator Dole's did not. George W. Bush's folksy way of speaking as an attempt to connect to the American public was often spoofed in comedy routines. In the election between John McCain and Barack Obama, some say President Obama's smooth oratory style contributed greatly to his winning the presidency.

The following include some habits thought to adversely affect specific perceptions of authoritativeness and sociability include:

George W. Bush's folksy way of speaking was often spoofed in comedy routines.

1.    Use of hedges such as "sort of" or "kind of"

2.    Hesitations such as "um" or "er"

3.    Meaningless verbalizations such as "oh well" or "you know"

4.    Intensifiers such as "quite," "really," or "very"[3]

Displaying a pseudo sense of humility—"In this person's humble opinion…"—can also turn off audiences. Golda Meir put it bluntly: "Don't be humble. You're not that great."

Sometimes the right message or word can change even some of these faults. Listen to Dave Powers, an aide of John F. Kennedy.

I set it up for him to make a speech to the Gold Star Mothers, and you never in your life heard such a speech. He's hemming and hawing and you'd need a pair of pliers to drag the next sentence out of him. The women are all sitting there, waiting to hear him say something, and very little is coming out. Worse than that, it looks like he never learned how to end a speech. It's going on and on and I'm beginning to perspire.

All of a sudden he says it. The right words come to him and he says it. He says: "Well, I think I know how you ladies feel. My mother, too, lost a son in the war."… They broke into applause; some of them started to cry and the mothers rushed forward to grab his hand and hug him. That was his first campaign, and from that minute onward, you could see the tide turn his way.[4]

Probably the best advice comes from a pro like Gerald Gardner. "Be open and easy; treat your audience like old friends…be yourself."[5]

# TYPES OF DELIVERY

Aristotle's fourth canon, *memory,* describes the importance of knowing what and how you intend to move through your message. The four principal ways of delivering a speech are (1) by reading from a manuscript, (2) by memorization, (3) by impromptu delivery, and (4) by speaking extemporaneously. The subject and the occasion are important factors in determining which one or which combination should be used at a given time.

## Reading from a Manuscript

Fortunately, the subjects and occasions that demand this method of delivery and preparation are few, for this is probably the most difficult of all the types of delivery. However, such occasions are increasing in number. A **manuscript** speech stems from a prepared document from which the speaker reads word for word while still maintaining connection to the audience. An important policy speech by the United States Secretary of State may be dissected word by word by foreign governments; therefore, it calls for maximum accuracy in wording and a minimum of opportunity for angry misstatement.

> *Speak when you're angry and you'll make the best speech you'll ever regret.*
>
> **Henry Ward Beecher**

The mass media make further demands on a speaker's flexibility. Very often a copy of the manuscript is distributed before the speech is given, and thus the newspapers can print or quote the speech almost before it has been delivered. If the speaker then deviates from the manuscript, he or she invites trouble and confusion. Certain highly complicated and technical subjects demanding absolute accuracy may call for manuscript reading.

The problems of manuscript reading, even for a classroom speech, are apparent. There is little chance for spontaneity or for instant adaptation of the material to the ever-changing demands of the audience. Except for very exceptional readers, the actual delivery is hamstrung by a lack of eye contact and directness. Your eyes are typically glued to your manuscript, except for furtive glances into outer space, which only cause you to lose your place. This embarrassment may cause you to lose emphasis and vocal variety. For some the word is *dull.*

One of the ironies in speech training is that the beginner, apparently in an effort to avoid the inevitable confrontation with the audience, may use the manuscript as something to hide behind. Doing this only delays self-development because it usually results in an unsuccessful audience experience, which is extremely frustrating for the beginner.

When preparing a manuscript that is to be read aloud to an audience, you have to make some fundamental stylistic changes in the writing. The language of writers, for example, is typically less direct. They use *wording such as a person, people, and the reader;* a speaker uses the words *you, they, I* and the like. The other differences are not as obvious. Although we extemporize in short, simple sentences, we tend to write in longer, more complex ones. When we are engaged in literary writing (material that will be read silently by the receiver), we have less of a problem with this "longer" style, for the receiver can reread and review. In a speech, however, the necessity for shorter, less complex sentences is critical—as is the use of repetition, restatement, and reinforcement. Remember that the listener, unlike the reader, cannot stop and go back over the material or use a dictionary. The spoken words must be instantly clear to the listener. Therefore, they require more illustrations, examples, analogies, contrasts, and vividness than a written essay does. The secret is to write "out loud."

The delivery of a speech from a manuscript is also somewhat different. Normal eye contact and vocal patterns are often disrupted. The manuscript may be hard to see if the lighting is bad or your vision is otherwise reduced. A fan has been known to distract a speaker. The position of the manuscript also creates problems. You may either hold your manuscript in your hand at about waist level or put it on a lectern. In the first case, you inhibit your hand gestures; in the other, you hide most of your body. Either way, the problem is to let your eyes drop to the paper while keeping your head erect.

Most good manuscript reading requires a generous amount of memorization, but *partial* memorization only—that is, of blocks of language that are held together for you by meaning. This permits you more time to look at the audience. When your memory fails, you refer back to the manuscript for the next memorized language group. The problem is trying to find your place. Marginal notes, underlining, and various markings can help. The only real insurance is a thorough understanding of your message and—practice, practice, practice! To achieve successful oral communication, you must learn to spend considerably more time looking at your audience than at your manuscript.

Problems of voice may also be apparent in manuscript reading. Most people do not read well without practice and training, and this is why we have courses in interpretative reading. Beginners may singsong (speak in a monotonous rhythm of rising and falling tones), use stress and inflection separate from meaning, or project a sleepy monotone. Varying the rate, loudness, pitch, and quality, along with the careful use of pauses, are essential to manuscript reading. It is most important to join these vocal variations to the pertinent meanings. The secret is to try to develop a wide-ranging eye–voice correspondence.

## Memorization

**Memorization** was expected in times of oral documentation. Each pause and emphasis was employed for dramatic ends and was anticipated by the audience. When a story was told without the anticipated emphases, pauses, or even particular phraseology, the speaker lost credibility. Now, however, except among actors who work hard at sounding spontaneous, there is little justification for a completely memorized speech. A memorized speech is the direct effort of word-for-word recall. This effort, however, is enormous. The delivery, unless done by professionals, is typically stilted, overly rhythmical, and impersonal. Moreover, memorization does not offer any easy way to adapt the material to the audience. However, just as they will choose to read from a manuscript, many frightened beginners will undertake the enormous task of memorization. This method can result in panic if their memory fails. There is neither a place to go nor a specific thing to do. Grade schoolers repeating a memorized poem are in far better shape than most speakers because they have a prompter. Besides, it is only a poem, not a personal message, which is in danger.

This is not to say that you should not memorize *parts* of your speech. A dramatic introduction, a conclusion that includes poetry, a piece of testimony, and a complicated group of statistics (when visual aids are unavailable or awkward)—are all likely passages for memorization.

## Impromptu Delivery

An **impromptu** speech is one that is delivered on the spur of the moment, without advance notice or time for detailed preparation. Usually you will not be asked to make an impromptu speech unless it pertains to your special knowledge, experience, or training. If you have such expertise that makes you vulnerable to unexpected requests for a "few words," you had better carry at least a mental outline with you at all times. In this way you reduce the risks of being caught completely off guard.

A student from Kenya once observed that even in the most informal gatherings he was routinely asked to explain something about Kenya and his reaction to America. On these occasions, he eventually found himself in a true speaking situation, as more and more people gathered around and as he did more and more of the talking. To improve these presentations, he prepared several highly adaptable speech outlines, committed the outlines to memory, and then tried to anticipate each situation and group in which he was apt to find himself. He explained that he has become so expert at this that he is now disappointed if he is *not* asked to say a few words. People are amazed at his fluent and well-organized "impromptu" remarks!

Your instructor may give you some experience in impromptu speaking by simply stating two or three speech topics and then telling you to choose one topic, to take a minute to collect your wits, and then to start talking. Here are some general rules that may help if you find yourself in this or any other potentially impromptu situation:

> It usually takes me more than three weeks to prepare a good impromptu speech.
>
> **Mark Twain**

1.  *Anticipate the situation.* Try to avoid having to present a true impromptu speech. Figure the odds on your being called, and try to determine on what topic you will be asked to speak.

2.  *Relate the topic under consideration to your experience.* You will tend to speak more easily and confidently about something with which you have had specific experience.

3.  *When in doubt, summarize.* There may be moments when you lose the thread of what you were saying or where you were going. At this moment, a quick review or summary often restores perspective and allows your mind to get back on the right track.

4.  *Be brief!* The less time you speak impromptu, the less chance for you to lose track of what you are saying.

5.  *Quit when you are ahead!* All too often we make a good impromptu speech and then, either because we feel we have not said enough or

because our momentary success has given us false confidence, we continue to ramble on until we eventually ruin whatever communication we had achieved.

6.  *If you really have nothing to say then don't speak!* Better to be thought a fool than to open your mouth and remove all doubt.

# Extemporaneous Delivery

The **extemporaneous** speaking method involves the preparation of a thorough but flexible outline, the cataloguing of much potentially usable material, and the use of a speaking outline that is either memorized or carried by the speaker. The language and wording of the speech are adaptable, as is the use of speech materials and details.

> There are some who speak one moment before they think.
>
> **Jean de LaBruyere**

In this method the emphasis is on knowing your subject and knowing your audience. This method typically requires collecting a lot more material than you will need. Thus, if one illustration or piece of evidence does not satisfy your audience, you will immediately be able to select another. If one strategy of organization is unclear, you will have a previously determined alternative to adapt to the audience confusion of the moment.

The chief advantage of extemporaneous preparation and delivery is that they give you *flexibility* and *adaptability.* You are able to respond successfully to the communication problems as they develop. You are thinking on your feet in the best sense of that term. These are the essential qualities of good conversation; they should be present in all good speeches as well. The speaker who seeks to inspire need not sound artificial or pompous. A speaker can be eloquent without sounding like divine certainty. On the other hand, adapting conversational qualities to public speaking does not mean employing a matter-of-fact voice, poor preparation, or careless language. Public speaking is more structured, uses more polished language, and relies on more formal body action and delivery than does a conversation.

A famous speech teacher, James A. Winans, once noted, "It is not true that a public speech to be conversational need sound like conversation. Conventional differences may make it sound very different." We are seeking the best qualities and moods of conversation, not a stylized version of conversation.

An extemporaneous speech is most effective when given from a brief but meaningful outline, which is carried in either your head or your hand and which is supported by thorough preparation. This is the type of preparation and delivery expected of you except in those special exercises your instructor may announce.

# The Nature of Nonverbals

Nonverbals of whatever kind—conscious or unconscious—may be characterized as follows:

1.    They always communicate something.

2.    They are bound to the situation.

3.    They are believed.

4.    They are seldom isolated.

5.    They affect our relationships.

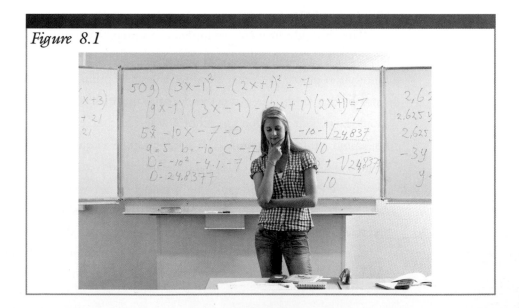

*Figure 8.1*

## Nonverbals Always Communicate Something

Assuming some kind of human interaction, we cannot *not* behave; and because behavior is nonverbal communication, we *cannot not communicate.* A blank stare communicates something to the audience, even it if is just confusion. This fact is not always appreciated by less sensitive personalities. These behaviors may be conveyed consciously or unconsciously, but one way or another they communicate.

## Nonverbals Are Bound to the Situation

The context or situation makes a lot of difference. The baby's smile might indicate pleasure in one situation or gas in another. A thumb in the air might mean A-OK on the launch pad or a request for a ride on the highway. When the context or situation is not considered, nonverbals can be confusing indeed. When it is obvious, our nonverbals are most clear. Is there any doubt about what this listener is expressing in Figure 8.2?

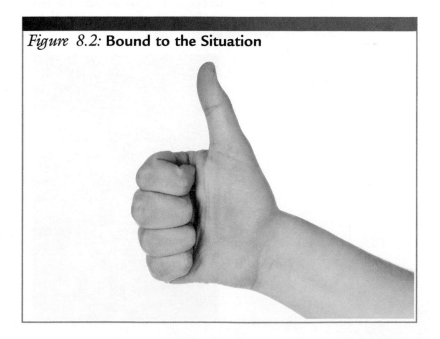

*Figure 8.2:* **Bound to the Situation**

## Nonverbals Are Believed

Perhaps nonverbals should not be believed, but this tendency exists. Con men have always taken advantage of this fact. Perhaps nonverbals are harder to fake for most of us, but certainly not for good actors. When what you say disagrees with how you *look* or *sound,* people tend to believe the nonverbals—"Trust me; you'll love it! Would I lie?" (Figure 8.3).

## Nonverbals Are Seldom Isolated

Communication comes in packages. It is very difficult for most of us to be boiling mad and yet control our actions and voice so that we appear calm. A glisten of perspiration, a faster eye-blink, a slight tremble, dryness in the voice—these and more give us away. Even when you are laughing on the outside and crying on the inside, the character of your laughter probably gives you away. These other nonverbals tend to be related, consistent, and supportive of one another. When they are not, when they are *incongruent,* suspicions about your intent are raised. Even in pictures or audiotapes, nonverbals are difficult to isolate.

*Figure 8.3*: **Nonverbals are believed more than words spoken when the two are incongruent**

## Nonverbals Affect Our Relationships

We decide three important things about people largely on the basis of nonverbal communication: (1) personal liking or attraction, (2) evaluation of power relationships, and (3) evaluation of the response we get from others. Let's review each of these as nonverbal codes:

1.  Sometimes we feel attracted toward another by nonverbal cues alone. That person seems "a likeable sort," "a good guy," and is easy to be with. That the opposite also happens is all too clear.

2.  Power assessment is your evaluation of the other person's status, influence, or clout. Nonverbal cues become important, particularly in the absence of verbal information. Several of these will be discussed shortly.

3.  Another nonverbal area is your perception of a responsive listener, a person who can and will appreciate your position or your problem.

# BODY ACTION COMMUNICATION (KINESICS)

## Unconscious Nonverbal Communication

The way a person walks, sits, or stands at a given moment may demonstrate that person's mood more adequately than his or her words do. When we try to avoid looking awkward, we usually communicate even more awkwardness and look unnatural and ridiculous; in addition, such holding back may lead to poor control of our emotions. Lack of action often makes the message less clear. There is no point in trying to avoid body action; there are many good reasons to try to *understand* it, *control* it, and *use* it.

**EMPATHY**    If your instructor runs his fingernails sharply across the chalkboard, you probably cringe and grit your teeth. If you've ever huddled in the stands, alternately shivering and cheering as your team made a goal-line stand against the Oakland Raiders or the Miami Dolphins, you can understand empathy. If you've ever seen a youngster take a violent and bruising fall, you probably "felt" the pain as you projected yourself into the youngster's situation.

This type of projection is the basis of empathy. Empathy includes a muscular reaction; to an extent, an audience imitates the actions of the speaker. When a speaker appears mortally afraid and tense, the audience dies a little. When the speaker acts tired, the audience feels tired or bored. When a person paces the floor like a caged lion, the audience usually tires before the speaker does. You should take the audience into account when considering body action and should attempt to use the kind and amount of action that will help achieve the purpose of your speech.

**EMOTION**    Good actors, dancers, and capable speakers appear to communicate emotions effectively. The actor has the script, the set, other actors, and the stylized conceptions of the audience as aids. If the cause of whatever emotion the actor is portraying is also seen (for example, a gun producing fear), the communication is easier to interpret.

In addition to communicating emotion, you can also drain off pent-up tension or emotion through the use of body action. This is why some speakers pace the floor or fidget constantly. Instead of acting in distracting ways, try to use *meaningful* body action that will help you control your speech fright at the same time that it helps communicate your message.

In this section we shall discuss the patterns of physical behavior that make up total body action. Although these patterns most often occur at the same time, we are separating them here for the purpose of explanation.

## Types of Body Action

**GENERAL IMPRESSION**    The general impression you create is a combination not only of all the signals that you communicate to your audience but also of the things in the system over which you may not always have control—for example, the lighting, the building, the platform,

Highly trained dancers put in long hours of practice to be able to communicate emotions with movement effectively. They acquire the ability to tell stories with their bodies.

and the person who introduces you. However, there are some relatively simple things over which you *do* have some control, things that may contribute much to the general impression you make. (See Figure 8.4)

Dress is one of these. In considering what to wear, the watchword is *appropriate. Appropriate dress* is attire that the audience would expect for the occasion, your level of expertise, and the topic. You don't want to appear conspicuous, yet you do wish to live up to your audience's expectations regarding the dress of its speakers. Your physical and psychological comforts affect your body action. However, there's a lesson to be learned if the audience remembers your leotard instead of your speech. We discuss attire further, and the adornments we don, under Object Language.

When thinking about general impression, another problem is deciding how to *position yourself*—whether you will address the audience from a sitting or a standing position. You might feel awkward standing on a platform with only three or four listeners at your feet, and some small, informal audiences may prefer that you sit while speaking to them. However, other small groups are insulted if the speaker sits. The impression they receive, apparently, is that they are not considered important enough for a stand-up speech. Your decision depends a lot

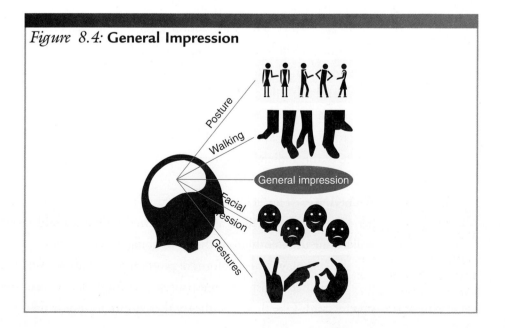

*Figure 8.4:* **General Impression**

upon how well you know the group and how well they know you. As a general rule there is less risk in standing, even before a very small group. If the audience appears uncomfortable, it is much easier to sit down after a speech has started than to stand up. In an Effective Supervision course in which eight to twelve students rated the teachers, the evaluations of the instructors favored those who stood while speaking. Whether you're sitting, standing, or walking, the way you do it is revealing. It can draw people to you or drive them away.

**POSTURE**    Posture is an important part of the general impression you make. It affects the empathy of the audience and what they conclude from your signals. The way you carry yourself tends to show whether or not you have confidence in yourself. Whether you slouch and cower or whether you stand with military bearing affects your outlook, sense of power, and your control over yourself. A slouching posture can tire the audience as quickly as it can the speaker.

In general, *good posture* involves the distribution of your body weight in a comfortable and poised way consistent with the impression you wish to make as a speaker. You should be erect without looking stiff, comfortable without appearing limp. Your bearing should be alert, self-possessed, and communicative. Good posture and poise reflect a kind of cool unconcern. The great danger, as with all stylized body action, is appearing artificial, overly noticeable, or out of place.

A satisfactory standing position should be a balanced one; it should allow you to recover quickly if you were suddenly pushed. Your feet should be fairly close together, one foot slightly ahead of the other. Keep your hips straight, shoulders back, and chin in. Try to find a poised, natural speaking stance. There is not one way that is right for every speech. The stance you finally select will have to be modified to meet changing speech circumstances, such as the size and nature of the audience, the formality of the occasion, and so on.

**WALKING**    The "femme fatale" actress has a walk that clearly communicates her role; the sneaky villain also has a stylized walk; the child about to be scolded walks quite differently from the child going to the movies.

*Walking* may serve as a form of physical punctuation. A few steps to the side may strengthen transitions and pauses, and emphasis may be strengthened by a step forward. Like the actor, the speaker wishes to appear natural, not awkward.

If your walking is ungraceful or mechanical, it will distract rather than accomplish its intended purpose; if it is random, it will detract from the general purpose of your speech. In short, the way you walk tells a lot about you. It can communicate energy, enthusiasm, sloppiness, indifference, fatigue, or any number of other things.

Walking also has empathic value—it can offer physical relief to a suffering audience. On the other hand, too much walking can wear an audience out. One instructor was known for pacing across the front of the classroom during his entire lecture. Students reported being dizzy after every class. The right amount of planned, purposeful walking, however, is an outlet for muscular tension for both the speaker and the audience.

The question of the desirable amount and kind of walking requires the same considerations that apply to all body action: the subject, the speaker, the size of the audience, the formality of the occasion, and so on. In general, the more formal the speech, the less pronounced your walking should be; the larger the audience, the more definite your steps should be. Remember also that walking, like all body action, begins before you actually start to speak. When you leave your chair to approach the speaker's stand, your communication has already begun. You are not finished until you have walked off the platform.

**FACIAL EXPRESSION**    Two scholars who have spent a lifetime studying the recognition of emotions from facial expressions insist that there are *universal facial expressions* of emotions. Ekman and Friesen identify them as *happiness, sadness, surprise, fear, anger and disgust.*[6] Others have argued that these expressions should be regarded as cultural artifacts rather than as universals;[7] context is the overriding variable.[8] **Facial expressions** result from one or more muscle motions or positions on the face. The facial muscles can create four thousand to five thousand different muscle combinations. Perhaps these minute variations lend to the individual differences of expression we see on each other's faces.

We all have heard of "the face that launched a thousand ships" and been told, "The eyes are the mirror of the soul." The problem is that the speaker may unintentionally use stylized facial expressions unsuitable to the subject Figure 8.5, Facial Tics). One speech student had a temporary facial disorder that caused one eye to wink uncontrollably about every sixty seconds. Even after the class

*Figure 8.5:* **Facial Tics**

discovered the real cause of the winking, the signal confusion remained alarming. Once the student learned to blink both eyes, most of the problem was solved. Closing one eye in a wink has a stereotyped meaning. Closing both eyes at the same time in a blink has no stereotyped meaning (unless done in rapid succession) and was, in this case, not confusing or particularly distracting. An emotionally tense person might tighten the jaw and unconsciously take on a crocodile grin. This usually passes as one relaxes, but the first moments of a serious speech by a grinning speaker can be most confusing.

The speaker's eyes, at least for relatively small audiences, are very communicative. Audiences are wary of shifty eyes—"She avoids my eyes" is a frequent classroom criticism. The audience expects to be looked at—not stared at constantly, but looked at occasionally. Many define directness of delivery as being based on eye contact.

The lessons are (1) avoid unintentional or inappropriate facial stereotypes, (2) make eye contact with the audience, and (3) free your natural and spontaneous facial expressions so that they strengthen your message.

**GESTURES**    U.S. speech education in the nineteenth century suffered from a highly mechanical approach. It was a period of flamboyant language and highly stylized gestures. Delsarte devised a system of gesturing during this time that contained some eighty-one gestures for practically all parts of the body, including specific ones for the nose, eyebrows, and feet. In reaction against this movement, the famous School of Expression of S. S. Curry was born. This view taught, "Every action of face or hand … is simply an outward effect of an inward condition. Any motion or tone that is otherwise is not expression." In other words, speakers should be so involved in the subject that their expression is always dynamic and spontaneous.

*Reinforcing Gestures*   It seems natural to clench our fist or perhaps even pound the lectern when we are trying to communicate a strong feeling. Such actions emphasize our words. In disagreeing verbally we might routinely turn our palms down or out. In appealing we might naturally turn our palms up or in. These types of gestures reinforce through *emphasis.* Other gestures reinforce through *suggestion.* In communicating a scolding attitude toward the other political party, we might shake a finger in much the same stereotyped way that a scolding parent does. Speakers may emphasize a separation of points by using first one hand ("On the one hand it can be said …") and then the other. We might, also, only use one hand, suggesting several categories by slicing the air with a vertical palm and moving our hand on a level plane from left to right. No two persons use these reinforcing gestures exactly alike, but the stereotype is usually recognized. These also are called **emblems. Emblems** are hand gestures translated to specific words or meaning rather directly, as with the hitchhike or A-OK sign.

School of Expression of S. S. Curry, every action of face or hand is simply an outward effect of an inward condition.

*Descriptive Gestures*   When you are asked to describe the size or shape of something, it is natural to use your hands to indicate the dimensions. Ekman and Friesen refer to these gestures as **illustrators.** If you could not use your hands, it would be difficult to describe a circular staircase to a person who had never seen one. All descriptive gestures are also partly reinforcing. If you really didn't like circular staircases, you might also subconsciously communicate a message of approval or disapproval.

***Standards of Good Body Action***    Good body action is as important as the words we choose, the gestures we employ to accentuate meaning, and the expressions our faces reveal. Therefore, we need to  consider the ways in which we move our body. We need to ensure that they are appropriate to the audience, that they are varied (and not stale), that all body movements are physically coordinated with each other, and that they are coordinated with our words (Figure 8.6).

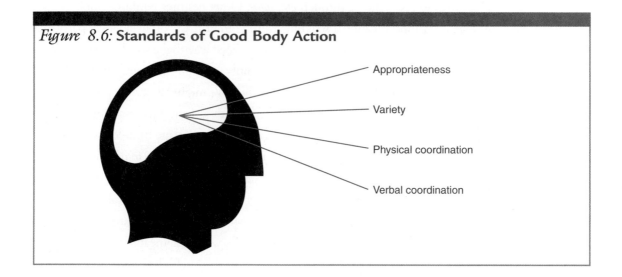

*Figure 8.6:* **Standards of Good Body Action**

- Appropriateness
- Variety
- Physical coordination
- Verbal coordination

**APPROPRIATENESS**    Your subject, the context, and the size and nature of your audience determine what kind of body action is appropriate. A very formal subject, particularly when combined with a formal occasion and a small, older audience, generally calls for poised but relatively restricted body action. Grand sweeps of the arms and other showy movements would be out of place. Other things being equal, the larger the audience, the more unrestricted your body action may be. Cross-cultural problems abound when it comes to appropriate body actions and gestures (Figure 8.7).

*Figure 8.7:* **Cultural Appropriateness**

- The thumbs-up gesture is offensive to Arabs.

- The left-hand gesture is considered unclean in many cultures.

- Waving goodbye is a good way to summon a Filipino.

Most speakers use too little body action, whatever the speech occasion. When you are finally free of your inhibitions, remember to match your body actions with the expectations of your audience.

**VARIETY**    Any body action, but particularly gestures, should be varied occasionally. Otherwise the routineness of the action may call attention to it and become a distraction. Speakers who pound the table *every* time they make a point, regardless of its importance, soon lose the reinforcing effect.

All of us tend to repeat our favorite gestures. We must periodically ask ourselves if we are overworking some of them and if our body action really reflects the message we would like to project. If necessary, your instructor will feed this information back to you so that you can correct such distracting habits.

**PHYSICAL COORDINATION**    Physical coordination refers to the combination of all parts of your body in expressing yourself. You can appear ridiculous by locking your elbows to your sides and moving only your forearms and hands.

A "detachment" such as this makes you appear mechanical. The whole body is always involved in any body action.

**VERBAL COORDINATION**   By verbal coordination we mean timing your words and actions so as to achieve the greatest reinforcement of your message. This includes rehearsed body action. A lack of verbal coordination can be quite humorous. Try saying "Uncle Sam needs *you,*" but instead of pointing on the word *you,* wait three seconds and then point!

# VOICE AND ARTICULATION (PARALANGUAGE)

Can we express emotions through the voice alone? You bet we can. Consider a piercing scream—"Help, murder, rape!" Even without the words we get the emotional message of *fear.* "YUCK, what a gruesome sight," we hear as someone observes the picture in Figure 8.8. *Disgust* is in the voice.

## Voice and Personality

What do you *hear?* Is it fear or disgust? The voice clearly expresses emotions. It is so effective at conveying attitudes that often we don't need the language. Aristotle said it plainly, "The art of delivery has to do with the

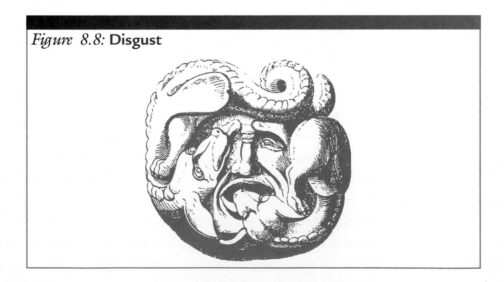

*Figure 8.8:* **Disgust**

voice." Tone, pitch, and inflection say it all. As a matter of fact, when the voice contradicts the words—"She said *NO,* but there was *YES* in her voice"—we tend to believe the voice. The voice is thought to be a harder signal to fake yet the old radio actors were great fakers. This suggests that voice has a lot to do with self-presentation, and that you can do something about it. As in pantomime, there are certain long-standing stereotypes that we take for granted in the use of the voice. We recognize certain radio roles as voice stereotypes: the mean character, the hero, the coward, and the dunce. The very great danger in using voice stereotypes is that one might take on an artificial voice permanently. Of course, we all occasionally fail to match the voice we "put on" with the situation in which we find ourselves. Listen to yourself on occasion. If you sound "arty" when talking about fertilizer, your voice habits may be altering your personality in ways that will seriously affect your communication.

The voice contributes much to the total communication signal. It may be the single most important code we use. Studies of voice and persuasion indicate the importance and the communication potential of this nonverbal code.[9] There is evidence that one's social status can be determined in large part by the signals we receive from the voice alone, apart from language. There is also evidence that Americans tend to downgrade a person who speaks with a foreign accent.

## Variable Characteristics of Voice

You have considerable control over certain characteristics of your voice. You can change your *rate* of speaking; you can adjust your *loudness* almost as you would that of a radio; you can speak at different *pitch* levels; you can alter the overtones or partial tones of your voice, which represent a kind of *quality* control often called *timbre* or *vocal color*. Along with *intonation* (sounding the vowels), these characteristics are the nonverbal signals that help a listener determine the structure and meaning of what you say. They are also known as vocal qualifiers.

**RATE**    Test passages have been devised for measuring verbal speed in wpm (words per minute). In general, a rate of more than 185 wpm is considered too rapid for a normal public speaking situation, and a rate of less than 140 wpm is considered too slow. A poor speaker is more apt to use short, abrupt speech consistently. Really slow talking young speakers may injure their impressions of competence.[10] Research also indicates that reasonably fast talkers were usually perceived as competent and socially attractive, particularly if their listeners were also known to have fast rates.[11] Unreasonably fast talkers across all contexts and audiences are another matter.

A further problem associated with verbal rate is that words are not really separately formed units but tend to flow from one sound to another; this affects both articulation and pronunciation. Take the phrase, "Did you eat?" If really speeded up, it becomes "Jeet?" This process is called *assimilation*. The length of sounds or tones is also a factor in verbal rate, as are pauses, phrasing, and general rhythm patterns.

The *duration* of sounds and words normally varies with our moods. We generally use tones of relatively short duration when expressing anger and more prolonged tones for expressing love.

Your use of *pauses* and phrases is a factor in your rate of speaking. A **phrase** is a group of words that forms a thought unit. **Pauses** occur between words and between phrases, and the number and duration of pauses seriously alter the meaning of what you say. The complexity and nature of your speech material should also affect your decisions regarding the use of phrases and pauses. The "*pregnant pause*" is no idle jest; it has much to do with our communication. If you were to use a long pause after a phrase for emphasis, fine, but if the phrase were relatively silly you might appear ridiculous. If you were to use long pauses in a random manner not related to meaning (not an uncommon error), you would then *confuse* your listener. Short pauses generally indicate that there is more to come. If you routinely use a rather intermediate-length pause without consistently relating it to what you are saying, you run the added danger of *monotony* a tiresome lack of variation.

Increasing our rates in normal conversation, alone, carries a message. In addition, our pitch goes up, articulation suffers, and pauses take on less significance or are lost altogether. It becomes, in large part, a question of self-presentation. If your fast rate is done rhetorically with full awareness of the *relationship* risks, that's one thing. If it's done simply as a bad habit, you risk that others may construe it as compensatory or tactless.

**LOUDNESS**    Loudness is a measure of the total signal. You may think of loudness generally as volume, but speech science indicates that volume is related so intimately to pitch that the term loudness may be misleading. Your volume is easier to increase as your pitch goes up. Furthermore, it is possible to speak with more force or intensity without altering your volume proportionately.

Extreme loudness has strong *relationship* ramifications for most people. We reserve it for emergencies or issues of great concern—and sometimes for conflicts that "get away from us." As Chief illustrates in Figure 8.9, loudness also expresses emotion.

There is another side to this loudness question. Sometimes we speak very softly. Among the psychological reasons for a lack of voice projection is a form of avoidance of the speech situation. People tend to *withdraw* from threatening situations. It is almost as if speaking with a soft, barely audible voice is the next best thing to not being in the situation at all. This may cause an audience to infer a lack of competence.[12]

Your receivers will help you adjust your loudness. Look at them for feedback signs. Are they straining to hear? Are they withdrawing?

Much of what we call *vocal variety* is related to loudness. The force with which you utter certain phrases or words is a form of oral punctuation and can add much to another's understanding of what you say. The manner in which you

*Figure 8.9:* **Loudness can express emotion**

apply force to what you say is also a factor in vocal variety. An audible whisper can be a powerful nonverbal as well as verbal emphasis in some interactions. Reducing volume can be just as effective as increasing it to make your point.

**PITCH**   We can pretty accurately determine sex and, to a point, age through pitch alone.[13] Normal pitch changes as we move from childhood to adolescence to adulthood, and these pitches are generally recognizable as belonging to the appropriate age groups.

Interestingly, men's voices reach their lowest pitch during middle age and then rise slightly with age. It appears that the same may not be true of women; pitch remains more constant during their adult years.

A drop in pitch at the end of a statement frequently indicates that a person is ready to yield the floor. If you are maintaining the floor in part through rapid rate, your pitch rises. When we speak, we use a variety of pitches that are normally distributed in terms of amount of usage. If we were to plot the number of occurrences of the different pitches we use, we would find a central pitch around which the others vary in relatively predictable amounts.

For most people, optimum pitch should be the habitual or central pitch. Often, our optimum pitch is found a little below the habitual or normally used pitch because of tensions that restrict the vocal apparatus.

**QUALITY**   Voice quality is a product of modification and modulation of the vocal-cord tone by the resonators. It is that attribute of tone and sound waves that enables us to distinguish between two sounds that are alike in pitch, duration, and loudness.

Other things being equal, we can easily distinguish the overly nasal, breathy, or harsh voice. In addition, we are able to make nonverbal distinctions of a much more subtle nature. For example, we recognize the voice of a person who is sincerely touched by a tribute or the voice of a person who is suppressing anger. Emotional moods affect voice quality and may have a profound effect upon emphasis and meaning. In this context, voice quality is often referred to as *timbre*.

Voice quality is considered faulty when an individual's voice contains consistent deviations that detract from the message or its meaning. Certain organic disorders, such as a cleft palate or nasal obstructions, can cause defects in voice quality. Emotional moods may also result in temporary deviations in voice quality. In addition, voice quality may be affected by the strictly temporary physical problems caused by head colds, sore throats, and the like.

An expert in voice and diction training once said, "Bluntly stated, one may have a dull, uninteresting, or unpleasant voice because his voice is defective or improperly used; but he may also have such a voice because he is a dull, uninteresting, or unpleasant person." Vocal training, like all speech training, cannot take place in a vacuum; rather it is intimately related to the whole personality. Just as personality affects voice, voice improvement may affect personality, or at least others' perceptions of one's personality.

Some have argued that former President Clinton had an advantage over Senator Dole on voice alone (when the President didn't lose his voice). One critic commented that no matter what Bob Dole said, it always sounded like a raucous, "Get off my grass." Good evidence indicates that when persuasion and social goals are in jeopardy, one's quality of speech rate and vocal intensity tend to be the first to suffer.[14]

## Articulation Control

The word *articulation* refers in general to a flexible fitting of things together. For example, the bones and cartilages in your elbow are said to articulate. The word is well suited to the action of the speech organs as they *interact* with one another and help join the various sound units into accepted patterns that we call speech.

**COMMON ARTICULATORY FAULTS**    Some of the more common mechanical causes of careless articulation are (1) locked jaw, (2) slack lips, and (3) muffled mouth.

The **locked jaw** problem is caused by a failure to open the mouth wide enough. The jaw is tight and seems locked in position. The speaker talks through his or her teeth and nose because the sound has to escape somehow. Projection is reduced; resonance is increased; vowel quality in particular is injured. This problem may be caused in part by tension and speech fright, but in any case the remedy is the same—unlock your jaw and open your mouth!

In the case of **slack lips** the lips are so loose that they do not adequately shape the mouth opening for proper vowel production or for proper articulation of the lip consonants (*p, b, m, w, f,* and *v*). The rule is simple: allow your lips to perform their necessary functions. In addition, an inability to see the speaker's lips move is frustrating to many listeners. Unless you are a ventriloquist, free your lips. Articulation, of course, can also suffer from very tight or tense lips.

The **muffled mouth** problem is caused principally by weak or slow tongue activity. Because the tongue is your most important organ of articulation, you may ruin a large part of your speech if you are guilty of this fault. The production of the fine shades of tone that distinguish the vowels from one another is endangered by a muffled mouth, since the tongue position decides in large part the shape and size of the oral cavity. Many consonants also depend upon vigorous and precise tongue action. A *th* sound (these) easily becomes a *d* sound (dese) if the tongue is lazy and does not move forward far enough to articulate with the teeth. Other consonants, such as *d, l, r,* and *s,* also call for vigorous and specific tongue action. Vigorous and firm articulation of your tongue with your teeth is your best safeguard against muffled quality.

## Pronunciation

**Pronunciation** is the act of expressing the sounds and accents of words so that they conform to accepted standards. In addition to aiding understanding, appropriate pronunciation influences how an audience judges a speaker. Adapting to the varying standards and groups to which you belong again points out the value of using two dialects. In old Milwaukee the word *theater* was typically pronounced "the-*ay*-ter," a compromised carryover from the German pronunciation of "das Theater" (tay-*ah*-ter). In Detroit we hear "thee-*uh*-ter." Some localities may say "drammer" for "drama."

The extremely valuable dictionary is sometimes ambiguous on some pronunciations because there are three generally accepted dialects in the United States (*eastern, southern,* and standard *American*). The most widespread dialect is standard American, and our dictionaries and national mass media are geared to this dialect. Sometimes the use of a second dialect has social and practical advantages.

The problem of showing on paper the desired or different pronunciations of a word is awkward at best. One way is to agree upon and memorize a common code of symbols based strictly upon sound, which is how the International Phonetic Alphabet was born. It has one symbol for every different sound in the language. The news services use a system of *respelling* similar to what was used for the word *theater* two paragraphs above. Dictionaries use *diacritical marks* and relatively stable words as bases of pronunciation. Accent or stress is indicated as primary or secondary . A guide to pronunciation and to the diacritical system used in dictionaries is carefully explained in the introduction to any good dictionary and is well worth reading. (See Table 8.1.)

*Table 8.1:* **Guide to Pronunciation**

| WORD | DIACRITICAL SYSTEM | INTERNATIONAL PHONETIC SYSTEM | RESPELLING SYSTEM |
|---|---|---|---|
| chaotic | /kā-ät-ik/ | [ke atik] | kay-otic |
| theater | / thē- ət- ər/ | [ θiətɚ] | thee-uh-ter |
| nativity | /nə- tiv- t-ē/ | [ne tivati] | nay-tiv-ity |

Some of the more common pronunciation errors are a result of improper stress, errors in spelling-phonetics (pronouncing words as they are spelled), sound substitutions, additions reversals, and subtractions.

# RELATED NONVERBAL BEHAVIORS

## Object Language (Clothes and Things)

In one clever study a young woman was dressed and made up attractively for one group of receivers and was then dressed and made up to look unattractive to a similar audience. The young woman was judged to be more believable and was generally found to be more persuasive and more desirable when presented attractively.[15]

The "times" and context make a difference; sometimes, casual dress works as well as more formal attire. At least it did in one study of student perceptions of their instructors.[16] Of course, if you're the only person without a coat at a formal party, you may not come off too well.

How we dress ourselves, what jewelry we wear, or tattoos we don are referred to as **artifacts**. Artifacts represent our culture, our beliefs, and our attitudes They also are associated with stereotypes. One circuit judge was so annoyed with a man who showed up for a court date wearing four gold chains, a gold charm, and six gold rings that he sentenced him to six months on an electronic tether. "It offended me, wearing all of that jewelry," said the judge.

Right or wrong, many stereotypes are associated with clothes and things. Research helps us define even these. People who wear bizarre clothes are considered more radical and activist. People who wear more conventional dress are associated with everyday jobs and "traditional fun."[17] The problem is in knowing what kind of clothes and things are conventional, in style, or expected of us. Not having this knowledge is a potential problem of *all* communication, whether nonverbal or verbal. The nonverbals of our artifacts make a big difference in the way we are seen totally—that is, socially, vocationally, sexually, and so on. The key word is *appropriate*. We usually do not wish to stand out in a crowd, yet we want to be fashionable and appropriate to what is expected of us at any given time or in any particular situation.

## Space and Distance (Proxemics)

Audience arrangement—the physical setting, seating, and so on as discussed in Chapter 4, "Audience Considerations"—are a large part of proxemics. So too is our vocal behavior. We use our voices differently according to distance, message, and mood. Figure 8.10 depicts various speech situations a person might encounter with a description of appropriate volume and style.

## Time (Chronemics)

Time is another element over which you have some control. Seldom are you in trouble for being early, but occasionally you may get in trouble for being late! A speaker who is ready for his or her presentation at the appropriate time, speaks within the given time parameters, and reveals regard for the time he or she is spending with the audience increases credibility.

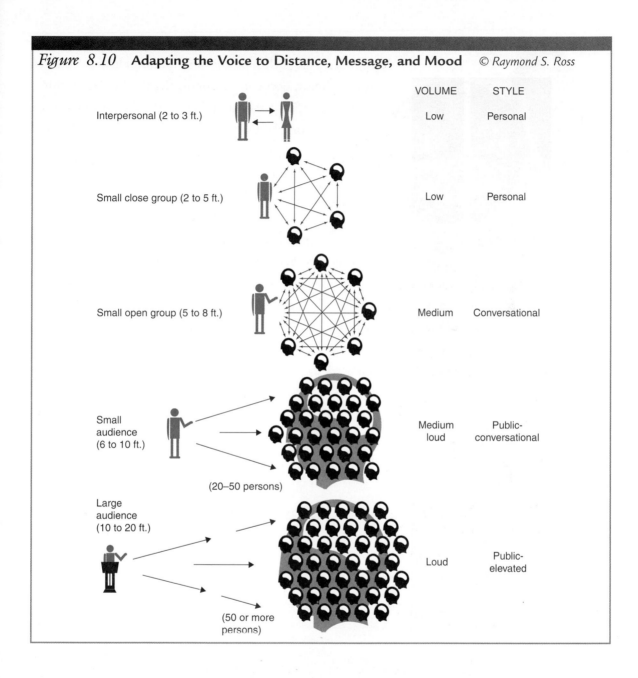

Figure 8.10    Adapting the Voice to Distance, Message, and Mood    © Raymond S. Ross

| | VOLUME | STYLE |
|---|---|---|
| Interpersonal (2 to 3 ft.) | Low | Personal |
| Small close group (2 to 5 ft.) | Low | Personal |
| Small open group (5 to 8 ft.) | Medium | Conversational |
| Small audience (6 to 10 ft.) (20–50 persons) | Medium loud | Public-conversational |
| Large audience (10 to 20 ft.) (50 or more persons) | Loud | Public-elevated |

One famous American general who had risen from the ranks claimed that one of the secrets of his success was always being fifteen minutes early for appointments. Almost every interview form includes an evaluation of the subject's dependability, which often translates into his or her attitude toward being on time. American culture tends to stress promptness and is considered a monochronic culture. In **monochronic** cultures, time is linear, occurring chronologically. We expect things to occur "in time" and "on time." Television viewers complain by the thousands when a scheduled program is delayed by a news special or a sports event that runs into overtime.

Lateness results in low regard for the sender, the situation, or the message. We can often save strained relations by giving good reason when we are late. Knowing when to stop talking is also a *time* consideration. In **polychronic** cultures, time is not seen as linear, but rather as occurring simultaneously. When visiting Costa Rica, friends of the family with whom one of the authors was staying indicated they would be over for cake and coffee in the afternoon. The host family explained that would be anytime after 12:00PM and before 6:00PM. Indeed, they arrived at 5:40PM.

# CHAPTER REVIEW
*Wrapping it up*

## Summary

A well-paced, moving delivery, maintenance of eye contact, and a clear, pleasant, well-articulated voice are associated with effective speaking. The four principal ways of delivering a speech are reading from a manuscript; memorization (Aristotle's fourth canon, often referred to as "the lost canon"); impromptu delivery; and speaking extemporaneously.

Our nonverbals may be conscious or unconscious and have five important characteristics: (1) They always communicate something. (2) They are bound to the situation. (3) They are believed. (4) They are seldom isolated. (5) They affect our relationships. We decide three important things about people largely on the basis of nonverbal communication: (1) personal liking or attraction, (2) evaluation of power relationships, and (3) the feelings of responsiveness we get from them. If the verbal and nonverbal messages are incongruent (contradictory), we are more likely to believe the nonverbal message.

Much unconscious body action accompanies most speeches, yet a lack of action often makes your message less clear. There is, therefore, no point in trying to restrain body action, and there are many good reasons for trying to understand it, control it, and use it.

Empathy, the projection of oneself into the situation of another, includes a muscular reaction; the audience imitates, in part, the actions of the speaker. Speakers should adapt their body action to the empathy of the audience. Constant pacing, for example, should be avoided, because it will probably wear out the audience before it does the speaker.

Prolonged restraint on the use of normal body action can result in emotional disintegration. We should use constructive body action to help control our speech fright as well as to communicate our message. The following are types of body action: posture, walking, facial expression, and gestures.

Check out our website
**www.bvtlab.com**
for flashcards,
summaries,
self-quizzes and speeches.

Posture is an important part of the general impression you make. It affects the empathy of the audience and what they conclude from your speech. Good posture and poise present a picture of cool unconcern. The great danger is in appearing artificial, overly noticeable, or out of place.

Walking is an important way to express various moods and degree of emphasis. It serves as a form of physical punctuation for the speaker. Walking also has empathic value; it can offer physical relief to a cramped or suffering audience.

Good facial expression includes the avoidance of unintentional or inappropriate facial stereotypes, eye contact with the audience, and natural and spontaneous expressions that will reinforce your message.

Some gestures are used to emphasize parts of the message. These are reinforcing gestures. Others are used to describe the shape or size of objects and are called descriptive gestures.

In general, speakers should be so involved in their subject and audience that their body action language will be both dynamic and spontaneous. It is evident that we communicate through many learned stereotypes of body action and that a speaker must use these stereotypes.

The standards of good body action include 1) appropriateness, 2) variety, 3) physical coordination, and 4) verbal coordination.

Paralanguage contributes much to your nonverbal signal and thus to your total communication signal; it may be the most important code you use. Voice and articulation are thought to be faulty when they deviate so far from the norm that they call too much attention to themselves. Some common problems of voice are fast rate, wrong pitch, improper level of loudness, and faulty articulation.

There are certain attributes of voice over which you have considerable control. These are rate, loudness, pitch, and quality. Rate is influenced by assimilation, duration, pauses, phrases, and rhythm. Loudness is a product of intensity, volume, and vocal variety. There are central, habitual, and optimum levels of pitch. Your pitch range includes all the pitches you can sing without a complete loss of quality. The most critical problems affecting quality are nasality, breathiness, and harshness.

Articulation is the interacting of the speech organs as they help join the various sound units into accepted patterns that we call speech. Your training of such organs as teeth, tongue, lips, palate, and jaw are of great importance to proper articulation. Some of the more common mechanical faults in articulation are locked jaw, slack lips, and muffled mouth.

Pronunciation is the act of expressing the sounds and accents of words so that they are best adapted to your total communication. There are three general dialects in the United States: eastern, southern, and standard American. Our mass media and dictionaries are geared to the standard

American dialect. The problem of showing different pronunciations in print is solved in part through pronouncing systems such as the International Phonetic Association alphabet, the re-spelling system, and the diacritical-mark system. Our dictionaries prefer the last of these.

Some of the more common pronunciation errors in the English language are improper stress, errors of spelling-phonetics, sound substitutions, sound additions, sound reversals, and sound subtractions.

Object language uses the influence and display of material things or artifacts. It includes the clothes you wear, jewelry, tattoos, cosmetics, and so forth that say something. The key to thinking about using artifacts is determining what is appropriate to the speaker, the subject, the occasion, and the audience.

Space and distance (proxemics) are the personal space or territory we deem acceptable. Our preferences are culture-bound. Space and distance are closely related to the message, situation, and mood. We adapt our voices in rather set ways to these aspects.

Time as a nonverbal varies with cultures and situations. In our monochronic cultures, such as the United States, promptness is stressed. Lateness results in low regard for the sender, the situation, or the message. In polychronic cultures, like Costa Rica, they are more forgiving of lateness, as time is not viewed in terms of linearity, but rather simultaneously occurring events.

# *Notes*

1.  For a fuller treatment of nonverbal communication see: Judee K. Burgoon, David B. Buller, W. Gill Woodall, *Nonverbal Communication: The Unspoken Dialogue* (New York: Harper & Row, 1989); Mark Knapp, "Nonverbal Communication," in *Human Communication: Theory and Research,* eds., Gordon L. Dahnke and Glen W. Clatterbuck (Belmont, California: Wadsworth, 1990), pp. 50–90.

2.  Jerold L. Hale and James B. Stiff, "Nonverbal Primacy in Veracity Judgments," *Communication Reports,* 3, no. 2 (Summer 1990), 75–83.

3.  See especially Lawrence A. Hosman, "The Evaluative Consequences of Hedges, Hesitations, and Intensifiers: Powerful and Powerless Speech Styles," *Human Communication Research,* 15, no. 3 (Spring 1989), 383–406.

4.  Jim Bishop, *A Day in the Life of President Kennedy* (New York: Random House, 1964), p. 35.

5.  Gerald Gardner, *Speech Is Golden* (New York: St. Martin's Press, 1992), p. 107.

6.  Paul Ekman and Wallace B. Friesen, *Unmasking the face,* 2nd ed. (Englewood Cliffs, N.J.: Prentice Hall, 1984), pp. 22–25; also see Paul Ekman, "Facial Expression and Emotion," *American Psychologist,* 48, no. 4 (April 1993), 384–92.

7.  See Catherine A. Lutz, *Unnatural Emotions: Everyday Sentiments on a Micronesian Atoll and Their Challenge to Western Theory* (Chicago: Chicago University Press, 1988). For more on this debate, see Alan J. Fridlund and Ross Buck, "Reviews and Comments," *Communication Theory,* 5, no. 4 (November 1995), 393–401.

8.  Michael T. Motley, "Facial Affect and Verbal Context in Conversation: Facial Expression as Interjection," *Human Communication Research,* 17, no. 1 (Fall 1990), 140–69. See also Stanford Gregory and Stephen Webster, "A Nonverbal Signal in the Voices of Interview Partners Effectively Predicts Communication Accommodation and Social Status Perceptions," *Journal of Personality and Social Psychology,* 70, no. 6 (June 1996), 1231–40.

9.  Judee K. Burgoon, Thomas Birk, Miachael Pfau, "Nonverbal Behaviors, Persuasion, and Credibility," *Human Communication Research,* 17 no. 1 (Fall 1990), 140-69. See also Stanford Gregory and Stephen Webster, "A Nonverbal Signal in the Voices of Interview Partners Effectively Predicts Communication Accommodation and Social Status Perceptions," *Journal of Personality and Social Psychology,* 70, no. 6 (June 1996), 1231-40.

10.  Howard Giles, Karen Henwood, Nikolas Coupland, Jim Harriman, and Justine Coupland, "Language Attitudes and Cognitive Mediation," *Human Communication Research,* 18, no. 4 (June 1992), 500–27.

11.  David B. Buller, Beth A. LePoire, R. Kelly Aune, and Sylvie V. Elvoy, "Social Perceptions as Mediators of the Effect of Speech Rate Similarity on Compliance," *Human Communication Research,* 19, no. 2 (December 1992), 286–311.

12.  Charles E. Kimble and Steven D. Seidel, "Vocal Signs of Confidence," *Journal of Nonverbal Behavior,* 15, no. 2 (Summer 1991), 99–105.

13.  N. J. Lass, K. R. Huges, M. D. Bowyer, L. T. Waters, and V. T. Broune, "Speaker Sex Identification from Voiced, Whispered and Filtered Isolated Vowels," *Journal of the Acoustical Society of America,* 59 (1976), 675–78.

14.  Charles R. Berger, Steven W. Knowlton, and Matthew E. Abrahams, "The Hierarchy Principle in Strategic Communication," *Communication Theory,* 6, no. 2 (May 1996), 111–42.

15.  William I. Gorden, Craig D. Tengler, and Dominic A. Infante, "Women's Clothing Predispositions as Predictors of Dress at Work, Job Satisfaction, and Career Advancement," *Southern Speech Communication Journal,* 47 (Summer 1982), 422–34.

16.  T. L. Morris, J. Gorham, S. H. Cohen, and D. Huffman, "Fashion in the Classroom: Effects of Attire on Student Perceptions of Instructors in College Classes," *Communication Education,* 45, no. 2 (April 1996), 135–48.

17.  For more on these matters, see Mark L. Knapp and Judith A. Hall, *Nonverbal Communication in Human Interaction,* 4th ed. (Fort Worth, Texas: HJB College Publishers, 1997).

# USING VISUAL AIDS

# Chapter 9

## Chapter Objectives

### Classifying Visual Aids

Functional Levels of Visual Aids

Selecting the General Level

### Representational Aids

Graphics

Practical Rules

Making Transparency Graphics

Computer-Technology

### Demonstrations

### Experiential Presentations

### Using Electronic Assistance

Overhead Projection

As we learned earlier, visual aids can enhance feelings of self-confidence, protect your memory, increase audience interest and attention, and generally improve the content and quality of your performance—all of which lead to greater credibility.[1] The *thinking about* and *preparation* of the aid may be more valuable than the aid itself. The goal of this chapter is to aid speakers in achieving highly successful presentations and in avoiding common pitfalls when using visual aids.

# CLASSIFYING VISUAL AIDS

## Functional Levels of Visual Aids

There are three functional levels of visual aids: the **experiential** level, the **demonstrational** level, and the **representational** level. The **experiential level** of visual aids provides a forum for the audience to directly experience some element of the message. A student of yoga who explains to the class how to do particular yoga poses by having each member of the audience do the poses with her is providing real-life or hands-on experience. This concrete teaching method utilizes participation to make the subject clearer and more interesting. Had the yoga student shown the class the series of poses, she would be demonstrating instead of having the class experiencing the poses. The **demonstrational level** is a show and tell level of visual aids. Had she simply used a picture that depicted the different yoga poses, while explaining them, she would be employing the **representational level** of visual aids.

Figure 9.1 describes these levels in terms of function and degree of audience involvement. The most concrete level is learning by *experience,* that is, actually participating in an activity as described above. In the first picture, the students are learning the upward dog pose experientially. The woman in the second picture is showing the upward dog pose, explaining how it is done. This functional level of *demonstration* is less concrete (more abstract) for the audience than had they participated. The third picture is a characteristic drawing that represents what upward dog looks like. Visual aids that *represent* something (like pictures, pie charts, or graphs) are the most abstract of the three levels and also the most popular for classroom speeches, usually due to time parameters. It is possible and, time permitting, often advisable to use two or more of the levels to reinforce one another.

*Figure 9.1*  **Functional Levels of Visual Aids**

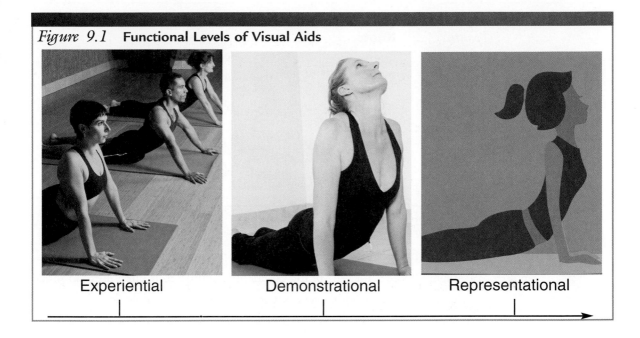

Experiential          Demonstrational          Representational

Most visual aids are used to clarify, build interest, reinforce, and sometimes help sell your message. On all counts they are valuable to the speaker although they are not without some hazards and problems. Knowledge of the types of aid available—and the function for which each kind of aid is best suited—helps one determine what to use in a given situation.

Effective visual aids at any level are simple, relevant, and reinforce the content of the speech. The mere presence of visual aids in a speech does not make a speech better, however. Deliberate consideration and planning are required to effectively incorporate visual aids into a speech. The best visual aids are only as good as the presenter is at transitioning between and within the visual aids while delivering the speech.

## Selecting the General Level

When making a speech, you are not restricted to just one classification level of visual aids. For instance, the yoga student had the class practicing a pose on an *experiential* level, while her showing the pose was on the *demonstrational* level. A simple graphic of the pose on an overhead would suffice as clear at the *representational* level (see Figure 9.2).

*Figure 9.2*   **Knots**

If your speech topic lends itself to audience participation of even a limited kind, you might choose some part of the experiential approach. It often uses too much time in a short classroom speech; but it can work, for example, in a knot-tying demonstration (pass out a length of rope for everyone). We will talk later about the pitfalls of passing visual aids around the classroom during your speech.

Your topic will direct your decision making if you're considering a demonstration speech. Some topics lend themselves to "show and tell" better than others, such as "Basic Tennis Shots," "Dance Steps," "Folding a Flag," and so on. Others are awkward or impossible because of space, ventilation, or rules. The flag-burning speech in a Pennsylvania classroom survived the legal system, but not the fire marshal.

The *representational* type of visual aids—graphs, charts, flat pictures—fit most topical areas but not all. Eulogies, if conducted with great ritual, may call for representational decoration, music, or perhaps a picture, but rarely a diagram on a flip chart.

It is important to consider the occasion as well as the size of your audience and its expectations in planning your visual aids. Physical arrangements play a large part in your decision to use visual aids. A large audience may not be the best for the *experiential* choice. An audience distanced from the podium may not always be conducive to a demonstration. The lighting, wiring, or ceiling height may not permit some electronic visual aids.

Select your general function and level of visual aids in terms of your topic, your specific purpose, the occasion, physical arrangements, and your audience analysis. In the following sections, we will discuss the types and practicalities

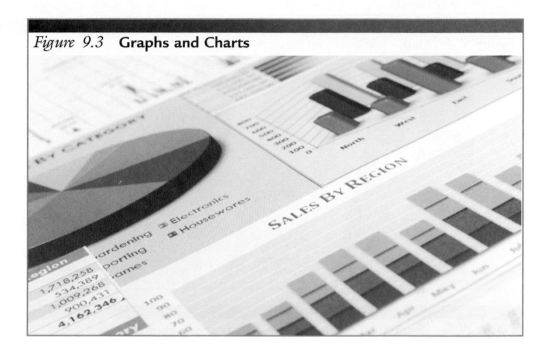

*Figure 9.3*    **Graphs and Charts**

of each functional level. Since most classroom speeches use representational aids, we will start there at the most abstract level, move through demonstrational level, end at the most concrete level–experiential.

# REPRESENTATIONAL AIDS

These visual aids represent something—a process, some information, an object—in graphic form, occasionally as a three-dimensional model. Standard graphics include charts, tables, maps, drawings, and photographs that are displayed on posters, flip charts, slides, or within computer presentation software.

## Graphics

Samples of graphics that a speaker might use are shown in Figures 9.4 to 9.10.

## Practical Rules

Your instructor may prefer that you not use the chalkboard as a primary aid. Information on the board may be erased or smudged; preparing and protecting

*Figure 9.4*   **Map**    Predictions on the earth's shifting crust

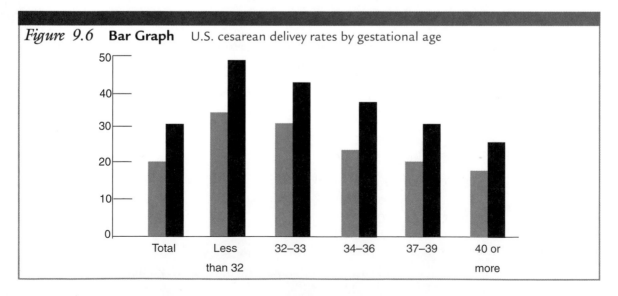

Wash.
Ore.
Calif.
Nev.
San Francisco
San Andreas Fault
Los Angeles
San Diego
Ariz.
Mex.
Pacific Ocean
**Present**

10 million years

20 million years

50 million years

*Figure 9.5*   **Pictogram**    Great Lakes ore carriers: the new and the old

Typical Great Lakes carrier: 620 feet long, 60 feet wide, carries 16,000 tons of cargo
New ore carrier: 1,000 feet long, 105 feet wide, carries 55,000 tons of cargo

*Figure 9.6*   **Bar Graph**    U.S. cesarean delivery rates by gestational age

| | Total | Less than 32 | 32–33 | 34–36 | 37–39 | 40 or more |
|---|---|---|---|---|---|---|

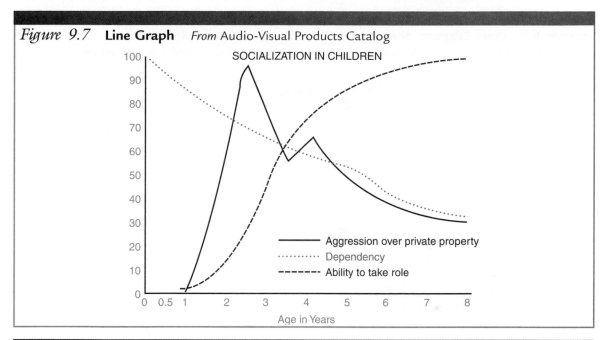

*Figure 9.7*  **Line Graph**    *From* Audio-Visual Products Catalog

SOCIALIZATION IN CHILDREN

——— Aggression over private property
·········· Dependency
– – – – Ability to take role

Age in Years

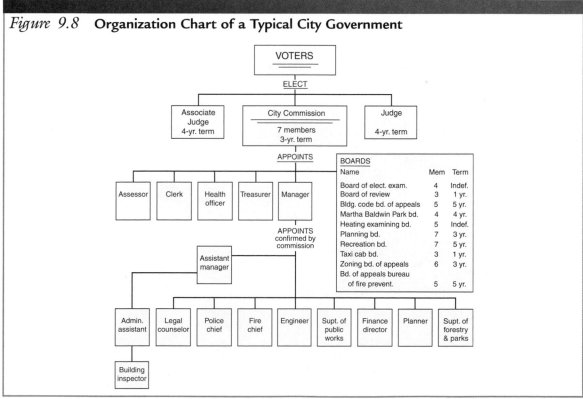

*Figure 9.8*    **Organization Chart of a Typical City Government**

VOTERS

ELECT

Associate Judge
4-yr. term

City Commission
7 members
3-yr. term

Judge
4-yr. term

APPOINTS

Assessor

Clerk

Health officer

Treasurer

Manager

| BOARDS | | |
| --- | --- | --- |
| Name | Mem | Term |
| Board of elect. exam. | 4 | Indef. |
| Board of review | 3 | 1 yr. |
| Bldg. code bd. of appeals | 5 | 5 yr. |
| Martha Baldwin Park bd. | 4 | 4 yr. |
| Heating examining bd. | 5 | Indef. |
| Planning bd. | 7 | 3 yr. |
| Recreation bd. | 7 | 5 yr. |
| Taxi cab bd. | 3 | 1 yr. |
| Zoning bd. of appeals | 6 | 3 yr. |
| Bd. of appeals bureau of fire prevent. | 5 | 5 yr. |

APPOINTS
confirmed by
commission

Assistant manager

Admin. assistant

Legal counselor

Police chief

Fire chief

Engineer

Supt. of public works

Finance director

Planner

Supt. of forestry & parks

Building inspector

**Figure 9.9    Area Diagram Showing the Four Zones of Earth's Interior**

*Special permission granted by* My Weekly Reader, *no. 5. Published by Xerox Publications.*

© *Xerox Corporation*

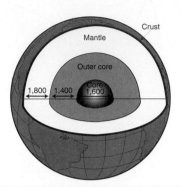

**Figure 9.10    Stream or Tree Chart Representing Plant Life on the Left Side and Animal Life on the Right**

*From Trumon J. Moon, Paul B. Mann, and James H. Otto,* Modern Biology *(New York: Henry Holt and Company). Reproduced by special permission of Holt, Rinehart & Winston.*

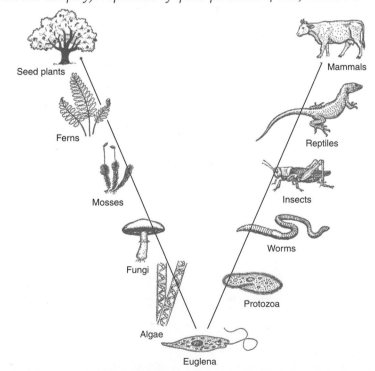

your chalk graphics in advance is difficult. There is also the tendency for you to turn your back to the audience.

## PREPARING GRAPHICS

1.    Start early, rough draft your artwork, and coordinate it with your outline.

2.    Label only the significant parts. Restrict details.

    a.    One point or relationship per visual

    b.    Maximum of six words per line

    c.    Maximum of six lines per visual[2]

3.    Make a visual aid readily visible. Is it big enough? Are the lines heavy and dark enough (one-eighth to one-half inch thick)?

4.    Practice with your final version.

## USING PREPARED GRAPHICS

1.    Display them where all members of your audience can see them.

2.    Display them only when they are relevant.

3.    Face and talk to the audience. Make sure to stand to the side of your visual aid and turn your head toward your visual only to signal the audience to look at it.

4.    Orient your audience. For example, "This is a top view."

5.    Arrive early and check the display area.

Today, many exciting and effective graphics are possible thanks to electronic copiers and computer-generated graphics packages.

**COMPUTER-GENERATED GRAPHICS**    If you do not have a personal computer with graphics capability, most libraries, student computer labs, and campus bookstores do. Graphics created on a computer are far more professional than ones designed by hand before class and can be printed at home and enlarged at a printing lab, usually for a nominal fee. Many classrooms are now equipped

*Figure 9.11*　**Face and Talk to Audience**

with large screen projectors which allow your graphics to go directly from your laptop to a screen or a TV monitor. If you do have such technology available, take care that the medium doesn't become more important than your message. We'll have more to say about computers in the "Computer Technology" section.

## DEMONSTRATIONS

Demonstrations don't always work as planned. A student once demonstrated a tear-gas pencil in an overheated, poorly ventilated classroom with the temperature outside about zero. Talk about audience involvement! Another student, demonstrating the toughness of unbreakable, bulletproof glass, dropped it on a concrete floor. It did not break—it exploded—producing one badly shaken speaker! (A glass company spokesman informed us later that the chances of the angle of impact, the temperature, the force, and other factors being perfectly co-ordinated—which caused the shattering—were about one in ten thousand.)

The obvious questions are "What can I do to reduce the probability of things going wrong?" and "If something does go wrong in spite of careful planning, what do I do at that moment of truth?"

The answer to the first question is careful *planning*. Plan exactly *how* you will perform the demonstration. Make sure you have all your equipment and have it in the right sequence. Be sure the demonstration *works* in your practice sessions. Emphasize safety precautions. Check for conditions that may vary from the practice session (for example, electric current). Finally, be sure you can do the demonstration. A flight instructor was teaching cadets the principles of airfoil and how an airplane develops lift. To demonstrate, he put a piece of paper between his lower lip and his chin. He then blew over it, creating a partial vacuum on top of the paper, which caused the paper to lift.

A new instructor who had observed this demonstration rushed to the next class with no time for practice. Confident that he could do it, he proceeded to blow—with no movement from the paper and with an audience of well-disciplined cadets trying not to explode with laughter. There are some moments when defeat is very evident.

The answer to the second question, "What if it goes wrong anyway?" is again to be found in planning. More specifically, calculate the extent and nature of the risk and then plan emergency alternative procedures for every disaster you can think of. This is a must. You have no time to change your plans when something does go wrong, and the shock and confusion may cause you to react emotionally rather than rationally.

The student with the "unbreakable" glass had a calculated risk of one in ten thousand. You can hardly blame him for not being thorough in planning alternate procedures. Those are probably better odds than a pedestrian has on the Los Angeles Freeway. Nevertheless, this student could have had two pieces of glass, just as you should always have two bulbs for your slide or movie projector.

Extra equipment or spare parts are only part of the answer. The real problem is what you will say. Plan your communication strategy very carefully. *When and if the glass breaks I will say, "The odds on that happening were one in ten thousand. Let me prove it by beating the next piece of glass with this hammer."* If the next piece breaks, you may have to resort to an alternate plan using prayer. You can't win them all!

*Figure 9.12*    **Principles of Airfoil**

Lift

The value of demonstration is that the audience can see and hear your explanation. It appeals to several senses, reinforces your message, saves time, has dramatic appeal, and is more concrete than just telling. Demonstration also helps speakers remember their material.

## EXPERIENTIAL PRESENTATIONS

At this level your audience actually participates, whether it is handling an object, working through a process, or acting out a dramatic presentation in role-playing. These presentations are a must for professional trainers and teachers. They are the most concrete but also the most difficult. You probably will not often use the experiential level in your speech class because of the time, cost, difficulty, surprise, and confusion inherent in most audience participation. Your advanced courses may be smaller in size and therefore more amenable to this level of presentation. Any time the audience is asked to physically participate, their focus turns from your message to their personal involvement and all of the judgments that accompany their involvement. Therefore, more time is needed to bring the audience back to the message at hand, connecting the experience and the message.

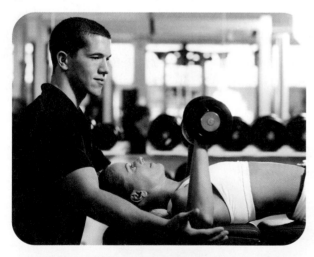

At the Experiential level, your audience actually participates. The audience may work through a process, such as a client would with a personal trainer.

## USING ELECTRONIC ASSISTANCE

The title of this section refers to the use of overhead projectors, computers, computer presentation software including PowerPoint® and Key Note®, and Internet presentations. Certainly, one can also use an excerpt from a video or a DVD to exemplify a particular point. Some beginning speechmaking classes may limit the use of electronic equipment because it involves a complex overload of learning objectives. A speech with simple graphics is challenge enough for most of us. The problems of darkened rooms, visuals that replace the speaker, and the inevitable equipment problems abound. Of all of the electronic options, the overhead projector is by far the least complex and most amenable to public speaking.

## Overhead Projection

One advantage of using an overhead projector is that it is positioned at the front of a lighted room, allowing the speaker to face the audience and still *see* the visual aid by simply looking down at the transparency. If the physical arrangement is set up properly, every audience member has an unobstructed view of the screen. You will notice in figure 9.13 that the best set-up for the screen is the corner of the room. Although this is not what you will find in all classrooms, it is what you should strive for when projecting your visual aid.

If you are considering putting your graphics on overhead transparencies (slides), be sure to check with your instructor first. Although there are a growing number of schools that require an "overhead-projector" speech, many are still restricted by time, cost, equipment, and policy.

Some other advantages you should know about for the world beyond this course include the following:

1. Whatever you can do with charts, you can also do with transparencies and an overhead projector.

   > *Audiovisuals are not intended to be your presentation. They're intended to support it.*
   > **Lani Arrendondo,**
   > **Corporate trainer**

2. An overhead projector poses little likelihood of a mechanical failure. There is a much greater possibility of mechanical failure or operator problems with other, more complicated equipment.

3. The overhead projector can be easily turned on and off, directing the attention of the audience from the screen back to the speaker.

4. Material can be revealed point by point (a technique known as "revelation"), so that attention is fixed and participants cannot read ahead.

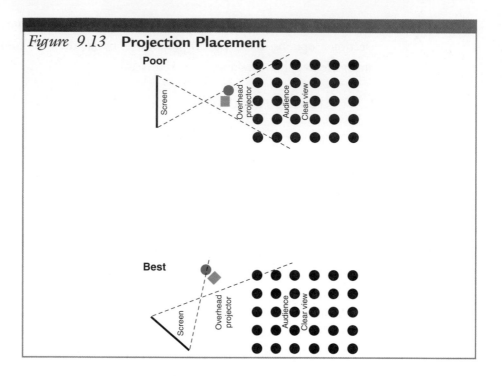

Figure 9.13   **Projection Placement**

5.    The overhead projector does not require expensive and time-consuming technical processing or knowledge.

## Making Transparency Graphics

The single factor maintaining the popularity of overhead projectors is that transparencies can be made easily, quickly, and inexpensively. Transparencies are celluloid sheets onto which you can directly print using your home printer or onto which you can copy using a copier. It is imperative that you use the correct transparency slide for the printer or copier you have, or you run the risk of damaging your equipment.

If you have access to a personal computer and the right software, you can generate graphics and then convert them into transparencies for an overhead projector. Computer-generated graphics can also be made poster size if you have a photocopy machine with this capability. A PosterPrinter is now available which will create in seconds a presentation poster or flip chart page up to eight times the original size, in your choice of seven color combinations. Printing labs can also assist you in creating presentational materials.

Using computer presentation programs (such as PowerPoint®), DVD or film clips, and using overhead projectors, can greatly enhance the delivery of your speech. However, there are some drawbacks that may deter students from relying on technology to present their visual aids.

## Computer-Technology

Technology now provides the flexibility of preparing visual aids on a computer, at home or in the library, and downloading the work to a CD or a USB jump-drive. The CD or jump-drive can then be used on laptops or classroom computers, which are connected to projection devices that project images to a screen. One can then "mouse" excerpts for dramatic illustrations, incorporating everything from pictures to sound bites and music. In many colleges and universities, standard classroom equipment now includes a computer, a projection unit for digital-visual presentation equipment, video players, DVD players, and an Internet connection with display and sound. A student can now access real-time Internet examples for his or her speech. In some classrooms, the ever reliable overhead projector is no longer available, and digital-visual presentation equipment has taken its place. Make sure to know what equipment is available in your classroom and practice using it *before* giving your speech.

Over the last twenty years personal computers have become powerful communication tools. The bar has been raised in terms of expectations for professional presentations and visual aids. A speaker's credibility can be enhanced or diminished based on the quality of his or her visual aids. Software tools give anyone the ability to create professionally looking visual aids, but ability does not necessarily translate into results. When designing your visual aid, some suggestions to enhance the professional appearance include choosing the right art and avoiding the overuse of animation.

**STOCK-PHOTOGRAPHY VS. CLIP-ART**    Early software programs for creating visual aids had limited graphic capacity—and thus the "rise of bullet points." With the introduction of clip-art for desktop publishing and presentation software, individuals were able to insert images, yet these images were mostly cartoon-like in nature. They were often unprofessional and overused. Over the years, the quality of the clip art has improved; however, the tendency to overuse images, in general, has not changed. If you choose to use images, there are several free and commercial websites for obtaining quality professional images to use in a presentation (see Additional Resources at the end of this chapter). The use of such images increases the professional appearance and visual impact of the presentation.

**MOTION AND ANIMATION EFFECTS**    Computer-presentation software also provides the ability for transition effects and animations. Purposeful animation and transitions can be quite effective if used in moderation. Yet, of all the tools in these software programs, animation is probably the most misused. In 2000, General Sheldon, chairman of the Joint Chiefs of Staff, issued an unusual order to U.S. military to avoid "Venetian-blind effects or fancy backdrops."[3] The general was concerned that Pentagon presenters were focusing too much on style rather than on substance. His concern is still relevant, as many presentations contain useless transition effects and animations.

In the words of one high-tech corporate trainer:

> *The success of your presentation doesn't lie solely in projecting whiz-bang graphics. It still lies primarily in your relational skills—in how well you relate, and relate your message to people.*[4]
>
> **Lani Arrendondo**

# CHAPTER REVIEW
## Wrapping it up

## Summary

Visual aids are used to help make a subject clearer, to build interest, and to reinforce a message. These aids can be classified in terms of functional level as *representational, demonstrational,* and *experiential.* Representational is the most abstract and uses visual symbolization in the form of graphics and pictures. Demonstrational can be described as "show and tell"; experiential as audience participation or "doing." Select the functional level of your aids in terms of topic, purpose, occasion, physical arrangement, and audience analysis.

Representational aids *represent* something typically in graphic form or occasionally as a model. Standard graphics include the following: pictures, drawings, charts, maps, diagrams, and bar graphs that are displayed on a poster or flip-chart or computer screen.

The following are rules for using prepared graphics include: 1) Don't obstruct. 2) Let them reinforce not distract. 3) Talk to the audience not the chart. 4) Orient your audience to the chart. Rules for preparing charts include 1) relate them to the topic, 2) make sure they are visible, 3) keep them simple and uncluttered, and 4) organize the aid so it helps your memory.

A demonstration speech combines showing with telling. Its purpose is to show how a skill, procedure, process, or device is used. Demonstration appeals to several senses. It reinforces, saves time, and has dramatic appeal. Plan carefully, make sure you can do it, calculate the risks of things going wrong, and plan alternate procedures.

You are least likely to use visual aids at the *experiential* level because of time, cost, surprise, and confusion inherent in audience participation.

Graphics can be computer-generated. Some classrooms are equipped to project your graphics directly from your laptop computer or are designed for CDs, DVDs, and USB jump-drives.

Overhead projectors are advantageous because they allow for fully lit classrooms, speaker visibility, and are less complicated than other aids. Digital-visual presentation equipment, however, is making stand-alone overhead projectors obsolete in some schools.

Thanks to photocopy machines, transparencies for overhead projectors or digital-visual presentation equipment are simple to make and can replace the larger charts and graphs. They allow a speaker to face the audience and still see the visual aid. They also allow material to be revealed point by point, and are relatively inexpensive.

Presentational software, including PowerPoint® and Key Note®, can be a wonderful tool if used judiciously. Cartoon-like clip-art, an abundance of images, and overused animation can hinder a presentation by reducing its professionalism and losing the message.

## Notes

1. See Kent E. Menzel and Lori J. Carrell, "The Relationship between Preparation and Performance in Public Speaking," *Communication Education,* 43, no. 2 (January 1994), 17–26.
2. The 3M Meeting Management Team, *Mastering Meetings* (New York: McGraw-Hill Inc., 1994), p. 142.
3. Greg Jaffe, "What's Your Point Lieutenant? Please Cut to the Pie Charts," *Wall Street Journal,* (April 26, 2000). P. 1.
4. Lani Arrendondo, *How to Present Like a Pro* (New York: McGraw-Hill, Inc., 1991), p. 101.

## Additional Resources

1. iStockPhoto (www.istockphoto.com)
2. Microsoft Office Clipart (office.microsoft.com/clipart/)
3. slideshare (www.slideshare.com)

SPEECHES TO INFORM

# Chapter 10

## Chapter Objectives

# TYPES OF INFORMATIVE SPEECHES

You're asked to give a *class report* on "Systems Theory" for your management course. As a student teacher you must *lecture* on "Attribution Theory." You're called upon to give a *book* or *play review* for the Little Theater group. You're required to make a *committee report* to your fraternity or sorority. You're *instructing* Boy or Girl Scouts on the merit badge in ornithology. You're reporting and *explaining* the results of your physics class experiment. You're *demonstrating* aerobic exercise in your speech class. You're making *announcements* at the local 4-H club. We can report on places where we've been, things we've done, people we've met, and so on. We can instruct and/or demonstrate about everything from dancing and tennis to cooking and magical sleight of hand. We can explain the rationale behind hypnosis, cult behavior, or other concepts from existentialism to Keynesian economics. All these and more are speaking situations where the primary purpose is to inform. The most frequent of these are *reporting, instructing,* and *explaining.* An informative speech may use parts of all of these types.

## Reporting

Reporting, instructing, and explaining are forms of speaking situations where the primary purpose is to inform. An informative speech may use parts of all of these types. Instructing about preparing and cooking a meal would be considered an informative speech.

When reporting, one is giving an account or description of events, places, special objects, interesting people, and the like. If you are reporting specifically on the "United Nations Building Floor Plan," you will probably use mostly a spatial order to organize your speech. If you are talking about the "History of the United Nations Building," you will probably use a chronological order. Note how your organizational options change as your specific purpose sharpens. The various, organizational-order options were discussed in Chapter 6, "Organizing the Speech."

- Chronological order
- Difficulty order
- Spatial order

- Logical order

- Topical order

# Instructing

Although all informative presentations involve some instruction and explanation, our efforts here concentrate on having our audience learn about and/or understand a process, or perhaps "how to" actually perform a process or special set of actions. In addition, the helpful suggestions on demonstration speeches given in Chapter 9, "Using Visual Aids," are reviewed here:

1. Plan it very carefully.

2. Try it. Make sure it works.

3. Check the facilities: power, light, space, and so forth.

4. Calculate the risks.

5. Plan alternative procedures.

Topics are usually concrete and can range from "How to Program a VCR" to "How to Prepare for a Job Interview." The chronological order fits most of these speeches.

# Explaining

In this case, we explain ideas and concepts that are more abstract such as theories of persuasion, principles of navigation, transcendental meditation, hermetic philosophy, aesthetics, and so forth by providing concrete examples, descriptions and familiar experiences to connect to the abstract ideas. Restrict your speech purpose and central idea in this type of information sharing. One theory of persuasion is very adequate for a short speech. "Shooting an Azimuth" may be enough for navigation. "Modernistic Art" is probably more than enough for aesthetics. The topical order, with considerable definition of the main elements, is primary in this kind of explaining.

Your problems with informative speeches are similar to those a teacher confronts: meaty and intellectual, but not over people's heads; factual but not too technical; theoretical but not obtuse; objective and accurate, but not dull and tedious.

In the business world this is frequently called presentational speaking. How to organize such speeches or presentations and how to make them clear and interesting are primary objectives of this chapter. Visual aids can be of immense help so you may wish to reread Chapter 9. Because learning is involved, let's start there.

# LEARNING PRINCIPLES

Not all students and audiences are eagerly waiting to hear what you have to say, however Most need to hear some reason whether it is exploring personal growth and development, making money, saving effort, or simply satisfying curiosity. In short, you first need to explain why someone should listen to your topic. Remember audiences are egocentric: they want to know how the information pertains to and affects them. Geometry seemed stupid to Dr. Ross until the teacher pointed out that it could be used to plot navigation courses for his Power Squadron boating course. Leonard, on the other hand, found geometry to be effective in honing her pool table skills. Trigonometry was really dull for Dr. Ross until he relearned it in artillery school. Environmentalists were far-out until he visited Los Angeles during the smog season and found he couldn't eat the fish in Lake St. Clair. Yet, Leonard's mother was recycling before the environmentalist movement coined the term, so environmentalists weren't as far-out as they were "behind-the-times."

Presenting information is the most common speech purpose. In a sense, you are a teacher. You must motivate your audience to listen. You must present your material not only in a clear and interesting way but also in a way that makes it easy for your audience to learn, remember, and apply the information.

## From the Known to the Unknown

In Chapter 1 we learned that people understand a message primarily by applying their previous experience and knowledge to it. It follows that teachers or speakers must select and arrange their material so that they best utilize the knowledge and experience the audience already have. The rule might be stated as follows: *Go from the known to the unknown.* For example, in trying to explain the relationship between wire size and electric current, a speaker compared the wire size to a garden hose (known) and the excess strain put upon the hose when someone restricts the opening with the nozzle. The listeners, having probably once burst a garden hose by turning the nozzle off, understood this explanation. It was clear, interesting, and easy to apply. Similarly, assuming that everybody knows the size of an English sparrow, a robin, and a crow, bird watchers typically relate the size of all unknown or unidentified birds to one of these three. This simple relating of known to unknown has made the communicating and sharing of much information far less frustrating for serious bird watchers.

## Serial Learning

People tend to learn more readily when things are arranged in some sequence or serial order, especially when they are aware of the order. We teach youngsters addition and subtraction before multiplication and division; we could start with algebra, but we have found that it is more efficient to use a sequence based on difficulty. In history courses we often use a chronological order, but a sequence based on social issues might also be used.

The previous knowledge of the audience, the difficulty of the subject, and the specific information the speaker is presenting determine the particular order of the material to be learned. The audience is said to be learning serially when it is able to connect each portion of the sequence to the one immediately following it. In learning to drive a car, you must learn a great many details, but you have not really learned to drive until you have connected clutching, braking, steering, and other operations in such a way that one action is followed automatically by the next appropriate action.

## Reinforcement and Emphasis

Perhaps in an education or psychology course you have heard the expression **SRX.** In discussing the subject of learning, theorists use S to stand for **stimulus,** R for **response**, and X for **reinforcement.** This X may be a reward for responding in the desired way, a punishment for incorrect behavior, some form of known association, or perhaps some form of repetition. The teacher that feeds back criticism with a smile, a frown, or a high or low grade practices reinforcement. The drill sergeant with a loud, booming voice is also practicing reinforcement. The enhancement of a desired response is an application of reinforcement whether it is by repetition, loud voice, or some other form of emphasis.

In the term *SRX*, *X* represents reinforcement. This *X* may be a reward or punishment for behavior that is desired or discouraged behavior. A drill sergeant with a loud, booming voice is emphatically practicing reinforcement.

In an experiment, a fifteen-minute informative speech was given to student audiences in a relatively neutral or emphasis-free mode. Then experimental speeches, each loaded with various amounts of repetition and verbal emphasis, were given to similar audiences. Retention of material was significantly better when the following reinforcers were used.[1]

| Rank | Form of Emphasis |
|------|------------------|
| 1 | For example, "Now get this" (verbal emphasis preceding a remark) |
| 2 | Three distributed repetitions |
| 3 | Repetition (early in speech) |
| 4 | Speaking slowly (half normal rate) |
| 5 | Repetition (late in speech) |
| 6 | Pause |
| 7 | Gesture |

These results are strong evidence of the value of emphasis—whether verbal, vocal, gestural, organizational, or some combination of the above.

The evidence also contains some serious warnings for speakers.

1.   Although three repetitions were a significant factor in retention, four repetitions were much less of a factor, and two repetitions appeared to cause no effect. Although the results of one limited experiment in no way suggest that three repetitions are a magic number, they do imply that too much repetition is as bad as too little. All of us have grown weary of certain TV commercials that continually repeat a product name. On the other hand, we all appreciate the teacher who repeats and reviews course work, making it easier to understand and recall the important items. Optimal repetitions offer more opportunities for cognitive processing.[2]

2.     It was found that voice, especially volume, made a difference. In the case of a loud, almost bombastic voice used for emphasis, the difference was negative. It hurt retention. A really soft voice for emphasis didn't seem to make much difference. Although the results do not mean that we should never use a loud voice, they do demonstrate that in certain communication circumstances a loud voice may interfere with recall of information.

In sum, take care not to overdo a good thing or to draw overly specific rules from limited experiences. Reinforcement in the form of verbal, vocal, gestural, and organizational emphasis can be a real asset to speakers presenting information—as long as they are careful to adapt the amount and kind of reinforcement to the particular subject, situation, and audience. "Now get this" might be a little strong for some audiences!

# CLARITY AND INTEREST

In seeking *clarity* we utilize what we know about learning to make understanding easier. Perhaps not quite so evident is the fact that an audience's *interest* or *motivation* to learn may have an important effect on how much they remember.

Your speech topic should be chosen with your own interests in mind, but you should also be considering audience interests and topic orientation at the same time. Following are key questions to consider:

1.     How important is the subject to the audience?

2.     What does the audience know about the subject?

3.     How do they know what they know?

4.     What is their attitude toward the subject?

5.     How do they assess my topical credibility?

## Achieving Clarity

The *scope* of your purpose (the amount of information you wish to cover in a given period of time) is a vital factor in clarity as is the organization of the material. The philosopher H. P. Grice offers nine maxims that communicators share which make understanding possible. Good speakers apply them to achieve clarity and understanding.

1.    Make your speech as informative as is required considering purpose and time restraints.

2.    Do not make your contributions more informative than is necessary.

3.    Do not say what you believe to be false.

4.    Do not say that for which you lack adequate evidence.

5.    Be relevant to your topic and your listeners.

6.    Avoid obscurity of expression.

7.    Avoid ambiguity.

8.    Avoid unnecessary prolixity (wordiness).

9.    Be well organized.[3]

The use of visual aids is still another method of improving clarity (Chapter 9). Clarity is also enhanced by the use of the forms of support discussed in Chapter 5: illustrations, examples, analogies, statistics, testimony, restatement, and, of course, effective organization (Chapter 6). The goal of clarity is to provide a situation in which your audience achieves understanding.

## Developing Interest

*Interest,* the second primary objective in a speech to inform, refers to the motivation of the audience to want to listen or learn. The problem is to hold the attention of your audience while you are practicing all of the suggestions for clarity. What are the categories of things that tend to interest all of us? How can they be applied to your subject in such a way as to motivate the audience to pay attention and want to learn? Much of a speaker's interest depends upon his or her style of delivery and use of vocal variety; however, we are concerned here mainly with speech *content.* Some of the more useful qualities of speech content that stimulate interest are specificity, conflict, novelty, curiosity, immediacy, vital concerns, and humor.

**SPECIFICITY**   When a speaker says, "Let me give you an example of what I mean by dog-tired," you probably pay closer attention than if he or she were simply to give you some general, academic explanation. Suppose the speaker used the following example:

> The men of Hurricane Katrina's Red Cross rescue group thought after two days of forced march through wreckage-strewn coastal areas that they were dog-tired. Then they saw the remote victims of the storm, who seemed to be moving on sheer instinct and determination alone. They staggered through their broken homes with drooping shoulders, so physically drained that it seemed to take every last ounce of strength to put one foot in front of the other.

*Specificity, reality,* and *concreteness* are more interesting than clichés, vague generalities, or abstractions. Instead of saying, "A boy was run over," be specific. Call him by name; indicate his age; identify the car: "When Mark Scott, age 6, ran into the street to greet his mother approaching from the other side, he was dashed to the pavement by a 1997 Explorer traveling in excess of the 30-mile speed limit."

**CONFLICT**   TV stories always seem to pit "bad guys" against "good guys." This conflict and fighting pay off in viewer interest. Can you imagine *NYPD*

*Figure 10.1*

*Blue* or a daytime soap opera without conflict or uncertainty? What would *Court TV* or *Judge Judy* be without conflict?

Sporting contests create interest for many people in Western cultures, but not all cultures share the same view of competition to win. The Japanese attitude toward athletics differs greatly from the North American attitude. The Japanese goal of baseball is not to have one team win but to achieve a tie![4] Although, conflict is interesting, you might want to use examples of it carefully and sparingly. If you can use conflict in your examples, illustrations, and explanations without seeming to set up nonexistent battles, your speech should have added interest for the audience.

**NOVELTY**   Something that is novel is *different, unusual, contrasting,* or *strange.* Of course, if the subject is so exotic that listeners cannot relate it to their previous knowledge and experience, interest may be lost rather than gained.

Novelty is not limited to the exotic. Relatively average things become novel if the world about them is in contrast. At one time a bikini would have been a novelty, mostly because of its contrast to more conservative swimsuits. In our time, a man or woman would probably gain more attention wearing one of the old-fashioned neck-to-ankle suits of the early 1900s. New Yorkers find nothing unusual or novel about their skyscrapers, but the Empire State Building entrances visitors. The Tower of Pisa, however, is a novelty even to New Yorkers.

Television shows always seem to pit "bad guys" against "good guys." Programs like *Judge Judy* maintain interest through drama and conflict.

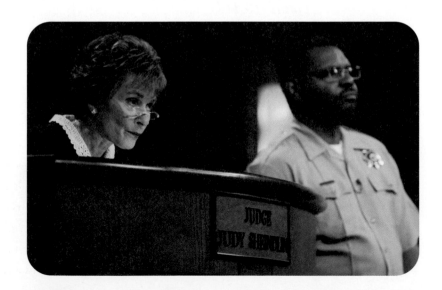

The unusual, the contrasting, the exotic, the strange, the rare, and the generally different things in life are more interesting than the run-of-the-mill. Let your examples, analogies, and explanations be novel for added audience interest.

**CURIOSITY**   One of the more marvelous and exasperating aspects of young children is the seemingly endless series of questions they ask. Grownup children (men and women) are not really much different, except that they may become a little more precise about the subjects they want to know about and the questions they ask. Humans seem to desire finding out what lies around the corner or beyond the stars. Each new discovery in space leads to added suspense about what the universe is really like and to the big question, "Is there life out there?"

*Unanswered questions, uncertainty, and suspense*—these are the ingredients of curiosity that may be used effectively by speakers to arouse interest. Posing a question early in your speech that you return to answer later is one way to pique your audience's curiosity, creating suspense.

**IMMEDIACY**   By immediacy we mean the use of *issues of the moment* or of the specific occasion that will quickly arouse and maintain attention and interest when related to a speaker's subject. A company's training director had the rare ability to memorize names of individuals along with other relevant facts after just one informal meeting. She once startled a group of forty executives on the second day of a course by randomly calling them by name throughout a two-hour period: "Mr. John Kolon, what do you think of…?" Needless to say, interest was high. Her listeners never knew when she would call their name, cite their job description, or ask their opinion.

A reference to a recent incident that is known to the audience may also heighten interest. In a speech to a business audience in Flint, Michigan, a speaker was interrupted by two window-rattling sonic booms. The audience stirred nervously. The speaker walked to the window and said, "Just a couple of young jet jockeys from the air base. I'll want to talk to them at the next briefing!" The audience quickly returned its attention. Not only had the distraction been acknowledged but the audience also felt closer to the speaker.

Learning about the occasion, the audience, last-minute headlines, the community (proximity of the air base), and all other matters of the moment is time well spent in helping to make your speech interesting. In your classroom speech, you might want to refer to an earlier speaker or topic. You might hearken back to the last exam in class or something the professor has said. These moments of shared experiences increases your immediacy with the audience.

**VITAL CONCERNS**    If, while reading this book you had the FM radio playing and the announcer suddenly broke in to say, "Alert! Alert! Please turn to your emergency frequencies at the civilian-defense white triangles on your radio dial," you would undoubtedly stop reading and turn the dial as instructed. The reason is obvious: Staying alive, protecting your loved ones, defending your home—all these are vital concerns to you. You are interested because you have to be.

Vital concerns, if truly vital, will gain attention because of personal involvement. Create interest in your speeches by using arguments, examples, and illustrations that affect your audience's self-preservation, reputation, property, sources of livelihood, and freedoms. More will be said about the role of these factors in Chapter 11, "Speeches to Persuade."

**HUMOR**    If you feel you do not tell a joke well or you find it difficult to be a humorous speaker, perhaps you need not be too concerned. Long-standing research on the impact of humor on an audience seems to indicate mixed results. A series of more recent studies produced similar mixed results, except that humor did seem to improve the character ratings of the speaker and better student retention of humorous informative lectures was demonstrated.

Remember that humor, when offensive, can work against you so, too, if it confuses the mood or is in some other way a distraction from the message. Related, funny anecdotes (if told well and in good taste) have probably helped hold attention and increased retention.

If you do decide to try humor make it as professional as possible. There is no feeling quite as desperate as viewing a poker-faced audience after you have told your best joke. Make sure that the material is related to either the subject or the occasion; make sure you can tell it fluently; make sure you remember the punch line; and make sure that it will not offend your audience. The best advice of all— try it out on a small group of friends first. In other words, *practice* and *polish!* More will be said about humor in Chapter 13 under "After-Dinner Speeches."

# ORGANIZING EFFECTIVELY

When Chauncey Depew, a gifted speaker and state senator from New York, was asked to reveal the secret of his oratorical success, he replied:

"First, tell them what you are going to tell them; second, tell them; and third, tell them you have told them." I'm sure Mr. Depew would allow another

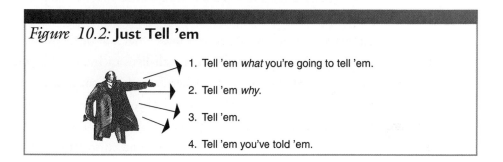

*Figure 10.2:* **Just Tell 'em**

1. Tell 'em *what* you're going to tell 'em.

2. Tell 'em *why*.

3. Tell 'em.

4. Tell 'em you've told 'em.

step involving *why* someone needs to know what someone is about to say. Mr. Depew didn't need that additional step as much as the rest of us because his audiences were usually eagerly awaiting what he had to say.

The learning principles discussed in this chapter should assist in organizing information. What does it tell us? First, it tells us of the need to grab listeners' attention early and to motivate them to listen. In addition, it tells us of the value of serially ordered material, Moreover, it tells us of the need for reinforcement and for preparing states of readiness to learn or listen.

Your immediate purpose is to create a desire in the listeners to hear more about the information you have to offer. If the audience is already highly motivated, your attention step and part of the orientation becomes

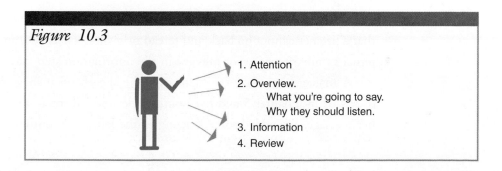

*Figure 10.3*

1. Attention
2. Overview.
   What you're going to say.
   Why they should listen.
3. Information
4. Review

proportionately less important. When interest is a serious problem you may wish to move the *why* up to the attention step.

If you have some natural credibility about your topic, it usually motivates the audience to listen—an athlete talking about her sport, a pilot explaining flying, a premed student discussing health care, and so on.

In a student speech "to inform the class about some of the sociological problems facing India," the speaker first explained that he had lived in India for three years. (Your introducer can also help here.) He then opened with the following (*attention* and *interest*): "Did you know that half of the world's population is illiterate and that one-third of this half lives in India? Did you know that over three hundred languages are spoken in India? That fourteen thousand babies a day are born in India? That Indians feel Americans are uncaring? Americans do care—they are just poorly informed."

The speaker used startling statistics and curiosity to gain attention. Notice the suggestion on why the audience needs to know—because we are perceived as uncaring. His *central idea* is that "Americans do care—they are just poorly informed." The student previewed his four main points, letting the audience know what he would cover. He then explained each of his points in detail, and in order, in the body of the speech. At the close of the speech, he repeated the four points; and, in addition, he briefly summarized some of the important details from the information step. In other words, he *reviewed* the speech, or "told 'em what he told 'em." The completeness or amount of detail you put into your summary or review will depend upon the complexity of the subject, the time allotted, and your purpose. In some speeches you may prefer to deliver a brief summary of the points you have tried to make; in more complex or elaborate speeches, you may want to add details to your review to sum up your speech.

The *reinforcement value* of this approach is obvious. Once more, remember that a listener cannot go back and reread or review. Therefore, an occasional internal summary, review, or preview in the information step may help.

A management major student gave the speech on management functions discussed in Chapter 5 and her point of view added interest and credibility to her message. We added some labeling to the left of her outline to assist you in understanding the development of her speech as she provided necessary elaboration to make her points complete.

## THE ROLE OF THE MANAGER

INTRODUCTION

| | | |
|---|---|---|
| Attention | **I.** | In a well-run organization, confusion pertains 25 percent of the time. |
| | | **A.** Use visual aid with data and another with list of functions. |
| Credibility | | **B.** Studies show that communication breakdowns occur foolishly. |
| Orientation | **II.** | Management is getting work done through others. |
| | | **A.** That makes communication the heart of all management functions. |
| Central Idea | | **B.** That takes knowledge of the five basic functions. |
| Preview | |     **1.** Planning |
| | |     **2.** Organizing |
| | |     **3.** Directing |
| | |     **4.** Coordinating |
| | |     **5.** Controlling |

```
1. Planning.
2. Organization.
3. Directing.
4. Coordinating.
5. Controlling.
```

Visual aid

BODY

| | | |
|---|---|---|
| Main Point | **I.** | The planning function |
| Subpoint | | **A.** Determine objective |
| Subpoint | | **B.** Consider tools available |
| Detailed Explanation | |     **1.** Time |
| of Subpoint | |     **2.** Space |
| | |     **3.** Personnel |
| | |     **4.** Material available |
| | | **C.** Consider possible lines of action. |
| | | **D.** Select the best line of action. |
| | | **E.** Determine the actual process. |
| | |     **1.** Who? |
| | |     **2.** When? |
| | |     **3.** What? |
| | |     **4.** Where? |
| | |     **5.** How? |

Main Point  **II.**  The organizing function

         **A.** Line of authority

         **B.** Span of Control

             **1.** Number of personnel

Further Elaboration        a. Nature of job

                    b. Ratios (1–20, 3, 7)

             **2.** Distance

             **3.** Time

Visual aid

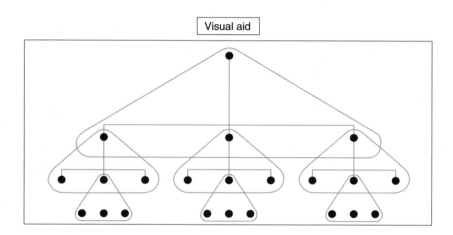

         **C.** Homogeneous assignment

             **1.** Group like functions together.

             **2.** Avoid several unrelated responsibilities.

         **D.** Delegation of authority

             **1.** Cannot delegate responsibility

             **2.** Clearly define limits of delegated authority.

Main Point  **III.**  The directing function

         **A.** Communication

         **B.** Understanding people

Main Point  **IV.**  The coordinating function

         **A.** Relating to lateral organizations

         **B.** Relating to the parent organization

III, IV, V

Human relations and communication area

Visual aid

Main Point    **V.**    The controlling function

                 **A.** Reporting

                 **B.** Inspecting and evaluating

CONCLUSION

Review    **I.**    I have tried to make clear the five basic management functions.

                 **A.** Planning

                 **B.** Organizing

                 **C.** Directing

                 **D.** Coordinating

                 **E.** Controlling

Impact    **II.**    Communication is the heart of all management functions! It has to be— management is getting work done through people—and that takes communication.

It is helpful to remember that organization is key in putting your information together so the audience can follow and make sense of your topic. Some points need more support and elaboration than others—although all should be of fairly equal weight if they are to stand as independent main points. The job of the informative speech is to provide as much detail on the chosen topic as is necessary for your particular audience. That is no easy task.

A sample Informative Speech, in its manuscripted form, can be found in the back of the book. "COIK" which stands for "Clear Only If Known" is the title of a speech by Edgar Dale, a former professor of education at Ohio State University. It is a classic illustration showing how to apply the principles covered in this chapter: learning, motivation, clarity, interest, and even humor. The speech provides a lesson in planning and preparing an informative speech and should prove helpful to you, not just in its content and advice, but in its organization as well.

# CHAPTER REVIEW
## Wrapping it up

## Summary

The most frequent types of informative speeches involve reporting, instructing, and explaining. Useful learning principles related to communicating information include 1) relating new information to what an audience already knows; 2) ordering the material in some serial progression that makes it easier for people to follow and relate the significant points; and; 3) reinforcing the message and the response through a sensible amount of repetition, verbal emphasis, organization, and voice—all of which communicate importance, reward, punishment, or some other meaning. The final lesson to be gained from learning theory is that there appears to be a point of diminishing returns with all these devices; too much repetition can be as harmful as too little. This point of diminishing returns depends upon the specific and total communication circumstance.

The primary goals in informative speaking are achieving clarity and interest. Methods of achieving clarity include illustration or example, analogy or comparison, statistics, testimony, and restatement — all of which allow understanding to occur. The factors that create or add interest are specificity, conflict, novelty, curiosity, immediacy, vital concerns of the audience, and humor. Maxims that promote understanding are as follows: present an appropriate amount of information; avoid false statements; use evidence for what you say, be relevant to your audience as well as your topic, avoid obscurity, ambiguity and prolixity; and be well organized.

The importance of organizing your speech effectively is to ensure understanding by your audience; to grab their attention early and motivate them to listen. The rule of thumb is to 1) tell them what you are going to tell them 2) tell them why it is important to them 3) tell them and 4) tell them what you have told them. The job of the informative speech is to provide as much detail as is necessary for your given audience.

The "COIK" model speech, found in the appendix, is an excellent illustration of how to apply the principles covered in this chapter.

# *Notes*

1.  Raymond Ehrensberger, "An Experimental Study of the Relative Effectiveness of Certain Forms of Emphasis in Public Speaking," *Speech Monographs,* 12, no. 2 (1945), 94–111.

2.  J. T. Cacioppo and R. E. Petty, "Effects of Message Repetition and Position on Cognitive Responses, Recall, and Persuasion," *Journal of Personality and Social Psychology,* 37 (1979), 97–109.

3.  Adapted from H. P. Grice, *Studies in the Way of Words* (Cambridge, Mass.: Harvard University Press, 1984), pp. 26–27.

4   Julia T. Wood, *Interpersonal Communication Everyday Encounters,* 2nd edition (Belmont, CA: Wadsworth, 1999), p. 295.

5.  Gerald Gardner, *Speech Is Golden* (New York: St. Martin's Press, 1992), p. 73.

6.  Reprinted by permission of Edgar Dale.

SPEECHES TO PERSUADE

# Chapter 11

## Chapter Objectives

### Types of Persuasive Speeches

Disputed Facts Speech
Belief and Value Speeches
Action and Policy Speeches

### The Nature of Persuasion

Influence, Motivation, and
  Persuasion

Engaging the Consistency
  Principle
Using Both-Sides Persuasion
Using Evidence and Logical
  Reasoning

### Organizing the Persuasive Speech

Natural-Order Method
Both-Sides Method

The Concept of Attitude
Intrapersonal Responses to
  Persuasion

### Routes to Effective Persuasion

Improving Perceptions of
  Credibility
Appeals to Human Needs

### Speaker Integrity

Being Communicationally
  Sensitive
Culpable Ignorance
Affording Clues and Choice
Democracy and Demagoguery

# TYPES OF PERSUASIVE SPEECHES

All speeches to persuade involve efforts to get receivers to (1) accept your interpretation of *disputed facts;* (2) align their *beliefs, attitudes,* and *values* more closely with yours; and/or (3) move them to *action* on your proposition. Some speeches may involve efforts in all three areas.

> When Isocrates taught rhetoric to his Greek schoolboys he empowered them; he helped them see avenues for making their minds count in the affairs of society.
>
> **Roderick P. Hart,**
>
> **College of Communication Dean,**
>
> **University of Texas at Austin**

The more closely you can define the type of speech and audience with which you're dealing, the more efficiently you can seek out information and arrange it into an effective strategy. As we shall see shortly, if your audience thinks differently than you do about these critical dimensions, you'd better find that out as quickly as you can.

## Disputed Facts Speech

What is or is not the case? Facts are actions, events, or conditions, that have been *properly* observed, described, classified, and reported. Space travel is now a *fact* since it meets the definition above, but what of flying saucers (UFOs)? The saucers fail for most people on the word *properly* but clearly not for all. UFOs become (for believers) a persuasive speech using their version of the disputed facts.

Of course, people may not agree with the definition of fact given above. One dictionary definition allows for "information presented as having objective reality." An argument over the Koran or the Bible might be a question of disputed fact for one person and a question of belief or value for another. All questions are not as complex as these, but they may involve inconclusive facts. "Is there life out there in space?" "What causes Alzheimer's disease?" "Why can't Johnny read?" "Is the defendant guilty of the crime?" These are all questions of fact, asking what is or is not the case—and where persuasive efforts are possible, sometimes difficult, and sometimes frustrating.

Some facts really aren't worth arguing about—"Which is higher, the Andes, the Alps, or the Rockies?" An encyclopedia or a quick Internet query can solve that one. You could measure them yourself! A fact which can be determined to be true through proper observation is not one that fits the parameters of persuasion. Where there is no disagreement, there is no need for persuasion. In all cases of fact, do your audience analysis even when you think things are obvious. There are still many people who do not accept the "fact" that Neil Armstrong set foot on the moon.

## Belief and Value Speeches

What is better, right, or moral? Beliefs are constructs we hold about the world; they give rise to related attitudes. A strong belief in protecting the environment can affect one's attitudes about a wide range of things from political candidates to spotted owls. Values, as we learned in Chapter 3, "Audience Considerations," are still larger, more important frames of reference that hold our belief and attitude systems together.

These speeches do not necessarily ask audiences to take action, although it is often implied. One can argue the case (pro or con) for assisted suicide in an effort to change people's beliefs without detailing what they should do. The same is true of other controversial topics, which typically engage people's belief and value systems: capital punishment, abortion, birth control, life supports, and so forth. Your speeches should include many facts and much information if you are to give responsible and effective belief speeches. Some real-world speeches on questions of strong values sometimes rely on overly emotional efforts. When this occurs, the argument often pits itself against the opposition, rather than inviting the opposition to see a different viewpoint.

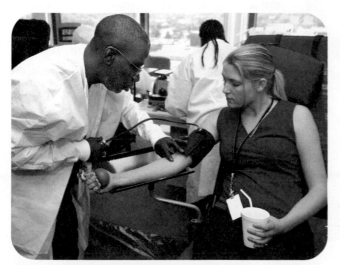

Statements like "Give Blood" are designed to actuate, that is, to encourage people to take some action.

## Action and Policy Speeches

What should or should not be done? Action and policy speeches are designed to **actuate**, which is to move people to action. For example:

Sign this petition.

Vote for Senator Foghorn.

Enlist in the Marines.

Buy this Chevrolet.

Give blood.

Beliefs and attitudes may also be involved, but the bottom line is some kind of action—even if it is only a "yes" response indicating a strong intention to ultimately take the action you are suggesting.

When we deal with more involved and specific courses of action, we're talking about policy. Facts, beliefs, values, and attitudes—all are involved here, but now we're talking about what *should* or *should not* be done over time.

What should be our school system's position on funding public education?

How should the USA deal with the proliferation of nuclear arms?

What should be our policy regarding national health care?

Most policy questions involve some controversy. For some audiences on some topics the mood can be downright hostile: abortion, feminism, secular humanism, gays in the military, gay marriage, church and state, tax reform, and so forth. There are special strategies for antagonistic groups that sometimes work. These strategies will be discussed later in this chapter.

Most policy questions involve some controversy. Some topics are known to be downright hostile, such as, abortion.

In persuasive speeches, from a sales talk to one of controversial policy, you will have to demonstrate a need or a problem that calls for a solution. You will then have to provide a solution or plan that meets the need you've hopefully made clear, and finally to show the practicality of your solution. In other words, show how your solution works. This is usually the more difficult part because not only must you show that your solution is practical but also that it is more sensible than other practical solutions that may be available. Our need for health care reform seems obvious to most citizens, but the precise nature of the specific needs is open to argument. Certainly the range of solutions from rationing to socialized medicine is daunting.

Audience analysis is very important for these speeches because even a few people who take severe issue with your stand or are seriously offended by it can be disruptive. "You can't win 'em all" but you don't always have to. Attitudes, as we shall see shortly, are usually changed incrementally.

# THE NATURE OF PERSUASION

Persuasion is just one part of very large systems of influence and motivation, but its emphasis on reasoned, intentional messages and its insistence on ethical choice for receivers makes it a very special part indeed.

## Influence, Motivation, and Persuasion

**Influence**, the most general of these terms, refers to a power that affects a person or a course of events, usually indirectly. It can be positive or negative, human or nonhuman, intentional or unintentional, ethical or unethical. Influence includes mood setters like lighting, music, and pictures as well as the actions or presence of other people.

**Motivation** pertains to *any* stimulation or inducement that leads to an act or belief. It could be caused by drives to reduce tension, achieve goals, or grow as a person, or by a need for self-understanding. These various causes suggest that we are motivated both by need and by plenty. Success and satisfaction usually foster motivation. So frequently do failure and dissatisfaction. We are often motivated through argument or social compliance and laws. We have avoidance needs as well as growth needs. Human motives have been defined by Krech and Crutchfield as *survival, security, satisfaction,* and *stimulation.*[1] These motives are grouped into deficiency motives (survival and security) and abundancy motives (satisfaction and stimulation). **Deficiency motivation** is characterized by needs to *avoid* danger, threat, disruption, and discomfort. **Abundancy motivation** is characterized by desire to grow, discover, create, enjoy, and achieve. The various motivators are *verbal* and *nonverbal, logical* and *emotional.*

Motivation need not be intentional; it can be accidental. Furthermore, it is essentially **amoral**—that is, not particularly concerned with notions of right or wrong, fair or unfair.

**Persuasion** is certainly concerned with social influence and human motivation but in a very special way. Persuasion is a change process resulting mostly from shared, symbolic-thinking activity. Whereas this text is concerned mostly

*Abundancy motivation* is characterized by desire to grow, discover, create, enjoy, and achieve. We see this demonstrated in how children seek out new activites, learn new words, or play.

with spoken messages, the effects of persuasion are in the thoughts and behaviors, the sociology, of the receivers. This fact suggests that receivers have some bias and also some choice in these matters. Persuasive messages attempt to influence *how* receivers choose or decide which information to process and respond to.

A persuader has an ethical responsibility for the strategies and for their social consequences. Techniques and strategies are ethical unless they are dishonest, unfair to the facts, or so subtle that they give no clue to the receiver. The clue is important. It protects the receiver's fundamental right of choice. There is no lasting persuasion without honesty, pressure free of violence, receiver choice, tolerance for strategy, fair hearing, and a willingness to comply with persuasion from legitimate authority. In a democracy, ethical persuasion is the major means of social influence.

*In this context persuasion is a nonviolent means of ethically influencing and motivating others through messages.* It is an instrument for obtaining reasoned adherence to rational propositions. By these definitions, persuasive influence must clearly protect a receiver's right to choice. "Your money or your life" may involve influence and motivation, but it does not afford a viable choice. We will talk further about ethical responsibility later in the chapter, under the section Speaker Integrity.

## The Concept of Attitude

Persuasive efforts are directed in large part at changing or maintaining the attitudes of others. These efforts are usually directed at producing some related behavior: a vote, the sale of a product, some compliant action. Does oral argument (speech) affect attitudes? For centuries we have answered, "yes" on the basis of subjective observations. Objective observations and research as early as 1931 have also clearly indicated that persuasive speaking can make a difference.[2] Logical arguments work but so do the psychological and more emotional speeches.

**Attitude** refers to the thinking, feeling, and behavioral intentions that govern our predispositions toward people, situations, and things. Attitude has also been defined as a tendency to respond in a given way. This response may be **cognitive** (how one thinks), **affective** (how one feels), or **behavioral** (how one behaves or intends to behave). The altering of attitudes is for some the altering of a receiver's cognitive, schematic structures as well as behaviors as a result of message processing.

We are also persuaded by **logical appeals**, where the messages are focused on reasoning, as well as by **emotional appeals**, in which the messages are focused on feelings and emotions. When we are persuaded to buy a product, take a position, or join a cause, how much of our behavior is based on reasoned discourse? How much on appeals to our emotions? There is strong evidence that people are multi-motivated.

Many of our attitudes are expressions of our experience and our values. They maintain and promote our value systems and our **self-identity**, the ways in which we see ourselves. For example, if we value our health and clean air highly, we will probably have unfavorable attitudes toward smoking and fluorocarbons and would see ourselves as health conscious and as environmentalists.

All of us are somewhat directed by **self-interest** or **egoism.** Egoism is thought by some to be a major motivator of all human conduct. We defend our own egos, our own welfare, and our own advancement. Take care of Number One! This behavior has been explained as an ego-defensive function. The more ego-defensive one is, the more destructive it can be and the harder it is to change attitude or motivate action.

Some theorists view attitudes as being underlaid by *belief systems.* **Beliefs** *are sets of inferences* we make about the world. *Beliefs are nonevaluative.* They are probability statements we hold about the world.

Consider the following belief statement: Smoking and heart disease are related. This statement is a belief because it makes a probability inference between smoking and heart disease. Now consider the following attitude statement that might grow out of that belief: Smoking is bad. The statement is an attitude because it makes an evaluation of one of the objects (smoking) in the belief statement. The significant point is that our *attitudes are evaluative and grow out of our belief systems.*

A single point on a scale, however, cannot always represent attitudes adequately. They represent different strengths and different ranges or latitudes of acceptance. Consider Figure 11.1. This scale indicates a strong leaning toward objecting to abolishing all men's clubs.

This person would be difficult to persuade to support the statement since the range of objection (or rejection 3-7) is so large. Suppose, however, that the data looked like Figure 11.2. This scale reveals less commitment to strong attitudes. The more acceptable (√) or uncommitted positions one indicates, the wider the latitude of acceptance and, therefore, the greater likelihood of attitude change.

Research on how we make judgments about physical objects also gives us insights into our social judgments. If you put your hand in a pail of hot water for a minute or so and then put it in a pail of lukewarm water, you tend to judge the water *colder* than it is. If you go from cold to a pail of warm water, you tend to judge it *warmer* than it is. The hot pail (or cold) serves as a **reference point**

*Figure 11.1*    **Strong and Committed Attitude Indicators**

I think all "men only" clubs should be abolished

| √ | √ | × | × | × | × | × |
|---|---|---|---|---|---|---|
| 1 | 2 | 3 | 4 | 5 | 6 | 7 |

Strongly disagree        Neutral        Strongly agree

MARK:
(×) *All* positions you find objectionable
(√) All positions you can live with (acceptable)

*Figure 11.2*    **Less Committed Attitude Indicators**

| × | | √ | √ | √ | | |
|---|---|---|---|---|---|---|
| 1 | 2 | 3 | 4 | 5 | 6 | 7 |

or anchor for our succeeding judgments. When the temperature is sharply contrasted from that of the anchor, you tend to perceive it as farther from the anchor or colder than it really is; when temperatures are close to that of the anchor, you tend to assimilate it, to perceive it as warmer than it really is.

This tendency for assimilation and contrast has been applied to attitude change. A receiver's *initial* attitude toward the persuasion serves as a reference point, or anchor, for making judgments about the message. In general, the more extreme the initial attitude (anchor), the less attitude change you can expect. The less extreme the anchor, the more change you can expect.[3]

## Intrapersonal Responses to Persuasion

Successful persuasion evokes favorable thoughts or internal responses from receivers. These thoughts may then affect favorable behaviors, feelings, or ideas (cognitions). This familiar notion of communication as a process suggests that listeners, in their decoding, sort, select, and elicit from their storehouse of knowledge those things they feel relate best to the message elements. **Cognitive-Response Theory** helps show how people may respond to a persuasive message by evoking thoughts from their own storehouses of experience and knowledge that may not be contained in the message sent. If these "cognitive responses" (thoughts) agree with the persuader's purpose, they should promote attitude change in the desired direction. If, on the other hand, the message somehow backfires and evokes unfavorable or disagreeing thoughts, the sender's purpose may be defeated or at least inhibited attitudinally. The **Elaboration Likelihood Method (ELM)** of persuasion is based on this approach; namely, that the more elaborately a receiver responds cognitively, the greater the likelihood of attitude change.[4]

Cognitive-response theory suggests that just as personal growth and development are often considered to be really self-growth and self-development (or that learning is in the final analysis self-generated), we really persuade ourselves through these cognitive reevaluations.[5] This theory explains why the receivers of highly polarized attitudes are sometimes so busy processing, repeating, and rehearsing their own thoughts and views that they really do not hear the message. Highly polarized audiences may have quite different constructions of reality than yours based on different experiences and a different sociology of knowledge. Analyzing an audience's cognitive responses from their view of reality should help us better decide the kind, the length, and the ordering of arguments that will promote favorable "self-generated" responses.

*Enthymematic* persuasion seems to be a logical extension of the strategy implicit in cognitive-response theory. **Enthymemes** are syllogistic arguments with unstated premises. Their rhetorical function is to let the audience correctly supply the desired missing premises. Like cognitive-response theory, enthymematic persuasion assumes that thoughts are often more influential if they are our own rather than if they were explicitly stated in the message by others.

Cognitive-response researchers Richard Petty and John Cacioppo suggest two components or "routes" to persuasion: *central* and *peripheral*.[6] *Central* is characterized by more "elaborative" reasoning about issue-relevant matters; *peripheral* refers to the more affective, nonissue-relevant, contextual cues. Of the two routes, the more thoughtful *central* route resulted in more enduring and resistant persuasion than did the peripheral route.[7] This is not to say that the affective domain is unimportant. Advertising research suggests that the peripheral affective cues and the cognitive central cues are both important indicants of overall message effectiveness.[8]

Aristotle's explanation of the enthymeme and his routes to persuasion make clear that he too was most interested in a receiver's intrapersonal responses. He called them *modes.*

> Of the modes of persuasion furnished by the spoken word there are three kinds. The first kind depends on the personal characteristics of the speaker, ETHOS; the second on putting the audience into a certain frame of mind, PATHOS; the third on the proof or apparent proof provided by the words of the speech itself, LOGOS.[9]

These are strikingly similar to the dimensions of attitude discussed earlier: cognitive (*Logos*), affective (*Pathos*), and behavioral (*Ethos*). By *ethos,* Aristotle meant speaker credibility or persuasion based on a person's behavior, past and present. We'll have more to say about credibility in the next section.

There are, then, three basic intrapersonal responses to persuasion and, therefore, three related methods or modes a speaker should consider.

In the model shown in Figure 11.3, **cognitive** refers to logical thoughts, to thinking, to the mental process (cognition) by which knowledge is acquired, constructed, and elaborated. **Affective** refers to feelings, thoughts, and things more emotional. **Behavioral** can be an action, an action intention, or a

*Figure 11.3*  **Intrapersonal Response**

thought response to the past behavior of the speaker (credibility) or the current speaking behavior (ethical proof).

*Persuasion, in this context, is a process of skillfully and ethically using logical thoughts, affective appeals, credibility, and ethical proof to influence and motivate others to respond as you wish them to.* Persuasive methods or modes can then be described as logical (Aristotle's logos), affective (Aristotle's pathos), and behavioral (Aristotle's ethos). The *logical* mode (cognitive component) includes reasoning, evidence, argument, and logical consistency. The *affective* mode (affective component) includes the feelings induced by emotional and motivational appeals, personal involvement, and needs reduction.[10] The *behavioral* mode is concerned with (1) credibility and ethical proof, that is, speaker behavior, past and present, and (2) a receiver's personal involvement (behavior or behavioral intention) with the message, speaker, or situation.

Your first goal as an ethical speaker is to support your specific purpose with logical, consistent reasoning and argument. However, the affective and behavioral modes are not unethical as long as they reasonably relate to your logical argument and are fair to the facts.

Persuasion is like an arrow. The shaft is evidence and reasoning; the feathers are ethics and credibility, which provide direction; the arrowhead is attention and emotional appeal, which promote target response. The arrow must be properly assembled, balanced, and then skillfully aimed. If the flight of such an arrow of persuasion is true, and its target a rightful one, then its prospects are favorable. (Figure 11.4)

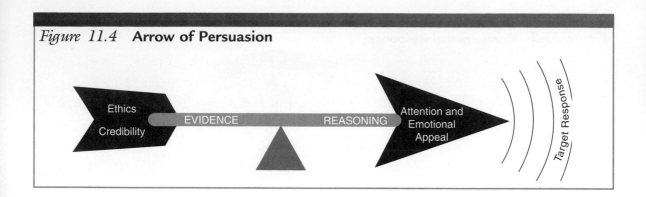

Figure 11.4    **Arrow of Persuasion**

This chapter mostly concerns the feathers and the arrowhead—that is, the more psychological, the more peripheral route to successful persuasion (pathos and ethos). The more logical, more central route (logos) will be discussed more fully in Chapter 12, "Logical Reasoning and Argument."

Most persuasive speeches use a combination of logical, affective, and behavioral elements. It is, of course, possible to have a speech based almost entirely on evidence and closely reasoned argument. On the other hand, many of our radio and television commercials make it abundantly clear that some efforts are based almost entirely on affective appeals. Some of these elements, such as source credibility, ethical proof, and personal involvement, embody both affective and cognitive dimensions and are difficult to divide. How much of one's perception of intent, trust, expertise, or status is based on affect? How much on evidence and logical deduction?

Persuasive efforts can be complex—sometimes very subtle, sometimes blatant. Consider the persuasion efforts of political campaigns. How much is logical persuasion? How much is affective? How much is based on source credibility? Aristotle reminds us of the importance of utilizing all three modes.

## ROUTES TO EFFECTIVE PERSUASION

Getting an audience to think or, more specifically, to rethink a proposition is the goal of most persuasive efforts. However, internal reevaluation, as we just learned, is triggered by affective as well as cognitive arguments.

# Improving Perceptions of Credibility

*Credibility* refers to a receiver's acceptance of or disposition toward the source. Aristotle used the term ethos to designate the audience's perception of the speaker. Ethos can be separated into three dimensions of which the speaker should be aware: *character, competence,* and *charisma.* In regard to ethical proof, Aristotle set forth the general rule that "there is no proof so effective as that of the *character.*" **Character** refers to the audience's perception of the speakers' honesty and trustworthiness. It may be more fact than fiction that "what you are speaks so loudly I can't hear what you're saying." Perhaps it's also true for some that "if you're not part of my group (or party), I won't hear what you're saying." **Competence** refers to the audience's perception of the speakers' skills, ability, and knowledge. A speaker's **charisma** is his or her personality that is seen by the audience as attractive, engaging, and dynamic. These characteristics are further explored in this section.

**SOURCE CREDIBILITY**    **Source credibility** is related to Aristotle's concepts of goodwill, good moral character, and good sense; as they are perceived and evaluated by receivers. Goodwill and good moral *character* refer to the audience's perception of the speaker's honesty and trustworthiness. Good sense refers to the audience's perception of the speaker's *competence,* his or her knowledge of the topic and the ability to communicate the message. In both cases, the determination of source credibility lies in the hands of the audience. Providing the audience with reason to see the speaker as a credible source offers a stronger platform from which the message can be received. High source credibility generally produces more attitude change in the receiver.

Both reason and research tell us that an obviously untrustworthy speaker, regardless of his or her other qualities, will be viewed as a questionable message source. However, many special aspects and conditions also affect people's perceptions of credibility. Although a convicted, hard-core, experienced car thief may not meet the classical tests of credibility (goodwill, good moral character, good sense), if he were to speak (or write) about the secrets of his trade, he might indeed be perceived as having a special credibility. After all, he is an expert!

Characteristics that we infer about a source may cancel all or some credibility. Jesse Delia hypothesizes that "many persons hearing a militant speaker openly and

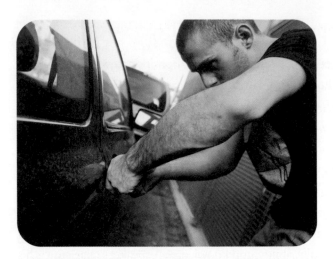

Determination of source credibility lies with the audience. A car thief may not meet the classical tests of credibility, though he does possess special credibility, being an expert in his field.

explicitly advocate an abhorrent position on an issue important to them would make with equal certainty the attributions that the speaker is honest and forthright, but also very misguided and unsafe."[11]

The receiver's perception of a sender's intent appears to influence credibility. A persuasive message was prepared on the topic of raising the minimum driving age, and the same speech was given to two groups of teenagers. One group of subjects was told that the purpose of the program was to study the speaker's personality. The other group was told that the speaker considered teenage drivers a menace. In the first group the speaker's intent to persuade was made less clear; in the second it was made abundantly clear. The second group saw the communicator as more biased, as might be expected; the first group made a greater attitude change in the direction advocated.[12]

In a study designed to persuade eighth graders to take a more conservative attitude about drugs, a law enforcement officer was less successful than others.[13] Perhaps his intent was perceived in a way that injured his credibility. His presentation may have been too threatening for his audience, or perhaps his status as a law officer didn't carry over to his expertise (if he had any) about drugs.

People's status may also vary with the issue. We may have high status in one role and low in another. George Patton had high status as a combat general but low status as a diplomat.

Apparently people form their general impressions of a sender's credibility on the basis of a wide array of variables: Intent, trust, and competence are only the beginning. We should view credibility as an interactive process among sources, messages, and receivers. It is no wonder that research evidence on credibility is sometimes inconsistent. However, when high source credibility is *perceived,* and when it is *relevant* to the message and the situation, it generally produces more favorable attitude change in the receivers.

There is also a practical credibility or likability that can be established or re-inforced by the speaker's charismatic characteristics and behavior during the sending of the message. These speaker behaviors have been referred to as "ethical proofs" and are thought to be closely related to an audience's impressions of the honesty, character, wisdom, and goodwill of the speaker.

**ETHICAL PROOF AND SELF-PRESENTATION**    Other things being equal, persuaders may be most influential when the receivers perceive them as having attitudes *similar to their own*. *Ethical proofs* also include the speaker's *self-presentation* in terms of voice, language, humor, information, and evidence; in other words, the speaker's *charisma* or dynamism impacts how the audience perceives the speaker.

Conan O'Brien is a speaker who is primarily known for his charisma and humor.

Studies have found that excess verbalizations and signals indicating disorganization detract from a speaker's credibility.[14] Recall that even social status may be inferred. Yet, audiences tend to respond to speakers who have dynamic and energetic personalities and presentations.

The use of humor may enhance speakers' pragmatic ethical proof, if not their persuasion, as measured by attitude shifts among the audience. Humor and satire, when used with a professional touch, can affect audience interest and attention and thereby retention. That they can boomerang when not used properly is very clear from research and common experience.

Can we manage these impressions? One sociologist thinks so. According to Erving Goffman, **impression management** is a doable part of how you present yourself to receivers.[15] Impression management suggests that in our efforts to present our best and most persuasive self, we try to give appropriate performances on the stage of life. Let us consider a college student presenting his senior thesis before the faculty or a potential employer. He may attempt an impression of maturity, self-confidence, knowledge, and dependability. According to Goffman, this can be done in the following general ways:

1.    *An appropriate front*    This is general behavior that is designed (or natural) to better define (persuasively, we hope) who you are. Your personal front includes

such things as appearance and manner. It also includes things over which you have only limited control, such as sex, age, and size. Clothes, posture, gestures, facial expressions, and language patterns are more modifiable dimensions of your front. Should our college student appear in dirty shorts, needing a shave, and using the English language profanely, would that front offend or reassure his audience?

2.    *Dramatic realization*    According to Goffman, we must clearly realize the role expected of us and work it into the performance. We may have to put on an act to hide our lack of confidence. If the role calls for attentiveness, we had better give such an impression. We may be paying attention; but if we are not perceived that way, then we have done a poor job of impression management. A patient may suspiciously view a flip physician that writes a fast prescription, however accurate the quick diagnosis.

3.    *Mystification*    This aspect of impression management refers to perceptions of *social distance* between the actor and the audience. Our physician above is more apt to be concerned with this kind of impression than is our student presenter. That is, the physician must not become too folksy lest he or she lose some of the mystery of the medical role. Our college student, however, must accommodate the real or fancied social-distance factors of the theater in which he finds himself.

The point of those various examples is that we *do* present ourselves to others; and others *do* form impressions—good, bad, and indifferent. If, as a student of persuasion, you understand this dramaturgical model, you should be better equipped to deal with impression management. The important lesson is that credibility and ethical proof also involve impressions of trust and confidence based on the perceived intent, position, knowledge, and sincerity of the source.

# Appeals to Human Needs

We have discussed the relevance of ethos or credibility in proving one's argument. We move now to **pathos**, what Aristotle describes as the appeal to the emotions or motivations of the audience. To a great extent, the sources of affective persuasion are found in an understanding of human needs and behavior. Some are learned; some are thought to be innate. Ever since ancient times, humankind has tried to find simple explanations of what motivates people to do what they do. If you could discover these explanations and determine universal systems of human motivation, you could theoretically control the behaviors of others in many ways. In modern times we speak of reducing internal tensions, but are wary of surefire manipulations of those tensions. We're not only interested in the message sent but also the message received. In a systems view there is an interaction—something mutual about persuasion.

To some poets and philosophers, most notably Aristotle, "the proper study of man is man himself." The assumption is that all humans, at least in a general sense, are much alike. At the physiological level this assumption presents few problems, for despite obvious individual differences in height, weight, color, and other physical attributes, all people exhibit a striking physical similarity. We could hardly have a science of medicine were this not true. In the nonphysiological realm the problem is more complicated. Plato argued that to study humans one must investigate their environment; for Plato, "man" was but a reflection of his own society, a view not unlike the social constructionist theories of today. Both Plato and Aristotle make sense. We can learn much from studying the similarities among all of us; perhaps even more by studying the social environments that produce many of our differences.

Any attempt to classify similar human needs must begin with biological needs. A. H. Maslow has supplied such a system.[16] His notions synthesize much of the tension-reduction theorizing and also extend our understanding by suggesting that human needs are arranged hierarchically.

These five general categories of needs, in the order of their importance, are *physiological, safety, love, esteem,* and *self-actualization.* As each need in the sequence is satisfied, a person seeks out the next highest level. This hierarchy of needs may be thought of as a pyramid, with the basic needs foundationally at the bottom and the higher needs appearing in order up to the top of the pyramid shown in Figure 11.5.

If members of your audience cannot fulfill even the basic needs at the bottom of the pyramid, they theoretically are not as likely to be persuaded by the higher levels of needs appeals. Starving people are thought to be almost blind to all appeals except those promising food and drink. However, once fat and full, they become concerned with safety. After achieving a feeling of safety, they can

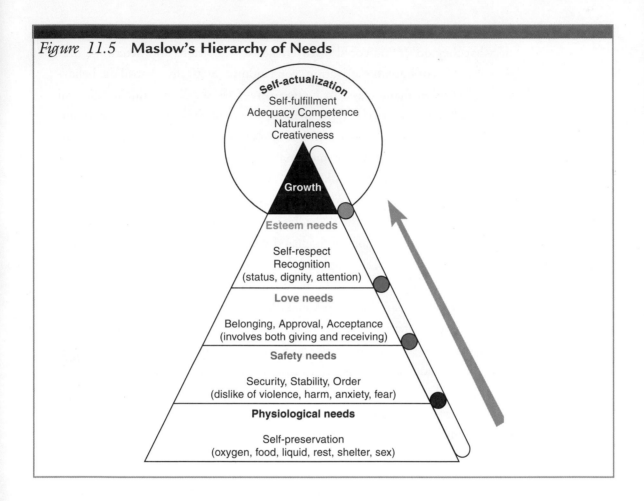

Figure 11.5   Maslow's Hierarchy of Needs

be appealed to more easily by the higher needs. In simple terms, individuals are no longer motivated by needs (however basic) that are pretty much satisfied. These needs can all be operating at one time but with varying strengths.

Certain prerequisites in the Maslow system are so important that they themselves become strong motivators when denied or endangered.[17] The environmental prerequisites include such things as free speech, intellectual freedom, the right to self-defense, and a desire for justice, honesty, and orderliness.

In Chapter 1 we pointed out that receivers decode according to their past experiences, emotions, and attitudes. More specifically, they decode in terms of their interacting needs. At one time the need for love may predominate, coloring the meaning listeners attach to a communication; at another

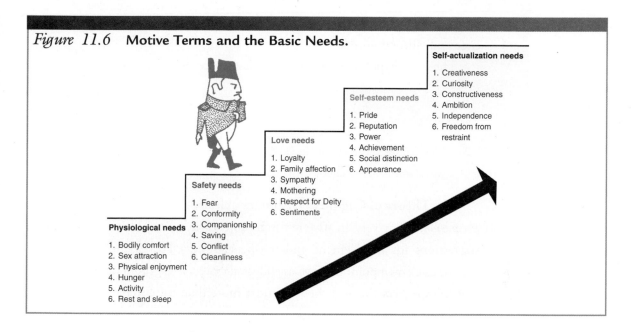

*Figure 11.6*    **Motive Terms and the Basic Needs.**

**Self-actualization needs**
1. Creativeness
2. Curiosity
3. Constructiveness
4. Ambition
5. Independence
6. Freedom from restraint

**Self-esteem needs**
1. Pride
2. Reputation
3. Power
4. Achievement
5. Social distinction
6. Appearance

**Love needs**
1. Loyalty
2. Family affection
3. Sympathy
4. Mothering
5. Respect for Deity
6. Sentiments

**Safety needs**
1. Fear
2. Conformity
3. Companionship
4. Saving
5. Conflict
6. Cleanliness

**Physiological needs**
1. Bodily comfort
2. Sex attraction
3. Physical enjoyment
4. Hunger
5. Activity
6. Rest and sleep

time the need for esteem may be foremost, and their openness to persuasion is altered accordingly.

Specific needs, motives, appeals, and so forth can be roughly sorted under the five basic needs as shown in Figure 11.6; Napoleon headed toward the self-esteem needs and internal-tension reduction.

## Engaging the Consistency Principle

Our thought systems seek an agreeable, balanced set of relationships between our view of the world and our latest information. This search for consistency suggests that speakers can persuade by using reasoning that causes an audience feelings of dissonance with their own point of view. The word **dissonance** refers to these ill-fitting, inconsistent thoughts. Sources of such dissonance range from logical argument to emotion and mixed feelings.

**COGNITIVE DISSONANCE**    Leon Festinger, chief architect of cognitive-dissonance theory, points out that we could substitute the words *frustration* and *disequilibrium,* among others, for *dissonance.*[18] Whatever the label, the word refers to ill-fitting, inconsistent relationships among our thoughts and beliefs. *Logical* inconsistency is a typical source of dissonance. There are, of course, other sources of dissonance between beliefs based, for example, on past experience and cultural norms.

The basic hypotheses of cognitive-dissonance theory are as follows:

1.    The existence of dissonance, being psychologically uncomfortable, will motivate the person to try to reduce the dissonance and achieve consonance.

2.    When dissonance is present, in addition to trying to reduce it, the person will actively avoid situations and information that would likely increase the dissonance.[19]

The **Theory of Cognitive Dissonance** clearly states that *behavior can cause persuasion.* Many very creative research projects support this point and provide suggestions for involvement and self-persuasion.[20] For example, in arguing against one's own point of view, as college debaters must often do, it was found that the speakers changed their attitudes more than the listeners. This kind of logical inconsistency apparently creates intrapersonal dissonance and, often as a result, self-persuasion.

The practical suggestions stemming from cognitive consistency indicate that a persuader may need to create dissonance through argument (a need) and then show how to achieve consonance (a plan). Audience analysis is needed to see how much need may already exist. The second hypothesis suggests that *too many* dissonance-provoking arguments might induce avoidance. How many are too many? That is not easily answered because an audience's *personal involvement* or commitment, especially a public one, to an issue or its source (pro or con) can make a real difference in how a receiver is apt to respond.[21] A superficial opinion on the number of beans in a jar doesn't represent much personal involvement; a lightly held belief or attitude, such as a preference for one brand of coffee over another, suggests only a modest personal involvement. A public commitment to a religion, family, country, or lifestyle is quite another matter. Here we are dealing with values and serious social constructions of reality. Values were defined earlier as *frameworks that hold attitudes together.* Values involve us very personally. They help define our self-concept. They are ego-centered.

Recent research suggests that when receivers perceive your message as having high personal relevance for them, three really strong arguments are better standing alone than adding another two or three weak ones. Interestingly, when listeners had low personal involvement with the issue, the combination of strong and weak arguments was more persuasive than the strong arguments alone.[22] When people don't see much personal relevance in an issue but *like* the speaker, one good strong argument is often sufficient. It was found more effective than a *disliked* speaker using even as many as five strong arguments.[23]

It seems clear that one is well advised to adapt one's message to the personal interests of the audience. Clarify early why your message is relevant to audience members.

**AFFECTIVE/COGNITIVE DISSONANCE**   Both research and experience suggest that people suffer dissonance when what they feel (affective) and what they believe (cognitive) do not agree.[24] If clear evidence is suddenly discovered that long-time Representative Smith is receiving kickbacks from his staff after their salaries have been padded, you may suffer considerable dissonance (or inconsistency) in supporting him. Your new information (he's dishonest) is inconsistent with your longtime affection for Smith, the man.

Scandals involving politicians, political candidates, and even televangelists have caused many Americans to suffer pangs of affective/cognitive dissonance. How does one reduce such tensions and achieve consistency in such dilemmas? Affective/cognitive theory suggests three things that one can do. All have implications for speakers who would use this merged-mode of persuasion.

Upon hearing the evidence regarding Representative Smith a receiver might (1) reject the data and communication that brought about the difficulty: "I simply don't believe it"; (2) *fragment* the original attitude by trying to isolate the affective and cognitive elements: "Others do it. He just got caught," or "The good he's done outweighs the bad"; or (3) *change* your attitude by accommodating the dilemma in such a way that your feelings and beliefs are consistent: "I'll not vote for him. My feelings have changed. I don't believe in dishonesty." Presumably you could also escape by trying not to think about the inconsistency.

As we learned earlier, the amount of your *involvement* with or *commitment* to Representative Smith could make a difference. A heavily involved person might simply stop at choice 1, that is, reject the news of Representative Smith's dishonesty as preposterous. A lightly involved person might briefly test choices 1 and 2 and then decide on choice 3 and change his or her attitude. Indeed, a hierarchical sequence is suggested here. One's first tendency is to reject, then fragment, and then change one's attitude.

## Using Both-Sides Persuasion

When you feel that you have good, solid arguments to support your position but also know that your audience clearly doesn't agree, is it better to stick with just your one-sided arguments? Or is it better to acknowledge opposing arguments as well?

The advertisement by Seagram Distillers not only acknowledges but also concedes the disrupting effects of too much alcohol. The handwriting in the Seagram ad (Figure 11.7) is also a clear and interesting use of the logical supports of persuasion.

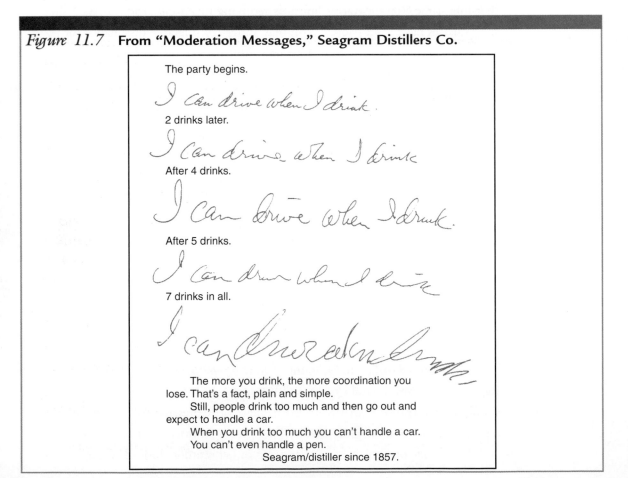

*Figure 11.7*  **From "Moderation Messages," Seagram Distillers Co.**

**Both-sides persuasion** presents arguments both pro and con to the point you are making. This method of organization typically opens with the "other" side, that is, a conceding of some of the obvious arguments against (con) your position. It is a particularly good method when there is obvious antagonism or opposition toward your point of view or when the audience has been *inoculated* against your position.

The effects of argument arrangement on antagonistic receivers when their initial attitudes are known have been generalized as follows:

1. Presenting arguments on both sides of an issue is more effective than giving only the arguments supporting the point being made.

2. Audiences previously persuaded by both-sides argumentation are more resistant to counterpersuasion than those persuaded with one-sided argumentation.

The supporting research concludes that a two-sided presentation is more effective in the long run than a one-sided one (1) when, regardless of initial opinion, the audience is exposed to subsequent counterpersuasion, or (2) when, regardless of subsequent exposure to counterpersuasion, the audience initially disagrees with the speaker's position.[25]

Both-sides persuasion has the appeal of objective, rational evaluation. It is a subtle yet honest call for fair play. Opposing arguments are not omitted; therefore, opposed listeners are less antagonized. Listening should be more favorable because the listener will not be rehearsing as many counterarguments during the positive persuasion. Both-sides persuasion not only helps insulate or inoculate audiences against counterarguments but also forces speakers to be more audience oriented. Successful both-sides speakers are more sensitive to their audience's attitudes and to all the relevant arguments and issues. One student speaker, after much research on both sides of his speech topic, reported that he was now convinced of the other side.

> *He who knows only his side of the story doesn't know that—*
>
> **J. S. Mill,**
> **English philosopher and political economist**

Some specific characteristics of a both-sides persuasive speaker are as follows:

1. *Objectivity* is fair, bases bias on evidence, concedes the obvious, and refutes equitably.

2.  *Suspended judgment* avoids superpositive statements, creates doubt, and frequently uses the hypothesis form.

3.  *Nonspecific opponents* does not stress audience opposition and seeks common ground.

4.  *Critical willingness* promotes common reevaluation and motivates receiver to reconsider the other side.

5.  *Qualified language* avoids overgeneralized statements and avoids harsh criticism.

6.  *Audience sensitivity* adapts the presentation to feedback signs and considers alternative actions before making the speech.

7.  *Ethical conduct* above all, is honest and acknowledges or concedes significant opposing arguments in an objective manner.

If the opposition to the topic bleeds over to include you, the speaker, you should try in some way to establish common ground. The experience of professional speakers pretty much agrees with the more academic suggestions:

1.  Be friendly and modest. (Avoid "I think...")

2.  Refer to common experiences.

3.  Compliment tactfully.

4.  Use tasteful humor (especially at your own expense).

5.  Point out agreements with their beliefs and attitudes.

6.  Commit reasonable time for opposing arguments.[26]

7.  Make sure your facts are absolutely correct and supported.

8.  Let your introducer help establish your credibility.

In its simplest form the both-sides strategy appears as follows:

INTRODUCTION

> **Thesis or Claim:** (Unless obvious, this is typically withheld until the transition.)

BODY

I.  Acknowledgments (con side)
  A. Arguments against your claim

   **B.** Concessions when obvious

**II.**    Transition (An appeal for a fair hearing of your side of the issue)

**III.**    Pro side arguments and appeals

   **A.**
   **B.**    } (Pro)
   **C.**
   **D.** Meeting objections

CONCLUSION

   More detailed organizational methods and illustrations will follow shortly.

# Using Evidence and Logical Reasoning

The intrapersonal and cognitive response models discussed earlier argued that when receivers could be induced to think or elaborate about issue-relevant arguments they were most likely to be persuaded. This was the more central versus the peripheral route to effective persuasion. Clearly a responsible and ethical persuader needs intelligent arguments supported by valid evidence, logical reasoning, and critical thinking. Aristotle refers to this proof of argument as **logos**: reasoning, valid evidence, and arrangement. We will save "Logical Reasoning and Argument," for its own chapter (Chapter 12) but will discuss arrangement (organization methods) next.

# ORGANIZING THE PERSUASIVE SPEECH

## Natural-Order Method

The most famous natural-order or common thinking system is what John Dewey called *reflective thinking*. This pattern is used frequently in group problem solving. It includes the following:

1.    Attention and awareness of felt difficulty

2.    Recognition of a problem or need

3.    Sorting of objections and counterplans in search of the best solution

4.    Working out and visualizing the proposed solution

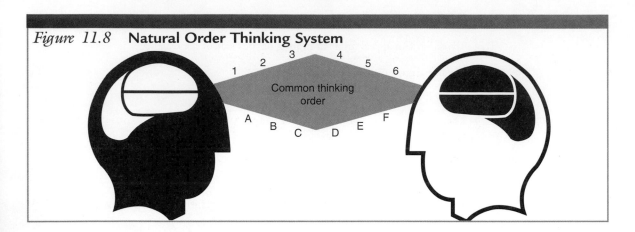

*Figure 11.8*  **Natural Order Thinking System**

Common thinking order

5.    Evaluation of the solution, leading to its acceptance or rejection

If the goal of the speaker is to motivate an audience to action or changed attitudes and beliefs, then following the natural way humans think should help make the argument understandable and hopefully acceptable to the audience. Persuaders and speech scholars have made many adaptations to the model of reflective thinking. One suggests that the fundamental tasks of a speaker are attention, interest, impression, conviction, and direction. Some other popular organization systems based on natural order follow:

Alan H. Monroe called his popular method the motivated sequence, the sequence of ideas that, by following the normal process of thinking, motivates the audience to respond to the speaker's purpose.[28] The key steps are (1) attention, (2) need, (3) satisfaction, (4) visualization, and (5) action. This system argues that, first, our attention must be caught; second, we must be made to feel a definite need; third, we must be shown a way to satisfy this need; fourth, we must be made to see how the proposal applies to us personally; finally, we must be shown how we should act. This system is really a need-plan or need-solution system, as explained in Chapter 6. Most of our TV commercials follow this format.

If you look at Monroe's Motivated Sequence carefully (Figure 11.9), you will see that it is organized very similarly to the descriptions of all our outlines. Section "I" is the introduction with necessary elements to situate and connect to the audience, state the thesis, and preview the main points. "II," "III," and "IV" are main points requiring support, elaboration, and examples. Section "V" is the conclusion that requires a summary, a specific call

*Figure 11.9*    **Monroe's Motivated Sequence**

Introduction

I.  Preview the Persuasive Intent (within the introduction)

    A.  Gain attention of the audience

    B.  Reveal the theme or thesis from which your entire speech flows or to which your requested action is tied

    C.  Signify the importance or significance of the subject to the audience

    D.  Establish credibility of yourself, the speaker

    E.  Preview the persuasive intent and organization.

Body

II.  Present the Need

    A.  Statement: State the nature of the problem.

    B.  Illustration: Illustrate problem with relevant detailed examples.

    C.  Ramification: Show the extent of the problem with statistics and testimony.

    D.  Pointing: Point out the personal implications for the audience members.

III.  Satisfy Problem with a Solution

    A.  Statement: State the attitude, belief or action you want your audience to adopt.

    B.  Explanation: Make your proposal understandable with examples and visual aids.

    C.  Theoretical Demonstration: Show the logical connection between the problem and the solution.

    D.  Reference to Practical Experience: Show where your proposal (or one similar) has worked in past or in similar situations.

    E.  Meeting Objections: Reveal how your proposal overcomes known or anticipated objections (inoculation).

IV.  Visualize the Results

    A.  Positive Method: Describe what the future will look like if your solution is adopted.

    B.  Negative Method: Describe what the future will look like if your solution is NOT adopted.

    C.  Contrast Method: Compare and contrast what the future will look like if the solution is not adopted and how that differs from the adoption of the solution.

Conclusion

V.  Request Action

    A.  Call for overt action, attitude, or belief with which you want audience members to comply. (This is a good place to include a summary of your points, reminding your audience why they should comply.)

    B.  State personal intention to act accordingly.

    C.  End with impact.

to action and a resounding closing statement. It is not always necessary to address each supporting step within the sequence, and sometimes time limitations make it impossible to do so. However, the more clarification and explanation you can provide to the problem and the solution, the more likely your message will be influential.

Natural-order systems for organizing persuasion make much of the attention concept. William James once said, "What holds attention determines action …" This readiness to respond does not, of course, follow every good attention step, but the research on emphasis and its use in successful advertising does suggest its importance. Attention is also selective and often fleeting. It is necessary to concentrate on keeping an audience attentive and interested throughout the steps in the organizing process.

In Chapter 10 we discussed the forms of emphasis useful in transferring information to the audience. Audiences were better able to remember things that they had been told with emphasis. Granted, an improvement in an audience's remembering or interest does not necessarily mean that their attitudes have been changed, or even that they are more open to change. However, if attention and interest do help determine action and a readiness to respond, as James says, then the suggestions for presenting information fit here also.

Whatever specific organization adaptation you decide upon, the following *psychological order* is used, at least theoretically, in all persuasion speeches:

1. Creation of attention and location or establishment of need

2. Arousal of interest and problem awareness by relating the need to the specific audience

3. Explanation of the solution in terms of the problem, need, previous experience, knowledge, and personality of the audience

4. Evaluation, when necessary, of all important objections, counterarguments, or alternative solutions

5. Reinforcement of your message throughout your speech, particularly toward the end of it, through verbal reminders, reviews, summaries, and visualizations

Any message-arrangement prescription is a simplification of a very complex persuasion system. Nevertheless, the popular practices shown in Table 11.1 are

**Table 11.1  A Comparison of Natural-Order Systems**

| | HOLLING-WORTH | MCGEE[27] | MONROE | ROSS |
|---|---|---|---|---|
| **Introduction** | Attention | Attention | Attention | Attention |
| | Interest | Problem | Need | Need |
| **Body** | Impression | Solution | Satisfaction | Plan |
| | Conviction | Visualization | Visualization | Reinforcement |
| **Conclusion** | Direction | Action | Action | Direction |

very useful in showing the relationship of message, receiver, sender, and how one begins to organize the parts of a message.

A speaker's outline on the subject of "Dutch Treating" follows. He used the motivated sequence arrangement method and labeled his motive appeals. You will see that he did not address all supporting elements of the sequence. This outline would have been stronger with a more developed introduction.

MODEL OUTLINE

**Topic:** Dutch-Style Dating

**General Purpose:** To persuade

**Specific Purpose:** To persuade the audience that both men and women reap benefits by "Dutch Treating"

**Central Idea:** Male treating engenders fears of unequal date obligations.

DUTCH IT UP A LITTLE

**INTRODUCTION**

ATTENTION     I.  Women, have you ever dated men whom you really never got to know that well?

(Conflict)     **A.** Have you ever experienced an odd feeling of indebtedness after or even during a first or second date?

    **B.** Have you ever found yourself pushing to enjoy yourself rather than simply being yourself?

|           |       |
|-----------|-------|
| (Conflict) | **II.** Men, have you been discouraged by costly dates?<br>**A.** Since you're paying, do you ever feel chauvinistic?<br>**B.** Have you ever thought that your mixed feelings had stopped the real you from shining through? |
| Credibility | **III.** Our Student Council survey on dating found that women felt indebted when men paid and men took pride in being able to pay. |
| Central Idea | **IV.** Male treating engenders fears of unequal date obligations. |
| Preview | **V.** The question is what can we do about these fears? First, I will describe in more detail wherein lies the problem and then a simple solution that can ultimately benefit everyone. |

**BODY**

|           |       |
|-----------|-------|
| NEED<br>(Conflict) | **I.** To pay or not to pay is a real fear.<br>**A.** Women may appear pushy if they attempt to pay or a pushover if they don't offer.<br>**B.** Men may appear stupid by assuming a woman can't pay or chauvinistic by assuming she shouldn't. |
| (Saftey) | **II.** Whether male or female, students are not usually independently wealthy.<br>**A.** To have one pay the whole bill and the other nothing creates financial stress.<br>   **1.** This stress can cause a feeling of responsibility in the one who pays.<br>   **2.** And can cause a sense of obligation in the one who is treated.<br>**B.** Due to most of face financial limitations, this arrangement might also reduce the number of dates the couple can go on. |
| SATISFACTION | **III.** Only through the practice of the "Dutch Treat" can these fears be alleviated. |
| (Safety) | **A.** Women need not feel uneasy or dependent in any way on men they hardly know. |
| (Love) | **B.** Men are able to say, in a special way, "I'd like to treat you tonight because I enjoy your company." |

      **1.** Contrast to our taken for granted, "He always treats."

      **2.** A way of saying something special we all like to hear

**IV.** Both men and women benefit from "Dutch"-style dating.

(Self-actualization)     **A.** Only when two people are equal in a relationship can they really reach for the sky together.

    **B.** Neither men nor women feel an unnecessary indebtedness with "Dutch"-style dating.

(Love)       **1.** They are thus able to concentrate on how they really interact with each other.

(Self actualization)       **2.** Fulfilling relationships can develop under these conditions.

VISUALIZATION   **V.** The "He always pays" way of dating has gone too far.

    **A.** If a woman wishes to pay her own bill, her date often feels that her action is a form of rejection.

(Safety)       **1.** Why shouldn't she have this right to independence?

      **2.** Couldn't her gesture mean she cares for him and his financial situation?

**VI.** I've experienced this situation myself (personal illustration)

    **A.** Mabel was misunderstood.

    **B.** I had not been forthright.

**CONCLUSION**

ACTION    **I.** Try dating "Dutch" next time, but heed two warnings:

(Fear)     **A.** Misunderstanding may result due to assumed status quo.

    **B.** Misunderstanding may result from a lack of forth-rightness.

**II.** One way to avoid these misunderstanding is to talk about the dinner date before you sit down to dinner.

**III.** Make your dates as enjoyable as my second one with Mabel!

    The next speaker outline followed the more standard introduction-body-conclusion format for the outline and labeled the persuasive modes "logical" and "affective."

MODEL OUTLINE

|  |  |
|---|---|
| **Topic:** | Global Warming |
| **General Purpose:** | To persuade |
| **Specific Purpose:** | To persuade the audience to decrease reliance on fossil fuels |
| **Central Idea:** | Reliance on fossil fuels to maintain our standard of living must be curbed in order to slow the greenhouse effect and global warming. |

BE COOL; LAY OFF THE FUEL

**INTRODUCTION**

I. The greenhouse effect is what makes life sustainable on our planet, by insulating the earth's surface from the cold of space; but too much greenhouse effect can destroy us.

  A. The earth's atmosphere contains trace gases that absorb heat, warming air temperatures, making life livable.

Logical Mode   B. Too much increase in surface air temperatures appears to cause glaciers to speed up their melting process.

  C. Reduction in glaciers contributes to rising sea levels and is said to increase global warming by replacing the bright reflective properties of snow with the dark heat absorbing properties of the sea.

II. Our reliance on fossil fuels is contributing to global warming which is speeding up the greenhouse effect.

  A. Fossil fuels provide our homes with warmth and light and our cars with gas.

Affective Mode   B. Yet, burning these fuels releases carbon dioxide gases which had previously remained trapped.

  C. These carbon dioxide gases absorb heat, which increases the earth's air and water temperature; therein lies the problem.

**BODY**

(Problem)   I. The use of fossil fuels has increased earth's air and water temperature.

  A. This increase in surface temperature increases glacier melt resulting in increased sea level.

      **1.** Glaciers react quickly to temperature changes.

      **2.** Two-thirds of the 54 cubic miles of ice lost by Greenland in 2005 is proposed to be due to rising surface temperatures.

Affective Mode      **B.** Ocean temperatures are also rising.

      **1.** Linking global warming to increased sea levels and temperatures, Kevin Trenberth at the National Center for Atmospheric Science suggests that these warmer temperatures increase water vapors into the atmosphere contributing to stronger storms.

      **2.** Some scientists suggest that this results in increased numbers of strong hurricanes.

      **C.** This is deleterious to animals and plants.

**II.** Fossil fuels are hydrocarbons that are formed from the remains of dead plants and animals and are safely buried deep in the earth's crust.

Logical Mode      **A.** These remains are buried or frozen in the tundra for years.

      **B.** We mine for these fuels in the form of natural gas, coal, and fuel oil.

      **C.** We then use these fuels to generate electricity, power our cars, and heat our homes.

      **1.** Human's reliance on fossil fuels is said to be the largest source of emissions of carbon dioxide, one of the sources of greenhouse gases leading to global warming.

      **2.** According to the US EPA, 85–90 percent of greenhouse gas emissions come from the combustion of fossil fuels.

(Solution)  **III.** Decreasing your consumption of fossil fuels can slow the greenhouse effect and stave off global warming.

      **A.** Everyone can choose to simply modify his or her behaviors.

      **1.** Choose to ride your bike or walk for short errands.

Logical Mode      **2.** Carpool or use the bus for regular routines to and from school or work.

      **3.** Reduce the number of vehicles your family depends on.

      **4.** Make sure that you run errands in a circle, or on the way home from a daily routine.

      **B.** Replace fossil fuels with alternative fuels.

      **1.** Use an alternative fuel vehicle.

Logical Mode    **2.** If more people demanded alternative fuel vehicles, car companies would be more likely to research and market these vehicles.

**CONCLUSION**

Merged Mode    **I.** The increased greenhouse effect and its resulting global warming are decreasing the sustainability of our planet.

    **A.** Human's reliance on fossil fuels is said to be the largest source of emissions of carbon dioxide, a major contributor to Global Warming.

(Visualization)    **B.** If we don't make changes now, our future is in peril.

    **II.** Reducing impact on the Earth's resources is everyone's responsibility.

    **A.** Re-evaluate your behavior.

    **B.** Make sound choices in how you use energy.

    **C.** Support renewable energy sources like alternative fuels.

    **D.** Do your part to be a part of our planet!

# Both-Sides Method

There are three general ways to organize two-sided messages 1) acknowledge and concede first (con); 2) present your side first (pro); and 3) repeat the con-pro order with each issue (con/pro, con/pro, and so forth).

The research evidence discussed earlier generally supports the *con-pro* order, that is, acknowledge and concede first, then refute and explain your side. This is an especially good choice when audiences are antagonistic, ill humored, or hostile. When audiences are not unusually troubled with your position, it may be enough to simply discuss and meet objections to your case at the end of the speech. If your speech involves multiple issues each of which is in contention, it may be advisable to interweave the con-pro strategy as you take up each new issue.

A useful format for the con-pro order follows. First, acknowledge or concede opposing arguments and then refute and support your own claim.

        **Topic:**

    **General Purpose:**    Persuade (both-sides persuasion)

    **Specific Purpose:**

    **Thesis or Claim:**

INTRODUCTION

Attention

Orientation (Note: you may hold back the central idea in the intro)

Credibility

Preview of the persuasive intent

BODY (CON)

Acknowledge con arguments

Concede con arguments

TRANSITION

The bridge between the con and pro:
an appeal for fair hearing
and reciprocity

BODY (PRO)

Refutation and arguments supporting your claim

CONCLUSION

Review and/or visualization

Final pro-side appeal

If your speech has two or three major arguments or contentious issues that pretty much stand alone, the "con-pro-repeat" organization might be preferable:

INTRODUCTION

BODY

Argument A

Con side

Pro side

Argument B

Con side

Pro side

Argument C

    Con side

    Pro side

CONCLUSION

    A sample student outline showing both-sides organization follows. Note that it opens with a concession and the critical arguments against (con) the position. The state of Michigan has a deposit law on beer and soft drink containers. A campaign to repeal the deposit law was under way, supported by both the Can Manufacturing Institute and some consumers who objected to the extra cost. Many in the audience supported the repeal and all would be exposed to media counterpersuasion—a good time for both-sides persuasion.

## MODEL BOTH-SIDES OUTLINE

| | |
|---|---|
| **Topic:** | Repeal of deposit law |
| **General Purpose:** | To persuade (both-sides persuasion) |
| **Specific Purpose:** | To persuade the audience to retain the deposit law |
| **Central Idea:** | We should resist the campaign to repeal the deposit law because the law protects the environment at a reasonable cost. |

## MANY HAPPY RETURNS

### INTRODUCTION

(Attention)    **I.** Are these a familiar sight to you? (Exhibits: several bottles and cans).

(Credibility)      **A.** As you know, last December 3rd the deposit law went into effect.

          **1.** It requires a deposit on all beer and soft drink containers.

          **2.** Deposits are then repaid when consumers return the containers for reuse or recycling.

     **B.** Since most of you probably drink soft drinks or beer, this law affects you directly.

BODY (CON SIDE)

   **I.** You, as consumers know this law does affect your pocketbook.

     **A.** The Can Manufacturing Institute's recent survey of shelf prices indicates that beer and soft drinks cost about one dollar a case more in Michigan than in states that don't have deposit laws.

(Acknowledgments and Concessions)

     **B.** The Stroh Brewing Company and Coca-Cola of Detroit concede: "Unfortunately the cost of doing business has to be passed on."

   **II.** Industry representatives show that the price increases are due to the extra handling which the law creates.

     **A.** When the consumer returns the bottles and cans, the retailer has to store them until the bottler picks them up.

     **B.** Many retailers and bottlers are complaining about storage problems and sanitation problems, which increase costs.

       **1.** They need more warehouse space to store empties.

       **2.** They need bottle washers.

       **3.** They need additional delivery trucks to transport the empties.

       **4.** They also need to hire more drivers.

   **III.** There are other complaints about the law.

     **A.** It eliminates some jobs in glassmaking (bottles are reused).

     **B.** The law probably wastes energy by forcing trucks to make additional trips with empty containers.

**Transition to Pro Side**  But if you really think about it, what are we supposed to do?

     **A.** Repeal the law like the Associated Food Dealers want to do.

     **B.** Then go back to all the cans, bottles, and broken glass on our streets, highways, and landscaping.

     **C.** I think not; listen to the reasons for supporting our deposit law.

BODY (PRO SIDE)

   **I.** Volunteers have recently staged a cleanup throughout the state.

     **A.** Of nine thousand items picked up, only nine were returnables.

(Evidence)       **B.** Look at the differences in our roadsides and our neighborhoods (before and after pictures).

                 **C.** Our penalty litter fines obviously were not doing the job.

**II.** Five other states now have deposit laws.

                 **A.** A survey in Oregon (which has a long-standing deposit law) says that 95 percent of the people still favor the law.

                 **B.** Oregon's deposit return rate is 94 percent.

                 **C.** In Vermont (which also has a deposit law) a study shows the following:

                     **1.** A 76 percent decline in beverage litter

                     **2.** A 35 percent reduction in total litter volume

(Evidence)           **3.** A 31 percent decline in state costs for litter pick-up

                     **4.** The law has created about four hundred new jobs in sorting, storing, and truck driving.

                     **5.** Vermont figures that the container manufacturers save 708 million BTUs in energy annually as a result of recycling and reuse. (That's enough energy to heat the homes of fifteen thousand people.)

(Meeting **III.** The increase in the prices of beer and soft
Objections) drinks may also be caused by other factors.

                 **A.** The Michigan United Conservation Clubs recently asked the Attorney General to investigate the increases in prices. They found that:

                     **1.** Many bottlers changed their product designs.

                     **2.** Bottlers switched to metric volumes. (Display 1/2 liter Coke bottle.)

                     **3.** Bottlers installed new equipment.

                 **B.** These are new and mostly one-time costs.

                 **C.** Once these costs are assimilated, bottle and can prices should drop.

                     **1.** The average bottle is used over and over (about fifteen times).

                     **2.** The aluminum cans are recycled over and over and over, which reduces the cost of aluminum and saves our natural resources.

                     **3.** A Faygo spokesman said that the deposit law would result in some reduced prices after the new equipment is paid for.

CONCLUSION

I.   The deposit law is a way to deal with the problem of litter from beverage containers.

   **A.** Isn't it nice to see the Michigan streets cleaner again?

   **B.** Wouldn't it be even nicer to see the whole country cleaner?

(Visualization)   **C.** Because people have to pay a deposit on a container, it's more than likely they will return it rather than throw it around.

   **D.** As we have seen, the deposit law is not solely responsible for our current price increases.

   **E.** It may be inconvenient returning the containers but isn't it worth the trouble?

II.   This law is a major step in cleaning up this country. Support the deposit law—resist the repeal campaign.

   **A.** If someone asks you to sign a petition to repeal the law, DON'T DO IT.

(Final Appeal)   **B.** If, by some chance, it comes on the ballot in 1998, vote to keep our deposit law.

   **C.** There is talk of a nationwide deposit law to clean up the whole country. I urge your support.

III.   The benefits greatly outweigh the inconvenience.

   **A.** Help keep Michigan and the nation clean.

   **B.** "Many Happy Returns"

In the back of the text you find a manuscripted persuasive speech written for Former President Jimmy Carter. It is his undelivered Energy Speech, originally scheduled for July 5, 1979, during one of the country's worst fuel crises. You can analyze the speech to see what format most closely indicates the organization he followed.

# SPEAKER INTEGRITY

We cannot conclude this chapter without a section on speaker integrity. In the world of persuasion, a speaker has the personal and cultural values, beliefs, and attitudes to concern himself with. These are deeply entrenched and are woven together to create the tapestry of our perceived lives. This section places speaker integrity in its right context.

## Being Communicationally Sensitive

A persuasive appeal is only as good as its "fit" or match to a given audience. Ironically, unethical persuaders have usually learned this lesson well. The patent medicine salesperson takes care to avoid the medically informed or quickly fails. Honest salespersons can fail just as readily if insensitive to their audiences and become unintentionally unethical by selling a product or idea to unknowns who will injure themselves or others. The bartender is interested in your age; the handgun seller in your permit; the doctor in your medical history, and so on. For any of these people not to care about these matters is clearly an ethical matter.

*Communication sensitivity* involves effectively and ethically matching the message we are sending to the requirements of the receivers, the situation, and the context. It is a measure of a speaker's willingness to consider carefully the psychological environment before encoding messages. It is the ability to judge public and interpersonal encounters accurately and to sense when to be rhetorically sensitive and when to be rhetorically assertive.

For a speaker to use complicated statistics to impress a sophisticated audience is one thing; to use them as a deceptive strategy on an unsophisticated audience is unethical. To use inflated statistics to raise consciousness or because the cause is just, is also unethical. Politicians and even spokespeople for very worthy causes often overlook this fact.

We learned earlier that a given message does not mean the same thing to all people and that perceptions and understandings vary within contexts and situations. Without some consideration of the receivers, we stand a good chance of confusing or unintentionally deceiving our receivers. A child may decode a message quite differently from that of a mature adult. How a particular person will interpret a particular message is also an ethical consideration.

## Culpable Ignorance

Most moral, professional, and legal codes carefully consider *intent* in passing judgments. However, our legal systems are harsh on people who are expected to "know better" and to "behave better." Witness the large number of medical and legal malpractice suits or our treatment of political, religious, and even sports figures who stray from expected behaviors. Trained, educated speakers have special ethical obligations beyond intent. Listeners, like patients and clients, also have responsibilities to society and to themselves.

The role or status of a speaker enters into ethical evaluations of that speaker. A qualified person serving in a leadership role has special ethical obligations. We expect our political and religious leaders and our professional people to be responsible, regardless of intent. A doctor convicted of malpractice rarely intended to do harm. An incompetent teacher may have good intentions. We hold such people ethically responsible, even though their intent may have been good. As one jokester put it, "Congress has the Ten Commandments bottled up in the ethics committee." They had better "unbottle" them since our laws accommodate these premises, not just for political leaders and professionals, but for all public figures as well. Senators, representatives, and other public figures have less protection from libel and slander than does the average citizen. (They do, of course, have their protective immunities.)

All of us have some ethical obligations beyond intent. Those who "meant well" have hurt many people. All of us have an obligation to get our facts straight before sending messages that might capriciously misinform or injure the receiver. Moralists call this **culpable ignorance**, that is, ignorance that comes from carelessness and thus deserves blame.[5]

## Affording Clues and Choice

The following postulates are offered as guidance. If there were such a thing as a covering law, it would be that speakers are ethically responsible for the strategies employed, inferred, or attributed.

It is unethical for a speaker to simply conceal his or her real purpose, the organization represented, or to pretend to speak objectively when really an advocate of only one point of view. This postulate or rule is obvious in some contexts but not as clear in others. A man posing as a minister to bilk a senior citizen of her money, a Marxist pretending to be a capitalist—these are unethical if the concealment or deception is *total* (that is, if there is no real clue), whether the concealed entity is purpose, organization, or point of view. What of legitimate strategy? Perhaps rhetorically one should not be too quick to shout out one's point of view or purpose. To do so might prohibit any kind of a hearing. The emerging theorem is that you are rhetorically ethical as long as your concealment is not total or is not so delayed that it has no chance of being heard.

As process-oriented receivers we should be on guard and perhaps expect some overstatement when listening to a person with an obvious ax to grind—a politician, salesperson, or promoter. If that person is within the law (no false claims, misrepresentative statistics, slander, and so on) and does not falsely or totally conceal the purpose or the organization represented, he or she is probably meeting this ethical postulate.

Honest clues protect the receiver's fundamental right of choice. Even in social compliance situations, one usually has some choice. When choice is minimal, one usually has some alternatives (the courts, when necessary). The ultimate decision on how to behave, act, interpret, or believe must be in some way, however small, left to the receiver. That choice must be a viable one. "Your money or your life" is no real choice. In a democracy choice is a very special ethical consideration for speakers, especially when their purpose is to persuade.

**USE OF EMOTIONAL APPEALS**    Appealing to the emotions is not a new ethical question. Plato and Aristotle argued it long ago. Plato counseled that emotional appeals should be avoided because they detract from the truth. Aristotle felt that it was a speaker's moral *purpose*, not his or her art, that made such appeals unethical. The use of emotional arguments when there is *no* evidence to support one's point is for Aristotle (and most modern rhetoricians) unethical. It is also unethical if the emotional argument clearly flies in the face of what the receivers, given time, would find in their own investigations.

In an angry speech one is not always searching for truth. One may not intend to distort unfairly, but it happens. As receivers we should be reminded that humans are emotional as well as rational and that free citizens have a right to sound off and frequently do. Our ethical tolerance should include a healthy discounting of legitimate emotional appeals.

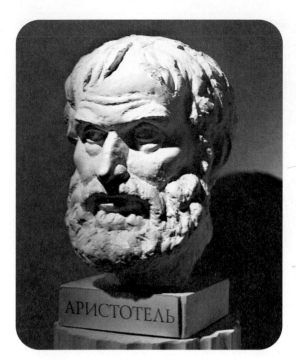

Aristotle felt that it was a speaker's moral purpose, not his or her art, that made emotional appeals unethical.

**FAIR HEARING**   As receivers we have an obligation to seek out clues and choices, to question and clarify, to give a fair hearing once we have committed ourselves to some legitimate interest in an issue. We must make an effort to understand the sender's biases and intent. We should show tolerance. Fair hearing replaces force in a free society. The listener must also help decide what constitutes valid proof and a legitimate appeal to the emotions.

To give fair hearing we must also analyze our range of acceptance. Are we really stuck with a "hard" attitude? Is there some latitude in our position? Giving a fair hearing also means allowing the other person some chance to talk. Ethical communication doesn't outlaw aggressive arguing, but it does outlaw excessive monologuing; it does necessitate giving the sender some chance to make and explain his or her point. Fair hearing also calls for fair fighting. Sandbagging or setting people up for obvious embarrassment borders on unethical (and often illegal) entrapment. Dragging in every superfluous issue in order to deliberately confuse is another violation of ethics.

**LIES AND FALSE FACTS**   A lie is a statement intended to deceive. "He tells a lie who has one thing in his mind and says something else by words or by any signs whatsoever." To some moral philosophers, the natural end of speech is to communicate with our thoughts, and a lie is evil because it frustrates the very purpose of speech. A speaker is responsible for telling the truth and for the social consequences that result if the truth is not told. This view includes not only our words, but all of our nonverbal communication.

**FALSE PRETENSE**   A person posing as a doctor of medicine may do considerable harm through such a charade. Speaking as a qualified economist or engineer while lacking the background to do so is also dangerous and unethical. This is not

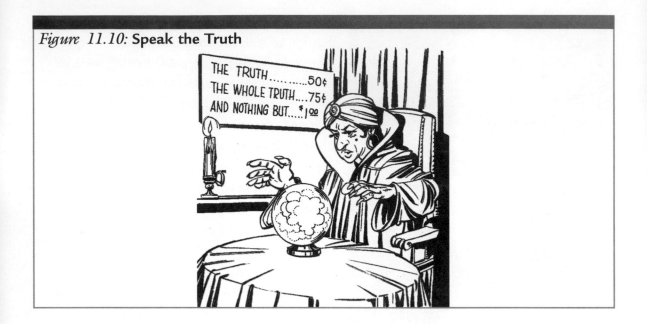

*Figure 11.10*: **Speak the Truth**

to say (assuming we are not posing) that we must remain silent on taxes, wage concessions, automotive engineering, and the like. The point is that we should not mis-
lead others about our *qualifications* to expound.

Someone may be a brilliant NBA star but not an expert on foreign policy.
This individual has as much right as anyone else to speak his mind, but less so
if he's *posing* as an authority or if we've paid thirty dollars to hear him speak
about basketball. There are, however, several clues for us here; and so he may
be guilty of poor judgment but not unethical communication (unless he was
grossly in breach of his contract).

**UNSUPPORTED PERSONAL ATTACKS**    When a speaker attacks the character of an opponent rather than the issue at hand, that person is guilty of *ad
hominem* argument (unless the character of the person *is* the issue). When ***ad
hominem*** is used solely to change the argument from one of issues to one of personalities, as a rule it is considered unethical. Our legal system calls it *slander* if the
personal charges are unsupported and *libel* if the charges are put in writing—clearly
serious matters of ethics (and legality) for responsible speakers. It is unethical for a
speaker to divert attention from weaknesses in his or her argument by unsupported
attacks on an opponent.

# Democracy and Demagoguery

A democratic system based on a sound legal system is designed to avoid decay by welcoming free speech and often, harsh criticism. It needs that input to adapt to a changing world. However, there is a limit. Free speech turned to license and irresponsible rhetoric is demagoguery. Such speaking injures and threatens the integrity of any speechmaking subsystem; but more, it threatens the social, political, and legal systems of all of us. Articulate demagogues like Hitler and Mussolini have destroyed political systems, in large part, through deliberately using irresponsible speech. The United States has had its eloquent demagogues as well: Huey Long, Joseph McCarthy, Charles Coughlin, and some zealots still on the scene. Their *intent*, then and now, was ostensibly to preserve the system through intemperate criticism or impassioned calls for radical behavior, which in reality threatened the system.

> *"Every wicked man is in a state of ignorance as to what he ought to do and what he should refrain from doing, and it is due to this kind of error that men become unjust and, in general, immoral."*
>
> **Aristotle**

Being honest and fair to the facts are agreed-upon rules for most of us. We must play by the rules and obey the law. The use of outright lies, manufactured facts, and "dirty tricks" is unethical.

Hitler was a demagogue who used rhetoric irresponsibly to promote ideas of hate.

It is also possible to be fair to a legal statute and yet lose sight of one's ethical responsibilities to a larger system. Meeting the letter but not the spirit of the law is an example.

# CHAPTER REVIEW
## *Wrapping it up*

## *Summary*

Check out our website
**www.bvtlab.com**
for flashcards,
summaries,
self-quizzes and speeches.

All speeches to persuade involve efforts to get receivers to do the following: 1) accept your interpretation of *disputed facts—what is or is not the case;* or 2) align their *beliefs, attitudes,* and *values* more closely with yours—what is better, worse, right or wrong; and/or 3) move them to *action* on your proposition. When we deal with more involved courses of action, we are talking about policy—speeches on what *should* or *should not* be done over time. In action speeches one must demonstrate a need or problem and then provide a plan or solution and show the practically of the plan in fixing the problem. Most attitudes are changed incrementally.

Influence refers to any power that affects a person or course of events. Motivation pertains to any stimulation or inducement that leads to an act or belief. Motivation need not be intentional and is essentially amoral. Persuasion is an ethical, nonviolent means of influencing and motivating others through messages. It is an instrument for obtaining reasoned adherence to rational propositions.

Attitudes refer to thinking, feeling, and behavioral intentions that govern our predispositions toward people, situations, and things. An attitude may also be defined as a tendency to respond in a given way. The dimensions of attitude have been described as cognitive, affective, and behavioral. Attitudes are underlaid by belief systems, which have vertical and horizontal structures; that is, we can engage them at different levels. A single point on a scale cannot always adequately represent attitudes. They have different ranges or latitudes of acceptance. There is also a tendency for attitude response to have assimilation or contrast effect depending on how discrepant one's initial attitude is.

The *Elaboration Likelihood Method* (ELM) of persuasion suggests that the more elaborately a receiver responds cognitively, the greater the likelihood of attitude change. *Cognitive-response theory* suggests that people really persuade themselves through cognitive (or thought) reevaluations. The basic speaker strategy is to develop messages that 1) evoke favorable thoughts and 2) induce people to rehearse and remember these thoughts.

In the *intrapersonal-response model,* these responses may be affective and behavioral as well as cognitive. *Persuasion,* in this context, *is a process of skillfully and ethically using logical thoughts, affective appeals, credibility, and ethical proof to influence and motivate others to respond as you wish them to.*

Five routes to effective persuasion include credibility (ethos), human needs (pathos), consistency theory, both-sides persuasion, and logical reasoning (logos).

Credibility (referred to as proof of *ethos* by Aristotle) refers to the audience's acceptance of or disposition toward the source. It is related to Aristotle's notions of goodwill, good moral character, and good sense—which can be described as the speaker's character and competence. High source credibility generally produces more attitude change. Ethical proof includes attitude similarity, language, humor, voice, evidence, and general impression—which can be described as the speaker's charisma.

Impression management includes practical facts on how you present yourself to receivers. Front is your appearance and manner. *Dramatic realization* is the role you play on the stage of life. *Mystification* refers to the social distance between you and the audience.

Maslow's theory provides us with a useful classification of human needs. From the basic to the higher order needs, these needs are physiological, safety, love, esteem, and self-actualization. A satisfied need is no longer a motivator according to this theory. Motive appeals (what Aristotle refers to as proof of *pathos*) are useful triggers of human needs.

Cognitive-dissonance theory assumes that when new information is contradictory to or inconsistent with a person's ideas and attitudes, some psychological confusion and tension will result. This tension motivates people to adjust their attitudes or behavior in order to reduce this inconsistency. (A persuader needs to create enough dissonance [or need] and then show how to achieve consonance [a plan].) However, too many dissonance-provoking arguments might induce avoidance. Other variables that may intrude are speaker likability and the personal involvement of the audience.

An audience's personal involvement or commitment to an issue or its source makes a difference in how they are apt to respond. The number and strength of arguments used by a sender should vary with the personal relevance perceived by receivers.

Affective/cognitive consistency theory suggests that when our beliefs are in conflict with our feelings, the resulting dissonance can be relieved by 1) rejecting the data, 2) fragmenting the original attitude, or 3) changing our attitude.

How one organizes or arranges the message as well as the logic and reasoning provided is what Aristotle refers to as *logos.* Both-sides persuasion has been shown to be superior to one-sided persuasion when the audience is initially opposed to the point of view being presented or when, regardless of initial attitude, the audience is exposed to counterargument. A rational form of persuasion, the both-sides approach is characterized by objectivity, suspended judgment, nonspecific opponents, critical willingness, qualified language, audience sensitivity, and ethical conduct.

A natural thinking order suggest the following procedure for organizing persuasive messages:

1. Creation of attention and location or establishment of need

2. Arousal of interest and problem awareness by relating the need to the specific audience

3. Explanation of the solution in terms of the problem, need, previous experience, knowledge, and personality of the audience

4. Evaluation, when necessary, of all important objections, counterarguments, or alternative solutions

5. Reinforcement of the message throughout the speech, particularly toward the end, through verbal reminders, reviews, summaries, and visualizations

There are many plans similar to this one. Hollingworth suggests that the fundamental tasks of a speaker are attention, interest, impression, conviction, and direction.

Alan H. Monroe calls his system the motivated sequence, "the sequence of ideas which, by following the normal process of thinking, motivates the audience to respond to the speaker's purpose." The key steps are 1) attention, 2) need, 3) satisfaction, 4) visualization, and 5) action.

There are three ways to organize two-sided messages: 1) acknowledge opposition and concede first (con); 2) present your side first (pro); and 3) repeat the con-pro order with each argument (con-pro, con-pro, and so forth). The con-pro order works best when audiences are antagonistic or ill-humored. When audiences are not unusually troubled it is often enough to state your case and meet objections to it at the close. In multiple argument or issue speeches, the interwoven con-pro strategy may work best.

Responsible speakers and listeners should know that a democratic system based on a sound legal system is designed to avoid decay by welcoming both free speech and harsh criticism. However, free speech turned to license and irresponsible rhetoric is demagoguery. A qualified person serving in a leadership role has special ethical obligations. All of us have some obligation to get our facts straight before sending messages that might capriciously misinform or injure the receiver. Moralists call this culpable ignorance—that is, ignorance usually arising from carelessness and deserving of blame.

A communicator is responsible for telling the truth and for the social consequences that result if the truth is not told. Using outright lies, manufactured facts, and dirty tricks is clearly unethical. Some mental reservations are allowed as long as there are fair and sufficient clues within the special contexts and situations. A strict mental reservation without any clue is a lie in any context. The ultimate decision or choice on how to behave, act, interpret, or believe must in some way, however small, be left to the receiver.

As receivers we have an obligation to give fair hearing once we have committed ourselves to some legitimate interest in an issue. Ethical communications preserve the integrity of the ego, provide the information needed, permit and encourage the expression of thought and feeling, and reveal respect for the person as a person.

## *Notes*

1.  David Krech, Richard S. Crutchfield, Norman Livson, William A. Wilson, Jr., and Allen Parducci, *Elements of Psychology* 4th ed. (New York: Alfred A Knopf, 1982), p. 435.

2.  See Raymond S. Ross, *Understanding Persuasion,* 4th ed. (Englewood Cliffs, N.J.: Prentice Hall, 1994), pp. 65–68.

3.  For more on this theory, see Ross, *Understanding Persuasion,* pp. 79–83; also see Carolyn Sherif, Muzafer Sherif, and Roger Nebergall, Attitude and Attitude Change (Philadelphia: Saunders, 1965; reprint 1982), p. 226.

4.  See Richard E. Petty and John T. Cacioppo, "The Elaboration Likelihood Model of Persuasion," *Advances in Experimental Social Psychology,* vol. 19 (New York: Academic Press, 1986), p. 175.

5.  Richard M. Perloff and Timothy C. Brock, "…'And Thinking Makes It So': Cognitive Responses to Persuasion," in *Persuasion: New Directions in Theory and Research,* ed. Michael E. Roloff and Gerald R. Miller (Beverly Hills, Calif.: Sage Publications, Inc., 1980), p. 90. For a modified view, see Daniel J. Breti and James Price Dillard, "Persuasion and the Internality Dimension of Cognitive Responses," *Communication Studies,* 42, no. 2 (Summer 1991), 103–13.

6.  John T. Cacioppo and Richard E. Petty, "Central and Peripheral Routes to Persuasion: The Role of Message Repetition," in *Psychological Processes and Advertising Effects,* eds. Linda F. Alwitt and Andrew A. Mitchell (Hillsdale, N.J.: Erlbaum, 1985), pp. 91–111.

7.  Petty and Cacioppo, "Elaboration Likelihood Model."

8.  Richard J. Lutz, "Affective and Cognitive Antecedents of Attitude Toward the Ad: A Conceptual Framework," in Alwitt and Mitchell, *Psychological Processes and Advertising Effects,* pp. 45–63; also see R. P. Bagozzi, "An Examination of the Validity of Two Models of Attitude," *Multivariate Behavioral Research,* 16 (1981), 323–59; and R. R Bagozzi, A. M. Tybout, C. S. Craig, and B. Sternthal, "The Construct Validity of the Tripartite Classification of Attitudes," *Journal of Marketing Research,* 16 (1979), 88–95.

9.  See Lane Cooper, *The Rhetoric of Aristotle* (New York: Appleton-Century-Crofts, 1932), pp. 24–25.

10. See Rajeev Batra and Michael L. Ray, "How Advertising Works," in Alwitt and Mitchell, *Psychological Processes and Advertising Effects,* pp. 13–43.

11.  Jesse G. Delia, "A Constructivist Analysis of the Concept of Credibility," *The Quarterly Journal of Speech,* 62, no. 4 (December 1976), 361–75.

12.  Jane Allyn and Leon Festinger, "The Effectiveness of Unanticipated Persuasive Communications," *Journal of Abnormal and Social Psychology* 62 (1961), 35–40.

13.  James E. McCLeaf and Margaret A. Colby, "The Effects of Students' Perceptions of a Speaker's Role on Their Recall of Drug Facts and Their Opinions and Attitudes about Drugs," *Journal of Educational Research,* 68 (July 1975), 382–86.

14.  James J. Bradac, Catherine W. Konsky, and Robert A. Davies, "Two Studies of the Efforts of Linguistic Diversity upon the Judgments of Communicator Attributes and Message Effectiveness," *Communication Monographs,* 43 (March 1976), 70–79.

15.  Erving Goffman, *The Presentation of Self in Everyday Life* (Garden City, N.Y: Doubleday & Company, 1959; New York: Overlook Press, 1974), p. 208.

16.  Abraham H. Maslow, "A Theory of Human Motivation," *Psychological Review,* 50 (1943), 370–96.

17.  Abraham H. Maslow, *Toward a Psychology of Being,* (New York: Van Nostrand Reinhold Company, 1968), p.25.

18.  Leon Festinger, *A Theory of Cognitive Dissonance* (Stanford, Calif.: Stanford University Press, 1957), p. 14; also see Tori DeAngelis, "Cognitive Dissonance Alive and Well," *APA Monitor* August, 1990, p. 10.

19.  Ibid., p. 3.

20.  Ross, *Understanding Persuasion,* pp. 76–79.

21.  See Chris A. Dickerson, Ruth Thibodeau, Elliot Aronson, and Dayna Miller, "Using Cognitive Dissonance to Encourage Water Conservation," *Journal of Applied Social Psychology* 22, no. 11 (June 1992), 841–54.

22.  R. E. Petty and J. T. Cacioppo, "The Effects of Involvement on Responses to Argument Quantity and Quality: Central and Peripheral Routes to Persuasion," *Journal of Personality and Social Psychology* 46 (984), 69–81.

23.  S. Chaiken, "Heuristic Versus Systematic Information Processing and the Use of Source Versus Message Cues in Persuasion," *Journal of Personality and Social Psychology,* 39 (1980), 752–66.

24.  Milton Rosenberg and Robert Abelson, "An Analysis of Cognitive Balancing," in *Attitude Organization and Change,* eds. Carl Hovland and Milton Rosenberg (New Haven: Yale University Press, 1960; Westport, Conn.: Greenwood Press, Inc., 1980), pp. 112–63; see also M. Rosenberg, "An Analysis of Affective-Cognitive Consistency," in *Attitude Organization and Change,* pp. 15–64.

25.  For a review of the classic Yale studies, see Ross, *Understanding Persuasion,* pp. 189–96; also see Mike Allen, Jerold Hale, Paul Mongeau, Sandra Berkowitz-Stafford, Shane Stafford, William Shanahan, Philip Agee, Kelly Dillon, Robert Jackson, and Cynthia Ray, "Testing a Model of Message Sidedness: Three Replications," *Communication Monographs,* 57, no. 4 (December 1990), 275–91.

26.  See Mike Allen, "Meta-Analysis Comparing the Persuasiveness of One-sided and Two-sided Messages," *Western Journal of Speech Communication,* 55, no. 4, (Fall 1991), 390–404.

27.  John A. McGee, *Persuasive Speaking* (New York: Charles Scribner's Sons, 1929).

28.  B. E. Gronbeck, R. E. McKerrow, D. Ehninger, and A. H. Monroe, *Principles and Types of Speech Communication,* 13th ed. (New York: Addison Wesley Longman Publishers, 1996), p. 175.

29.  Richard L. Johannesen, *Ethics in Human Communication,* 4th ed. (Prospect Heights, Ill.: Waveland Press, 1997), p.10.

# LOGICAL REASONING AND ARGUMENT

# Chapter 12

## Chapter Objectives

# COGNITIVE PERSUASION

## The "Mostly" Central Route

In our last chapter, we introduced Aristotle's *three proofs of an argument (ethos, pathos, and logos)* and explained how arrangement or organization works toward fulfilling the proof of logos. In this chapter we look further into logos by describing the thinking and reasoning process. In the cognitive or more "central route" of the persuasion process, we are concerned primarily with evidence, rational reasoning, critical thinking, and argument—that is, with the logical rather than the psychological and emotive modes of persuasion.

When we speak of arguments, we are speaking of *making* arguments rather than *having* them. In other words, we aren't talking about fighting over who does the dishes. Nonetheless, when we are in a heated argument over the dishes, we are using the same intrapersonal thinking process that we use when making a point in a debate on the best candidate for president; unfortunately we often don't take the time to extricate our emotions from the argument over the dishes. In either case, fighting over who does the dishes or debating who should be president, the internal efforts of the listener to evaluate the reasons, evidence, and argument, if elaborated positively by receivers, lead to persuasion. How we, as speakers, construct and support a particular claim we are

*Figure 12.1:* **Human Processes to Persuasion**

making through our organization and our reasoning helps the listener evaluate it for acceptance or rejection.

Humans are clearly different from animals in that they have the capacity to reason at higher levels of abstraction. They are, as a result, vulnerable to unethical or confused appeals that only *sound* logical. Those who intentionally muddle their arguments or befuddle their receivers are perhaps the most unethical persuaders of all. Those who don't analyze their audiences and check their assumptions are not far behind.

Ms. Clocko put the new student in the first grade in Traverse City, Michigan, on the spot when she asked, "Scott, when do the robins come to your home?" An uncomfortable six-year-old seemed evasive and confused. "Come, come Scott, you know the answer. Think hard."

In a tentative, trembling voice, Scott answered, "Fall."

"No, no, no. You think for a moment. Mark, can you answer the question?"

"Yes, Ms. Clocko—spring."

The sad part of this story is that Ms. Clocko was reasoning only from her view of the situation. Scott had recently moved from New Orleans, his home of birth, where the robins indeed do come in the fall.

As humans, capable of higher reasoning, we are often vulnerable to unethical or confusing appeals that only sound logical. Ms. Clocko, who asked Scott about the robins, demonstrated an example of this concept.

The discussions that follow should help us avoid Ms. Clocko's problems (and Scott's) and also protect us from those who would intentionally use deceptive reasoning and argument.

We should be aware of unethical or confused arguments and the overlapping nature of emotive and rational appeals as we study the *primarily* logical, central modes of persuasion. Other things being equal; good, clear evidence, reasoning, and argument are critical to the quality and stature of your persuasion.

## Evidence

In Chapter 4, we discussed the different types of evidence and the importance in supplying what is necessary for your audience to understand your message. If you recall, evidence may be observable objects or phenomena or reliable reports from experts on such things. Three major forms of evidence utilized in persuasion include examples, testimony, and statistics. In persuasion, evidence takes on a particularly important role. First, it helps to explain the points you are making; second, it provides the support needed to secure your argument in the minds of your listeners; and third, evidence is at the crux of the reasoning process that we will explain momentarily.

A speaker's use of good *evidence* may significantly increase immediate attitude change and credibility when the message is delivered well, and particularly when the audience has little or no prior familiarity with the evidence. Evidence also appears to make listeners less easily persuaded by future counterargument. Assuming a message has information of some essential worth, the delivery of it and its accompanying ethical proof are also important to how the audience finally evaluates the evidence.[1]

## How We Reason

We might have many clear examples, strong testimony and coherent statistics that can be used to support our claim, but how we tie these pieces of evidence to our claim is just as important as the evidence itself. This process of connecting the evidence to the claim is called reasoning. How we reason tells the listener a lot about who we are and how we think. Since we have learned that public speaking is primarily an audience-centered activity, we must carefully consider what reasoning our audience will most likely follow and understand.

In the following section we will discuss some of the major western reasoning patterns. It should be noted, however, that cultures vary in what constitutes support for an argument. In some native cultures, storytelling by the learned or respected member of the tribe is a reasoning pattern that is accepted as proof for the claim being made. In the case of storytelling, the conclusion is often drawn by the audience rather than provided by the speaker.

# FORMS OF REASONING

## From Generalization

Reasoning from generalization involves inducting from fair and sufficient samples or examples. "Induction is a type of reasoning that begins with specific instances and through the process of synthesis arrives at conclusions that are probable."[2]

*Generalization* rests on the assumption of regularity of a characteristic within a class. If a new Mazda automobile shows up with a defective motor mount, we may have an atypical or special case. If fifty of the identical models show up with the same defect, it is probably time to argue for a recall. The argument is based on the assumption that if defective mounts are found in these known cases then they will probably show up in the unknown cases.

The following are some tests for good generalizing from specific cases:

1.    Are there a reasonable number of cases?

2.    Are the cases typical?

3.    Are the negative cases accounted for?

Whenever you argue from "accepted" to particular cases, you are reasoning *deductively.* If we agree on the generalization or first premise that "all birds have wings," then our deduction appears as follows:

**Premise 1:**    All birds have wings.

**Premise 2:**    All ostriches are birds.

**Conclusion:**    Therefore, all ostriches have wings.

The preceding example is called a *categorical syllogism.* A syllogism may only have three terms, and the middle term may not appear in the conclusion. *Wings* is the major term, *birds* the middle term, and *ostriches* the minor term.

Most of your speeches that use deductive argument will not follow such a strict syllogistic form. However, the testing of your deduction, and perhaps your entire speech purpose, may be aided by utilizing the syllogistic form.

Suppose your specific purpose is to persuade the audience that smoking should be made illegal. The general premises you are considering include the following

*Actions that cause cancer are evil.*

*Smoking is an action that causes cancer.*

Your conclusion:

*Therefore, smoking is evil.*

The conclusion now becomes a premise in another syllogism.

*That which is evil should be made illegal.*

*Smoking is evil.*

*Therefore, smoking should be made illegal.*

More likely your deductive argument would appear in the form of an *enthymeme,* that is, an abbreviated syllogism.

*Any action that causes cancer is evil, and therefore smoking should be made illegal.*

Note that you have also logically tested your central idea (or discovered it).

Of course your premises may not always be accepted at face value, and you may have to establish their validity with valid evidence and critical thinking efforts. Knowing your audience, what they know, and what they think about your topic will help you decide how much effort you will need to provide to supporting the "agreed-upon" premise.

> To reason correctly from a false principle is the perfection of sophistry.
>
> **Nathaniel Emmons,**
> **American Theologian**

## From Analogy

Analogies can make things clear, vivid, and interesting. Some analogies are figurative or emotive, others more literal. All offer support, but the literal are thought to be the more logical.

A *literal* analogy is open to less argument but is nevertheless always imperfect proof. Its effectiveness depends on how close the comparison really is. In arguing for gun control, Senator Edward Kennedy tried the following *literal* analogy:

> Opponents of firearms laws insist that gun licenses and record-keeping requirements are burdensome and inconvenient. Yet they don't object to licensing automobile drivers, hunters, or those who enjoy fishing. If the only price of gun licensing or record-keeping requirements is the inconvenience to gun users, then the public will have received a special bargain. Certainly sportsmen will gladly tolerate minor inconvenience in order to protect the lives of their families, friends, and neighbors.

George Ziegelmueller and Jack Kay analyzed this analogy as follows: "Senator Kennedy asserts that gun licensing is like automobile, hunting, and fishing licensing in an essential characteristic (inconvenience), and he suggests that it will be like the other forms of licensing with regard to the characteristic (tolerance) known in the other forms but not known in the instance of guns."[3]

*Figurative* analogy is often persuasive but not always very logical.

Some tests of argument by analogy follow:

1. Are the compared cases essentially similar?

2. Are the compared cases accurately described?

3. Are there other analogous cases?[4]

# From Cause

Suppose you found a dead man (the effect of something) with a bullet in his heart. Can we conclude absolutely that the bullet is the cause? This is reasoning from *effect to cause—a posteriori* reasoning. The bullet is certainly a possible cause, but as any *Law and Order* fan knows, the man might have been killed by arsenic poisoning, then shot after his death as a means of hiding the real cause. We should expect causes to be complex and interrelated. Coincidence is frequently mistaken for cause. Just because two or more things occur near or at the same time does not mean that the first to occur necessarily caused the second to occur.

Your car battery is weak, you observe that it's ten degrees below zero, and you conclude that your car isn't going to start. This is before the fact, or *a priori* reasoning. The conclusion is based upon circumstances you observed before the disputed fact. You are reasoning from *cause to effect*.

If when you get up tomorrow morning you say, "It's ten below zero; my car won't start; I'll be late for school," you are reasoning from *effect to effect*. Both your faltering battery and your tardiness (as well as the thermometer reading) are the effects of a common cause—low temperature. In arguing from effect to effect, you must first sort out the *effect-to-cause and cause-to-effect* elements and then apply the general requirements for arguments based on causal relations. These are as follows:

1.    Is there a consistent association between alleged causes and attributed effects?

2.    Is the association strong and dependable across different circumstances?

3.    Do the alleged causes and effects appear in logical order over a reasonable time frame?

4.    Does the relationship hold up in the light of other known data?

## From Signs

We reason from circumstances or clues that act as signs. We use sign reasoning every day, often without applying proper tests.

*He drives a Porsche; he must be wealthy.*

*She is wet; it must be raining.*

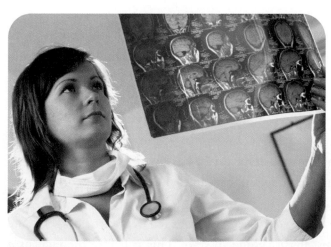

Medical diagnosis is an example of sign reasoning.

**Wrong!** The man is a car thief, and "she" fell in the swimming pool! However, all sign reasoning isn't confused. A trained auto mechanic knows how to interpret the growl signs in the front end of your car and quickly deduces that it is a wheel bearing. Medical diagnosis is another example of sign reasoning. In both cases sign reasoning is strengthened if there are multiple signs available. The mechanic also reads signs from alignment, wheel shimmy, and the absence of other growl sounds. The doctor finds special pain signs, elevated white blood cell count, and others that lead to the suspicion of appendicitis.

A really good detective has to be an expert at sign reasoning. His or her minimal list includes the following:

Are the signs reliable? (That is, not accidental or coincidental.)

Are they in sufficient number?

Do any contradict one another?

# ELEMENTS OF ARGUMENT

If reasoning is how we go about generating and testing ideas that support a position we are taking, or a claim we are making, then argument is the scheme by which we link and demonstrate the logic of our claims.

## The Toulmin Pattern

Stephen Toulmin devised a descriptive model of argument that presents how a persuasive argument is constructed. [5] His model depicts a system of logic and critical thinking, which gets one from evidence to inference and avoids symbolic relationships seen in the more syllogistic models. The process avoids the "all-ness" problem often associated with formal syllogisms.

The three main elements found in the model include the *claim*, the *grounds*, and the *warrant*. The **claim** is the statement you want your audience to accept. Essentially, it is the thesis of your argument. The **grounds** are the evidence you are using to support your claim. Grounds are made up of data and facts. Information is a powerful element of persuasion; however the information must be seen as clearly connected to the claim. The **warrant** is the link between the information (grounds) and the claim. Warrants are often implicit, based on shared ethos, logos, and pathos with the audience; hence they often need not be stated. Think of the warrant as the presumption (or declared statement) that the grounds are relevant to the claim. According to this model, we reason from evidence or fact to the claim. Some speakers will state the claim first and then present the evidence. Others will state the evidence first and build to the claim. The former approach can often result in the audience building its defense, rather than offering a fair hearing.

Four additional supporting elements include qualifiers, reservations, backing, and rebuttals. **Qualifiers** limit how universally the claim applies. These are statements that help us avoid the "all-ness" problem previously mentioned. Words like "most," "usually," "typically," "sometimes" are all qualifiers indicating that this claim is not necessarily true in ALL situations. **Reservations** are statements that allow for the possibility that the claim may be incorrect. Words like "should," "likely," "expect"—all might be found in a claim as a reservation. **Backing** is sometimes necessary to provide support or further explain the warrant. **Rebuttals** are the prepared responses to counterarguments. Think of the rebuttal in speech employing the Toulmin model as meeting objections. Toulmin symbolizes the relationship between the data (grounds) and the claim in support of which they are produced by an arrow, and indicates the authority for taking the step from one to the other by writing the warrant below the arrow and including qualifiers, reservations, backing, and rebuttals where necessary.

For example, let's take a look at Figure 12.2

The claim being made is that "George is likely to develop cancer." Note that the reservation "likely" is imbedded in the claim—meaning the claim could be wrong. The grounds used to support this claim is that "George smokes heavily." Additional grounds might have included data that supports what is meant by "heavy." Note that the arrow from grounds to claim symbolizes the relationship between the heavy smoking and the developing cancer and the warrant listed below is the authority for taking that leap: "Heavy smokers are more apt to develop cancer than those who do not smoke." In this argument, using the U.S. Department of Health to strengthen the warrant is the backing for the warrant. Even though the warrant is strong and the claim includes a reservation, this argument also includes a qualifier, "so, probably," decreasing the leap from the grounds to the claim. The qualifier reduces the all-ness problem. Finally, rebuttals are put in place to answer counterclaims that might emerge in the audience.

This system stresses the reservations and qualifiers and should suggest caution to both speakers and listeners in making claims. It also puts a priority on *warrants* (Is your claim warranted?), that is, the explicit justification of

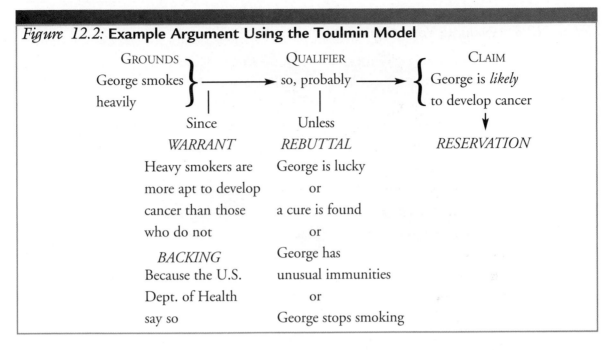

*Figure 12.2:* **Example Argument Using the Toulmin Model**

GROUNDS

George smokes heavily

QUALIFIER

so, probably

CLAIM

George is *likely* to develop cancer

Since

WARRANT

Heavy smokers are more apt to develop cancer than those who do not

BACKING

Because the U.S. Dept. of Health say so

Unless

REBUTTAL

George is lucky

or

a cure is found

or

George has unusual immunities

or

George stops smoking

RESERVATION

the reasoning between data and claim. A speaker is advised to first determine the underlying purpose of the argument and then to evaluate it. First, the grounds must be sufficient to support the claim. Second, the warrant must be applicable and based on solid backing. Third, exceptions and possible rebuttals must be considered. The questions in Figure 12.3 can guide you in evaluating your argument. These are the kinds of questions to ask yourself before you advance your thinking in a formal speech.

# CRITICAL THINKING ERRORS

## Common Reasoning Errors

**FALSE ASSUMPTIONS**   Galileo's claim that Earth was not the center of the solar system put him under house arrest for the last eight years of his life.

Clearly the assumptions of otherwise good thinkers were in error. That the Earth was the center was absolutely obvious and they were supported in that false assumption by another—"God would not have had it any other way." Galileo has, of course, been vindicated but perhaps, more importantly, forgiven. Close-minded,

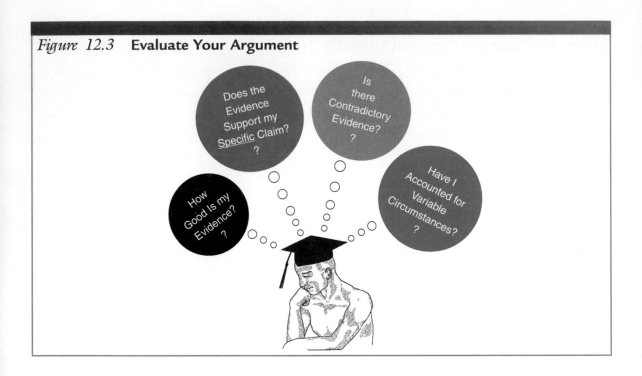

*Figure 12.3*    **Evaluate Your Argument**

false assumptions have been changed and a lesson in critical thinking learned. Be vigilant about your beliefs and do be objectively *skeptical* of new or strange ideas but do *not* be close-minded about either. The famous counselor and therapist Carl Rogers advised, "Always allow a 1-5 percent chance that you're wrong." In other words, maybe the patient is sane and "I'm losing it." This is not to say that we shouldn't hold strong beliefs, attitudes, and values, but it does mean that they should be based on evidence, logical reasoning, and a willingness to update and reevaluate. Unfortunately, Galileo's early critics would not even look at his evidence and his reasoning. Modern scientists and the U.S. Air Force are very skeptical about the presence of UFOs but they are eternally looking "out there."

> Most people would rather die than think; indeed most of them do.
>
> **Bertrand Russell,**
> **Philosopher and writer**

**DEFINITIONAL CONFUSION**    If you define *sound* as "free from error," how does it affect your answer to the question, "When a big tree falls in isolation in a distant forest, does it make a sound?" Not a very helpful definition you say. Try this one: "Acoustic sensation perceived by the sense of hearing."

If no one was around to hear it, then there was no sound. Hold on. It must have sounded like thunder! Try the scientific definition: "Mechanical radiant energy that is transmitted by longitudinal pressure waves in a material medium (as air)." *Now* the tree has made a sound. Nothing really changed in the forest, only the reasoning from different and yet "sound" definitions.

> As dysfunctional as they may be on occasion, our theories, preconceptions, and biases are what make us smart.
>
> **Thomas Gilovich, Cornell Professor of Psychology and Author**

It gets worse. When does life begin? At birth? When brain life begins? At conception? When survival outside the womb is possible? Clearly there are strong differences of opinion here, and also some people who haven't considered any definition but their own.

We even have definitional questions about *death.* Some states are still debating that definition because of the problem of organ transplants. "Brain function" defines death in many states, breath or heart function in others.

You can save yourself and your audience considerable confusion if you carefully consider your definition of terms. An example often helps. "By the Federal Government, I mean the Federal Trade Commission." Explanations of what you *don't* mean often help. "By intervention, I do not include military operations." One can also find definitional help from authority. "Poverty as defined by the *Statistical Abstract of the United States.*" "Tax-sharing as defined by Rush Limbaugh." Here all authorities are not created equal. On topics involving religion, it may be a church leader, the Koran, the Bible, or a distinguished theologian; for some, it may be a secular humanist.

Terms and words, even definitions, do not mean the same thing in all senses and in all situations. If you think they do, you are guilty of the fallacy of equivocation.

**MISATTRIBUTIONS**   One weather-weary backwoods Michigander called the popular local meteorologist and told him that he'd had enough and that if the ice was not off the bay by April 15th, he was coming after him with a chain saw. A real case of misattribution—in this case, guilt by association. Did our backwoodsman really think that the weather forecaster was causal? Thank goodness the ice went out on April 14th.

All misattributions aren't as harmless as the one above. Accidental physical association alone may lead to more serious false attributions or accusations of guilt. You are seated in a fancy restaurant one table behind a table of known gangsters. The aggressive reporters capture you as background in all of their videotape. How easy it is to infer false notions of guilt by association.

As we learned in the language chapter, loose word association causes much confusion. For some, a humanist, a secular humanist, a social psychologist, a Darwinian, an empiricist, and a behavioralist are all identical bad people who do not believe in God. They attribute the beliefs and traits of some to all. For the record, Edison, Einstein, and even Darwin made it very clear that they believed in God. Critical thinking demands some effort to distinguish fact from judgment and belief from knowledge.

The suggestions given to listeners in Chapter 3, "Critical Listening," also apply to persuaders seeking logical supports of their claims. Beware of misinterpreting chance events, second-hand information, wishful thinking, conventional wisdom, and language confusion.

**SINGLE PERSPECTIVE**    Single perspectives usually produce simplistic, singular answers to most questions. They are sometimes viable, rarely wise, and almost always undemocratic.

Single perspectives are attractive to some people who find they allow one to eliminate much of the dissonance caused by having to think critically or, in some cases, to think at all. Surely the followers of self-appointed Messiah David Koresh and the Branch Davidians found it so.

All single perspective errors are not as far-reaching and as dangerous. Some are applied more gently to single issues where one may have had a traumatic experience. Phobias apply here, but so do issues where one has simply a sincere concern: the spotted owl, wetlands, ozone layer, and so forth.

*For every complex problem there is an easy answer, and it is wrong.*

**H. L. Mencken**

Critical thinkers, for example, will consider the perspectives of the logging and lumber industries as well as those of the environmentalists. Considering more than one perspective, however, may not, perhaps should not, always lead to compromise. The plea is not to accept; the plea is to *consider.*

There are ways to expand our perspectives and improve our critical thinking. One is called playing *devil's advocate.* The early Roman Catholic Church used this device to make sure they heard arguments from a different perspective in making canonization or beatification decisions. It is, in this case, the appointing of someone to use arguments and perspectives with which they did not personally agree—a role-play. In individual cases, it is prevailing upon yourself to search out and seriously consider the best relevant arguments of perspectives other than your own.

Another way to avoid the single perspective error is double-checking your facts or what you presume to be the facts. We prefer to believe what we prefer to be true. A second, more dispassionate look at the facts is often a real eye opener. You studied *Romeo and Juliet* in high school and you are startled to hear someone say that you really did not—that is, your version was considerably different from Shakespeare's original version. A close examination of high school anthologies shows that over three hundred lines have indeed been dropped. All sexual material was removed—even words like *bosom* and *maidenhood.* The love story was mostly lost as were most lines that in any way associated religion with violence.[6]

Verify your facts. Are yours the only facts? Are your sources reliable? Are they up-to-date? Are you blinded by your beliefs? When absolutely sure, look again.

A third way of expanding a single perspective is to seek out the opinions of people holding more neutral views or broader perspectives than your own on the issue at hand. An uncensored library is another source of second opinions and multiple perspectives.

## Common Argument Errors

Errors in reasoning and argument are called fallacies. **Fallacies** represent reasoning too far removed from the facts, a tangle of generalizations based on inadequate facts, or even a purposeful misrepresentation of the claim. The unscrupulous may deliberately use fallacious errors hoping that they will not be detected. Our cognitive systems are sometimes easily deceived by these fallacious messages. To complicate matters even more, fallacies are very often unintentional or accidental. They are usually plausible-sounding arguments using false, inadequate, or invalid

Another way to avoid the single perspective error is double-checking your facts or what you presume to be the facts. Many original lines in Shakespeare's *Romeo and Juliet* have been excluded from the present day version studied in high schools.

evidence. Once detected by an audience, a careless or unethical speaker is in for a difficult time. When noted by the listener, fallacies destroy a claim.

Aristotle devised a classification of fallacies that has been the springboard for all classification systems to this day. He divided fallacies into two principal types: those in the *language* of the argument and those in the content or matter of the argument. Fallacies of language were discussed in Chapter 7. There are seven fallacies of *matter*, or "beyond language." Aristotle himself admitted that there were problems in his system, so we may presume to rearrange his list. For our purposes we shall examine four major types of fallacies, together with their respective subtypes. The four are ***overgeneralization*** ("They're all dumb."); ***false cause*** ("The dance caused the rain."); ***begging the question*** ("Everybody knows they're crooks); and ***ignoring or ducking the issue*** ("What discrimination?").

"They're all dumb."

**OVERGENERALIZATION**    Snap judgments or generalizations based on insufficient evidence or experience belong in the category of overgeneralization. We are not talking here about language and the dangers of the word *all*, but rather the concept of *allness* itself. This fallacy results in our going from the general case to a specific case or vice versa. It is similar to the problems of induction and deduction.

It is in the *exceptions* to generally accepted rules that overgeneralization causes the most trouble. We would all agree that it is wrong to kill a person. However, a specific case of killing in self-defense can be an exception to this rule.

To take another example, there could be exceptions to the rule, "Alcohol is harmful." Not if it's used for fuel.

**Sampling**   A group of star high school football players was being oriented to a certain Big Ten campus when they observed a dozen devastatingly chic females coming out of a campus building. To a man, the generalization was, "Wow! What coeds this place has!" The coach did not bother to tell them that these women were all professional fashion models who had just come from a faculty spouses' program.

Consider the size and representativeness of your sample before generalizing. A rash of teenage delinquencies may cause some people to conclude that all teenagers are juvenile delinquents, but this would be an unfair generalization. The most treacherous part of this fallacy is that it does start with facts. There *were* twelve stylish females on a given campus; teenage delinquency *has been* recorded. It is the lack of objective analysis of the sample of experiences or subjects that causes the trouble.

**Extrapolation**   This "thin entering wedge" is also known as the "camel's nose in the tent." It too is a form of sampling trouble (as are all overgeneralizations), except that this one is keyed to *prediction* and *probability.*

Stuart Chase put it well: "You chart two or three points, draw a curve through them, and then extend it indefinitely!" Space scientists extrapolate or they do not predict at all. This is also true of economists and the weather forecasters. Scientists usually know the dangers of extrapolation; to offset these dangers, they generally phrase their predictions in terms of *statistical chance* or confidence. Scientists draw predictive curves only when they have found enough points to make a qualified prediction. We are well advised to do the same.

"The dance caused the rain".

**FALSE CAUSE**   This is the fallacy of assigning a wrong or false cause to a certain happening or effect. It also is refutation with irrelevant arguments. Superstitions belong here. If you blow on the dice and win, was it the blowing that brought you luck? Rabbits' feet are still being sold; and most hotels still have no thirteenth floor. Debaters call it *nonsequitur* (it does not follow).

***After This, Therefore Because Of This***    Superstitions fit here. In our saner moments we are aware of this fallacy. It arises from the subtle misuse of time sequence. For example, if a new city government comes into power after a particularly rough winter and is faced with badly damaged roads, you may hold them responsible as you survey one ruined $70 tire: "We didn't have roads like this until after their election." The great Roman Empire fell after the introduction of Christianity—care to try that one? You will hear it in Latin as *post hoc ergo propter hoc:* after this, therefore because of this.

***Thou Also***    This fallacy consists of making a similar, but essentially *irrelevant,* attack upon an accuser. A discussion between a Brazilian student and several Americans about Communist infiltration in Latin America became quite heated. Suddenly, the Brazilian said, "Communists? How about segregation in your country?" The retort was equally brilliant: "How about Nazis in Argentina?" This is also referred to as a **red herring fallacy**, diverting attention to an unrelated topic.

***Consequent***    This fallacy simply is the corruption of the reasoning or inferential process used in conditional syllogisms. The problem in conditional syllogisms is with possible, partial, or even probable truths. If he lies, he will be expelled from school; he was expelled; therefore, he lied. (In actuality, he may have been expelled for poor grades.) When we use conditional reasoning and argue from the truth of the consequent (what happened: he was expelled) to the truth of the antecedent (what preceded: he lied), or when we argue from the falsity of the antecedent to the falsity of the consequent, we are committing the fallacy of the *consequent.*

***Either/Or***    Certainly there are things in this world that are either one way or another? You are either living or dead; the lake is frozen or it is not. There is no such thing as being slightly pregnant. Even these can be argued in terms of definitions. Certainly, when a statement or problem with more than two possible solutions is put in an either/or context, we have a fallacy. "The fight is either Jan's or Jim's fault." It may be neither's fault, or it may be the fault of both. There are shades of gray in most things. All too often, we hear either/or arguments that only slow real solutions: science versus religion, capitalism versus socialism, suburban versus city living, and so forth.

*Loaded Question*   This trick assumes something has already happened; it usually asks two questions as if they were one. You're in trouble no matter how you answer. In a speech it may take the form of a great many questions, the combination of answers leading to fallacious reasoning. The answers sought are *yes* or *no*. "Have you stopped drinking? *Yes* or *No?*" If you answer *no,* you are an admitted drinker. If you answer yes, you are an admitted former drinker. Either way, the loaded question stacks the deck against you. "Heads I win, tails you lose."

"Everybody knows they're crooks."

**BEGGING THE QUESTION**   This fallacy assumes the truth or falsity of a statement *without proof.* A common form is the use of two or more unproved propositions to establish the validity of one another. Other forms are simple, unwarranted assumptions or statements. It is related to loaded questions.

*Arguing In A Circle*   This is the classic form of using two or more unproved propositions to prove one another. "Professional boxing should be outlawed because it is inhumane; we know it is inhumane because it is a practice that should be outlawed." "Detroit is to blame for the smog in Los Angeles since they make the cars we drive." This assumes cars are the major source of pollution, and that all the cars are made in Detroit—a vicious circle. We might just as easily accuse the Japanese carmakers.

*Direct Assumption*   In this form of question begging, language is carefully selected to conceal unsupported assumptions. Many statements may be used, or perhaps just a word or two are subtly inserted. In a discussion of big-time college football, an opposition speaker started with the words, "It is my purpose to show that buying professional players is not in the best interest of college football." This statement begged the whole proposition by assuming at the outset that colleges buy professional players. Unless the statement is proved, it remains an assertion.

"What discrimination?"

**IGNORING OR DUCKING THE ISSUE**    This fallacy can be a subtle, treacherous, and often vicious process. It almost always uses apparently relevant but objectively irrelevant arguments to cloud or duck the real issue of argument. This fallacy has several types, and each is worthy of a word of warning to the listener and unsophisticated speaker.

To argue the stage and screen abilities of Burt Reynolds by referencing his off-screen pursuits is a good example of *ad hominem*.

*Attacking Personalities*    This fallacy is also known as *ad hominem*. When a speaker attacks the personal character of an opponent rather than the issue at hand, that person is guilty of ad hominem argument. The purpose of ad hominem is to change the issue from an argument on the proposition to one of personalities. To argue the stage and screen abilities of Burt Reynolds by referring to him as "that self-centered woman-chasing louse" is a good example of ad hominem. Mr. Reynolds's stage and screen *abilities* have no direct logical connection to his alleged off-stage pursuits. This is not to say that every personal attack is unfair or illogical. If Mr. Reynolds were being evaluated on his public relations abilities, it might be a different matter.

***Appeals To Prejudice*** This is an appeal to the people through their biases and passions. The symbols of motherhood, the flag, race, and sin are typical themes. Vicious and often unsupported attacks have been made against liberal Americans in the name of un-Americanism, Romanism, Zionism, racism. The "ist" words—sexist, racist, feminist, abortionist, and socialist—are often misused in this type of appeal. The reason that these appeals have been known to work and cloud the reasoning is due to the strongly held biases of the listeners. *Ad populum* appeals should become less successful as the general population becomes better educated and more sophisticated.

***False Appeal To Authority*** This type of fallacy is an appeal to authority and dignity. When the authority is legitimately connected to the subject, as Aristotle is to logic, we have no problem. However, if in our reverence of Aristotle we use him to oppose modern probability theory, we are guilty of false appeal. Michael Jordan and John Elway are highly paid experts in their specialized fields. They are probably not authorities on laser theory or even beer or breakfast cereal. If you are impressed because Dr. Whosis says that alcohol causes cancer, find out if Whosis is an MD or an English professor.

***Appeals To Ignorance*** This is a mean trick, hiding weak arguments by overwhelming an audience with impressive materials about which they know little. A twelve-cylinder vocabulary can screen many a feeble argument. Improper use of statistics (or even proper use) for people ignorant of the theory or the numbers involved is a good example of an appeal to ignorance. This is not to say that vocabulary and statistics are the problem; it is the intent with which the speaker adapts them to the audience that is the problem.

# CHAPTER REVIEW
## *Wrapping it up*

## Summary

In the cognitive or more "central route" of the persuasion process, we are concerned primarily with evidence, rational reasoning, critical thinking, and argument—an expansion of Aristotle's *logos*.

Useful evidence to consider as particularly effective in persuasion, include the following 1) statements by authorities, 2) examples, and 3) statistics.

Four basic forms of reasoning are derived from 1) generalization, 2) analogy, 3) cause, and 4) sign. The Toulmin pattern of argument includes the following elements of argument: claims, grounds (data, evidence), warrants (the reasoning that links the grounds to the claim), backing (additional support to the warrant), qualifiers (limit how universally the claim applies), reservations (allow that the claim may be wrong), and rebuttals (claims prepared for counterarguments, or meeting objections in the audience). One is advised to first determine the underlying purpose of the argument and then to evaluate as follows: 1) the grounds must be sufficient to support the claim; 2) the warrant must be applicable and based on solid backing; and 3) exceptions and possible rebuttals must be considered

The following are some good questions for testing your arguments are:

1. How good is my evidence?

2. Does the evidence support my *specific* claim?

3. Is there contradictory evidence?

4. Have I accounted for variable circumstances?

Critical thinking errors include four major reasoning errors 1) false assumption, 2) definitional confusion, 3) misattributions, and 4) single perspective; and four argument errors 1) overgeneralization, 2) false cause, 3) begging the question, and 4) ducking the issue. Both errors in reasoning and errors in argument are referred to as fallacies.

# Notes

1.  See Raymond S. Ross, *Understanding Persuasion*, 4th ed. (Englewood Cliffs, N.J.: Prentice Hall, 1994), p. 113.

2.  George W. Ziegelmueller and Jack Kay, *Argumentation: Inquiry and Advocacy.* 3rd ed. (Boston: Allyn and Bacon, 1997), p. 349.

3.  Ziegelmueller and Kay, *Argumentation*, p. 105.

4.  See Austin J. Freeley, *Argumentation and Debate*, 9th ed. (Belmont, Calif.: Wadsworth, 1996), pp. 172–74.

5.  S. Toulmin, *The Users of Argument* (Cambridge, England: Cambridge University Press, 1958); see also Barbara Warnick and Edward S. Inch, *Critical Thinking and Communication*: The Use of Reason in Argument (New York: Macmillan, 1994), pp. 179–88.

6.  Joan Del Fattore, *What Johnny Shouldn't Read* (New Haven: Yale University Press, 1992), Chap. 1.

# UNIQUE FORMATS
# AND OCCASIONS

# Chapter **13**

## Chapter Objectives

### Audience Participation Occasions

General Rules

Rules for Answering Questions

Generating Participation

### Speaking with Humor

Humor

After-Dinner Speeches

### Introductions and Special Occasions

Speeches of Introduction

Speeches of Presentation and
  Acceptance

Speeches of Tribute and
  Commemoration

# AUDIENCE PARTICIPATION OCCASIONS

In a sense, every speech situation in a democracy represents potential audience participation, if not a formal open forum. Questions, comments, and objections from the audience may come at any time. You should always calculate the risk of being interrupted or even heckled. Some speakers ask for trouble by pleading with the audience to interrupt for any good reason whatsoever. A very large audience of perhaps hundreds can be a real nightmare if there is no prearranged system of handling questions.

> The way a question is asked limits and disposes the ways in which any answer to it—right or wrong—may be given.
>
> **Susanne K. Langer,**
>
> **Philosopher**

The Economic Club of Detroit has the audience of 800 to 1,000 people turn in written questions that are screened for duplication and relevance while the speaker is still on the platform. Of course, there are situations, such as certain discussion groups or small classes, in which you seek immediate audience participation. Although formal speakers should be democratic and focus on the audience, they must also cover their subject and stay within their allotted time. Unreasonable questions and interruptions have ruined many an otherwise good speech and have shaken even experienced speakers.

The solution to the general problem is in the word *control.* Speakers must stay in control of the communication situation. They must control audience

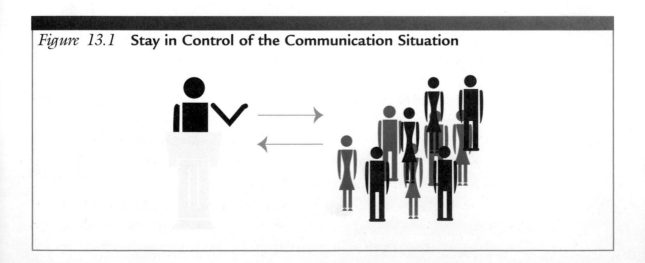

*Figure 13.1*   **Stay in Control of the Communication Situation**

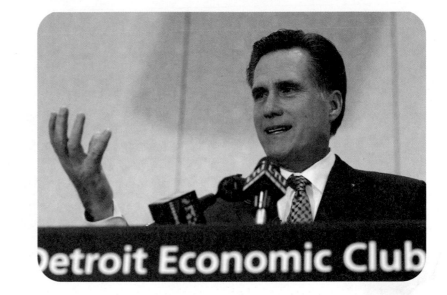

When speaking, be prepared to handle audience participation appropriately.

participation in such a way as to do justice to the audience, the material to be covered, and the time restrictions placed on their speech.

Most **business communication and training programs** use a great deal of audience participation. This is as it should be for educational psychology teaches us that *people learn faster and better when they have a feeling of participation and involvement.* The audience, particularly in training programs, is usually invited to interrupt the speaker or teacher. However, the speaker who chases after every question, relevant or not, will soon be in serious trouble. One inexperienced speaker pleaded sincerely for interruptions and he *got* them—some good, some bad, some ridiculous. He tried to react, answer, or comment on each equally. The result was that he covered only one-fourth of his material, and even this part was confused because of the free-for-all participation.

Another situation in which you may find yourself is the more typical **open forum** after a speech. Open forums allow for a question-answer period after the speech has concluded. The problems indicated above apply here, but perhaps to a lesser degree, because you have much better control of your time, and you have probably covered the points you set out to cover.

The third typical audience situation is the **symposium forum**. A symposium is made up of a panel of presenters and the forum usually allows one-third of the total time for questions from the general audience. Many

A symposium forum usually allows one-third of the total time for questions from the general audience.

convention programs are run this way. Once again, the rules and problems are similar to those of the two situations discussed above, except that a decision must often be made as to which of the panelists should respond to each question. The respondent must consider both the audience and fellow panel members. The size of the audience is again a key factor. If the audience is larger than was expected (say, one hundred instead of thirty-five), the moderator might have the panelists ask one another questions first, thereby ensuring some relevant questions. Furthermore, audience size alone may discourage members of the audience from asking questions.

## General Rules

The *first* rule regards your audience.

1.    *Know your occasion, subject, and audience.*

You are now in a position to apply the *second* rule:

2.    *Anticipate* the questions.

Try to guess what areas of your subject are most vulnerable to questions, and try to predict what questions this particular audience will ask.

3.    *Try sincerely to answer or at least react to all questions.*

Consider and respond courteously to even the irrelevant questions, and attempt, if necessary, to clarify or postpone the question. The *fourth* rule, and one that is very easy to overlook in your eagerness to meet the question asked, is:

**4.**    *Consider the rest of the audience.*

You must try to satisfy not only the person asking the question, but the total audience as well. Otherwise, you might satisfy the statistician, for example, while thoroughly confusing everybody else. *Fifth:*

**5.**    *Do not feel or act as if you have to know everything or win every argument.*

Finally:

**6.**    *When the situation calls for an open forum, encourage good questions and audience participation.*

It is very easy to discourage questions by a slightly overbearing attitude. However, it is possible to be so overbearing that the audience decides to interrogate you. People who assume leadership have to be constantly on guard not to intimidate others simply because of their position or rank. The sergeant who loosely followed the manual's advice to always ask, "Are there any *dumb* questions?" did not get many questions at all. That was why he said it! However, when such an overbearing attitude is *not* intended, the negative audience situation is even more unfortunate.

## Rules for Answering Questions

An audience of about four hundred students was listening to a famous philosopher speak. At the close of the speech the chairman asked for questions from the audience. Most of the hands raised were in the first row, where the Philosophy Club had gathered. The speaker pointed to a hand in the first row. To those near the middle of the audience the question sounded like, "I should zzum ug ask hrump zud Hegel?" The speaker moved to the lectern, stroked his chin, and then, speaking to the front row, said, "A very good question." He then proceeded to give what was probably a very good answer. The problem was that most of the audience did not know what the question was because they had not

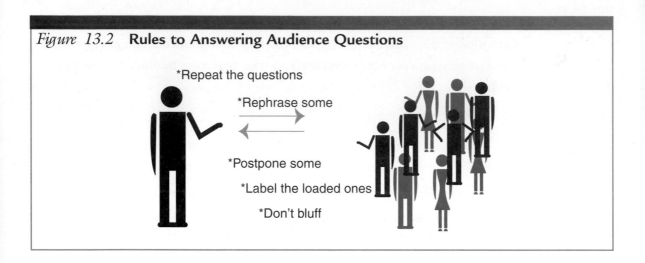

*Figure 13.2*   **Rules to Answering Audience Questions**

*heard* it. The speaker handled three or four more questions in the same manner with the audience becoming frustrated, then restless, and finally rude, as they started to leave.

One of the most elementary mistakes a speaker or panelist can make is to assume that everyone in the audience has heard and understood a question that is asked. Listening to misdirected answers without knowing the question is the height of frustration for most listeners. Speakers should communicate with the whole room, not just the questioner.

**REPEAT**    *Repeat the question* is the first rule. This is a good idea even with small audiences; for although the members are in a position to hear, they may not be listening. Another serious aspect of the all-too-common error illustrated above is that people will attempt to reconstruct what the question must have been in terms of the answer. Counterquestions based on inaccurately reconstructed questions can really raise confusion to a high level.

Sometimes a question may be asked in a loud, clear voice, but the wording is awkward or unclear. A famous army general was giving a speech at one university at the time of a Middle East crisis. In the large audience were foreign students from all of the countries involved, including Egypt, Iran, Kuwait, Iraq, and Israel. One of these students took the general to task in perfectly clear and audible English, except that the question was long and complicated. The general said, "I know what you're getting at," and proceeded to answer for about ten minutes. As the general completed his answer, the foreign student leaped to his feet and proceeded to give another short speech, which said, in effect, "But that's not what I asked." The general tried again, for five minutes this time, but still with no success. After one more unsuccessful attempt, the desperate general finally held up his hand and said, "Let's see if we can agree on what the question is."

**REPHRASE**    Sometimes it is necessary not only to repeat but also to *rephrase the question.* When rephrasing, you should gain the approval of the questioner. Ask the questioner if your phrasing is a fair statement of the question to see if the person objects verbally. You do not always have to rephrase questions; do so only when it is necessary for clarity, and then always seek approval.

Some long, complicated questions deserve careful attention if they are relevant to the issue and if you are capable of giving some kind of answer in the time available. When, however, you receive questions that are irrelevant, that demand a highly technical or complex answer, or that would consume all the open-forum time, you have a different kind of problem. Such questions can ruin an otherwise good speech. Though in principle you do not want to avoid questions, you also owe it to the rest of your audience to stay on the subject and to give more than one person a chance to ask a question.

**POSTPONE**    Let us, therefore, formulate a third rule: *Postpone the irrelevant, overly technical, or time-consuming questions.* Postpone such questions until after the official open-forum period, or until the end of the period if you have time remaining. This rule becomes more complex during interruptions of your speech. An audience member may interrupt to ask a question you intend to cover later in the speech. In this situation you should delay the answer until you arrive at that point: For example, you might say, "Allow me to hold the answer to that for a few minutes. I will cover the issue a little later." The problem is to remember the questions you may have postponed. One solution is to suggest that the person ask the question again, but after you have covered the point at hand.

**LABEL LOADED QUESTIONS**    Even the experienced and unflappable Gary Hart was jolted when he was asked, "Have you ever committed adultery?"

People sometimes deliberately ask the "Are you still beating your dog?" kind of question, but equally difficult are the questions that are unintentionally loaded. These are difficult to detect because they are often both subtle and naive at the same time, and people who are not troublemakers by reputation sometimes ask them. "Why is it that writers have such insatiable egos?" an author was once asked. If you are a writer, try to answer that without condemning yourself!

Thus, rule four is, *label a loaded question*. There are several ways to do this, if you are lucky enough to detect such a question in time. The most effective way is to pause long enough for the audience to label it for you. An audience is often quick to chuckle if they see the speaker faced with a "heads I win, tails you lose" situation. You could say frankly, "That's a loaded question." A more tactful way might be, "It looks like I'm in trouble no matter how I answer this." Another method is to ask the questioner to repeat the question. The audience will listen more closely and may label the loaded question for you, or the questioner may "unload" it. After you have successfully labeled or unloaded the question as courteously as possible, you should then attempt to answer. With the proper labels applied, the audience is not apt to be prejudiced by the question.

**DON'T BLUFF**   The surest way to get in trouble in an open-forum period is to try to bluff your way through a question for which you honestly do not have a satisfactory answer. Once an audience senses that you are bluffing, you can expect them to ask more questions on this bluff point. The solution is to know your subject thoroughly—but if you do not have an answer, say so right away and save yourself the embarrassment of being trapped later on. No speaker is expected to have all the answers to all the questions in the world. This rule, then, might simply be called the *"I don't know"* rule.

However, you cannot escape all the hard questions by simply saying, "I don't know." In some question-answer situations you may wish to say, "I don't know, but I have an opinion," or "I don't know, but I can answer in terms of my specialty." The point is that you should answer any question you are capable of answering and yet be honest enough to admit it when you cannot supply an answer.

Corollaries to "don't bluff" are "don't get belligerent" and "don't get defensive." Acknowledge honest differences of opinion and get on with the open forum.

# Generating Participation

> It will be a sad day for man when nobody is allowed to ask questions that do not have any answers.
>
> **Kenneth Boulding,**
> **Economist and Philosopher**

In some situations audiences just seem to spring into action; in other cases they must be given the proper stimulus for participation. Here are several techniques that might be useful for you.

**THE OVERHEAD QUESTION**   This is a direct question from the speaker or discussion leader to the entire audience. If no questions arise from the audience (or even if they do), you might say, "Let me ask this question in order to get some feedback. Given one million dollars, how would you use it to improve this university?" The problem is to make sure you choose a question that will cause a reaction, for if there is silence, you may be worse off than before. Sometimes you can react to your own question in such a way as to promote participation. "OK, then react to what I'd do with it." Consider a few, carefully worded overhead questions as a method of fostering participation.

**THE DIRECT QUESTION**   This technique consists of choosing a specific member of the audience and asking that person a direct question. This is often very effective if the individual is known to the rest of the audience or is in some special way qualified to answer. The size of your audience may present a problem in that

*Figure 13.3*   **Generate Audience Participation**

*Use overhead questions

*Use direct questions

*Redirect questions

*Prime the pump

the audience may have difficulty seeing or otherwise determining who has been singled out. Classroom audiences or larger groups that meet regularly respond well to this technique. Try not to call on the same person all the time, but do pick individuals who are most apt to get participation started. Try to tailor the question directly to the individual chosen. The question should be relatively short and clear and should demand more than a simple yes or no answer. If the situation is really desperate, however, you may have to settle for yes or no.

**THE REDIRECTED QUESTION**    This technique may also be called the *reverse method* or the *relay method*. In using the reverse technique, you simply redirect a question to the person who asked it: "That's a very good question. How would you answer it?" In using the relay method, you redirect the question to some other person: "A good question. Let's see how Mrs. Wright would answer it." A third approach is to overhead the question to the whole audience.

As a general rule, do not redirect a question unless you yourself know at least a partial answer to it. An exception to this rule is a simple question of fact upon which you can freely admit ignorance. Take heed of the story of the beginning teacher who redirected a tough question to which he did not have the answer to each individual of the class, only to find that it came right back to embarrass him.

**PRIMING THE PUMP**    This is the all-important technique of building questions into your speech. In the main body of your speech, your questions or implied questions should develop your point, stimulate audience thinking, and attract interest and attention. This can work to engender enthymematic participation from your audience, securing more attachment to your message.

# SPEAKING WITH HUMOR

## Humor

Other things being equal, a little showmanship is better than dull, hedged, powerless language and delivery. At the University of Arkansas business school, the final speaking assignment is a stand-up comedy routine. According to Professor Tabott, "If you can do that you can master any form of speaking."[1] However, some people are better at humor than others. They also have an advantage if they can discern when their humor may be *inappropriate*.[2] All "humorous" people do not tell jokes equally well.[3] If you're a poor jokester, perhaps you need not be too concerned. Long-standing research on the impact of such humor on audiences seems to indicate that at least in persuasive speeches for some people it may make little difference. Humor and showmanship include more than just jokes. A funny story if told well helps; so does relating an amusing experience you've had or someone else has had.

Comparing humorous and nonhumorous *information* lectures did show significantly better student retention of the humorous lecture over a period of six weeks.[4]

Remember that humor when offensive or tendentious[5] can work against you; so too, if it confuses the mood or is in some other way a distractor of the message. Related, funny anecdotes (if told well and in good taste) have probably helped hold attention for many an otherwise dull speaker. The professional writers of humorous lines certainly think so. They received $300 per minute of delivery time for the following:

(Roast of a successful clothing manufacturer)

Well, Tom, we managed to get all your friends together under one roof … they're outside in the car.

Actually Tom adores his wife and four children. He always wanted a big family … it saves on manikins.

(Introduction of a famous plastic surgeon)

Dr. Stevens has integrity. In fact, he's so honest he returns your old parts.

The head of this agency (Comedy Unlimited) describes how he goes about his work, and it makes for good advice.

A lot of research goes behind just one line. We do a thorough analysis of the client's needs before sitting down to the typewriter.

We look for lines that are perfectly appropriate for both the client and the audience. What might be hilariously funny and quite effective for a sales manager might be disastrous for the chairman of the board.

Practice is critical and this is where most speakers including some naturally humorous people fall down—the polishing.

The wit used by Comedy Unlimited was at least mildly disparaging. Research on deprecating and self-deprecating humor has been mixed. However, the last word seems to be that such humor if used sparingly and in good taste may help a speaker without damage to the traditional factors of ethos.[6] So much depends on the occasion, and on the people—the entire system must be considered. Research indicates that people differ on contexts perceived as appropriate for humor as well as on its type and spontaneity.[7]

Audiences seemed to find the self-deprecating humor of some of our presidents endearing: Kennedy mocked his wealth and his youth; Ford mocked his clumsiness; Reagan mocked his age; and Clinton his addiction to Big Macs. Even Lincoln was able to make fun of his homeliness. When during a debate Douglas accused him of being two-faced, without hesitation Lincoln calmly replied, "I leave it to my audience—if I had two faces, would I be wearing this one?"

The person has a lot to do with how an audience views appropriateness. A Jewish student evoked an appreciative response in a speech class with a joke about a bumblebee wearing a yarmulke. "The bee didn't want to be taken for a wasp." One must wonder if the story would have been as funny told by anyone else. Ethnic, racial, and sexual jokes are tricky and double-edged for speakers, yet research indicates that they are prevalent and, for some, popular.[8] No matter how popular the sexist jokes were rated, at least one rater was always turned off. The rule is "Sexism is just not funny." Racist jokes are no longer acceptable anywhere. One must marvel at what people will or will not laugh at when humor is involved. Joke A below was considered sexist by the majority surveyed. Joke B was a winner but still had at least one rater label it sexist.

|  **A** | **B** |
|---|---|
| "Is this the Salvation Army?" | The young husband was waiting outside a hospital room when the doctor emerged from his thorough examination of the wife to explain the sudden pain in her shoulders. The doctor said gravely to the husband, "I must tell you that your wife has acute angina." |
| "Yes." | |
| "Well, save me three for Saturday night." | |
| | "Yes, yes, I know. But what's wrong with her?" |

We laugh at unexpected deviations from scripted behavior. That's why bloopers or spoonerisms are funny for most people. We laugh at pratfalls if they happen to people in the public eye whether we like them or not. Try some of these bloopers.

Tonight's sermon: "What is hell?" Come early and listen to our choir practice.

This week's youth discussion will be on teen suicide in the church basement.

"This being Easter Sunday, we will ask Mrs. White to come forward and lay an egg on the altar."

Wednesday the Ladies Liturgy Society will meet. Mrs. Jones will sing, "Put Me in My Little Bed," accompanied by the pastor.

And from a newspaper, the headline CROWDS RUSHING TO SEE POPE TRAMPLE 6 TO DEATH.

If you're going to use humor, and especially jokes, take one more look at your audience. One person's belly laugh is another's yawn, or worse, a turnoff.

## After-Dinner Speeches

Today's after-dinner speeches are not what they used to be. For one thing they might be given after breakfast or after a luncheon banquet. Although a banquet may indeed be the setting for a very serious and profound speech to persuade or inform, there is a tradition of so-called "after-dinner" speaking that is rather special in our society. This is the good-humored, lighthearted, genial situation whose major purposes are a sociable meal and some relaxed enjoyment. This is the type of speech situation with which we are concerned here. The audience has been made content with good food and is tolerant and benevolent. It is not in a mood for argumentation, moral reevaluation, or complex issues. Such speeches are typically brief, light, and humorous. They are not easy speeches to deliver; for some, they appear almost impossible. You need not be a professional jokester; indeed, unless you tell a good relevant joke especially well, you are better advised to use your humor in another vein. Four general principles to guide you are:

1. *Select suitable topics.* "Great Snafus of the Civil War" was a delightful after-dinner speech at a history buff's banquet recently. The group was, of course, interested in the deeper aspects of the war, but not at this particular moment. Look on the lighter side of issues for your subject. If you are going to talk about teachers, concentrate on their eccentricities, not their educational philosophies.

2. *Be clear and brief.* Avoid complex organization; stick to one or two obvious main points. Do not use complicated forms of support. Use examples and entertaining illustrations. Above all, be brief. Plan several cutoff points in your speech should the whole program take more time than expected, or should the audience seem unusually restless or quiet (asleep).

3. *Be good-humored.* The diners are full of food and full of goodwill. Heighten the fellowship. Avoid bitter argument.

4. *Adapt to the audience.* Make sure you really know the audience, the occasion, and the program. Capitalize on this information. Tie your good humor appropriately and directly to your specific audience.

United States statesman Adlai Stevenson had an unflagging sense of humor and was a great after-dinner speaker. We can sympathize and laugh with him as he relates his experiences while campaigning for the presidency.

*Figure 13.4*   **After-Dinner Speeches Should be Brief and Light-hearted**

---

**THE CAMPAIGN SPEECH**

You must emerge, bright and bubbling with wisdom and well-being, every morning at 8 o'clock, just in time for a charming and profound breakfast talk, shake hands with hundreds, often literally thousands, of people, make several inspiring, newsworthy speeches during the day, and ride through city after city on the back of an open car, smiling until your mouth is dehydrated by the wind, waving until the blood runs out of your arm.

Then, you bounce gaily, confidently, masterfully into great howling halls, shaved and all made up for television with the right color shirt and tie—I always forgot—and a manuscript so defaced with chicken tracks and last minute jottings that you couldn't follow it, even if the spotlights weren't blinding and even if the still photographers didn't shoot you in the eye every time you looked at them. Then all you have to do is make a great, imperishable speech, get out through the pressing crowds with a few score autographs, your clothes intact, your hand bruised, and back to the hotel—in time to see a few important people.

And, too, there is mirth mingled with the misery all along the way. They shout, "Good old Adlie!" If you run for office and have a slightly unusual name, let me advise you to change it before you start, or be prepared to take other people's word for it. And I shall not soon forget about the woman in the crowd in San Francisco who reached into the car to shake hands with me, and not long after discovered that she had lost her diamond ring. Nor will I forget the warm welcome I received on a whistle stop in Bethlehem, Pennsylvania., and my thanks to "the people of Allentown."[9]

---

If you do decide to try humor to create interest, make the humor as professional as possible. There is no feeling quite as desperate as viewing a poker-faced audience after you have told your best joke. Make sure that the material is related to either the subject or the occasion; make sure you can tell it fluently; make sure you remember the punch line; and make sure that it will not offend your audience. The best advice of all—try it out on a small group of friends first. In other words, *practice* and *polish*!

# INTRODUCTIONS AND SPECIAL OCCASIONS

Weddings, funerals, graduations, award ceremonies, retirements—all call for special remarks from somebody. Sensitivity and appropriateness are among the most important watchwords. Speeches of introduction occur often enough and are so frequently unsuccessful that they will open our discussion. Mark Twain lost his patience with awkward introductions, and for a while he insisted that he not be introduced at all.

## Speeches of Introduction

"I just now met our speaker, who is a buddy of our president and a speaker on human relations. He teaches speech and should be a good example for all of you to follow. It gives me great pleasure to introduce Mr. Edwin J. Forsythe."

How would you like to speak to a strange audience after that introduction? It sounded as if the speaker were being foisted upon the group by a "buddy" in the organization. It was evident that the introducer in this case did not know anything about the speaker (not even that his name was Edward not Edwin!) and that he was not particularly interested in "human relations." Attention was called to the speaker's oratory instead of his subject and his credibility. The only good point about the introduction was its brevity.

Equally awkward is the overly dramatic, lavish praise introduction that overstates your credentials and piles on embarrassing flattery. A former Governor of Michigan was guilty of all of the above in introducing President Lyndon B. Johnson. The unflappable Johnson responded in a way that cut through the smoke and let him rejoin the human race. "Ah wish my parents were alive to hear that introduction. My father would have enjoyed it … and my mother would have believed it."

Even more devastating as a speech of introduction is a twenty-minute nightmare of poor jokes, trite language, and oral essays. This is especially cruel when the speaker intends to speak for only thirty minutes. What makes the situation really unfortunate is that the introducer is usually a well-intentioned, sincere person who is simply not skilled at introducing people. It is very difficult for speakers in this situation to undo the damage without appearing unkind. On one occasion a young instructor was introducing a distinguished professor to a group of university personnel who knew the professor. The instructor proceeded to give a speech that explained every entry on his bibliography. To make matters, worse, he proceeded to give an oral essay on the very topic on which the guest was supposed to speak. After some prodding from the chair-person, the introducer stopped abruptly and said, "Professor Monroe will now give his address." After a long pause, Professor Monroe rose and calmly said, "1714 Norfolk Drive, Lafayette, Indiana." He then sat down!

Remember that the major purpose of the speech of introduction is to *create harmony between the speaker and the audience,* which in turn creates a desire for the audience to want to hear the speaker's subject. You want the audience to like and respect the speaker and be inclined to listen attentively. Toward this end, follow these rules:

1. *Be brief but adequate.* Make sure that enough is said about the speaker and the subject to achieve harmony and advance the speaker's credibility. Do not overplay your role, for you are not the main speaker. Remember that your job is to focus attention on the speaker and the subject. You might introduce our president simply and adequately with "Ladies and gentlemen: the President of the United States." Seldom should a speech of introduction run more than three or four minutes.

2. *Stress the importance and appropriateness of the speaker's subject.* However, take care not to give the main speech! Do not explain the speaker's subject to the point of stifling curiosity and attention to the topic.

The major purpose of the speech of introduction is to create harmony between the speaker and the audience.

3.  *Make sure you know something about the speaker and the subject.* Consult the speaker before the meeting; see if there are some things the speaker prefers to be said or not said; and get his or her name right!

4.  *Consider the audience.* The length, language, and style of your speech should be carefully adapted to the audience. How well does the audience know the person? Are they friends, foes, or undecided? What do they already know about the speaker's topic?

5.  *Speak with sincerity and enthusiasm.* If you are not familiar with the speaker or the subject or are simply not interested, have someone else make the introduction. Do not stress the speaker's "oratorical" skills. Do not use trite language. In general, speak about accomplishments rather than about virtues.

6.  *Pay attention to the speaker.* After you have finished your speech of introduction, be a model listener. This suggests that the audience should also be good listeners. A gabby or hyperactive introducer can ruin audience concentration.

The introduction of a distinguished professor might be quite different for the following different audiences: 1) faculty colleagues, 2) graduating seniors, or 3) a local American Legion post. See the example introductions below.

**FACULTY COLLEAGUES**   "Chance favors the prepared mind." This statement by Louis Pasteur characterizes our distinguished colleague and seminar speaker. Professor Raymond is no stranger to any of us nor is most of his research, but how he bends lady luck to get these huge grants and research supports is a mystery to most of us. Friends, here's Mark Raymond to tell all, and perhaps explain what Pasteur was talking about, and whom he knows at the Ford Foundation.

**GRADUATING SENIORS**   "Chance favors the prepared mind." This statement by Louis Pasteur characterizes our commencement speaker. His research success in advertising and public relations effects was no more accidental than his winning the *Croix de Guerre*. His training has been arduous and thorough, with a bachelor's degree from the Annenberg School of Communication and a master's degree and doctorate in psychology from Yale University. Dr. Mark Raymond is currently a full professor of communication and psychology at the University of Michigan where he is a member of the Institute of Social Research, the Group Dynamics Research Center, and the Institute of Industrial Relations. Dr. Raymond has served as a research consultant to many government, business, and industrial organizations. He is the author of six textbooks and thirty-seven research monographs; he is listed in *Who's Who in America* and every other lexicon of important people in the world.

Dr. Raymond is not going to speak to you this evening on his latest research into cognitive-response persuasion, but rather about how post-commencement career preparation can help you bend fortune in your direction. Dr. Mark G. Raymond.

**AMERICAN LEGION POST**    "Chance favors the prepared mind." This statement by Louis Pasteur characterizes our speaker this afternoon. B.A., M.A., Ph.D., a half-dozen books are only half the story. How about the *Croix de Guerre,* the Silver Star, and two Purple Hearts? Here is a man who knows about chance and preparation as well as advertising and public relations. This man who rose from the ranks to lieutenant colonel has our best interests at heart, and is here to offer constructive feedback on our public relations efforts. His research on our current image is thorough, revealing, and a bit of a shocker—he wants to help change that for the better. And why not? He's a fellow legionnaire—Colonel Mark Raymond from the University of Michigan.

The commencement introduction to graduating seniors meets all of the rules and is longer and more formal than the other versions. The version for Dr. Raymond's colleagues is much shorter and even uses some humor; after all, they know the speaker. The American Legion audience calls for more adaptation. The speaker's military background is given more emphasis and, because criticism is forthcoming, pains are taken to make clear that he is a friend.

# SPEECHES OF PRESENTATION AND ACCEPTANCE

## The Presentation Speech

"Thanks for holding down the other end of the log" was engraved on a simple brass plaque and signed by four appreciative students. The students presented this award by simply placing it on the center of a professor's desk and saying "Thanks," as he retired from the University. With this close little group, a speech, a banquet, a formal meeting between professor and students was unnecessary. The recipient was honored and felt that his efforts were appreciated and recognized. The presentation was both sensitive and appropriate. Most often, however, a speech is called for when an award is given. The major purpose of a speech *of presentation* should be to show honor, appreciation, and recognition.

Goodwill and appreciation can be transmitted under considerably different circumstances. A five-minute formal speech read from a manuscript before a banquet audience of three hundred people concluded: "For these and his many other achievements, it was unanimously agreed by the Executive Faculty of the Marquette University of Speech that Dr. James W. Cleary was richly deserving of our Distinguished Alumni Award in the field of Speech Education."

The point is that presentations vary widely. The size of the group, the nature of the award, and the occasion all determine how much is said and how formally it is said. There are two general principles for most speeches of presentation:

1.   *The speech should sincerely communicate honor, appreciation, and recognition.* It should not stray from the facts; if so, it becomes insincere. Do not overpraise, overstate, or overemotionalize. Review the recipient's accomplishments honestly.

2.   *Adapt your speech to the occasion and the award.* For annual and routine service awards, only a short, straightforward word of congratulation may be necessary, even on a formal occasion. When many similar awards are given, as with contest winners, one short speech can often show honor and recognition for the entire group, each that might then step forward individually to receive a medal. This is not to say that a brief speech should be a less sincere speech. Make sure the speaker selected to present an award is thoroughly familiar with the kind of effort and achievement involved.

On some award occasions the speaker may also have to consider the donor of the gift. A university giving an honorary degree or a distinguished alumni award deserves some recognition and reflected glory. This is also true of business and industry that honor long-time employees. In situations in which the award may have a history or be unusual in some other way, a short description of these facts may be in order.

## The Acceptance Speech

An *acceptance* speech should measure up to the total communication situation, and especially to the expectations of those making the award. If you are representing a group or organization, make this clear and explain briefly why the others as well as yourself appreciate the award. If appropriate, you may wish to mention individuals and their specific efforts or merits related to the award. If the award is a personal gift, your response might vary from a simple but sincere "thank you" to a short statement of gratitude. So much depends on the nature of the award, the expectations of those honoring you, the total communication climate—and, of course, your own feelings. Two general principles should be observed in acceptance speeches.

1.  *Be humble.* This is the time to recognize the efforts of others who helped you achieve the award. We are rarely successful without the aid of others.

2.  *Be brief.* A long-winded acceptance speech takes the power out of the gift.

Presentations vary widely; how formal they should be depends on the size of the group, the nature of the award, and the occasion.

Below is a sample speech of presentation followed by its corresponding acceptance speech. Mr. Hope's speech is shortened slightly. While not all of us can or should accept with as much humor, Bob Hope is a special case. So too is the presenter, Ronald Reagan.

## Speeches of Tribute and Commemoration

This form of special-occasion speaking includes *eulogies, anniversary addresses, dedicatory speeches,* and some *nominating speeches.* The **eulogy** is typically a speech of tribute upon the death of a person or shortly thereafter. It may also apply to the anniversary of the birth or great moments in the life of a historical figure, such as Lincoln or Washington. **Anniversary addresses** celebrate an

---

### Television Presentation by President Reagan

This award honors a lifetime of service and achievement. It is appropriate that the first award should go to a gentleman who has practiced the liveliest of arts—comedy—for over six happy decades. Bob Hope has given generously of his valuable time and talent in support of worthy causes, perhaps more than any human being alive today. Bob recently returned from the Persian Gulf where he let some of our finest young people know how much we love them and how proud we are of the job they're doing.

So you see this award is not only in recognition of accomplishments past but is also an incentive to future generations to be inspired to carry on the traditions established by Bob Hope. It is my pleasure now to present this award to the man whose name is a description of life—Where there is life, there is Hope.

---

### Acceptance by Bob Hope

Thank you very much, Mr. President. You know you've done some nice things around this neighborhood. You've done many wonderful things out here (Palm Springs, California) and we like you around here, and I think that after you've finished your term you ought to come here and do a stage version of *King's Row*. No, I appreciate the nice things he said about me even if I'm not Russian (referring to the Gorbachev meetings).

*continued*

Naming a culture center for me is like naming a monastery for Gary Hart. (More political jokes followed). I bumped into former President Gerald Ford this afternoon. I said, "Pardon me," and he said, "I don't do that anymore."

As you know Mr. President, no one who gets this kind of recognition can ever claim solo credit for his career, and the list of people who have come into my life and allowed me to reach this point is long and impressive. Some of them are here this evening, and some of them appeared on that video we just saw. Some have been content to make their invaluable contributions from behind the scenes. I owe them all my deepest "thanks for the memories" and for the love and support they have shown me over the years. Once again, my thanks to all who are responsible for my receiving this impressive award, and I shall treasure it and try to live up to its meaning. Thank you, Mr. President and thank you, ladies and gentlemen.

event, persons, or an institution. They mark the occasion of time. **Dedicatory speeches** are usually tributes to buildings, monuments, ships, libraries, and other things that are generally dedicated in honor of some outstanding personality, institution, or group of people. In some **nominating speeches**, it is the practice to pay tribute to the nominee as a way of proving his or her qualifications for office. As most organizations now use nominating committees, nominations are made with less oral flourish.

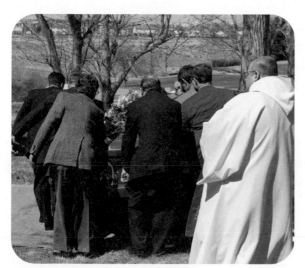

A eulogy is an example of a speech of tribute and commemoration.

All commemorative speeches are tributes. They serve to honor the memory or serve as a memorial to a person, an event, or a thing. Their purpose is to gain or increase respect, emulation, and appreciation for the people or institutions being honored and their impact upon society.

You can organize your speech according to the history of the person or institution being commemorated. Or, if time is short and the history is generally well known, you can concentrate on selected aspects of personality, achievement, or impact on society. Here are three general rules for most tributes and commemorative speeches:

1.    *Develop a sensitive understanding of the subject.* To deliver a funeral oration about a stranger would be awkward and embarrassing, if not disrespectful. Make sure you have more than just the immediate facts about the person, occasion, memorial, or building being commemorated. Try to capture the personality of the subject in both large and small incidents that typify the person's virtues or outlook on life. Know the outstanding achievements well, but do not lose sight of the personality.

2.    *Be objective and fair to the facts.* Perhaps we should not speak ill of the dead, but neither should we be totally dishonest. To eulogize a lazy, intemperate, hardheaded old lady as "this kind, generous model of moral simplicity" is apt to incite outright laughter and do a disservice to whatever virtues and respect the woman did have. No person is perfect in every way. Washington was not a model tactician at Valley Forge; young Lincoln was defeated so many times at the polls that his political future was in real danger. You will want to magnify and concentrate on the subject's virtues and achievements, but let the person be human.

3.    *Use a style of language and delivery that is in keeping with the occasion.* Commemorative occasions often demand a style that is slightly more elevated than the style generally prescribed in this book. The expectations audiences have of a speaker in a church or cemetery are somehow special. In paying tribute to someone tragically killed, the speaker's voice and measured cadence help express the grief, reverence, and solemnity of the occasion. On the other hand, there are many happy anniversaries, dedications, and tributes, and these call for a different style. Most commemorative speeches demand an elevated style at some point during the speech.

All eulogies should strike an emotional nerve and be in a special style that captures what the person meant to those assembled. It doesn't have to be a person. Consider this touching tribute by Steve Rubenstein who lost his dog.

## THE SPEECH OF COMMEMORATION

*The abridged model that follows helps illustrate the point above. It was delivered on the floor of the United States Senate by Senator Everett Dirksen after President Kennedy's assassination. A formal resolution was read, and Senator Dirksen was then recognized:*

MR. DIRKSEN: Mr. President, the memory of John Fitzgerald Kennedy lingers in this forum of the people. Here we knew his vigorous tread, his flashing smile, his ready wit, his keen mind, his zest for adventure. Here with quiet grief we mourn his departure. Here we shall remember him best as a colleague whose star of public service is indelibly inscribed on the roll of the U.S. Senate.

And here the eternal question confronts and confounds us. Why must it be? Why must the life of an amiable, friendly, aggressive young man, moved only by high motives, lighted on his way by high hopes, guided by broad plans, impelled by understanding and vision, be brought to an untimely end with his labors unfinished? And why, in a free land, untouched by the heel of dictatorship and oppression, where the humblest citizen may freely utter his grievances, must that life be cut short by an evil instrument, moved by malice, frustration, and hate? This is the incredible thing which leaves us bewildered and perplexed. On the tables of memory, we who knew him well as a friend and colleague can well inscribe this sentiment:

"Senator John Fitzgerald Kennedy, who became the 35th President of the United States—young, vigorous, aggressive, and scholarly—one who estimated the need of his country and the world and sought to fulfill that need—one who was wedded to peace and vigorously sought this greatest of all goals of mankind—one who sensed how catastrophic nuclear conflict could be and sought a realistic course to avert it—one who sensed the danger that lurked in a continuing inequality in our land and sought a rational and durable solution—one to whom the phrase 'the national interest' was more than a string of words—one who could disagree without vindictiveness—one who believed that the expansion of the enjoyment of living by all people was an achievable goal-one who believed that each generation must contribute its best to the fulfillment of the American dream."

The *te deums* which will be sung this day may be wafted away by the evening breeze which caresses the last resting place of those who served the Republic, but here in this Chamber where he served and prepared for higher responsibility, the memory of John Fitzgerald Kennedy will long linger to nourish the faith of all who serve that same great land.[10]

## THE EULOGY

*The combination of appreciation and eulogy is illustrated by the touching speech that Tom Hughes gave in tribute to his brother, football player Chuck Hughes, who died of a heart attack on the field while playing for the Detroit Lions. All of the Lions were at the funeral in San Antonio. Tom gathered the Lions around him and spoke.*

Words cannot express the gratitude for you that I now hold in my heart. Sunday you were names. Today you are and always will be in my heart and the hearts of all of those that I hold dear. The love we have for Chuck, I now feel, was shown by you, the Detroit Lions.

This to me is the finest tribute you could ever bestow on him. I have on numerous occasions heard that the Lions are a team of class. These past three days have shown it. Please try to continue this. You strike me, an outsider really, as being a tightly knit family. My personal family is this way too.

Please don't let this tragedy spoil the things that make you stand out so prominently. Chuck died doing the one thing he wanted to do for such a long time. It was his life.

I'd prefer it, and so would he, that he died on the field, rather than in some other tragic way. Forget the tragedy of Sunday and remember him as the man you knew personally. He'd like that. He gave his all and I know that if he had to die he would tell you, losing is the tragedy. Play it to win.[11]

## GOODBYE FROM WILLIE AND JOE

They met in the mud a long way from home, when Ike was a five-star general and Willie and Joe were GIs.

Willie and Joe had no use for generals. They were pen-and-ink people, cartoon characters dreamed up by an upstart Army artist named Bill Mauldin, and they did their talking from the pages of Stars and Stripes, the GI newspaper. They weren't happy about the war.

Always, Willie and Joe were hungry, filthy and fed-up. They never had clean socks or a decent meal; they smoked cigaret butts and never got their mail; their feet hurt, their bones ached and the rain always rained on them. In time, they were famous—the absolutely perfect prototypes of American soldiers everywhere.

The brass didn't like Willie and Joe much and Gen. George Patton once threatened to ban them from the newspaper. It was Ike who came to their

*continued*

rescue, the only time an officer ever did anything for Joe and Willie. Ike arranged a meeting between Mauldin and Patton. They talked things over and Willie and Joe stayed.

When the war was over, Ike came home and so did Mauldin, but Willie and Joe stayed behind. Some said they were just too tired to climb out of the foxhole they had shared so long; others figured Willie and Joe just decided to stay with their friends. There were 300,000 dead in the fields of France and the jungles of the Pacific and so Willie and Joe stayed on.

They met once again, when Ike was a president and Willie and Joe were in Korea, but the years passed and the friendship dimmed. Only in the battlefields now quiet and green, the crosses marching white to the horizon, was there time to remember the history they shared.

He was the only general they ever learned to like.[12]

## A VERY GOOD DOG IS WHAT SHE WAS

Annie was a good dog. This might surprise anyone who knew her, but newspapermen are not allowed to bend facts. The truth is that Annie was the best dog around. I loved her and that's true, too.

Annie died on Wednesday on an operating table in Corte Madera, and I suppose this is her obituary. If you don't want to hear an obituary about a yellow Labrador retriever, you might wish to leave, because that's what this is.

In obituaries you are supposed to mention how many years old the subject was when she died. Annie was 0. She had yet to reach her first birthday. She was 11 months and 3 days old when her gentle heart stopped beating. It's not a long time to live unless you lived life like my dog did, which was pleasurably if not particularly honorably.

Annie enjoyed her 0 years. She spent them on Ocean Beach, chasing tennis balls. She spent them in the lake behind Stern Grove, swimming for sticks. She spent them in a house in Miraloma Park, chewing sofa cushions.

Annie had her own way of doing things, and it was rarely the right way.

She knew how to heel well enough to know she didn't care for it. She could fetch the newspaper, only to drop it halfway up the steps. She learned to stop chewing phonograph records about the time she learned to start chewing compact discs.

In her 0 years, she attended three weddings. One of them was mine. She was the ring bearer, a duty she performed with her customary enthusiasm and

*continued*

absentmindedness. The moment the parcel was fastened to her collar, she took off down the beach in pursuit of a spaniel.

My dog was just getting the hang of things. She could catch a Frisbee, sometimes. She could roll over, if nudged. She was developing a taste for bananas. When you die at the age of 0, you leave a lot of bananas uneaten and many of them are in a bowl by the sink. She left many uneaten Milk Bones, too, one of which I just pulled out of my windbreaker pocket.

Annie liked ice cubes, especially the way they slid like hockey pucks across the kitchen floor. We called them water bones. She especially liked kicking them under the stove and watching me crawl around and fish them out.

And she liked to travel. In her 0 years, she climbed to the top of Multnomah Falls in Oregon, swam in the Rogue River, romped through a snowstorm near Truckee and ate a barbecue beef sandwich in San Luis Obispo. She visited Los Angeles, too, because she was in the back of my car and had no choice. She forgave me, in exchange for a Milk Bone.

On her last day we visited the dog run in Mill Valley. It was a favorite place, located enticingly close to the sewage plant. We played fetch with a tennis ball and then it was time to drop her off for her ankle operation. I kissed her on the top of her head before the man led her away. I was always kissing her on the top of her soft, fuzzy head. People said I kissed my dog too much, but it's not really any of their business, being as the practice was conducted between consenting parties.

A few hours later, the call came from the surgeon. The anesthesia reaction that had stopped Annie's heart was a 10,000-to-1 occurrence. And the bone chip in her ankle, which necessitated the operation, was a 100-to-1 chance.

You can work it out for yourself. You multiply 10,000 by 100 and you find that Annie was one dog in a million. That's what she was, officially certified. She was a good dog, too, but that's not official. You only have my word on it.[13]

# CHAPTER REVIEW
## *Wrapping it up*

## Summary

There are six general rules for handling audience participation speeches includeing 1) know your occasion, subject, and question format, 2) second-guess the questions, 3) answer or react to all questions, 4) consider the rest of the audience, 5) don't act as if you must know everything or win every argument, and 6) encourage participation in open forums. Rules for answering questions include 1) repeat, 2) rephrase when necessary, 3) postpone the irrelevant or time-consuming, 4) label loaded questions, and 5) don't bluff. To help generate participation use 1) overhead questions, 2) direct questions, 3) redirected questions, and 4) prime the pump by building questions into your speech.

Other things being equal, a little showmanship is better than dull, hedged, powerless language and delivery. Some people are better at humor than others. All humorous people do not tell jokes well. Humor is more than jokes and is helpful when appropriate. Research also indicates that people differ on contexts perceived as appropriate for humor as well as on its type and spontaneity.

The after-dinner speeches with which we are concerned take place in a good-humored, light-hearted, genial situation whose major purpose is a sociable dinner and relaxed enjoyment. These speeches should be brief, light, and humorous. Some principles to follow are 1) select suitable topics; look on the lighter side of issues; 2) be clear and brief; stick to one or two obvious main points; 3) be genuinely good-humored; avoid bitter argument; and, 4) adapt to the specific audience; tie your message and humor directly to the audience at hand. Beware of jokes that injure people. Practice and polish all attempts at humor.

The major purpose of a speech of introduction is to create harmony between speaker and audience, which makes the audience want to hear about the speaker's subject. Toward this end, 1) be brief but adequate, 2) stress the importance and appropriateness of the speaker's subject, 3) make sure that you know something about the speaker and the subject, 4) consider the audience, 5) speak with sincerity and enthusiasm, and 6) pay attention to the speaker after he or she starts to speak.

# *Notes*

1.  Edith Paal, "Communication Skills Lauded," *The San Diego Union-Tribune,* November 25, 1996, C, 2. Also see Craig Johnson and Larry Vinson, "Placement and Frequency of Powerless Talk and Impression Formation," *Communication Quarterly,* 38, no. 4 (Fall 1990), 325–33.

2.  Melissa Wanzer, Melanie Booth-Butterfield, and Steven Booth-Butterfield, "The Funny People: A Source Orientation to the Communication of Humor," *Communication Quarterly*, 43, no. 2 (Spring 1995), 142–54.

3.  Ibid.

4.  R. M. Kaplan and G. C. Pascoe, "Humorous Lectures and Humorous Examples: Some Effects upon Comprehension and Retention," *Journal of Educational Psychology*, 69 (1977), 61–65.

5.  Joan Gorham and Diane M. Christophel, "The Relationship of Teachers' Use of Humor in the Classroom to Immediacy and Student Learning," *Communication Education*, 39, no. 1 (January 1990), 46–62.

6.  Charles R. Gruner, "Self- and Other-Disparaging Wit/Humor and Speaker Ethos: Three Experiments," paper delivered at the Fourth International Conference on Humor, Tel Aviv Israel, June 1984.

7.  Steven Booth-Butterfield and Melanie Booth-Butterfield, "Individual Differences in the Communication of Humorous Messages," *Southern Communication Journal*, 56, no. 3 (Spring 1991), 205–18.

8.  James Hassett and John Houlihan, "Different Jokes for Different Folks," *Psychology Today*, January 1979, 64–71.

9.  Bill Adler, "Adlai Stevenson's Wit," *This Week* Magazine, September 12, 1965, p. 5. Copyrighted 1965 by the United Newspaper Corporation. Reprinted with the permission of the author and his agents, Scott Meredith Literary Agency, Inc., 580 Fifth Ave., New York, New York 10036.

10. Congressional Record, 1964, pp. 21, 596–97.

11. Quoted by Jerry Green, *Detroit News*, October 28, 1971, p. 5D.

12. By permission of The *Detroit Free Press*.

13. Steve Rubenstein, "A Very Good Dog Is What She Was," © The *San Francisco Chronicle*. Reprinted with permission.

# SPEAKING IN GROUP SETTINGS

# Chapter 14

## Chapter Objectives

### The Nature of Meetings and Groups

Small Coacting Groups

Discussion/Debate Continuum

### Contemporary Forms of Discussion

### Group Presenting and Leadership

Personal Preparation

Sources of Leadership

Functions of Leadership

Styles of Leadership

Other Leadership Theories

# THE NATURE OF MEETINGS AND GROUPS

(Phone rings) "Hello. Larry Logan here."

"Larry, this is Ed Brock, your old biology teacher at Groves High School."

"Yes, Mr. Brock. What can I do for you?"

"Well, Larry, you know that the PTA, the school board, and the community are considering the merits of sex education. Since you're in premed and were an honored graduate, I'd like your input at a discussion we're holding on Thursday night at the school."

"Sounds interesting. What time?"

"Seven thirty. Will you do it?"

"Sure, and thanks for thinking of me."

Good *luck* to *Larry Logan!* He never asked what he was really getting into, or how — or even if — he should prepare.

So Larry arrives promptly at 7:30 on Thursday. That's his second mistake. He has no time to adjust to what he finds. He thought a discussion was a few people informally kicking an idea around; sometimes it is, but not tonight.

The meeting is in the auditorium, which is already half full. The stage is set with seven chairs in a semicircle. It looks like a discussion set-up; but if it's a *panel,* it's also a *panel forum.* Why else are there microphones in the aisle?

Mr. Brock points to a chair and says, "Larry, you're third. Try to limit your opening remarks to three or four minutes:'

"Yikes," says Larry to himself, "I've got to give a speech." Right, Larry, and welcome to a *symposium forum.* A symposium, he discovers, calls for short, uninterrupted speeches.

After the speeches have been given the moderator (Brock) invites the participants to question one another. This is a panel format, but hardly a cohesive, unified, small group. Larry is challenged sharply on his words "human sexuality."

"What does that have to do with sex education?" demands Mrs. Himmler.

"Well, let me better define sex education," Larry replies.

Himmler interrupts. "Don't define sex education for me, young man. I know what it means."

Larry is no longer in a discussion (if he ever was). This is a debate, and a rough one at that. "Shouldn't we at least define what we're talking about?" mutters Larry. It is not one of Larry Logan's better nights.

"Thanks for coming to our roundtable discussion, Larry," says Brock.

Larry sneaks out as quickly as possible, thinking "Roundtable? What in thunder is a roundtable? Wasn't there a *Roundtable of the Air* on the radio years and years ago?"

The point of this horror story is that many people don't really know the differences between the various forms of discussion. As a leader, Mr. Brock was better at biology than at communication.

If you find yourself in Larry's place, check out the purpose, setting, audience, and agenda. Also be prepared for the possibility of a speech. At the very least, ask Brock what he means by "a discussion" and what the setting will be. Is it to be a single-form discussion? A panel perhaps? Is it apt to combine several forms? A multiform? Be prepared for him not to know that he was talking about a symposium forum rather than a panel discussion. (We'll review these definitions, and leadership functions shortly.)

## Small Coacting Groups

**Coacting groups** are more than just small, casual gatherings. *There must be some common purpose, intent, or problem that requires interaction.* Members share a kind of mutual identification that binds them together.[1] They are sensitive to their own behavior as well as to the behavior of others. Feedback is often swift and to the point in small groups; large audiences are sometimes slower to respond and more formal in their patterns of response. (Larry might argue that!)

An audience is sometimes passive; a good group is usually active and dynamic. The group's small size permits active and instant participation by all. Some members may, of course, have a greater desire to take charge than others do. If Larry Logan were a member of the local YMCA or CYO board, he might find himself involved in friendly problem solving at one meeting and in a rather stiff debate at another. Some boards are very large and only their executive committee meets as a coactive group. Their report to the whole board might very well be in the form of symposium speeches.

All small groups are *not* coacting groups; several characteristics help define coacting groups:

1.    They have a common purpose or goal.

2.    Members have interdependent, interactive communication.

3.    Members experience pressure to conform.

4.    Members decide and take action as a unit.

Some generalizations based on observation and research of coacting groups are:

1.    Group discussion can change attitudes and behavior.

2.    Group judgment is frequently better than individual judgment.

3.    Group communication can be improved through training.

This kind of small-group discussion has also been defined as "… a few people engaged in communication interaction over time, usually in face-to-face settings, who have common goals and norms, and have developed a communication pattern for meeting their goals in an interdependent manner."[2]

Assuming, then, that we have a real, interacting, face-to-face group—persons with some common goal, not just a loose collection of individuals—we might say that at its best *small-group discussion is cooperative thinking*. However, healthy argument and debate short of verbal aggression is also part of the definition.

A group of employees assigned a project at work could be considered a coacting group.

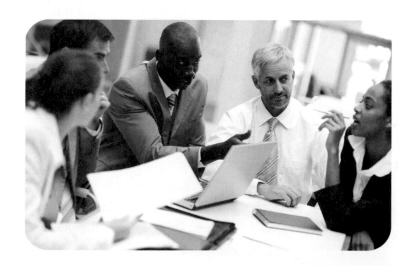

To enhance cooperation group members should:

1. Use tact when arguing.

2. Be enthusiastic and friendly.

3. Interact democratically and actively.

4. Seek agreement on procedures.

5. Share leadership.

6. Research the topic objectively.

## Discussion/Debate Continuum

Groups may generate little discussion on one issue and vigorous argument or debate on another. Some discussion/debate distinctions are helpful.

The term **discussion** is derived from the Latin *discussus*—to strike asunder, to pull apart, to separate and subordinate the elements and ideas that make up a question or topic. Discussion is many-sided. **Debate** is two-sided and more competitive. If decision is impossible through systematic discussion, then discussion may very well lead to useful debate. Debate may then lead to resolution. If it does not, the group very possibly will return to discussion. Premature, verbally aggressive, or unnecessary debate impedes problem solving. A discussion/debate continuum is illustrated in Figure 14.1.

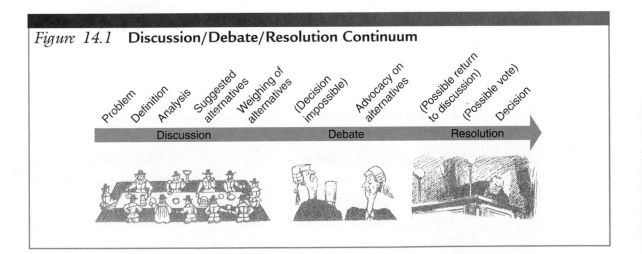

*Figure 14.1*    **Discussion/Debate/Resolution Continuum**

Problem · Definition · Analysis · Suggested alternatives · Weighing of alternatives · (Decision impossible) · Advocacy on alternatives · (Possible return to discussion) · (Possible vote) · Decision

Discussion          Debate          Resolution

Frequently a speaker goes from easygoing participant to an advocate. You may need to review Chapters 11 and 12 on persuasion and logic for certain situations. In some organizational settings you may also need to review parliamentary law.

# CONTEMPORARY FORMS OF DISCUSSION

The basic forms of group discussion are dialogue, panel, and symposium. A **forum** is simply that part of a discussion in which the audience may speak. It can be and often is included in any of the discussion forms. Rules for open-forum participation were discussed in Chapter 13, "Unique Formats and Occasions."

A **dialogue** is a two-person interaction, such as conversation, an interview, or counseling. If a dialogue is held before an audience and the audience is invited to participate, the interaction becomes a **dialogue forum**. (See Figure 14.2.)

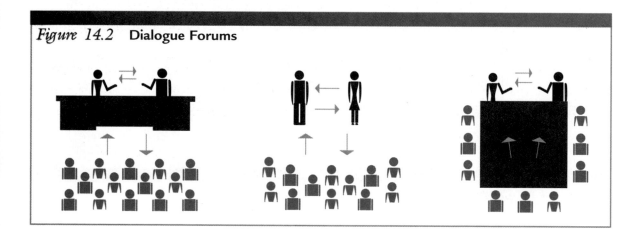

**Figure 14.2**   **Dialogue Forums**

The **panel discussion** is most often three to seven persons pursuing a common goal in an informal climate that promotes interaction. An audience may or may not be present. A panel discussion generally calls for a procedural leader, one who plans, starts, and ends the meeting. A simple program, or an **agenda,** might be called for. (See Figure 14.3.)

A **symposium** is a small group (three to five) that has special knowledge of different aspects of a broad topic. Each individual makes uninterrupted

*Figure 14.3*  **Panel Forums**

speeches before an audience. A procedural leader controls the order of speakers and the time limits. A forum usually follows, except when an audience is not physically present (as with radio or TV broadcasts). Frequently, the symposium speakers then relate to one another more informally in a panel discussion. (See Figure 14.4.)

These forms of discussion can be used for information sharing, problem solving or decision-making, as well as for instructional purposes. Examples of **information-sharing groups** are staff meetings, study groups, and workshops.

*Figure 14.4*  **Symposium Forums**

The overlap among these groups is evident and probably unavoidable. A workshop, for example, may be thought of as a study group that has concentrated its work into a couple of days or even a few hours.

**Problem-solving groups** include committees, conferences, and governing boards or councils. These discussion groups have the power of decision, or at least the power to recommend action. Their group discussions are usually closed to nonmembers. Groups engaged in problem solving and decision-making would be wise to follow formal procedures. Scholars and trainers offer variations on Dewey's Standard Agenda.

The basic steps of the Standard Agenda include:

1.    Define the problem by limiting and agreeing on the question that it presents.

2.    Analyze the problem by determining its separate elements, history, and possible causes.

3.    Establish criteria for solutions and recognize limitations.

4.    Generate and test solutions through brainstorming and research.

5.    Choose a solution for implementation and monitor results.

Following formal decision-making procedures helps to focus the group on the specific problem under consideration.

**Instructional formats** include case conferences, role-playing, and, to some extent, all the forms and techniques of discussion. A **case conference** is a discussion of a real or hypothetical incident that has a learning objective. It may or may not be conducted with an audience present.

Large groups in which wider, individual participation is desired may be divided into subgroups of four to six persons for more intimate, informal discussion. This technique is known as **buzz session** or "Phillips 66." The numbers refer to subgroups of six, which discuss a carefully worded question. The results of the individual buzz sessions are reported to the larger group by a spokesperson. The number of people in the subgroups seems to be important. A person is more apt to speak up in a group of six than of six hundred. (See Figure 14.5.)

The extemporaneous acting-out of assigned roles or dramatic parts in a group—often a case conference—it is known as **role-playing**. As a technique,

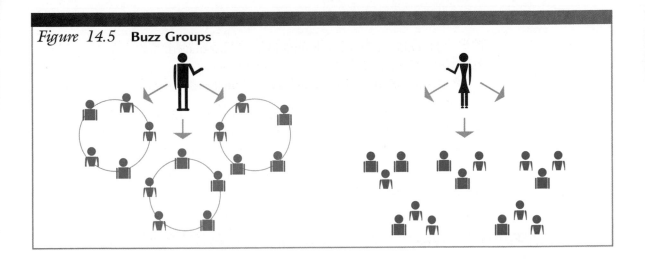

*Figure 14.5*  **Buzz Groups**

role-playing is often a good preliminary to the other forms of discussion. (See Figure 14.6.)

**Brainstorming** is a technique used when a group wants to generate a lot of ideas in a short period of time. This technique operates in an arbitrary psychological climate complete with penalties, the purpose of which is to prohibit immediate criticism of ideas. Its rules include:

1.    No criticism or discussion of ideas.

2.    No evaluation of any kind.

*Figure 14.6*  **Role-playing**

3.   The wilder the ideas, the better.

4.   "Hitchhiking" or combining ideas is encouraged.

5.   Record all ideas for later review and analysis.

Take the question, "What should this class use as a topic for a project discussion?" Under brainstorming rules, this question regularly produces sixty or seventy topics in ten minutes. No evaluative discussion of the topics is allowed until later. Using buzz groups to screen the list more systematically is a good follow-up (Figure 14.7).

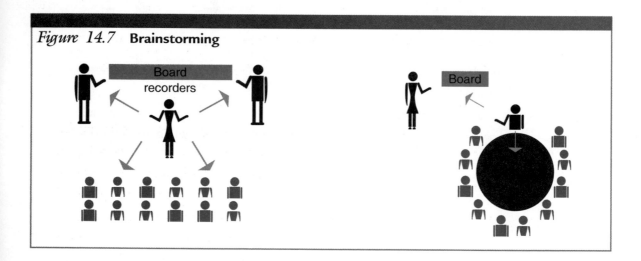

*Figure 14.7*   **Brainstorming**

# GROUP PRESENTING AND LEADERSHIP

## Personal Preparation

Recall the case of Larry Logan, "Merits of Sex Education," earlier in this chapter. He learned the hard way. To avoid his bad experience, you might ask the following questions:

1.   Who is in the group of speakers and in the possible audience? Do they have flexible or rigid positions? Do they view the purpose of the meeting differently than you do?

2.    Is it a large group meeting, or a small coaching group? What is the physical setup? Is there an audience? If so, will they participate?

> *What I wanted to be when I grew up—was in charge.*
> **Brigadier General Wilma Vaught**

3.    Is the format to be dialogue, panel, or symposium? If it's a symposium, you know you'll have to prepare a formal speech. Find out if you have been assigned to a specific aspect of the topic.

4.    Is there an "order of business"? Is there a prepared agenda of items to be covered? Do they have a formal statement of the problem?

As with formal speaking, researching the topic presumes you have a purpose, goal, or question in mind.

## Sources of Leadership

In general, **leadership** should be thought of as any significant action by any discussant that influences group achievement. A group may have an *assigned* leader, whose duties may range from a modest regulation of participation to strong goal control. It is possible to be in a leaderless group (that is, with no appointed leader) and still have considerable leadership, should this leadership emerge in some way from the group. By the same token, you could be in a group with a poor assigned leader. If no good leader(s) emerged, this group would really have no leadership. All group members have a stake and often a part in leadership. Thus, what follows applies to all group speakers, whether they are assigned as group leader, chairperson, moderator, or they emerge as a leader to fulfill the role for the group.

Leadership, however temporary, may fall upon a person in a group simply because he or she was appointed moderator. It may be assigned to a person only on certain issues because that person happens to be the best informed on those issues. It may befall a person by reason of *role, position,* or *status* in the group (for example, she happens to be the boss, or he is an expert).

Particularly in leaderless groups, leadership may fall to a person who happens to perform communication skills exceptionally well—who knows how to speak, how to assess people, how to build and apply agendas, how to keep the lines of communication open. Other members often see this individual as possessing skills and behaviors that represent leadership and therefore are willing to be guided by the individual.

# Functions of Leadership

Leadership, whatever its source, should help a group move toward its goal or help it find its goal. Leadership should also promote a healthy, democratic communication climate within the group.

If your perceived leadership role does not happen to agree with most of your receivers' expectations, you may not exert much influence. In relatively informal, short-lived groups, such as committees or subcommittees, it usually helps all concerned if there is some concordance about role expectations. If your role is strictly procedural and is a random appointment, don't emerge as a George Patton; not many will be expecting that of you. If, on the other hand, you have been handpicked because of your experience and expertise, you can look for different role expectations, but not always! Sometimes members do not know your qualifications, and sometimes they don't bother to do their homework. You may need to explain and assess your role in these situations. You may risk some embarrassment in so doing, but not to do so is to risk charges of entrapping or embarrassing the others in the group.

Even when people agree upon position descriptions (chairperson, president, supervisor, lawyer), they may not agree upon role expectations. Some people express antipathy toward formal leadership, but even such behavior is predictable if it shows up in your preliminary search for ***concordance*** (agreement between actual and expected role). To complicate things further, people change; their roles and their expectations change; not very long ago most formal leadership was gendered—male. Even today, males are more often chosen as leaders.

The major functions of leadership are goal achievement, procedural matters, and effective interpersonal relations (communication climate).

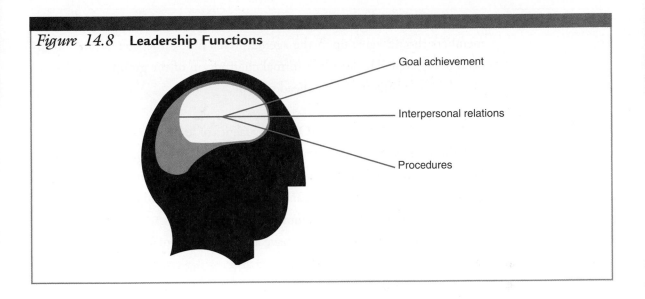

*Figure 14.8* **Leadership Functions**

**GOAL ACHIEVEMENT** This is leadership related primarily to *content* or *task*. It includes such things as contributing and evaluating ideas, locating issues and consensus, synthesizing and cross-relating the ideas of others, and generally seeking specific contributions toward a goal. It helps if you are enthusiastic about and personally committed to the task at hand.

**PROCEDURAL MATTERS** Leaders, particularly when assigned or designated, must also attend to the more practical functions, such as starting the meeting, drafting an order of business, clarifying statements, summarizing, and ending the meeting. Procedural functions may also include advance planning and physical arrangements.

As a procedural leader, you must review the purposes of the meeting. You should consider the members individually and decide the *degree of formality* necessary and the specific way you wish to open the discussion. You should consider group goals according to the time available. As a procedural leader you are also responsible for *participation*—that is, for preserving order, seeing that only one person speaks at a time, and gatekeeping—fairly distributing the right to speak. You may find it necessary on occasion to clarify what has been said as well as to remind the group of the agreed-upon items of business. The members should agree upon the agenda-items unless the agenda has already been designated. The leader or formal chairperson of the group often distributes the agreed-upon agenda ahead of time.

**INTERPERSONAL RELATIONS**    Qualities of leadership in this area include such things as establishing rapport, controlling emotions, establishing the communication and psychological climate, resolving conflict, regulating the too-talkative and the silent, reserved members, and generally promoting and facilitating those actions concerned with members' human or social problems.[3]

Leaders as well as participants have a responsibility to help the group whenever the situations shown in Figure 14.9 arise.

*Figure 14.9*

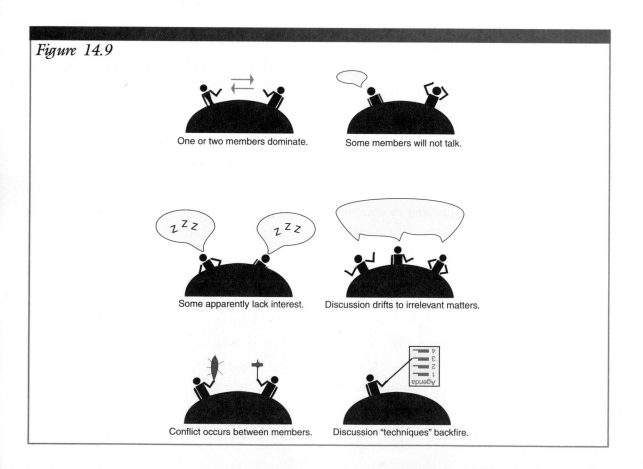

# Styles of Leadership

**Styles Leadership Theory** refers to a collection of specific leadership styles that we can identify in others and learn for ourselves. Different styles are attributed to different leaders, too.4 In this sense, style refers in part to method and in part to philosophy. Many times the type of organization in which you are operating determines style. For example, a Marine Corps drill instructor (D.I.) understands full well the autocratic-style expectations of the Corps, and the recruits put up with this highly directive style because, after all, that was what they expected.

Leadership styles are variously described as *laissez-faire, nondirective, permissive, democratic, supervisory, authoritarian,* and *autocratic.* These styles may be ordered on a continuum according to degree of control, as shown in Figure 14.10. However, Kurt Lewin's (1939) research on leadership found the three major leadership styles were laissez-faire, democratic, and autocratic.5 **Laissez-faire leadership** is represented by a participative but no control attitude. Laissez- faire is a French phrase that literally means to "let do." A laissez faire leader would let the group members decide for themselves and do as they

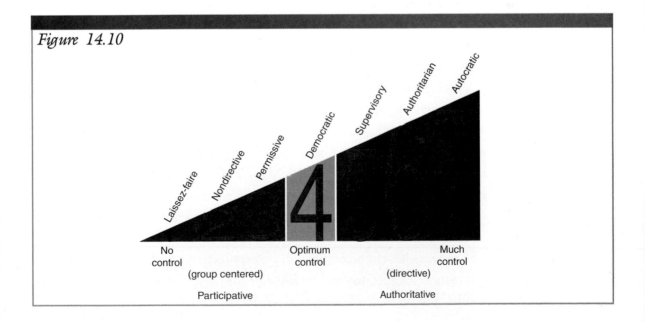

*Figure 14.10*

please. This is effective leadership when the group members are mature and have specific tasks they are already involved. This leadership style was found to be the least effective in promoting cooperation and motivation where roles or duties were even the least bit unclear. **Democratic leadership** is participative leadership wherein the leader motivates and guides the group to come to its own decisions. This leader promotes social equality amongst the members of the group, collaborative efforts and creative problem solving. **Autocratic leadership** is found at the far right of the control continuum. Autocratic leaders seek control to direct the outcome of group work. These leaders tend to make the decisions with or without group agreement or even input. They expect members of the group to obey their directives and ultimately take responsibility and credit for the results.[6]

Experience advises that a democratic style is generally superior to an absolute or nonresponsible style. Which leadership style we may occasionally use depends in part on the group's expectations, in part on the task, and in large part on the situation of the moment.

## Other Leadership Theories

Styles Leadership Theory is not the only theory on leadership, as you will find with even a precursory look at any textbook on group communication, or leadership, or a quick perusal on the Internet. In this section, we will briefly describe four other group leadership theories: trait leadership, functional leadership, situational leadership, and functional leadership.

**Trait Leadership Theory** is also referred to as "The Great Man" Theory. This theory suggests that leaders are born, not made and identifies innate *characteristics* of leaders. These characteristics would include self-confidence, humility, assertiveness, warmth, humor, emotional stability, far-sightedness, etc. – traits you might ascribe to a leader. Many leadership scholars reject this theory, even though many lay people still think there is some truth in it.

**Functional Leadership Theory** suggests that group members rise to fill leadership functions when necessary. Instead of focusing on the leader herself – who she *is* or her characteristics – this theory focuses on what the leader *does*. In this manner a leader may rise to make sure the tasks are getting completed, while another rises to motivate the group members.

**Situational Leadership Theory** combines the functional and styles approach and claims that effective leaders will combine the best style of leadership and functions with what the given situation calls for. Hence, our *style* might differ from member to member and situation to situation. Someone who needs lots of encouragement might require our patience. A member who is letting the task fall behind might need motivational style.

**Transformational Leadership Theory** looks at what leaders accomplish with the attributes they posses. Think of Martin Luther King, Jr. or Ghandi. Transformation means change. Transformational leaders make change happen. There are six attributes that transformational leaders tend to posses: 1) They are *charismatic*, which indicates they have an agreeable or dynamic personality, easy to listen to and follow. 2) They are *visionaries*, seeing the bigger picture – the goal to strive for and can help others see it too. 3) They are *supportive* by wanting members to strive for their own personal development and growth. 4) They empower members by involving them in important decision making and encouraging self-fulfillment. 5) They are innovative by encouraging creativity and helping members to understand the need for change. 6) They model member effectiveness, building a trust between themselves and other members.

# CHAPTER REVIEW
## *Wrapping it up*

## Summary

Many people tend to confuse the various forms of discussion, and do not understand coacting groups. Four main characteristics of coactive groups include the following: 1) sharing a common purpose or goal; 2) utilize interdependent, interactive communication; 3) tend to feel and pressure to conform; and 4) come to unitary decisions and actions. Other generalizations about small groups are 1) discussion can change attitudes and behavior, 2) group judgment tends to be better than that of individuals alone, and (3) group communications can be improved through training.

Assuming a group with a common goal, we can define group-discussion speaking as cooperative thinking. If decision is impossible through discussion, discussion may very well lead to debate. Discussion is cooperative and many-sided. Debate is two-sided.

The basic forms of group discussion are dialogue, panel, and symposium. Three techniques that may be used with any of these forms are the buzz group, role-playing, and brainstorming. A forum is simply that part of a discussion in which the audience may speak.

These forms of discussion may be used for information-sharing, problem solving, and instruction. Information-sharing groups include staff meetings, study groups, and workshops. Problem-solving groups include committees, conferences, and boards or councils and often rely upon formal procedures, like the Standard Agenda, to work through decision-making processes. Instructional forums include case conferences, role-playing, and, to some extent, all the forms and techniques of discussion.

Successful groups analyze before seeking solutions. Open communication that focuses on the task and related issues facilitates problem solving and decision-making.

Leadership can be considered as any significant action by any discussant that influences group achievement. It is possible to have no assigned leader and still have leadership; it is also

Check out our website
**www.bvtlab.com**
for flashcards,
summaries,
self-quizzes and speeches.

possible to have an assigned leader and no leadership. All group members have a stake and often a role in leadership.

Leadership may fall upon a person through designation or as a result of that person's superior information, role, position, or special ability to perform vital group functions.

The major functions of leadership are goal achievement and effective interpersonal relations. Leadership, particularly when designated, also has procedural functions. These functions may be planning, physical arrangements, purposes, degree of formality, goal setting, and the business agenda. The procedural leader is also responsible for general control of participation and for preserving order.

Styles Leadership Theory suggests there are three main styles of leadership may be described as autocratic, democratic, and laissez-faire. A leader's style is dependent upon group expectations, contingencies that arise, and participant behavior. A democratic style is generally preferred.

Four other leadership theories include: 1) trait theory – a leader is born, not made; 2) functional theory – a member rises to fulfill leadership functions when necessary; 3) situational theory –claims that a leader will combine the style and the necessary functions to the situation; and 4) transformational theory – suggest leaders accomplish change based on six characteristics (charisma, vision, supportive, empowering others, innovative, and modeling effectiveness).

## Notes

1.    Raymond S. Ross, *Small Groups in Organizational Settings* (Englewood Cliffs, N.J.: Prentice-Hall, 1989), p. 33.
2.    John F. Cragan and David W. Wright, *Communication in Small Group Discussions,* 4th ed. (St. Paul, Minn.: West Publishing Co., 1995), p. 7.
3.    For more on group facilitation techniques, see L. R. Frey, ed., *Innovations in Group Facilitation: Applications in Natural Settings* (Cresskill, N.J.: Hampton Press, 1995).
4.    Kurt Lewin, Ron Lippit, and R. K. White, "Patterns of Aggressive Behaviour in Experimentally Created Social Climates," Journal of Social Psychology, 10 (1939), pp. 271-299.
5.    Ibid.
6.    Jorge Correia Jesuino, "Leadership: Micro-macro Links," in Understanding Group Behavior, vol.2, ed. Erich H. White and James H. Davis (Mahwah, NJ: Lawrence Erlbaum Associates, 1996), p. 99.

# Speech Topic Locator

The *Idea Starters* (A) may be all you need to trigger a creative and manageable topic for your next speech. The *Idea Elaborators* (B) are meant to help you narrow your general topic and to suggest ways of dividing it into main points.

If you are still struggling to find a topic, consult the *Topic Inventory* (C) for help in finding a general topical area that interests you. Apply the *Idea Elaborators* to the topic chosen and proceed to narrow and refine it.

Shown are only 14 of the most obvious elaborators, but multiply those by the 500 topics in the inventory gives you a total of 7,000 ideas for speeches. There is plenty to talk about!

## A. IDEA STARTERS

| | | | | |
|---|---|---|---|---|
| People | Objects | Events | Problems | Issues |
| Policies | Definitions | Theories | Hobbies | Structures |
| Processes | Places | Concepts | Plans | Jobs |
| Your interests | Natural phenomena | Computers | Incredible phenomena | |

## B. IDEA ELABORATORS

| | | | |
|---|---|---|---|
| History of | Influence of | Current practices | Classic examples |
| Importance of | Differing views | How to do it | Who is involved |
| How to make it | Where it is located | How it works | |
| Implications of | Dangers of | Why it is done | |

## C. TOPIC INVENTORY

| | | | |
|---|---|---|---|
| Falconry | Home brew | Kuwait today | Birth control |
| Law clerks | Marxism | Dog breeding | Writers |
| Auto repairs | ESP | Hypnotism | Automobiles |
| Scuba diving | College athletics | Violence | Copyrights |
| Archery | Nuclear energy | Beatles | Floods |
| Acid rain | Laser disks | Volcanoes | FBI |
| Drunk drivers | Soul food | Handwriting | Hinduism |
| Leadership | Used cars | Ghosts | Infant mortality |
| Capital punishment | Pee-Wee hockey | Books | S & L's |
| Mummification | Ballooning | Missiles | Banks |
| Lasers | Ski racing | Karate | Macrame |
| Beijing | Handguns | Tai chi | War games |
| Bar Mitzvah | Pregnancy | Metaphysics | Mammoth Cave |
| Bas Mitzvah | Senior citizens | Hypnotherapy | Kremlin |
| Astrology | Iran | Jazz | United Nations |
| Witchcraft | Gun control | Camping | Stock market |
| Cheating | UFOs | Politics | Labor unions |
| Biological warfare | Marilyn Monroe | FCC | Military tactics |
| Martin Luther King | Pyramids | Alcoholism | Washington, D.C. |
| Peace Corps | Sleep research | Investments | Expressionism |
| Internships | Earthquakes | Divorce | Phenomenology |
| Working out | Ozone layer | Censorship | Word processing |
| Sailboarding | Cable cars | ROTC | Sailing |
| Birding | Solar energy | Acupuncture | Nelson Mandela |
| Child abuse | Dog training | Aliens | Public relations |
| Teen violence | Filmmaking | Boat navigation | Sex discrimination |
| Dutch treating | Umpiring | Dance | Diets |
| Dinosaurs | Kite flying | Advertising | Leisure |
| Iraq | World Series | Pollution | Buddhism |
| Organ donating | Drugs | Bottle laws | Bodybuilding |
| Cancer signs | Music | Architecture | Awards |
| Computers | Amnesia | Islam | Aerospace |

| | | | |
|---|---|---|---|
| Amnesty | Bermuda Triangle | Retirement | Biofeedback |
| Aggression | Counterfeiting | IQ | Bullfighting |
| Adoption | Ecology | NMCP | Forensic medicine |
| Kibbutzim | CIA | Olympics | Persuasibility |
| Koran | Health care | Pulitzer Prize | Titanic |
| Ku Klux Klan | Inflation | Scientology | Stamps |
| Knighthood | Esperanto | Suicide | Pygmies |
| AIDS | NOW | Whales | Mound builders |
| Fly tying | Nutrition | Tattooing | Jacques Cousteau |
| Chemical warfare | Papacy | Submarines | Magna Carta |
| Old Faithful | Royalty | Satellites | Native Americans |
| Word processing | Telepathy | Illusions | Comets |
| Existentialism | Transplants | Noah's Ark | Glaciers |
| Epistemology | Zen | Mormons | Fingerprints |
| Fidel Castro | Wind | Ghostwriting | Eskimos |
| Furniture | Telescopes | Knighthood | Etiquette |
|    refinishing | Boxing | Hot springs | Galileo |
| South Africa | Credit | Rain forests | Curling |
| Fairness doctrine | Economics | Voiceprints | Fossils |
| Smoking | KGB | Evolution | Flags |
| Crime | Nursing homes | Fencing | Death Valley |
| Day care centers | Health insurance | Abstract art | Dead Sea |
| Pornography | Maoism | Babe Ruth | Cave people |
| Marines | Nielsen ratings | Aesthetics | Castles |
| Robotics | Obscenity | C.I.O. | P. T. Barnum |
| Ageism | Population | Indian art | Aztecs |
| Statue of Liberty | Psychoanalysis | Bicycling | Pompeii |
| Rose Parade | Saints | Cholesterol | Abolitionists |
| Affirmative action | Slavery | Semantics | Railroads |
| Zone defense | Zodiac | Self-presentation | Henry Ford |
| Superdome | Waves | Collective behavior | Camouflage |
| World wonders | Recession | Propaganda | Wenkel engine |
| IRS | Chauvinism | Altruism | Eiffel Tower |
| Urban League | Cults | Family violence | Dead Sea Scrolls |
| Numerology | Gambling | Substance abuse | Cannibals |
| PLO | Acting | Desktop publishing | West Point |
| Psychic phenomena | Census | Herbs | Aborigines |
| Racism | Test-tube babies | Endangered species | Basilicas |
| Transcendental | Vitamins | Zero population | Apocalypse |
|    meditation | Zoos |    growth | Taj Mahal |
| Supreme Court | Ventriloquism | Future wonders | Rocket planes |
| Surrogates | NASA | Psychics | Speed |
| Weight lifting | Cloning | Arbitration | Panama |
| White House | Funerals | Ethics | Mermaids |
| Unknown soldier | ERA | America's Cup | Mayflower |
| Artists | Gay rights | Art deco | Harvard |

Everglades
Holocaust
Tar pits
Erosion
Creationism
Pigeon racing
Eclipses
Alchemy
Black death
Naval Academy
Alfred Nobel
H.M.S. Beagle
Casey Jones
Great Lakes
Fallacies
Riots
Kaizen
Apartheid
Rape
Terrorism
Torture today
Famines
Poisonous plants
Unusual
    monuments
Boxing
Baseball cards
Great imposters
Mediation
Agnosticism
Aptitude testing
Atlantis
Blood pressure
FFA
Grieving
Grievance
    procedure
Board membership
Child custody
Slang
Recycling
Waste disposal
Super tankers
Toxic substances
Noninvasive surgery
Hi-definition TV

Exceptional
    children
Firearms
Bonsai
Rug hooking
Colors
Early radio
Puppetry
Infrared
Ergonomics
Time management
Study skills
Genealogy
Body massage
Family boating
Volunteerism
Student
    government
Financial aid
Extracurricular
    activities
Commercial art
Criminal justice
Hospitality
    management
Law enforcement
Maritime
    academies
Pilot training
Travel agents
Fitness labs
Container
    gardening
Correctional
    institutions
Card weaving
Calligraphy
Databases
Happiness
Magic
Wildlife rescue
Edible flowers
Graphoanalysis
Kuntaw
Law aptitudes
    (LSAT)

Shamanism
Human sexuality
Pottery
Sign language
Dowsing
Clowning
Assertiveness
Aikido
Yoga
Loom weaving
Judo
Blacksmithing
Basketry
Flower arrangement
Shiatsu
Citizenship
Hurricanes
Social Security
Norplant
Centenarians
Eagle Scouts
U.S. acquisitions
Acropolis
Nature trails
Lyme Disease
Camping
Glasnost
Parochiad
Police brutality
Stonehenge
Population
Alzheimer's disease
Canning/freezing
Microfilms
    International
Genetically
    Modified Foods
Prostitution
ADC
Ecumenicism
Open housing
Rapid transit
Inner cities
States' rights
"As one"
DT/DCC

Boxing
Pentagon
Head Start
Cost of living
Blight
Budgeting
Terrariums
Circus
Shakespeare
Ergology
Phobias
Diabetes
Welfare
Parachuting
Frostbite
Bridges
Churches
Grand Canyon
Graffiti
Posters
Instant replays
Lightning
Esalen
Tiananmen Square
Gay marriage
Communal living
Gerontology
Poverty
Marijuana
Tuition costs
Forest fires
Avalanches
Bonding
Salvation
Systems theory
Mushrooms
Auto safety
E.T.V.
Common law
    marriage
Foreign imports
Multimedia
Shintoism
Branch Davidians
Yugoslavia
Somalia

| | | | |
|---|---|---|---|
| Fundamentalism | Health care | Bio-lite | Sports salaries |
| Feminism | Taxes | Madonna | Privacy act |
| Haiti | Movies | Gold | Credit cards |
| Breast cancer | Internet browsing | Floods | Homelessness |
| Prostate cancer | Flash cooking | Landfills | Internet Fraud |
| Cuba | Fuel cells | Fires | |
| Panama Canal | Virtual vision | Charter schools | |
| NAFTA | Virtual reality | Custody battles | |

# Example Speeches

Martin Luther King, Jr. was known for his exquisite use of rhetoric. His use of metaphor and vivid language moved his audiences by providing concrete imagery. He chose different words and metaphors depending on his audience and the occasion. On August 28, 1963, he delivered his "I Have a Dream" speech to some 200,000 people from the steps of the Lincoln Memorial in Washington, D.C. This speech was a persuasive speech organized in two main parts: the problem and the solution. He describes the American nightmare of slavery and injustice in the first part and the dream of a better future in the second part. Notice how he uses repetition, quotations, allusions, specific examples, and metaphors. The speech, in its entirety, follows.

## MARTIN LUTHER KING, JR. SPEECH AT THE MARCH ON WASHINGTON FOR JOBS AND FREEDOM (28TH AUGUST, 1963)

I am happy to join with you today in what will go down in history as the greatest demonstration for freedom in the history of our nation.

Five score years ago, a great American, in whose symbolic shadow we stand today, signed the Emancipation Proclamation. This momentous decree came as a great beacon light of hope to millions of Negro slaves who had been seared in the flames of withering injustice. It came as a joyous daybreak to end the long night of their captivity.

But one hundred years later, the Negro still is not free. One hundred years later, the life of the Negro is still sadly crippled by the manacles of segregation and the chains of discrimination. One hundred years later, the Negro lives on a lonely island of poverty in the midst of a vast ocean of material prosperity. One hundred years later, the Negro is still languished in the corners of American society and finds himself an exile in his own land. And so we've come here today to dramatize a shameful condition.

In a sense we've come to our nation's capital to cash a check. When the architects of our republic wrote the magnificent words of the Constitution and the Declaration of Independence, they were signing a promissory note to which every American was to fall heir. This note was a promise that all men, yes, black men as well as white men, would be guaranteed the "unalienable Rights of Life, Liberty, and the pursuit of Happiness." It is obvious today that America has defaulted on this promissory note insofar as her citizens of color are concerned. Instead of honoring this sacred obligation, America has given the Negro people a bad check, a check which has come back marked "insufficient funds."

But we refuse to believe that the bank of justice is bankrupt. We refuse to believe that there are insufficient funds in the great vaults of opportunity of this nation. And so we've come to cash this check, a check that will give us upon demand the riches of freedom and the security of justice.

We have also come to this hallowed spot to remind America of the fierce urgency of now. This is no time to engage in the luxury of cooling off or to take the tranquilizing drug of gradualism. Now is the time to make real the promises of democracy. Now is the time to rise from the dark and desolate valley of segregation to the sunlit path of racial justice. Now is the time to lift our nation from the quicksands of racial injustice to the solid rock of brotherhood. Now is the time to make justice a reality for all of God's children.

It would be fatal for the nation to overlook the urgency of the moment. This sweltering summer of the Negro's legitimate discontent will not pass until there is an invigorating autumn of freedom and equality. Nineteen sixty-three is not an end, but a beginning. And those who hope that the Negro needed to blow off steam and will now be content will have a rude awakening if the nation returns to business as usual. [Applause] There will be neither rest nor tranquillity in America until the Negro is granted his citizenship rights. The whirlwinds of revolt will continue to shake the foundations of our nation until the bright day of justice emerges.

But there is something that I must say to my people, who stand on the warm threshold which leads into the palace of justice: in the process of gaining our rightful place, we must not be guilty of wrongful deeds. Let us not seek to satisfy our thirst for freedom by drinking from the cup of bitterness and hatred. [Applause] We must forever conduct our struggle on the high plane of dignity and discipline. We must not allow our creative protest to degenerate into physical violence. Again and again, we must rise to the majestic heights of meeting physical force with soul force. The marvelous new militancy which has engulfed the Negro community must not lead us to a distrust of all white people, for many of our white brothers, as evidenced by their presence here today, have come to realize that their destiny is tied up with our destiny. And they have come to realize that their freedom is inextricably bound to our freedom. We cannot walk alone.

And as we walk, we must make the pledge that we shall always march ahead. We cannot turn back. There are those who are asking the devotees of civil rights, "When will you be satisfied?"

We can never be satisfied as long as the Negro is the victim of the unspeakable horrors of police brutality. We can never be satisfied as long as our bodies, heavy with the fatigue of travel, cannot gain lodging in the motels of the highways and the hotels of the cities. We cannot be satisfied as long as the Negro's basic mobility is from a smaller ghetto to a larger one. We can never be satisfied as long as our children are stripped of their selfhood and robbed of their dignity by signs stating "for whites only." We cannot be satisfied as long as a Negro in Mississippi cannot vote and a Negro in New York believes he has nothing for which to vote. No, no, we are not satisfied and we will not be satisfied until justice rolls down like waters and righteousness like a mighty stream.

I am not unmindful that some of you have come here out of great trials and tribulations. Some of you have come fresh from narrow jail cells. Some of you have come from areas where your quest for freedom left you battered by the storms of persecution and staggered by the winds of police brutality. You have been the veterans of creative suffering. Continue to work with the faith that unearned suffering is redemptive. Go back to Mississippi, go back to Alabama, go back to South Carolina, go back to Georgia, go back to Louisiana, go back to the slums and ghettos of our northern cities, knowing that somehow this situation can and will be changed. Let us not wallow in the valley of despair.

I say to you today, my friends, so even though we face the difficulties of today and tomorrow, I still have a dream. It is a dream deeply rooted in the American dream.

I have a dream that one day this nation will rise up and live out the true meaning of its creed: "We hold these truths to be self-evident, that all men are created equal.

I have a dream that one day on the red hills of Georgia, the sons of former slaves and the sons of former slave owners will be able to sit down together at the table of brotherhood.

I have a dream that one day even the state of Mississippi, a state sweltering with the heat of injustice, sweltering with the heat of oppression, will be transformed into an oasis of freedom and justice.

I have a dream that my four little children will one day live in a nation where they will not be judged by the color of their skin but by the content of their character. I have a dream today.

I have a dream that one day down in Alabama, with its vicious racists, with its governor having his lips dripping with the words of "interposition" and "nullification," one day right there in Alabama little black boys and black girls will be able to join hands with little white boys and white girls as sisters and brothers. I have a dream today.

I have a dream that one day every valley shall be exalted, every hill and mountain shall be made low, the rough places will be made plain, and the crooked places will be made straight, and the glory of the Lord shall be revealed, and all flesh shall see it together.

This is our hope. This is the faith that I go back to the South with. With this faith we will be able to hew out of the mountain of despair a stone of hope. With this faith we will be able to transform the jangling discords of our nation into a beautiful symphony of brotherhood. With this faith we will be able to work together, to pray together, to struggle together, to go to jail together, to stand up for freedom together, knowing that we will be free one day. This will be the day, this will be the day when all of God's children will be able to sing with new meaning:

My country, 'tis of thee, sweet land of liberty, of thee I sing.

Land where my fathers died, land of the pilgrim's pride,

From every mountainside, let freedom ring!

And if America is to be a great nation, this must become true.

So let freedom ring from the prodigious hilltops of New Hampshire.

Let freedom ring from the mighty mountains of New York.

Let freedom ring from the heightening Alleghenies of Pennsylvania.

Let freedom ring from the snow-capped Rockies of Colorado.

Let freedom ring from the curvaceous slopes of California.

But not only that: Let freedom ring from Stone Mountain of Georgia.

Let freedom ring from Lookout Mountain of Tennessee.

Let freedom ring from every hill and molehill of Mississippi.

From every mountainside, let freedom ring.

And when this happens, when we allow freedom ring, when we let it ring from every village and every hamlet, from every state and every city, we will be able to speed up that day when all of God's children, black men and white men, Jews and Gentiles, Protestants and Catholics, will be able to join hands and sing in the words of the old Negro spiritual: Free at last! Free at last! Thank God Almighty, we are free at last!

# COIK Speech: Edgar Dale, Former Professor At Ohio State University: COIK – Clear Only If Know

"COIK" which stands for "Clear Only If Known" is the title of a speech by Edgar Dale, a former professor of education at Ohio State University. It is a classic illustration showing how to apply the principles covered in chapter 10: learning, motivation, clarity, interest, and even humor. Dale grabs your attention quickly with an illustration with which most people can easily identify (paragraphs 1 and 2). Paragraph 4 clarifies what he's trying to say. He makes good use of relevant humor in paragraphs 5, 13, and 14). All of the paragraphs contain lessons that can help you as you plan and prepare your informative speech.

Attention | 1 | I have puzzled over the inept communication of simple directions, especially those given me when touring. I ask such seemingly easy questions as: "Where do I turn off Route 40 for the by-pass around St. Louis? How do I get to the planetarium? Is this the way to the Federal Security Building?" The individual whom I hail for directions either replies "I'm a stranger here myself," or gives you in kindly fashion the directions you request. He finishes by saying pleasantly, "You can't miss it."

Attention | 2 | But about half the time you do miss it. You turn at High Street instead of Ohio Street. It was six blocks to the turn, not seven. Many persons who give directions tell you to turn right when they mean left. You carefully count the indicated five stoplights before the turn and discover that your guide meant that blinkers should be counted as stoplights. Some of the directions exactly followed turn out to be inaccurate. Your guide himself didn't know how to get there.

3 | Now education is the problem of getting our bearings, of developing orientation, of discovering in what direction to go and how to get there. An inquiry into the problem of giving and receiving directions may help us discover something important about the educational process itself. Why do people give directions poorly and sometimes follow excellent directions inadequately?

Clarification | 4 | First of all, people who give directions do not always understand the complexity of what they are communicating. They think it a simple matter to get to the Hayden Planetarium because it is simple for them. When someone says,

"You can't miss it," he really means, "*I* can't miss it." He is suffering from what has been called the COIK fallacy—Clear Only If Known. It's easy to get to the place you are inquiring about if you already know how to get there.

Humor  5  We all suffer from the COIK fallacy. For example, during a World Series game a recording was made of a conversation between a rabid New York baseball fan and an Englishman seeing a baseball game for the first time.

The Englishman asked, "What is a pitcher?"

"He's the man down there pitching the ball to the catcher."

"But," said the Englishman, "all of the players pitch the ball and all of them catch the ball. There aren't just two persons who pitch and catch."

Later the Englishman asked, "How many strikes do you get before you are out?"

The Brooklyn fan said, "Three."

"But," replied the Englishman, "that man struck at the ball five times before he was out."

These directions about baseball, when given to the uninitiated, are clear only if known.

6  Try the experiment sometime of handing a person a coat and ask him to explain how to put it on. He must assume that you have lived in the tropics, have never seen a coat worn or put on, and that he is to tell you *verbally* how to do it. For example, he may say, "Pick it up by the collar." This you cannot do, since you do not know what a collar is. He may tell you to put your arm in the sleeve or to button up the coat. But you can't follow these directions because you have no previous experience with either a sleeve or a button.

7   The communication of teachers to pupils suffers from the COIK fallacy. An uninitiated person may think that the decimal system is easy to understand. It is—if you already know it. Students who are asked by an instructor to understand his explanation of the duodecimal system can gain some idea of the complexity of the decimal system—a system that some mathematicians will say is even simpler than the decimal system. It is not easy to understand with just one verbal explanation, I assure you.

8   A teacher of my acquaintance once presented a group of parents of first-grade children with the shorthand equivalents of the first-grade reader and asked them to read this material. It was a frustrating experience, but these parents no longer thought it was such a simple matter to learn how to read in the first grade. Reading, of course, is easy if you already know how to do it.

9   Sometimes our directions are overcomplex and introduce unnecessary elements. They do not follow the law of parsimony. Any unnecessary elements mentioned when giving directions may prove to be a distraction. Think of the directions given for solving problems in arithmetic or for making a piece of furniture or for operating a camera. Have all unrelated and unnecessary items been eliminated? Every unnecessary step or statement is likely to increase the difficulty of reading and understanding the directions. There is no need to overelaborate or labor the obvious.

10  In giving directions it is also easy to overestimate the experience of our questioner. It is hard indeed for a Philadelphian to understand that anyone doesn't know where the City Hall is. Certainly if you go down Broad Street, you can't miss it. We know where it is. Why doesn't our questioner?

11  It is easy, for example, to overestimate the historical experience of a student. The instructor often forgets that his students were toddling infants when Jimmy Carter was president. Events that the instructor has immediately experienced have only been read or heard about by the student. What was immediate knowledge to the instructor is mediated knowledge to the student.

12  We are surprised to discover that many college freshmen do not know such words as *abrogate, abscond, accrue, effigy, enigma, epitome, exigency*

*hierarchy, lucrative, pernicious, ruminate, fallacious, salient, codify, coerce,* and *cognizance.* College professors are surprised to discover that even their abler students do not know such words as *protean, shard, ad hoc, restrictive covenant,* and *prorogue.*

Joke   13   Another frequent reason for failure in the communication of directions is that explanations are more technical then necessary. Thus a plumber once wrote to a research bureau pointing out that he had used hydrochloric acid to clean out sewer pipes and inquired, "Was there any possible harm?" The first reply was as follows: "The efficacy of hydrochloric acid is indisputable, but the corrosive residue is incompatible with metallic permanence." The plumber then thanked them for the information approving his procedure. The dismayed research bureau tried again, saying, "We cannot assume responsibility for the production of toxic and noxious residue with hydrochloric acid and suggest you use an alternative procedure." Once more the plumber thanked them for their approval. Finally, the bureau, worried about the New York sewers, called in a third scientist who wrote: "Don't use hydrochloric acid. It eats hell out of the pipes."

Joke   14   Some words are not understood and others are misunderstood. For example, a woman confided to a friend that the doctor told her that she had "very close veins." A patient was puzzled as to how she could take two pills three times a day. A little girl told her mother that the superintendent of the Sunday school said he would drop them into the furnace if they missed three Sundays in succession. He had said that he would drop them from the register.

15   We know the vast difference between knowing how to do something and being able to communicate that knowledge to others, of being able to verbalize it. We know how to tie a bowknot but have trouble telling others how to do it.

16   Another difficulty in communicating directions lies in the unwillingness of a person to say that he doesn't know. Someone drives up and asks you where Oxford Road is. You realize that Oxford Road is somewhere in the vicinity and feel a sense of guilt about not knowing the streets in your own town. So you tend to give poor directions instead of admitting that you don't know.

17   Sometimes we use the wrong medium for communicating our directions. We make them entirely verbal, and the person is thus required to keep them in mind until he has followed out each of the parts of the directions. Think, for example, how hard it is to remember 426–7249 merely long enough to dial it after looking it up.

18   A crudely drawn map, of course, would serve the purpose. Some indication of distance would also help, although many people seem unable to give adequate estimates of distances in terms of miles. A chart or a graph can often give us an idea in a glance that is communicated verbally only with great difficulty.

19   However, we must not put too much of the blame for inadequate directions on those who give them. Sometimes the persons who ask for help are also at fault. Communication, we must remember, is a two-way process.

20   Sometimes an individual doesn't understand directions, but thinks he does. Only when he has lost his way does he realize that he wasn't careful enough to make sure that he really did understand. How often we let a speaker or instructor get by with such mouth-filling expressions as "emotional security," "audio-visual materials," "self-realization," without asking the questions that might clear them up for us. Even apparently simply terms like "needs" or "interests" have hidden many confusions. Our desire not to appear dumb, to be presumed "in the know," prevents us from really understanding what has been said.

21   We are often in too much of a hurry when we ask for directions. Like many tourists, we want to get to our destination quickly so that we can hurry back home. We don't bother to savor the trip or the scenery. So we impatiently rush off before our informant has really had time to catch his breath and make sure that we understand.

22   Similarly, we hurry through school subjects, getting a bird's-eye view of everything and a closeup of nothing. We aim to cover the ground when we should be uncovering it, looking for what is underneath the surface.

23   It is not easy to give directions for finding one's way around in a world whose values and directions are changing. Ancient landmarks have disappeared. What

appears to be a lighthouse on the horizon turns out to be a mirage. But those who do have genuine expertness, those who possess tested, authoritative data, have an obligation to be clear in their explanations. Whether the issue is that of atomic energy, UNESCO, the UN, or conservation of human and natural resources, clarity in the presentation of ideas is a necessity.

24    We must neither overestimate nor underestimate the knowledge of the inquiring traveler. We must avoid the COIK fallacy and realize that many of our communications are clear only if already known.[6]

# PRESIDENT JIMMY CARTER: UNDELIVERED ENERGY SPEECH ORIGINALLY SCHEDULED FOR DELIVERY ON JULY 5, 1979

Below is a manuscripted persuasive speech written for Former President Jimmy Carter. It is his undelivered Energy Speech, originally scheduled for July 5th, 1979, during one of the country's worse fuel crisis. You can analyze the speech to see what organizational pattern most closely indicates the organization he followed. Do you think this would have been an effective speech? Why or why not? Why do you suppose he decided not to give this speech and gave the alternative one, nicknamed, "The Malaise Speech" instead?

## ENERGY SPEECH

The long-predicted energy crisis has come. It is no longer something that experts say will happen sometime in the future. It is here. It is now.

Today, tens of thousands of Americans waited in gasoline lines -- as millions have done over the last several weeks. Many of you had to cancel holiday plans on Independence Day. Farmers and truckers have experienced shortages of diesel fuel. It is hard to get gasoline at any price -- and the price is rising fast.

People are asking: How did this happen to us -- and why? Will it be a permanent fixture of our lives? And what are we going to do about it?

Tonight I want to answer those questions. I want to speak to you honestly about the unpleasant realities of our short-term situation. And I want to point the way to a future of energy security.

The underlying cause of the crisis is the same as it has been for many years. That cause is our massive, deeply dangerous dependence on the OPEC oil cartel.

This cartel controls both the supply and the price of oil. It is increasingly willing to manipulate both, bleeding the industrial world of its wealth. Some of the OPEC countries are unstable or unreliable. The danger of interruptions in supply is a profound threat to our economic well-being and our national security.

A generation ago we sent more oil out of the country than we brought in. By 1973, just before the first oil embargo, we were still importing only one-third of our oil, and paying only $2 a barrel for it. Now we import nearly half of what we use.

And after last week's shocking OPEC price increase, we will be paying up to $23.50 a barrel -- compared to $12.50 only six or seven months ago.

The current gasoline lines are directly related to this vulnerability.

Seven months ago, the revolution in Iran cut off its oil production entirely. As a result, the United States lost a hundred million barrels of oil. We can never get that oil back, from which we draw gasoline and home heating oil. Iranian production has now been resumed, but at a much lower level. The result is a continuing shortage.

Before Iran, the world produced as much oil as it demanded Now, the world produces more than one and one-half million barrels less per day than it requires. This leaves our country with about 750,000 barrels per day less than we need. While OPEC production has dropped since the Iranian revolution, we have also had a steady decline for ten years in our domestic production.

The shortage is global. It is real. And because there is a shortage, there are gasoline lines.

The lines are an irritation and an inconvenience for millions of Americans. They are a threat to the livelihood of many of us. But the stakes are far higher than that.

Yesterday, we celebrated the anniversary of our independence as a nation. For 203 years, we have stood proud and free. We have met challenge after challenge -- and we have overcome them all.

Now our very independence is in danger. The threat is not military but economic -- but it is no less real, no less serious, no less grave.

Two years ago, I called the energy crisis the moral equivalent of war. Few were willing to heed the call. Now we are in that war, America must be ready to listen. We are now in a decisive fight for the independence and security of our nation. The battlefield is energy.

We must mobilize not only our resources but our spirits as well. We cannot afford business as usual. Beginning tonight, we must approach this crisis in a new way. We must recognize that only by pulling together, in a spirit of patriotism and of total common purpose will we be able to pull ourselves out of it.

I wish I could tell you tonight that the shortages will disappear soon. I wish I could tell you that the gasoline lines will vanish overnight. I wish I could tell you that our economy could sustain without damage the loss of tens of billions of dollars that will be drained away by the latest OPEC price increase.

I cannot tell you these things. I must tell you the truth.

The lines will not disappear quickly -- perhaps not fully until the end of the summer. When they disappear in one area, they may reappear somewhere else – because there is simply not enough gasoline to satisfy every demand.

My most important duty as President is to protect the health and safety of our citizens. That means I must first ensure that we have enough home heating oil for the winter and enough fuel to produce and deliver the food we eat. It means that I must ensure that police, fire, emergency, and defense needs are met. These simply have to be our first priorities.

We are urging refineries to increase their production of fuel and heating oil, and to distribute it as fairly as possible. The mechanisms by which we try to control the distribution of gasoline are clumsy and imperfect. They have a long response time.

Our allocations are based largely on past patterns of consumption; but the shortage itself changes those patterns. We have been working to improve our allocation system, and we will accelerate that effort. The best way to handle the immediate problem is for each citizen to conserve. The shortages will be with us for some time to come. We will not need to give up our way of life -but we will have to alter it. We will have to drive less. We will have to make sure that each trip we take is a necessary one, just as we did during Wrold [sic] War II. We will have to make greater use of public transportation and carpooling. When we reduce demand, the payoff is immediate.

(The people of California have demonstrated that when we voluntarily restrain our consumption, we can end the gas lines.)*

I again urge Congress to give me authority for standby gasoline rationing.

The need is now painfully obvious. It is absolutely crucial for us to arm ourselves against the possibility of further interruptions by OPEC in our energy supplies.

Also, I urge the Congress to act expeditiously to permit me to set mandatory state-by-state conservation goals, and enable the federal government to step in with mandatory conservation plans if a state fails to meet its target. I am also asking the governors to use the authority I have given them to impose minimum purchase requirements and odd/even and staggered hour plans at the earliest signs of spot shortages.

But let me repeat: spot shortages will continue to occur throughout the summer. And when the lines do disappear, the inconveniences will not.

Most likely, they will take some other, perhaps unexpected, form.

Many Americans ask whether some are trying to profit illegally from the crisis.

The answer is yes -- and it will always be yes as long as we reamin [sic] so desperately vulnerable. The ripoff artists, large and small, did not cause this crisis. But they cannot be permitted to take advantage of it -- and they will be brought to justice.

To produce more home heating oil and gasoline in the short-run, I am asking our independent energy regulatory agency and the states to remove all barriers to using natural gas to replace oil. If this request does not produce maximum results, I will seek mandatory authority to require such switching. I am instructing the Environmental Protection Agency to allow, where appropriate, the use of higher sulfur oil to free additional fuel oil supplies.

In addition, the increased production of natural gas and oil which decontrol will bring and the increased production of coal we will encourage will help make up our shortfall in the next year.

As for the economic impact of the almost sixty percent OPEC price rise since December, I will be equally blunt. The impact will be harsh. It will increase both inflation and unemployment. It will add l percent to our already severe inflation. By the end of 1980, it will add 800,000 people to our unemployment rolls. It will reduce economic growth substantially. Our economy has been wounded by OPEC and the wound will show in the months ahead. We cannot avoid these economic consequences. But we must act to make sure they are held to a minimum. I am setting up a series of consultations with the Congress, with labor, and with business over the next several weeks to work out our economic response to the OPEC price increase.

Nevertheless, our economy will remain the strongest in the world. It is now our solemn duty to mobilize that strength for ultimate victory in the energy war.

I went to the Tokyo Summit during this crisis because we need the cooperation of our closest allies to win this energy war. I got that cooperation when the world's major industrial nations pledged to reduce oil imports by specified amounts and to join in an international effort to develop alternatives to OPEC oil. That agreement means that there will be virtually no increase in demand for OPEC oil from now until 1985.

Now we must follow up with the speed and fervor of a nation at war -- not for the sake of other countries, but for our own.

Since my return, I have been working continuously to build on the proposals I made two and one-half years ago for our country to break its bondage to the whims of OPEC and to secure our economic and energy security. That work continues and will continue with the Congress when it returns next week.

But the general outline of a strategy for winning the energy war has now emerged -- and I feel it is important for me to brief you without delay on the steps we must now take.

First, I have ordered the preparation and submission to Congress of a bill creating a federally chartered private corporation to develop alternative energy sources to imported oil, such as synthetic liquid fuels. This corporation can be just as successful as the corporation the United States established in World War II to produce synthetic rubber. It will be funded at a multi-billion dollar level. It will accelerate our ability to turn our plentiful domestic resources -- such as coal, crops and organic products -- into gasoline and alcohol.

Second, we will accelerate the development and use of coal, unconventional oil and gas resources such as geopressurized methane, Eastern shales, tar sands, and heavy crude oils.

We have already tripled our investment in solar energy and I have set a goal of using solar energy for twenty percent of our energy within the next twenty years.

Third, I have ordered the development of a massive new conservation program to increase, on a greatly accelerated basis, the energy efficiency of our homes and buildings.

Fourth, I will seek the rapid creation of an Energy Mobilization Board, modeled on the War Production Board of World War II, to cut through the red tape and delays that are holding up crucial energy projects such as pipelines and refineries.

The details of these crucial projects will be hammered our [sic] in close consultation with the Congress. They will be submitted during the course of the next month. Congress has so far failed to deal with the oil imports problem. This inaction must now end.

Because these programs are central to long-term success in the battle for energy security, they must be put in place without delay.

These steps will be expensive. But unlike the billions we pay to OPEC, the costs of regaining our energy security will be paid by Americans to Americans. We will be creating jobs, not exporting our dollars overseas. We will be counter-acting recession -- not fueling it. We will be attacking one of the root causes of our inflation -- not increasing it. It will be money well spent.

These new production programs depend upon the passage of a strong wind-fall profits tax. The House has acted. The Senate must now give us the revenues from a permanent windfall tax to capture the billions of dollars decontrol will bring to the oil industry and to enable us to fully wage our energy war.

I close tonight with an urgent message -- a message that is as important as any program or policy.

Energy is an extraordinarily serious problem -- as serious as war itself and deserving of the same sustained national effort.

But our most serious problem is not a material one but a spiritual and psychological one. An atmosphere of fear, futility and foreboding has clouded our response to the energy crisis at hand.

Most citizens are facing the difficulties responsibly. But then we read of (people) being shoved and punched in (a) gasoline line.** We see reports of riots and shootings in strikes over diesel fuel. We see a political system seemingly par-alyzed by petty squabbling, so preoccupied with protecting special interests that the overall interest of the United States goes unserved. And we ask ourselves: Is this the shape of our future? Is this the kind of country we have become? Is this what it is going to be like from now on? The answer is NO.

There are many things we cannot control. We cannot dictate the price of foreign oil. We cannot make gasoline appear by magic when there is a world shortage of the oil from which it is made. But we can control the spiritual and moral destiny of our beloved nation -- and only if we do that can we control our material destiny as well.

The energy crisis has imposed suffering on our nation, and it will im-pose more before we have vanquished it. But if we can meet this crisis with determination, patriotism and common purpose -- as we have met so many crises in the two centuries of our history -- we can come out of it a stronger, prouder people than before. We will rally to each other and to the banner of our nation. We will tackle the long hard task ahead with the courage, the will, the vitality that are characteristic of the American people.

During this time of crisis, I have a responsibility to you that goes beyond the making of policy decisions and the submission of endless proposals to the Congress.

I have a responsibility to speak to you on a regular basis -- more frequently than I have in the past -- to explain where we stand and what we can expect in the future.

If I can have the cooperation of the radio and television networks, I will be speaking to you more frequently over the course of the summer -- not about false hopes or the painless solutions, but about the hard facts of our problems, and of how, if we work together as one nation, we will prevail.

Before this month is over, I will be talking to you again about the specific steps that we as a country must take to ensure our independence.

Franklin Roosevelt once said: "Lives of nations are determined, not by the count of years, but by the lifetime of the human spirit. The life of a man is three-score years and ten, a little more, a little less. But the life of a nation is the fullness of its will to live."

As a people, as a nation, let us meet the challenge of the energy crisis with the fullness of our will to live.

# GLOSSARY

**Abstract**   A summary of a journal article; used for information, never for citation

**Abstracting**   The process of thinking in which we selectively leave out details about concrete or real things

**Abstract Language**   Language that refers to concepts or ideas, not perceived by the senses

**Abundancy Motivation**   Characterized by desire to grow, discover, create, enjoy, and achieve

**Actuate**   The act of moving people to action, putting something into motion

**Affective**   Refers to feelings, thoughts, and things more emotional

**Agenda**   A simple program of items to be discussed and tasks to be accomplished at meetings

**Alliteration**   The repetition of initial consonant sounds in close or adjoining words

**Amoral**   Not particularly concerned with notions of right or wrong, fair or unfair

**Anniversary Address**   Celebrates an event, persons, or an institution

**Anonymity**   One who is lost in the press of the mob loses much of his or her sense of responsibility. This anonymity produces an inflated feeling of power

**Artifacts**   How we dress ourselves, what jewelry we wear, or tattoos we don

**Attitude**   Refers to the thinking, feeling, and behavioral intentions that govern our predispositions toward people, situations, and things

**Attribution Theory**   Deals with how and what we infer about the behaviors, attitudes, and intentions we observe or know, or think we know, in others and in ourselves

**Auding**   The process of listening to and comprehending spoken language

**Autocratic Leadership**   Leadership approach that employs power and authority to strictly control outcomes

**Back Channeling**   Uh-huh, hmmm, and other sounds that encourage the speaker to continue

**Backing**   Sometimes necessary to provide support or further explain the warrant in an argument

**Beliefs**   Sets of inferences we make about the world

**Bipolar**   Exhibiting two polar opposite attitudes, beliefs or behaviors

**Both-Sides Persuasion**
Presents arguments both pro and con to the point you are making

**Brainstorming**   A technique used when a group wants to generate a lot of ideas in a short period of time

**Buzz Session**   Large groups in which wider, individual participation is desired may be divided into subgroups of four to six persons for more intimate, informal discussion

**Call to Action**   Giving the audience specific actions they can adopt immediately

**Case Conference**   A discussion of a real or hypothetical incident that has a learning objective. It may or may not be conducted with an audience present

**Catachresis**   Somewhat abusive phraseology involving the misuse or misapplication of a word or phrase

**Character**   Refers to the audience's perception of the speakers' honestly and trustworthiness

**Charisma**   The speaker's engaging, dynamic and attractive personality, as perceived by the audience

**Claim**   The statement you want your audience to accept

**Coacting Groups**   More than just small, casual gatherings. There must be some common purpose, intent, or problem that requires interaction

**Cognitive**   Refers to logical thoughts, to thinking, to the mental process (cognition) by which knowledge is acquired, constructed, and elaborated

**Cognitive Restructuring**
Changing the way one thinks. A technique used to reduce communication apprehension

**Cognitive-Response Theory**
Explains how people may respond to a persuasive message by evoking thoughts from their own storehouses of experience and knowledge that may not be contained in the message sent

**Competence**   Refers to the audience's perception of the speakers' skills, ability, and knowledge

**Complete-Sentence Outline**
The most detailed and specific of all the forms

**Completeness**   The concept of completeness arises with our desire to fill in the missing pieces of a message or pattern to make a whole idea, picture, or message

**Concerted Audience** An audience whose members assemble with a common, active purpose in mind, with sympathetic interest in a mutual enterprise, but with no clear division of labor or rigid organization of authority

**Concomitant Signals** Nonverbals that accompany and operate at the same time as the words

**Concrete Language** language that is most descriptive, tangible, and closest to the referent, the thing itself

**Congruence** When things go together as we expect them to

**Connotation** The meaning of a word emerging by the feelings or emotional responses associated with it

**Context** The impact of the physical and psychological environment within which communication occurs

**Coordination** Means that a subordinate list of topics must have a common relationship

**Covariation Principle** Suggests that we often misattribute meanings and causes because we tend to work backward from behavior to inferences about causes and often overlook the other critical influences that covary

**Covary** Change together in a predictive manner over time

**Culpable Ignorance** Failure to acquire the necessary knowledge or understanding that results in wrong doing and therefore is blameworthy

**Debate** A formal method of a two-sided argument; often entered into competitively

**Decode** The sorting out, selecting, and eliciting meanings from one's storehouse of knowledge, experience, and training until he or she constructs in his or her own mind a notion of the images and ideas contained in the mind of the sender

**Dedicatory Speeches** Tributes to buildings, monuments, ships, libraries, and other things that are generally dedicated in honor of some outstanding personality, institution, or group of people

**Deficiency Motivation** Characterized by needs to avoid danger, threat, disruption, and discomfort

**Democratic Leadership** Participative leadership wherein the leader motivates and guides the group to come to its own decisions

**Demonstrational Visual Aids** A show and tell level of visual aids

**Denotation** The literal meaning or the dictionary definition of a word

**Dialogue** A two-person interaction, such as conversation, an interview, or counseling

**Dialogue Forum**   A dialogue held before an audience and the audience is invited to participate in the interaction

**Discounting Effect**   The discounting effect suggests a given cause should be discounted if other plausible causes are also present.

**Discreteness**   Each item in an outline should be a distinct point and not overlap other items

**Discussion**   Derived from the Latin discusses—to strike asunder, to pull apart, to separate and subordinate the elements and ideas that make up a question or topic

**Dissonance**   Lack of agreement; inconsistency between beliefs one holds or between their actions and their beliefs

**Doublespeak**   Used to soften bad news, shift blame, or, if completely unethical, to cover up the truth

**Either/Or Response**   Don't offer possibilities outside of the two or three provided, nor do they recognize individual differences

**Elaboration Likelihood Method (ELM)**   Persuasion is based on this approach; namely, that the more elaborately a receiver responds cognitively, the greater the likelihood of attitude change.

**Emblems**   Hand gestures translated to specific words or meaning rather directly, as with the hitch-hike or A-OK sign

**Emotional Appeals**   Appealing to the needs or the emotions of the audience when calling for agreement. Aristotle referred to this as the proof of pathos

**Encode**   To put together a message and convey it symbolically through words and nonverbals to an audience

**Ending with Impact**   All speeches should end with a strong final statement that leaves the audience with something to consider or resonates with the audience long after the speech is over.

**Enthymemes**   Syllogistic arguments with unstated premises

**Eulogy**   Typically a speech of tribute upon the death of a person or shortly thereafter

**Euphemism**   A mild, inoffensive substitute for a "bad" or negatively connoted word

**Everyday Values**   Specific value systems that might include ambition, independence, and altrusim.

**Experiential Field**   Humans exist in a sea of conscious and unconscious experiences that forms the way they perceive and understand phenomena. The perspective that develops extends to the social positions within which they engage, be it teacher, graduate student, housewife, or other.

**Experiential Visual Aids**
Visual aids that provide a forum for the audience to directly experience some element of the message

**Extemporaneous Speaking**  A speaking method involving the preparation of a thorough but flexible outline, prepared and practiced but not memorized or written out, except for key word reference.

**Facial Expressions**  Result from one or more muscle motions or positions on the face

**Fallacies**  Represent reasoning too far removed from the facts, a tangle of generalizations based on inadequate facts, or even a purposeful misrepresentation of the claim

**False-to-Fact**  Statements that cannot be supported by the fact

**Feedback**  Feedback is what the receiver provides to the speaker to let him or her know how the message is coming across to the audience and allows the speaker to make adjustments

**Feedback-Response**  The positive response to the efforts of the speaker

**Functional Leadership Theory**
Suggests that group members rise to fill leadership functions when necessary

**Grounds**  The evidence you are using to support your claim

**Hyperbole**  An exaggeration

**Idiom**  An accepted expression, shared by a culture or group of people, with a meaning different from the literal

**Illustrators**  Gestures that add clarity to the words being spoken. For instance showing with the hands the comparison of a large beach ball and a baseball.

**Imagery**  A form of vividness that employs language to produce mental pictures in the mind's eye of the listener

**Impression Management**
One's conscious presentation of self to others.

**Impromptu Speech**  Delivered on the spur of the moment, without advance notice or time for detailed preparation

**Incongruence**  What we expect to go together fails to do so; we notice the contradiction to our expectations.

**Indexing**  Used to disaggregate a group into individual members

**Inference**  Drawing a conclusion based on possibilities beyond what is observed

**Influence**  Refers to a power that affects a person or a course of events, usually indirectly

**Instructional Formats**  Include case conferences, role-playing, and, to some extent, all the forms and techniques of discussion

**Jargon**   Specialized language, accepted and used in a specific context or industry

**Key-Word Outline**   An abbreviated topical outline usually created out of the complete-sentence outline to be used as a speaking outline

**Laissez-Faire Leadership**   Represented by a no control attitude allowing the group to take charge of all actions and decisions

**Leveling**   De-emphasize less essential details

**Locked Jaw**   Caused by a failure to open the mouth wide enough to articulate or pronounce words clearly

**Logical Appeals**   Messages focused on reasoning and evidence to persuade the audience

**Logos**   One of Aristotle's three proofs of an argument. This proof is based on rational appeal by providing evidence and reasoning.

**Manuscript**   A prepared document from which the speaker reads word for word while still maintaining connection to the audience

**Memorization**   The direct effort of word-for-word recall

**Metaphor**   An implied comparison that transports the listener from the thing itself to a sensory image or experience

**Metonymy**   Substituting the name of an item associated with a larger concept for the idea

**Model**   Generally refers to a representation of a thing or a process

**Monochronic**   Linear time, occurring chronologically, one thing at a time.

**Mood**   Refers to feelings of the moment

**Motivation**   Pertains to any stimulation or inducement that leads to an act or belief

**Muffled Mouth**   Caused principally by weak or slow tongue activity

**Obfuscation**   To make obscure or unclear; to confuse

**Objectification**   An intellectualization or pragmatic explanation of what is happening to you

**Onomatopoeia**   Words that imitate the sounds to which they refer

**Overgeneralization**   (False generalization) stating a conclusion based on too little evidence

**Oxymoron**   Use of incongruous or contradicting details

**Paradox**   A seemingly self-contradictory, ironic, or absurd statement

**Pause**   Occurs between words and phrases; the number and duration of which seriously can alter the meaning of the message

**Pathos**   One of Aristotle's three proofs of an argument. This proof is based on emotional and motivational appeal to the audience.

**Pedestrian Audience**   A temporary audience, such as a group of pedestrians on a busy street corner

**Persuasion**   The art of convincing others to change their beliefs or adopt actions that are favorable to our purposes.

**Phenomenal Field**   (Subjective reality) Every individual exists in a continually changing world of experience of which he or she is the center

**Phrase**   A group of words that forms a thought unit

**Polarization**   Unusually homogeneous audience attitudes, polarized around a particular belief or attitude

**Polychronic**   Time occurring simultaneously rather than in a linear fashion. Lacks chronological order

**Presymbolic**   Communication behavior that functions without the formal symbols of language

**Progression**   Refers to the arrangement of related items in some sort of natural sequence, such as chronology, time, genre, or space

**Pronunciation**   The act of expressing the sounds and accents of words so that they conform to accepted standards

**Prosopopoeia**   Having the dead speak

**Qualifiers**   Limit how universally the claim applies

**Rebuttals**   The prepared responses to counterarguments

**Red Herring Fallacy**   Diverting attention to an unrelated topic

**Referent**   The thing itself before a word has been placed to describe or explain it. The heart of the difficulty with language is the confusion of the word with the thing for which it stands

**Representational Visual Aids**   Pictures, photos or graphs that depict the phenomenon being described or explained

**Reservations**   Statements that allow for the possibility that the claim may be incorrect

**Role Playing**   The extemporaneous acting-out of assigned roles or dramatic parts in a group—often a case conference

**Selected Audience**   An audience whose members are assembled for some common purpose, but not all are sympathetic to one another or to the speaker's point of view

**Self-Identity**    The ways in which we see ourselves

**Self-Interest/Egoism**    Focus on the gains to the self. Thought to be a major motivator for all human conduct

**Sharpening**    Emphasize the gist of the message

**Simile**    A comparison of things, similar to a metaphor, using "like" or "as" in the comparison

**Slack Lips**    The lips are so loose that they do not adequately shape the mouth opening for proper vowel production or for proper articulation of the lip consonants (p, b, m, w, f, and v)

**Social Facilitation**    An individual's desires are stimulated merely by the sight and sound of others making similar movements

**Source Credibility**    Related to Aristotle's concepts of goodwill, good moral character, and good sense; as they are perceived and evaluated by receivers

**State-Anxiety**    Anxiety due to the particular communication circumstance, not anxiety in general

**Styles Leadership Theory**    A theory that describes leadership based on specific behaviors or styles that can be learned. These behaviors are categorized as autocratic, democratic, and laissez-faire.

**Subordination**    The generally accepted requirement that information in an outline descends in importance from main points to sub-points, to elaborations, examples, and evidence, etc.

**Suggestibility**    A heightened emotional state that leads to hasty, thoughtless, and rash action, allowing us to get caught up in the moment. This human condition can contribute to crowds becoming mobs

**Symbolization**    Used in outlining to signify level of meaning and importance. Similar symbols (I, II, III; A, B, C, and so on) should represent similar items of equal importance; differing symbols (I, A, 1, a, and so on) should represent relative difference in importance

**Symposium**    A small group (three to five) that has special knowledge of different aspects of a broad topic

**Synecdoche**    A figure of speech whereby a part is meant to represent a whole or vice versa

**Syntax**    The arrangement of words to create well-formed sentences in a particular language

**Systematic Desensitization**    The process of reducing the sensitivity one has to anxiety provoking situations, by focusing on relaxation techniques while increasing the anxiety provoking situation

**Theory of Cognitive Dissonance**
Leon Festinger developed this theory to explain how we deal with the tension that emerges when we have two or more conflicting thoughts and behaviors. His theory proposes that people have a motivational drive to reduce the dissonance. This characteristic can be drawn upon for persuasive purposes

**Thought Speed**   The faster speed at which people think compared to the slower speed at which they speak

**Topical Outline**   The rough draft outline in which phrases or groups of words carry the essential meaning of the points in the process of development

**Trait Leadership Theory**   This theory suggests that leaders are born, not made and identifies innate characteristics of leaders.

**Trait-Anxiety**   Refers to anxiety across many or all communication situations

**Transactional**   A socially derived process involving an unending activity that simultaneously and reciprocally affects or influences both parties

**Transactional Model**   A transactional process of skillfully sharing, selecting, and sorting ideas, symbols, and signs in such a way as to help listeners elicit from their own minds a meaning or construction similar to that intended by the speaker

**Transformational Leadership Theory**   Examines the attributes that leaders possess that contribute to the ways leaders inspire followers to serve higher purposes than their self interests to become unified groups

**Ultimate Values**   The large value systems that hold our various beliefs and attitudes together

**Warrant**   The link between the information (grounds) and the claim

# PHOTO CREDITS

309; Wikimedia Commons, 310; iStockphoto, 312; iStockphoto, 320; AP Wide World, 321; iStockphoto, 349; AP Wide World, 351; shutterstock, 353.

**Chapter 12:**    iStockphoto, 358; iStockphoto, 361; iStockphoto, 366; Wikipedia, 374; AP Wide World, 378; shutterstock, 380.

**Chapter 13:**    AP Wide World, 382; AP Wide World, 385; iStockphoto. 386; iStockphoto, 399; iStockphoto, 403; iStockphoto, 405; shutterstock, 411.

**Chapter 14:**    iStockphoto, 414; iStockphoto, 418; shutterstock, 432.

**Chapter Appendix:**    shutterstock, 435; shutterstock, 440.

**Chapter Glossary:**    shutterstock, 459; shutterstock, 469

**Chapter Index:**    shutterstock, 471;

# INDEX